# ANOTHER EYESIGHT
# MULTI-SENSORY DESIGN IN CONTEXT

# ANOTHER EYESIGHT

## Multi-Sensory Design in Context

by
Julia Ionides MA
and
Peter Howell DiplArch Architect RIBA

with contributions from friends

**The Dog Rose Press
Ludlow
England**

**2005**

# Another Eyesight
## Multi-Sensory Design in Context
by
Julia Ionides and Peter Howell

Copyright 2005
The Dog Rose Trust
Charity Number 1053263
83 Greenacres
Ludlow
Shropshire, SY8 1LZ

Telephone 01584 874567

Published by
The Dog Rose Press
26 Bell Lane
Ludlow
Shropshire SY8 1BN

Telephone 01584 874567

Designed and set by the Dog Rose Press
in Times
Printed and bound by
Cambridge University Press

Published and Printed in the United Kingdom
Date of publication 2005

ISBN 0-9528367-3-4.

# CONTENTS

### Another Eyesight

## Chapter 3 Touch

# CONTENTS

## Chapter 6 Theatre

# *Architecture and the Human Condition by Juhani Pallasmaa*

### *Architect, professor, Helsinki*

Our western industrial culture is undoubtedly dominated by vision and the proliferation of visual imagery and information; Italo Calvino calls the current condition 'the rainfall of images'.[1] In addition to favouring the sense of vision, our culture suppresses other sensory modes, either deliberately or unintentionally. Even architecture, existentially the most central of art forms, is predominantly taught, theorized, practised and critiqued as an art of the eye. This unconditional privileging of one sense over the other four classically identified senses has its beginning already in Greek thought. 'The eyes are more exact witnesses that the ears', claimed the pre-Socratic philosopher Heraclitus in one of his fragments,[2] whereas Plato reckoned that 'the supreme benefit for which sight is responsible' is that through the cosmic revelations of vision man has acquired philosophy, 'the greatest gift the gods have ever given or will give to mortals'.[3] No wonder, that clear vision has become one of the most popular and charged metaphors in language, and synonymous to understanding.

Although our current obsessively ocularcentric culture has been supported by the western philosophical tradition, the suppression of the other senses has been a gradual process. There is plenty of evidence to determine that the senses of hearing, touch and smell dominated the human life world until the end of the eighteenth century – the era of the emergence of modernity according to one line of historical reasoning. Vision has gained power through numerous successive cultural developments and technical inventions. Walter J. Ong, for instance, relates the beginning of the dominance of vision with the invention of writing: '… [T]he shift from oral to written speech was essentially a shift from sound to visual space'.[4] 'Print replaced the lingering hearing-dominance in the world of thought and expression with the sight-dominance which had its beginning in writing […] This is an insistent world of cold, no-human facts', Ong argues suggesting that this shift implies a distinct loss of human quality.[5] It is evident that one´s experiential world based primarily on vision, the sense of isolation, distance and dominance, is fundamentally different from the world of hearing and touch which are both senses of integration, nearness and togetherness. The eye seeks and focuses, whereas sound approaches and embraces us.

In fact, it is misleading to think of the senses in isolation from each other. The senses interact and collaborate, and their interplay with each other and the body gives rise to more complex systems of perception, memory and consciousness than any one of the senses singly. 'My perception is [therefore] not a sum of visual, tactile and audible givens: I perceive in a total way with my whole being: I grasp a unique structure of the thing, a unique way of being, which speaks to all my senses at once', as Maurice Merleau-Ponty eloquently writes.[6]

In relation to its artistic essence, architecture has been regarded primarily as an aesthetic discipline based on visual composition, scale, rhythm and light. This visual understanding is concretised in Le Corbusier's famous credo: 'Architecture is the masterly, correct and magnificent play of masses brought together in light'.[7] This biased privileging of the eye has greatly contributed to the sense of isolation and sensory impoverishment that we frequently experience in setting of our time. It has become increasingly evident, that beyond mere visual aesthetics, architecture is grounded in the characteristics of the human existential condition, and it integrates all the sense modalities into an embodied experience, that projects a horizon for human perception and understanding. Beyond the articulation of matter and space, buildings also articulate our experiences of time and historicity; architecture domesticates both space and time for human habitation.

After decades, or centuries of neglect, the body and the senses are shifting into the center of today's architectural discourse. This fundamental change in our architectural consciousness echoes a more general growth of interest in sensuous qualities. 'We in the western world are beginning to discover our neglected senses. This growing awareness represents something of an overdue insurgency against the painful deprivation of sensory experience, we have suffered in our technologised world', writes Ashley Montagu, the anthropologist, who has powerfully argued for the primacy of the tactile sense in human environmental experience.[8] Tactility and hapticity seem to be a hidden and unconscious ingredients of all sensory experiences; all the senses are forms of touching, both literally and metaphorically. As Montagu points out, this fact is expressed 'in the age-old evaluation of touch as "the mother of the senses"'.[9]

We are only beginning to realize the deep mysteries of our bodily constitution, and its central role in our mental lives. Philosophers have suggested, for instance, that no human memory would be possible without a body memory,[10] and the body is an inseparable constituent of our very processes of thought.[11] Richard Rorty even argues that: 'If the body had been easier to understand, nobody would have thought that we had a mind.'[12]

In addition to its unquestioned visual hegemony, our current consumer culture idolises youth, health, strength, and success. As a consequence of this commercially motivated indoctrination, other groups of the population, such as children, the aged, the sick, and the handicapped tend to be neglected in normal situations of daily life, and they are dealt with as separate and isolated social groups. This is, of course, only one aspect of the alarming increase of segregation, inequality, polarization, and the disappearance of solidarity that we can currently witness in our increasingly surreal consumerist world. Modernity emerged from utopian social empathy and the ideal of democracy, but these values have been largely forgotten in our age of selfishness and narcissism.

Almost three decades ago, I had the opportunity to make a project for the Headquarters of the Central Union of the Blind in Helsinki. When working on the project, I naturally studied the problems as well as capabilities of individuals with a weakened or blinded eyesight, but I did not prepare myself to present my scheme to the project group, most of whom did not have a normal eyesight. To my great surprise, however, the blind members grasped my architectural intentions and proposals – through verbal description – better than the members with normal sensory capabilities, who even had the privilege of studying drawings and a model of the project. It seemed to me that the architectural objectives and motifs which would easily be interpreted (and frequently disregarded) as merely personal and subjective aesthetic aspirations, gained a new and objective validity, when such articulations turned into means of facilitating the environmental orientation and experience of persons weakened by a severe sensory loss. This observation suggested to me that aesthetic intentions and qualities are probably deeply grounded in the human existential condition: beauty is not, perhaps, a surplus characteristic of things, it is part of their very essence.

In his essay 'The Humanizing of Architecture' (1940), Alvar Aalto describes the process of designing the patient's room of the Paimio Tuberculosis Sanatorium (1929-33) 'for a person in the weakest possible condition' as follows: 'Scientists very often use exaggerated forms in analyses in order to obtain clearer, more visible results – bacteria are stained, and so on. The same methods can be adopted in architecture, also […] If we proceed from technical functionalism, we shall discover that a great many things in our present architecture are disfunctional from the point of view of psychology or a combination of psychology and physiology.'[13] Aalto continues to explain that during the design process of the sanatorium – he happened to be hospitalized himself for some time during that period – he came to a simple realization: 'the ordinary room is a room for a vertical person; a patient's room is a room for a horizontal human being, and colours, lighting, heating, and so on must be designed with that in mind'.[14]

Alvar Aalto's example of an architect's capacity for empathy and compassion has special value in our time, when even the most celebrated architecture often seems to have turned its back to the social and human reality. It is the noble task of architecture to stimulate authentic and autonomous experiences and defend human dignity.

[1] Italo Calvino, <u>Six Memos for the Next Millennium</u>, Vintage Books, New York, 1993, 57.

[2] Fragment 101a as quoted in David Michael Levin, <u>Modernity and the Hegemony of Vision</u>, University of California Press, Berkeley and Los Angeles, 1993,1.

[3] Plato, <u>Timaeus and Critias</u>, Penguin Books, London, 1977, 65.

[4] Walter J. Ong, <u>Orality & Literacy – The Technologizing of the World</u>, Routledge, London and New York, 1991, 117.

[5] Ibid., 121 and 122.

[6] Maurice Merleau-Ponty, 'The Film and the New Psychology', in Maurice Merleau-Ponty, <u>Sense and Non-Sense</u>, Northwestern University Press, Evanston, 1964, 48.

[7] Le Corbusier, <u>Towards a New Architecture</u>, The Architectural Press, London and Fredrik A. Praeger, New York, 1959, 31.

[8] Ashley Montagu, <u>Touching: The Human Significance of the Skin</u>, Harper & Row, New York, 1971, XIII.

[9] Ibid., 3.

[10] Edward S. Casey, <u>Remembering: A Phenomenological Study</u>, Indiana University Press, Bloomington and Indianapolis, 2000, 172.

[11] See, for instance, Mark Johnson, <u>The Body in the Mind: The Bodily Basis of Meaning, Imagination and Reason</u>, The University of Chicago Press, Chicago and London, 1987, and; George Lakoff and Mark Johnson, <u>Philosophy in the Flesh: The Embodied Mind and Its Challenge to Western Thought</u>, Basic Books, New York, 1999.

[12] Richard Rorty, <u>Philosophy and the Mirror of Nature</u>, Princeton University Press, Evanston, 1979, 239.

[13] Alvar Aalto, 'The Humanizing of Architecture' in Göran Schildt, editor, <u>Alvar Aalto in His Own Words</u>, Otava Publishing Company, Helsinki, 1997, 103.

[14] Ibid.

Professor Juhani Pallasmaa is one of the most prominent figures in contemporary architecture and design. He was Professor of Architecture at Helsinki University of Technology from 1991-1997 and Dean of the Faculty of Architecture from 1993-1996. He is the author of numerous articles and books, including <u>Eyes of the Skin: Architecture and the Senses</u> (1996). We have referred to this important book several times; in it Professor Pallasmaa emphasises the importance of multi-sensory design in architecture and the environment.

*From the eyesight proceeds another eyesight and from the hearing proceeds another hearing and from the voice proceeds another voice eternally curious of the harmony of things with man.*

Walt Whitman, Leaves of Grass, 1855.

This book is a personal journey, a journey which has enriched our lives. The book is based on our experience gained from working independently for about twenty years on ways to help those with sensory impairment and those whose problems lie in cognition. It is also a 10th birthday celebration of the Dog Rose Trust which was set up at a charity in November 1995.

Essentially the personnel of Dog Rose, later the Dog Rose Trust, were and still are Peter Howell and Julia Ionides and they are responsible for the contents of this book and any errors and opinions that there might be. If you do not agree with us, then let us know as we enjoy lively and constructive discussions. If you have any good ideas, then tell us about them. We are always learning and the more we learn, we realise how little we really know.

The subject covered by the book is very large and involves many fields of study and practice and it is not our intention to deal with all of these in detail. Indeed in some areas we would like to hear from specialists who have, and may not realise it, vital information to us. The days of academic isolation are gone; we now have to work together. For this reason we offer this book as a box of ideas and suggest that you get on with it. Certainly there is room for more thought and lots of research but essentially there is work to do which has to be done!

Much of this book is about the sensory environment, its appreciation and significance. Another aspect of the book is suggestions as to how one might carefully redesign the environment where necessary. This must be done with understanding and the process is currently called design. The Latin origin of this word, according to the <u>Oxford Dictionary of English Etymology</u>, is designare, to 'mark out'. The sensory world belongs to everyone and so we should all have a hand in its existence and change. Since we all have or should have a part in this, perhaps there should be a new word for design.

There is a need for us all to pull together and construct a set of understandable and usable concepts that will help us all to design. However, several writers come close to this and are mentioned in the text and many more who we feel will help when it is clear what is needed. Thus because the field of multi-sensory design and communication is relatively new, there are many avenues to explore and new thoughts to consider.

In some ways it is a plea to deal with design and communication in a different but holistic manner. This thought is not entirely new, as will become apparent in the text and through the books mentioned in each section; we do not suggest that all of these books should be read, but give you the information so that those taking a particular path should be able to set off in the right direction.

We do not have all the answers. What will we find when we have managed to return to the consideration of all senses as a point of departure for communication? Will we find that the commercial culture that currently imposes communication upon us is no longer relevant? One thing that we are sure of is that the centre of our understanding has to be the human being and its amazing and complex sensory ability.

Both of us have had considerable experience in the world of architecture and the environment. Julia was an actress and is now an architectural historian and Peter is an Architect. Julia runs the local Georgian Group and has written books on architecture. Peter had a career as an architect, a Research Fellow at the Building Research Establishment, at the Greater London Council Architects Department and the Department of the Environment Central and finally as a Planning Inspector before moving into sound. Both had worked on commercial sound recording before moving into the first phase of this work.

There is no beginning and no end to this road; it is simply punctuated with statements of what appears at a particular moment and hopefully has an aim to help fellow human beings. It is about providing a real environment for real people.

The first work carried out by us was to make guide tapes specifically for blind visitors to cathedrals. This opportunity came when, in 1988, Professor John Hull of the University of Birmingham set up Cathedrals through Touch and Hearing, an innovative and much-needed project. This provided an audio guide, a tactile model with a commentary and a Braille guide for as many cathedrals as possible so that these marvellous buildings could become accessible to people with visual impairments. Dr Hull wrote:

The basic concept of the project is not to try to convey to the blind person the sighted person's image of a cathedral but to enable the blind person to create his or her own impressions through sound and touch.

A proposal by Dog Rose Sound, as it was then, was sent to Professor Hull as a set of ideas to help with the work of providing audio guides. These ideas were based on experience, particularly with the research that Peter had carried out in the past. This was very much influenced by such people as Professor William Allen and Professor R G Hopkinson. Dog Rose Sound was appointed to carry out the work on this basis and produced guides to the following cathedrals: Coventry, Lichfield, Worcester, Hereford, Gloucester, Winchester (also a guide for sighted visitors), Exeter, Chichester and York. These guides, with permission from Professor Hull, are now available on the Dog Rose Trust radio station on the internet, in various file forms. They can be downloaded, with certain copyright restrictions, to assure that they can be used by anyone who needs them. The station is called Dog Rose Sound and the site address is www.dogrosesound.org. Other audio guides made by the Trust will also be made available in this way, as well as guides made by other organisations.

The Trust also has its own website which can be viewed and listened to via a screen reader on www.dogrose-trust.org.uk.We plan to put updates to this book on this site, so do check it.

In 1993 the Cathedrals through Touch and Hearing project closed. Dog Rose by this time was very experienced in the production of audio guides for blind visitors. To revert to other work would have been a loss in an area that desperately needs work and understanding and so it seemed important to continue. In spite of the uncertain future the organisation took the step of becoming a charity with the aims of researching and developing new methods and techniques of making all environments accessible to people with visual impairments.

As a result of this move, a group of Trustees were brought together and Julia Ionides became the Administrator of the Trust and Peter Howell became the consultant, both of them working in a voluntary capacity.

Because of the particular experience of the Trust most work has been done in the area of blindness. However, a study of Music and Deaf Culture was carried out for the University of Leicester in 1996. Experience with this research demonstrated the similarity of approach that is needed for this work and will form the basis of design. Several weekends spent at events concerning music and the deaf proved the point.

We have asked other people to contribute to this book from three continents: people whose work we admire and people we have enjoyed working with. What they have written might not always reflect the views of the Trust but we believe that they have something worthwhile to say. We have encouraged the contributors to use their own 'voices' and write from the heart. Their ideas may not always be ours but we appreciate what they say and respect their work. Their use of words may not be what we or you might choose, but we accept their choice. Owing to pressure of time, we have left the settings as the papers have been sent to us. This accounts for some inconsistency of the style of citing notes that appears.

This book has been written at a moment in time when there is a great opportunity to open museums and galleries to real people; but it can never be completed. There is no beginning, although one has one's own beginning, and there is no end because hopefully the concept and use of multi-sensory design will continue to develop into the future, The Dog Rose Press will continue to publish books and papers; Dog Rose Sound, our internet radio station, will continue to put together programmes and make available guides and information.

# ACKNOWLEDGEMENTS

The publication of this book has been made possible by the grant from Innovative Actions, a programme funded by Advantage West Midlands. The Dog Rose Trust is very grateful for this financial support and we would particularly like to thank Amanda Orchard and Nicole Lewis of the Innovation School in Coventry for the help, advice and support that the Trust has received from them.

This project is part funded by the European Regional Development Fund

There are many people who have worked with the Trust but not all of them feature in this book. This does not mean that their contribution to our work is any the less and our thanks are extended to everyone who has helped and advised us in any way. The Trust's four Trustees, Caroline Morris, Susan Bishop. Terry Stone and Bran Howell were appointed when the Trust was first set up and are still loyally serving it. Thanks to Terry for once again doing our proofing for us, to Caroline for her moral support during the frantic final weeks of getting this book together and to Mike Hancock for allowing us to use a photo of him at the Streets Alive Festival.

Special mention must go to our blind and visually impaired colleagues and their partners, some of whom have worked with us for many years and some we have met recently:

Eric Sayce and his Guide Dogs, Dorcas, Harry and Wills
Emilie Fane and her Guide Dogs, Ziggy, Sukie and Heather
Cambray and Heather Jones
Denise Collier and her Guide Dog Rebecca and Terry Collier
Anne Donnelly and her Guide Dog Rima and John Donnelly
John Fleming and his Guide Dog Oscar and Chris Fleming

Maureen Rowley
Geraldine and Peter Bounds
Liz Matthews
Michael and Brenda Campbell
Cath Simpson and Jim Agnew in Glasgow
And of course Professor John Hull who set us off on this adventurous path.

There are many other people who have contributed to our work in various ways including Susan and Geoffrey Taylor, Trudi and Len Graham, Betty Hooper, Dilwyn Morgan and our American friends Mary Brady, Ed Duggan, Karen Stone, Beth Ziebarth of the Smithsonian Institute, Paula Terry of National Endowment for the Arts and Stephanie Litvak of Very Special Arts in Washington DC, a member of the team who organised a very stimulating conference in Athens in 2003.

As you will see, we have included the covers of some of the books mentioned in the text; owing to a tight deadline, there was no time to contact the publishers and we apologise for this omission. However, we hope that this will bring the books to the attention of a wider audience, as they deserve. These covers are the copyright of the publishers.

We do not necessarily endorse the firms or manufacturers that we have included in the book, but many have been particularly helpful to us, especially Gardners of Cardiff and Photocast of Liverpool. Thanks Andrew, Kim and Pauline!

Please notice how often our garden has appeared in photographs in this book. It may not be to Royal Horticultural Society standards but it makes a good background for the objects being photographed and the birds love it.

We are very grateful to all the people who took part in the tactile research exercise. What they wrote about their work is almost as important as the pieces they have produced. We will be showing the Common Carp to as many visually impaired people as we can and get their comments and opinions. These will be posted on our website.

We are also grateful to all our contributors for writing papers for us and sending us photographs. Panic set in when large pictures arrived by email, filling up the mail box and even worse when 'cowboy' tree surgeons cut through the telephone cable with an uncontrolled chainsaw and we lost our broadband connection for two days.

# *Using all our Senses*

> *Between the half-wooded half naked hill, and the vague still horizon that its summit indistinctly commanded, was a mysterious sheet of fathomless shade – sounds from which suggested that what it concealed bore some reduced resemblance to features here. The thin grasses, more or less coating the hill, were touched by the wind in breezes of differing powers, and almost of differing natures – one rubbing the blades heavily, another raking them piercingly, another brushing them like a soft broom. The instinctive act of humankind was to stand and listen, and learn how the trees on the right and the trees on the left wailed or chaunted to each other in the regular antiphonies of a cathedral choir; how hedges and other shapes to leeward then plunged into the south, to be heard no more.*

Far from the Madding Crowd by Thomas Hardy[1]

This description by the 19th century writer, Thomas Hardy, is of a piece of countryside. The wind and the sound it produced are very much part of it. Although this is an inspired piece of writing it is also what most of us would wish to have written about the countryside. Although most of this extract is in terms of sound it does show how important all our senses are in such a description. But there is an idealism about it that was probably simply true when Hardy wrote this piece. Times have changed!

The Dog Rose Trust has a considerable experience in the design and provision of facilities that satisfy its aim to help people with sensory and cognitive difficulties. On this basis we, at the Trust, firmly believe that it is important to design for all senses and a combination of senses. In this way we will add to our lives and include disabled people in our world. This presupposes that people are aware that they have senses at all. Many of us, as children, were discouraged from using all our senses; for example, smell in our childhood was never to be mentioned and yet it is a major and significant sense. Therefore, it is also important that we make people aware of their senses. Certain multi-sensory artists do attempt to do this but in order for it to be successful it has to be something that we all appreciate, think about and consider. There is little doubt that perception forms a strange and powerful totality where all senses are used. For this reason care must be taken to make each 'track', or aspect of sensory communication, as meaningful or significant as possible. This means that there can be counterpoint between two or more senses, for example between touch and hearing, but it must be done with care. We have experience with this in the work we have done and further research is in hand. The hybrid vigour of using more than one sense will, we suggest, reward all of us. But it also means that we all need to learn to 'read and write' with all our senses.

On the other hand many writers, particularly of the romantic period, use descriptions of the world in the form of their own sensory reactions which are thought to be good. So what happened to our own first hand sensory reactions? As we have said, writers such as Thomas Hardy describe the environment very well. Since this is so successful then why do we not use the design of senses in real life?

An aspect of design that we need to understand is externalisation through one sense to another. We have to be looking at the totality of the senses and the bridges we can provide. It is possible to infer or simulate reactions of one sense through another. In a very interesting book The Skin of the Film, Laura Marks examines the memory of various senses and how these can be inferred in film. [2] She supports certain concepts of mimesis, in other words the use of one sense to describe another. Taking into account the limited presentation of film and television in terms of a very small screen, which is like looking down a cardboard tube, and sound that has at last spread about us, one can see the need for this sort of thinking. Nevertheless, it is very interesting to us and suggests areas for further study. In her introduction to the book she argues for multiculturalism and we would support this, every group of persons is individual and has its own culture. She says:

> There has been increasing interest in the past several years among film- and videomakers and visual artists to supplement vision with the experiences of hearing, touch, smell, taste, and kinasthesis.'[3]

So what more do we need to say – read the book!

In using multi-sensory design, and indeed universal communication, careful study is needed so that the psychophysical and perceptional differences between the senses are understood in relation to the persons for whom we are designing. No two persons are the same. In the same way we have to reconsider the anthropometrics and physical function of the individual person which are not generally understood. We need to add to this knowledge of the possible force that can be exerted by various categories of people, to set about the redesign of door furniture which has not moved forward since the end of the 18th century. As far as door furniture is concerned maybe we should be thinking of simple standardised automation and an audible proximity indicator. Department of Trade and Industry publications on anthropometrics have helped this forward. [4]

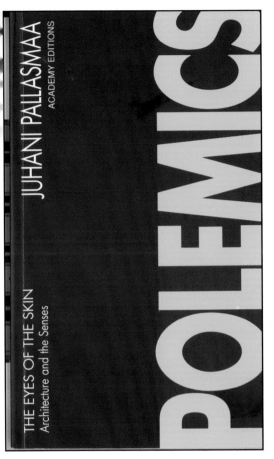

It is essential to get the concept of multi-sensory design across to designers and Architects and an overall awareness helps to do this. Sadly there is little sign that Architects and designers are really aware of the problems. One cannot exclude from this the necessary awareness of those who administrate museums and galleries since this is where it should all start. Again we have few examples of this, usually success is the result of one brave person who after a while, inevitably, leaves and the museum falls down the hole again.

Occasionally we find something written that we totally support. Such a piece of writing is a small book entitled The Eyes of the Skin by Juhani Pallasmaa.[5] We feel that this is a book that everyone in the design world should read.

So how does sound and touch fit into this? First one has to say that sound and touch are part of one's life and part of a whole range of senses that we are part of. They cannot be considered in total isolation. As I have already said sight is considered by most as the only useful sense. For this reason sound and hearing have not been considered in the same depth as light and seeing. Al Bregman in his very useful book entitled Auditory Scene Analysis remarked that when he started research on sound, hearing and perception some years ago he was amazed how little research had been done on sound perception as compared with work that had been done on light and its perception.[6]

AUDITORY SCENE ANALYSIS

The Perceptual Organization of Sound

Albert S. Bregman

In this book we are not dealing in detail with smell and taste but we have put in small sections which point out their importance. We occasionally find an opportunity to do something in this direction, but we need more forces for this. We firmly believe that smell and taste have tremendous potential and our limited experiences have shown this.

Touch is something that we are close to and much of our work is about communication by touch. However, touch has a special magic both in a personal sense and in the abstract. Other cultures seem to have reached out and have found this magic. If you touch a piece of Chinese jade then our argument for an abstract value of touch is completed. (Not many friends or relations have pieces of Chinese jade, but a look at the book <u>Chinese Jade</u> will also prove our point.[7]) Even the simple early forms, because of their shape and the material have a special magic.

*Launching the tactile model of York*

If you touch a fellow human being, a child, a wife or husband maybe, then the argument for personal touch is also completed. As a communication medium touch is very good. We have worked with true three-dimensional objects and this is very successful. Our bronze model outside the west end of the Minster in York is very popular. In fact it is so popular that it can be a problem taking photographs of it. Most of our work in this field has been in the creation of analogous models of architecture. However, at the simple communication level raised images and Braille can be very aesthetically pleasant, but also get the messages across very well. In all of these we try to provide sound to go with them either directly as interactive sound, as in the Palace of Westminster, or on a CDs. It would be possible with a suitable team to design a real interactive 'touch environment', but no one would give us the money!

Our work on sound and the sense of hearing has been going on for some time but it is only when sound is considered as a design tool, and its perception taken into account, that the whole falls into place and becomes useful in forming an environment. Music, which is a subculture of sound has been fairly well mutilated over the years but, as we say later, some composers are getting through. Given proper opportunities musicians, composers or sound designers could make real contributions to our environmentally unfriendly world.

Something that we have to do is to look for ideas and concepts that relate to multi-sensory design. In the past the connections relate to parts of the sensory world but only those where there was a practical or commercial aspect. Sound and touch are relative newcomers at new technical levels. Where should we look? One place is the world in which computer people make sound to indicate what is on the screen. In 1992 a group of similar people, mostly academics, met to discuss 'sonification, audification and auditory interfaces'. The resulting book entitled <u>Auditory Display</u> contains a wide range of essays many of which are very useful.[8] This was to blossom into ICAD, the International Community of Auditory Display. The transactions of their conferences held all over the world are worth looking at.

We can find some examples and a certain amount of thinking that support our case in different places. One source is the Bauhaus; this was a school set up in the Weimar Republic in Germany in 1919 after the terrible World War 1914-1918. It covered a vast range of subjects and the head was the well known Architect Walter Gropius. The school dealt with many of the facets of design in fields as they were defined then under the slogan 'art and technology – a new unity'. Gropius gathered a group of teachers such as Wassily Kandinsky, Paul Klee, and Josef Albers, most of whom were to become world famous. The school was overtaken by the Nazi party and most of the teachers left to go to other countries, many eventually to the United States of America. This can be seen as one of the most successful cultural enterprises ever established which provides the foundation of 20th century design. There are innumerable books on the subject of the Bauhaus; these are a necessary study.

In America, Lazlo Moholy-Nagy set up the New Bauhaus in Chicago in 1938. This, like the original school in Germany, was to have a great influence on design. Newer technologies such as photography were to become important. As a result from the basic course which, as in the German school, was very important, there came out workshops such as 'light, photography, film, publicity'. Clearly, this was moving towards multi-sensory design.

Moholy-Nagy himself had a tremendous influence and some of what he wrote is available in a book <u>Moholy-Nagy</u>.[9] Sadly he died in 1946 – it would be good to have him around now. Another book worth referring to is entitled <u>Laslo Moholy-Nagy</u>; it is subtitled Biographical Writings and that is what it is.[10] The book also provides many leads and an insight into his character.

After the 1914-18 war the world was in ferment and more radical thinking began to show. In Europe there were many 'movements' that provide sources for us. The constructivists were active in theatre and architecture. The futurists, particularly in Italy and Russia developed, or rather expressed, thoughts on sound and in particular noise. For example, Carlo Carla wrote about 'The painting of Sound, Noises, and Smell'. It is interesting to note in a book entitled <u>Le Livre Futurists de la Liberation du mot au poeme tactile</u>, that Marinetti in 1920 and Munari in 1931 and 1942 were working in tactile forms.[11] If one can define it as a movement, the DaDaists also need to be considered. Their radical demonstrations had a considerable effect. These movements belong to the past but we must remember that there is continuity of ideas through history. There is nothing new. For example what is the connection between Punk Rock and the Futurists?

More recently other people have also considered multi-sensory design and there is now a growing awareness of it. In the end we are faced with the problem of methodology. As Kandinsky and Franz Marc put it, through an essay on music by Th. v. Hartmann in the book they edited, The Blaue Reiter Almanac: 'Any combination of sounds, any sequence of tone combinations is possible. But here we encounter the great problem that exists not only in music but in all the arts. All methods can be equally right, but will they all together have the desired effect on the particular sense organ appropriate to each particular art?'[12]

There is a growing awareness in the art world that other media than flat saleable canvases are acceptable as usable materials. It is not a question of whether we approve or disapprove of the art itself, but that in this context we appreciate the extent of the media used.

[1] Thomas Hardy, Far from the Madding Crowd, 1874.

[2] Laura U Marks, The Skin of the Film; Intercultural Cinema, Embodiment, and The Senses, America 2000, ISBN 0-8223-2358-3.

[3] Marks, page 195.

[4] DTI Laura Peebles and Beverley Norris, Adultdata; DTI Stuart Smith, Beverley Norris and Laura Peebles, Older Adultdata; , DTI Stuart Smith, Beverley Norris and Laura Peebles, Older Adultdata. These useful books are produced by the Institute for Occupational Ergonomics, University of Nottingham.

[5] Juhani Pallasmaa, The Eyes of the Skin , Architecture and the Senses, London 1996, ISBN 1-85490-439-6. This book is now republished by Wiley & Sons, London.

[6] Albert S Bregman,. Auditory Scene Analysis, MIT Press, 1990, ISBN 0-262-02297-4.

[7] Jessica Rawson, Chinese Jade, From the Neolithic to the Qing, London 1995, ISBN 0-7141-2409-5.

[8] Edited by Gregory Kramer, Auditory Display, Reading USA, ISBN0-201-62603-9.

[9] Edited Richard Kostelanetz, Moholy-Nagy, New York 1970., ISBN 0-7139-0760-6.

[10] Louis Kaplan, Laslo Moholy-Nagy. USA 1995, ISBN 0-8223-1577-7.

[11] Giovanni Lista, Le Livre Futuriste, Modena, Italy.

[12] Edited by Wassily Kandinsky and Franz Marc, The Blaue Reiter Almanac (in English), New York 1974, ISBN 0-306-80346-1.

# *Design*

*All men are designers. All that we do, almost all the time, is design, for design is basic to all human activity.*

Design for the Real World by Victor Papanek.[1]

In this section we will discuss Design and the Design Cycle. In simple terms design is about thinking one's way through a series of requirements or parameters to find a solution. Design is something that applies to many disciplines and right across the senses. As Papanek says it applies to all men and we feel sure that this refers to women as well. The Trust designs in visual, tactile and auditory forms and so do many people. There are other people who are specialists such as exhibition designers, others who design machine tools and so it goes on. However, we feel very strongly that all designers, whatever their specialisation, should be designing in a multi-sensory form but they do not!

Some of you may not see yourselves as designers but we are quite sure that if a psychologist were to look at the straight-forward decisions we all make every day the mechanism of decision would be very similar to that used in a complex design situation. The missing factor is experience.

Design is not, emphatically not, anything to do with a style of clothes or logo. There are garments that are called 'designer' clothes that have little to do with design. There are many logos that tell the same story! Many of the forthright German logos designed during the Weimar days are excellent. It is not difficult to find good and bad examples.

# Design

What is designed might be considered as communication, or an artefact that aids communication, or simply an artefact. This artefact might, on the other hand, be some device to fulfil some function. In other words design covers a very broad spectrum. We design sound, we design books, we design objects that are themselves tactile analogues of the real thing for the purposes of communication. These last are generally haptic design, objects such as models and raised plans. Finally, we try to take into account that what we do is also a visual object that has to be attractive and communicate by sight.

Traditionally the designer made a visual analogue of the object to be produced. The drawing which is the classic basis for visual design is very similar in function to a script or sound design schedule. This used to take the form of a drawing. Most of us now use computers to design. Many of you will be aware of so-called CAD designs and those of you working in sound will know about the many exciting computer programmes that deal with sound. At the Trust we use very specific computer programmes to type-set and to produce graphics and tactile graphics. In the same way we use special computer programmes to design and modify sound; in fact the chequer-board pattern for a sound design is very similar to a physical design, but with a time-line.

Having designed something, the detailed concept has to be transmitted to the person who will make it or use it. We have seen much of the printing industry turned on its head and now we do on our computer what many skilled craftsmen used to provide. However, with this creativity there comes responsibility. Our proposed printing may be put on a carrier or transmitted down the telephone line. In certain circumstances it could feed direct to a machine; to give an example, we write, design and publish books. The books are set and the graphics designed using, say, the programme Adobe INDESIGN CS. This is transferred in Adobe PDF files and taken or sent to the printers at their factory where they then check over the technicalities and make the plates direct from our files. The PDF files can be routed direct to a digital printing machine.

While we have mentioned the specific programmes that we use now, these will change over time but the sequence could well stay the same. The point here is that in following such a procedure the designer carries the final responsibility for the work being absolutely correct. There has to be a checking system that lies outside the designer's organisation. Where the work is for other people then the person for whom the work is being done must finally check the work. We employ a very able sub-editor to check the text and the illustrations to make sure that we have not made serious errors. This will happen in other fields but what we have to remember is that we need to use the creative ability of people to its maximum and to position responsibility correctly. But then what is correct? It will vary according to what is being designed.

The correctness should be judged in relation to the brief for a start. The construction of a design brief in the first instance is another problem. Often it is straightforward. This has to include those who will use it to make money. On the other hand many designs have a social relevance. The accuracy of the brief and accuracy of the design in relation to the brief are both important. We found a book by Professor Robert E Goodin entitled <u>Reflective Democracy</u> of interest.[2] Another example of a useful approach is <u>The Oregon Experiment,</u> carried out at the University of Oregon.[3] This is a master plan for the development of the university which involves those who will occupy and work in the buildings.

You will come across people who call themselves designers. This is perfectly reasonable because instead of small designs that are part of everyday life, these people take on the design for large projects. They generally relate themselves to areas for which they 'profess' a special knowledge. An example to illustrate this point is an Architect who is trained for seven years to know about buildings. Similarly, many people train in other areas. We have to say that we have now spent over fifteen years specialising in the work we do now and feel we are beginning to know about what we are doing.

The spinning wheel is a joy to use and is an impressive machine. Perhaps in the later development of the spinning wheel before being overtaken by the more complex motor driven machines its design may have been committed to the drawing board. To draw the spinning wheel to scale is a way of modelling or making a useful analogue of the machine. However, before all of this the spinning wheel developed on a pragmatic step-by-step basis. In other words, each spinning wheel that was made probably incorporated a slight improvement which in turn was built into the next spinning wheel. At certain points in its development different routes were taken to produce slightly different end products. Nevertheless, most spinning wheels have similar characteristics.

Since those days of pragmatic development, seen by some as happy days, design has made use of many analogues of the real thing to take greater and greater steps forward at each stage. These analogues took far less time to work with than the actual manufacture of a piece. We have already mentioned the drawing board which created a visual analogue, but now CAD takes us forward in even bigger steps and shows us the design on the monitor of the computer.

While the reason for the need for these large steps was originally convenience, it has now become very commercial. It is good to make a larger step than your competitor because that way you can make more money. Another reason is that where the safety of people is a big consideration the analogue helps to judge this without putting a human being at risk. However, the major argument has to be that these new projection techniques also give better opportunities for accuracy and relevance in design and therefore provide more help for people who are disabled, but evidence suggests that they were not and are still not being considered anyway.

Any hand tool, and a spinning wheel is a complex hand tool, followed very much the same path except that they are even more fundamental; the connection between man and the tool is very strong. The ancient hand tools whose handles have been preserved by the peat for thousands of years are to be seen in the museums in Somerset. Hidden in all of this is the relationship of the tool with human beings. Until the beginning of the last century the pragmatic step-by-step development was thought of as normal evolution. However, 'design' or projection was to take over.

Part of the consideration of design is the parameters within which the design has to fit. Another aspect to be considered was the interchangeability of parts as first explored in the Winchester rifle in the United States. There has been a considerable amount of study of these parameters but rarely from the point of view of disability. Nevertheless, there are one or two indications that suggest that disability might become a matter to be considered, especially since it is an additional market for sales.

### Other ways of looking at design

Work study seems to have come into operation with Frank and Lillian Gilbreth who with their book, <u>Applied Motion Study</u> set off the American movement of work study from the 1920s, although Frank wrote a book on the subject in 1911.[4] There followed much research, basically on how things should be made to gain the maximum amount of profit. It is not surprising that the 'workers' were not enthusiastic about this movement which demanded greater efficiency all round. It did produce cheap goods and of course large profits. But more important, there has to be a set of theories that make a foundation for the study of use rather than assembly and this would be a help in design. After all, concepts of the process of assembly are not very far from the way something is used.

In the United Kingdom a broader study of this area, including assembly and use, is covered by the study of ergonomics. This discipline is formed by a gathering of many related disciplines; ergo means work and nomos means natural laws. Other phrases are used in the United States, as in other areas of study. All of these studies have something to offer and should be examined from the point of view of virtual projection of the function of a machine and the operation of a tool. We refer to a tool because there is more likelihood of a clear relationship appearing in one's consideration of this as compared with, say, a piece of art. When thinking of the spinning wheel again, the size and intricacy of the object is such that it is possible to make alterations and to test the effectiveness of these alterations, but with the design of an intricate machine tool, development of the ideas has to be virtual because it is not economically possible to build and rebuild these items to try out a new idea.

Ergonomics is a discipline that was developed during the 1939-45 war, and is related to the military significance of getting the job right when the life of people depends upon it. In fact it seems that wars force cooperation where none existed before. In this war, the research into ergonomics and the practice of ergonomics came into being. Of course, there is a difference between design of operations to manufacture and final product design for use, although much of the technical information is similar. Essentially we are looking at product design. Another heading that is useful is 'User Requirements'.

There is an active Ergonomics Society in the U.K. that you can check out on the internet. More or less the same subject is practised in the United States which seems to be called 'Human Engineering' and has an American way of looking at things. In the evolution of new disciplines names are important. 'Usability' is a useful word and there is a good summary of the practice in a book entitled <u>A Practical Guide to Usability Testing</u>, written by Dumas and Redish.[5] The tests as set out in this book can be carried out realistically.

### Anthropometrics

This is, on the face of it, straightforward since it refers to human dimensions which are clearly a significant aspect of physical design. In fact this is not as simple as it might be. Human dimensions are important because most activities are related to the interface of physical movement and effort with the world. For some reason the anthropometrics of people with disabilities has been almost completely overlooked. We suppose this is because no one saw the need to sell to those who are disabled or had unusual bodily dimensions. The majority of 'normal' people have been surveyed, but the more complex problem is that of people who are disabled.

To quote from the Cornell University Ergonomics website which comments on the current situation;

f. Disabilities – Worldwide, an estimated 400 million people cope with physical disability. In the U.S. in 1970 69 million citizens had some physical disability; 5.4 million were visual problems; 20.1 million auditory problems, 18.3 million arthritis, and 7 million with mobility problems (0 .5 million wheelchair users). There is very limited anthropometric data.

However, there has been some very useful work on the subject. There are few examples, but Selwyn Goldsmith wrote a monumental book entitled <u>Designing for the Disabled</u> in 1963 and there are subsequent updates.[6] Because the title belongs to 1963 it is not as politically correct as

I am sure Selwyn would like. This is a large book with much information and should be on every designer's shelf.

In 2002 the Rehabilitation Engineering Research Center on Universal Design in the School of Architecture and Planning at the University of Buffalo, NY State University, held a conference on the <u>Anthropometrics of Disability</u> and the report is available on the internet and is worth reading. There is an obvious need for the figures, but also for devices to aid design for the disabled. There are some of these for specific work and they can be anything from a set of tables to a computer programme that can take into account not only dimensions but limits of movement and force available to carry out an operation. This was clearly a very exciting 'workshop' and it is worth listing the immediate agenda that was identified as needing further research. They say: 'Here, we will focus on specific readily achievable actions that could advance the field in the near future'.

- Standardize methods for collecting data
- Improve data collection methods to provide better quality data and increased effectiveness
- Develop modelling methods that capitalize on current and future information technologies
- Organise anthropometric databases in more useful ways
- Develop mechanisms for further communications and dialogue among all the stakeholders

These goals are taken in turn and concrete action listed. If this action were taken then this could be a real benefit to the designers of products for people with disabilities.

**Experience**

In the February 2005 issue of <u>MCAD, Productivity Solutions for Mechanical Engineers and Designers</u>, Al Dean writes about programmes that can be applied to the design of machinery in respect to anthropometrics to provide the interface between man and machine. He points out that the NX Human Modelling programme can use anthropometrically accurate human models in CAD programmes, for example, to check the position of controls in vehicles. A similar programme with a broader basis of human information could be used to check the accessibility of vehicles for everyone. With very little alteration such a programme could be applied to many situations perhaps as a warranty that a design is accessible. Clearly before this happens we need more information.

It is not only initial training that is important. Experience is of great importance and we have to remember that a professional designer will retrain several times during his or her working life. The world does not stand still: new concepts, standards and technology move forward in a relentless manner. Most professional designers are obliged to carry out a minimum number of hours retraining each year. Architects in the U.K. have to fit a large amount of time in certified 'Continuing Professional Development' courses each year. If you employ a designer we do suggest that you check their credentials. Generally, the greater the experience that the designer has the better they will be able to carry out your work.

The designer is also responsible for the viability of the design, its cost, its function and its production timetable. To design within such parameters is, as you will all know, a critical issue. It can be argued that a spinning wheel did not need critical examination by expert designers, but then it developed over the equivalent of several lifetimes and undoubtedly a design procedure was used slowly and incrementally. Besides this, the maker and the user had considerable experience. Most designed objects are more complex than the spinning wheel, although not quite so elegant, and progress had to be much faster. Nevertheless, design by evolution is an interesting and significant concept.

### The Design Process

Serious designers, for obvious reasons, have considered the design process. Many have made small maps to show the recycling of various aspects of design to make up a complete process. In short at this simple level there are three words that occur time and again. You will see that this is a cycle of events. The steps are:

ANALYSIS
SYNTHESIS
EVALUATION

It does not take great intelligence to see how these words can make a simple map or diagram that constantly recycles. The way that decisions are made becomes continually more complex and with this, the map becomes more complex as well. However, the complexity is often made up of repeats of such a cycle.

At this point I will again raise the use of the analogue. Sketches on the back of envelopes are perfectly legitimate. However, there is a limit to their application. Often a good strategy is to make a physical model. Besides being looked at, the model has a tactile form. This adds another sense to the list of those involved in the 'evaluation'. Touching the material that is going to be used in the manufacture of the final object is important. There are many factors that are involved in this such as scale, materials, operation and aesthetics.

Techniques of 'rapid prototyping' can be used to save effort in making a physical model. The prototype can be evolved from a CAD programme. In many cases the display of the CAD programme is all that is needed since it can show the object in perspective. Physical models are not the only models that can be used in design. Parallel to the use of models as design analogues they can be used for pure communication on the existing form rather than the projected form.

### Sound prediction

There are computer programmes that can predict sound in particular environments; as yet these have not been developed as design tools but they certainly are used by acoustic consultants. They could be made to be more useful in normal design.

If we go back in time to at least the Roman architectural writer, Vitruvius, then we can see that design has been going on for a long time. In the 1950s Vern Knudsen developed a system of prediction that was based on long winded calculation. This is outlined in the book <u>Acoustical Designing in Architecture</u> by Vern Knudsen and Cyril Harris.[7] By using various factors, such as the frequency that would be reflected by a surface and the volume of the space, he worked out a method of predicting the reverberation time for a space. By using rather doubtful views on the ideal reverberation time for concert halls and different types of music it was possible to get some sort of clue as to whether a design might be reasonable. In fact the concert hall is a curious monster within which music is played. It is a commercial view of music that may or may not be justified. The history of music is fascinating and not at all related to a gathering of people who have purchased a ticket to hear music played to them. Indeed it is correct for that period when the concert hall, like the opera house, became a commercial possibility.

We know that John Bannister as late as 1602 'invented' concerts for which he charged money. This was picked up by a coal merchant by the name of Thomas Britton who also organised concerts. W. A. Mozart was one of the first freelance commercial musicians – and a very good one he was! Before this music was related to various social groups such as a King or a high official. Certainly musicians moved around the country to play 'folk music' where they could but not in formal concerts. Buskers in London until recently referred to the stage within a theatre as 'the green' and they felt that they were part of this.

Since the advert of electronic recording equipment which is economically available for all, a large proportion of music is now developed in small studios and put onto a CD. It is then circulated in this form and may not necessarily be part of a 'concert repertoire'. This is a whole complicated subject and we would refer you to <u>Ethnomusicology, an Introduction</u> In which Krister Malm gives a clear description of The Music Industry.[8] In fact the Scandinavian reaction to the big record companies was so strong that people took to the streets and demonstrated against imported music and the result is that there are many recording studios producing music that really belongs to these particular countries.

The above is by way of explaining why work was done on

acoustics and why the early methods of consideration and calculation came about. There is still tremendous skill and computer firepower used to design concert halls but the techniques were until now not readily available to simulate the acoustics of spaces.

Now the concert hall has been passed by because most music is available in perfect, if synthetic, acoustics on CDs. Most concert halls are too small for pop groups, or their promoters, who now make their own concert halls in the open air. Live concerts have developed the technology of speakers, power mixers and amplifiers to a very high degree. A concert situation can be created in an open field in a matter of days and removed in even less time.

Recently we worked with the University of York on the reconstruction of the acoustics of the virtually destroyed cathedral at Coventry. We supplied the University with the details of the building as it was in 1522 and a specialised recording of the mass as at that time. The University then produced an acoustic model in their computer and with this modelled a sound recording as though it were in the old cathedral. The detail of this technique is outlined elsewhere but here we need to note that virtual sound employed in this way, and for that matter other ways, is a powerful design tool.

### Design Concepts

There are various computer programmes that model thermal energy flow but do not, on the face of it, appear to provide design tools. There are many such ideas that could become useful as design tools as we move towards multi-sensory design. Clearly, a welcome development would be the integration of design 'tools' using more than one sense and function. The visual form of a space is closely related to its acoustic performance which makes this relationship possible. 'Virtual touch' could add to this both in the examination of analogues and real scale ideas. On the other hand the proper examination of real situations and their virtual replication and modification is also a promising approach.

Going back to the 1960s serious books began to be written about design. Many of the points that have been subsequently raised in a series of papers, are to be found in a book entitled The Design Method edited by S. A. Gregory.[9] People like Christopher Alexander in Notes on the Synthesis of Form take us into a much more complex situation.[10] Alexander leads us into new ways of thinking about generative architecture. Nigel Whitely in Design for Society deals with the need for industry to sell its concepts.[11] It follows from this the question, are products designed for the benefit of people or for the manufacturer? On the other side of the coin, Colin Campbell examines the culture that has been developed by the consumer in The Romantic Ethic and the Spirit of Modern Consumerism.[12] All these issues have relevance. At this point we have to note that we are in the midst of moral and political issues which we are not going to deal with, but the problems will not go away.

An aspect that we need to be aware of in design is the effectiveness of inter-modal design. Using more than one sense is important from many points of view. It will help those people with sensory and cognitive problems, but further to this it will have a tremendous effect on everyone. Our own experiments on the application of sound and touch, plus sight in the models we have made in the Dorcas Project set us thinking.

Here is a fast developing situation. We can only advise you to keep your eyes open. It is important to you to know what is going on. Our own thoughts are that besides the curious morality that surrounds design it will be the computer and communication systems that will bring to us the next series of design concepts.

[1] Victor Papanek, Design for the Real World, London 1997.
[2] Robert E Goodin, Reflective Democracy, Oxford 2003,
ISBN 0-19-925617-9.
[3] Alexander, Silverstein, Angel, Ishiwaka and Abrams, The Oregon Experiment, Oxford 1975, This the third of three volumes.
[4] Alexander, Silverstein, Angel, Ishiwaka and Abrams, The Oregon Experiment, Oxford 1975, This the third of three volumes.
[5] Dumas and Redish, A Practical Guide to Usability Testing, Exeter England 1993, ISBN 1-84150-020-8.
[6] Selwyn Goldsmith, Designing for the Disabled, London 1984,
ISBN 0-900630-50-7.
[7] Vern Knudsen and Cyril Harris, Acoustical Designing in Architecture, USA, 1950.
[8] Edited by Helen Myers, Ethnomusicology, an Introduction, UK 1992,
ISBN 0-333-57631-4; see The Music Industry by Krister Malm.
[9] S. A. Gregory, The Design Method,, London 1966.
[10] C. Alexander. Notes on the Synthesis of Form, Harvard 1994,
ISBN 0-674-62751-2
[11] N. Whitely, Design for Society, London 1993,ISBN 0-948462-47-7
[12] C. Campbell, The Romantic Ethic and the Spirit of Consumerism, Harvard 1994, ISBN 0-674-62751-2

## *Multi-Sensory Design*

> *Architecture is not only illuminated by light but by sound as well; in fact it is brought into relief for us through all our senses.*

Survival Through Design by Richard Neutra[1]

The Dog Rose Trust, and its predecessor Dog Rose, have been in operation for nearly seventeen years as a research and development organisation. One design that gained a Millennium Award was the 'Dorcas Project', named after the Guide Dog who was part of our research team. This work was about communicating information and the sense of space for an environment. The solution was interactive three-dimensional models that produced sound when touched. This is an example of multi-sensory design. In this section we present a simplified theoretical approach that we have adopted and could be useful to others in the future. We will list in this book the strategies that the Trust uses, which we believe will become particularly relevant in the future and so we wish to tell you about them.

The Trust is committed in its charitable aim to help those with perceptual and cognitive problems. It does this through the evolution of three major strategies. They are:

Universal Design.
Universal Communication.
The development of Multi-sensory Design.

In simple terms, Universal Design is already very much in operation, particularly in the USA, and many of us here have supported these concepts for some years. The use of Universal Communication is certainly in operation by the Trust, but multi-sensory design as a total concept is still evolving as an operative design concept. Multi-sensory design is, as we have defined it, a broader concept than Universal Communication since it covers all design. It should activate a substantial change as it comes into operation and will, we believe, eliminate many of the problems in the area of 'disability' communication.

In the consideration of these items two expressions need to be examined. The first is Universal and the second is Design. Since these expressions are used in a special way these need some explanation.

### Universal

Immediately this will be recognised as an important word that is now, for various reasons, quite rightly applied to what we do. This is not the place to remind you of current legislation and legislation in the past that failed, but rather to support a real provision for everyone. This can be seen either as an attitude that is politically more acceptable or a way to increase the market or perhaps both. We see it as a way to help people and communities.

In the development of an approach to design that has a socially acceptable breadth, the word Universal, as applied to people, has become current. The word universal is perhaps a bit over the top but as it can refer to 'ALL People' a dictionary assures me, then this use is permissible. For the designer the brief for his or her design should contain a detailed description of who the work is for. If the brief is what is termed inclusive, then it follows that it must be for everyone although this needs careful consideration. For example it is not satisfactory to design a ladies' lavatory in the same way as a gentlemen's lavatory. This aspect apart, in many ways we still do not know enough about the characteristics of our clients so it is not surprising that as a consequence we cannot pull together a reasonable brief.

However, people are very different. A simple statement, but to those of us who are presenting something to people in general, it is profoundly true and poses a major problem. The brief may have to cover all sorts of differences. In this context it is not a question of legislation, it is one of information and design. The brief for a design must state clearly whom the design is for. Certain information is available, even if not easily available, on which we should base our design work, whatever sense is under consideration. Mobility and physical ability is another fundamental issue.

Care must be taken in the manner in which one considers the concept of universal design. There are many situations where the natural differences between people make a natural segregation. Male and female is such a situation. It is a convention in England that public conveniences are segregated into those for male and those for female. As an aside, many of our blind friends have encountered problems of recognition of which sex a convenience is designated for to everyone's embarrassment. However, in some countries the customs of the communities are different and there might be no problem.

In the past, people who are blind have not been made to feel welcome in places like historic sites, art galleries and museums. But then neither have people who speak other languages or who are in any way different. The new awareness of disability was perhaps the beginning of a political move by those who were different. A new awareness of the needs of those who are different generally has yet to hit us, but it is certainly on its way. The Trust has designed signs for museums in Wales and quite reasonably both Welsh and English are used in the captioning. How many signs are also in Gujarati, let alone saying something relevant to other cultures?

The disabled veterans from the Vietnam War in the United States, quite understandably, felt left out in an inaccessible world and were bold enough to say so and to demonstrate what they felt. The impact was considerable and the idea was picked up by minorities elsewhere. Since then most of us are beginning to realise how important people are and so legislation has been devised both in the United States and Europe to make sure that people with disabilities are not left out. In fact it seems to us that none of the legislation works very well. Since the legislation has been put into operation it has served to demonstrate that almost every service or function in the community has failed to reach the community it is supposed to serve.

Coming from the world of architecture we were brought up assuming that most people were the same age as we were, about the same stature and so on. As an off-the-peg set of rules it was helpful but not definitive and its most important influence was the empathy that it suggested between the designer and the design. So what are the real characteristics of those we have to communicate with? The following is a simple and certainly not an exclusive list:

Because our clients are human every one has a different character
They come from different races
They speak different languages
They have different histories individually and collectively
People belong to different cultural systems and subsystems
They have different religions
They have different concepts of politics
They have different physical and mental characteristics
They have different perceptual and cognitive ability
They are of different ages
They have different degrees of mobility

Such a list is important and all these characteristics and more have to be considered in relation to all design work.

In our list above we have some, but certainly not all, the characteristics of people. Some aspects are physical. For example there is no point in designing a chair where the seat is two metres from the floor – but there are slight exceptions to this. Similarly a door handle has to turn easily otherwise a person with little strength will not be able to use it. It is not satisfactory to design a sign using words that are applicable to only one language where more than one language is spoken. Some people cannot see, some cannot hear, some cannot understand, some cannot reach. And that is not all. How then are we going to design for, communicate with or help our fellow human beings?

We believe that we can design for people by using Universal Design and Communication. We hope to convince you of this in the next few chapters of this book. You can also ask what is being done in this direction. The answer is quite a lot at a simple level but not much at a higher level.

There are areas where activity and study, often stimulated by commerce, are fruitful and we can learn from these. We even hope that specialists from these areas can help us. One such area is television and another allied one is cinema. We all appreciate the power of these cross-modal practices and academic studies, but in both cases a small square screen with albeit slightly improved sound than in the past constitutes a very minimal section of the environment. Clearly, there is much to be learned, even if the essence of what is to be learned is to kick over the commercial traces and move.

Even though we live in a society that is dysfunctional in both economic and social terms we have to look to the future and try to move forward. Right now no politicians or business operators show any signs of initiating a satisfactory system.

[1] Richard Neutra, Survival Through Design, New York 1969.

# *Universal Design*

This is a title and practice firmly established over quite a few years. It presents a more satisfactory answer to the problems of design than the provision of a special concept for people with disabilities. The implication is that all are equal and because of this everyone can use what is designed. To do this design parameters need to be stated. On the face of it Universal Design deals essentially with the mechanical or physical aspect of design but examination of the world of Universal Design shows that the concept is expanding.

There are many useful organisations in the USA where the field continues to expand. There are many publications on the subject but we would refer you to the web to keep up to date.

Progress so far with such ethical design is good and in the UK and the US it is becoming a component part of dealing with disability by making everything accessible to everyone. Some schools of architecture and design have adopted the idea and practice it in their teaching but this seems to be confined mainly to the US. The effect is achieved within a broad sensitive ethical design approach and the elimination of physical and control problems in the interface between the designed artefact or environment and the person. A statement defining Universal Design by The Center for Universal Design in North Carolina University, USA reads:

> The design of products and environments to be usable by all people to the greatest extent possible, without the need for adaption or specialized design.

It is important to look at the grain of this way of thinking. The specific headings that have been defined by The Center for Universal Design in North Carolina[1] in this subject are of importance. The list is set out below, however, there are likely to be detailed changes as time goes by:

1. **Equitable use**

The design is useful and marketable to people with diverse abilities.

2. **Flexibility in use**

The design accommodates a wide range of individual preferences and abilities

### 3.    Simple and Intuitive

Use of the design is easy to understand, regardless of the user's experience,

knowledge, language skills, or current concentration level

### 4.    Perceptible information

The design communicates necessary information effectively to the user,

regardless of ambient conditions of the user's sensory abilities

### 6.    Low Physical Effort

The design can be used efficiently and comfortably and with a minimum of

fatigue

### 5.    Tolerance for error

The design minimizes hazards and adverse consequences of accidental or

unintended actions

### 6.    Low physical effort

The design can be used efficiently and comfortably and with a minimum of

fatigue

### 7.    Size and space for approach and use

Appropriate size and space is provided for approach, reach, manipulation, and use regardless of the user's body size, posture, or mobility.

There are two important reasons for quoting this brief. First, it shows the ethical basis of Universal Design. Second, it is a good basis for the design of anything that has physical characteristics.

Another organisation of note in this field is the Adaptive Environments, 374 Congress Street, Suite 301, Boston, MA 02210 USA (www.info.adaptiveenvironments.org.) We have attended two of their conferences and in this way established links with other organisations with similar interests, particularly in the USA.

However, while universal design is a popular and is a useful approach there is still room for a broader consideration of design that needs some work to formulate. For example the concept could be extended to include communication issues.

[1] University of Carolina  www.design.ncsu.edu

# *Universal Communication*

Because of the history of the use of sight and its particular useful characteristics most designs are 'seen' as visual manifestations. This is because of the efficiency of sight compared with other senses on a superficial level; consequently other senses have been ignored. However, it is possible that before the Renaissance awareness of sight that other senses were more generally used. The fact that we say things are 'seen' is an indication of how deep rooted this view is. Nevertheless, it is clear that there are also design concepts that are based on other senses than sight. It is possible to design for touch. It is possible to design for hearing. It is possible to design for smell and taste. Further it is also possible to design using inter-sense design, that is designing for more than one sense at a time and in some ways it is impossible not to! This simple idea can be applied to both what we have termed Universal Communication and multi-sensory design.

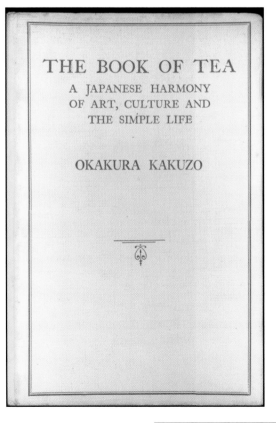

THE BOOK OF TEA

A JAPANESE HARMONY
OF ART, CULTURE AND
THE SIMPLE LIFE

OKAKURA KAKUZO

In practical terms if something is communicated though all senses those with a problem with one or even more senses can still understand it. This is a principle the Trust has used for some years and concepts and design ideas have evolved as we worked, as in the Dorcas Project. In operation the concept here is to provide communication through all senses primarily to help those with perceptual problems, such as people who are blind. However, while such communication is aimed at helping those with perceptual and cognitive problems it also helps those with all their senses and it makes it more enjoyable and rewarding for everyone! Such a concept of communication makes sense for everyone. Clearly, such a concept is related to Universal Design, which we have just talked about and might be seen as the sensory aspect of it. We have been very much concerned with sound as a part of this. In the long term there is no reason why this aspect of communication should not be built into the structure of Universal Design.

Let us take a closer look at an example where all senses are used. In the Book of Tea by Kakuzo Okakura, he says about the tea ceremony:

Quiet reigns with nothing to break the silence save the note of the boiling water in the iron kettle. The kettle sings well, for pieces of iron are so arranged in the bottom as to produce a peculiar melody in which one may hear a cataract muffled by clouds, of a distant sea breaking among the rocks, a rainstorm sweeping through a forest, or of the sighing of pines on some faraway hill. [1]

Here then is an elegant piece of multi-sensory design. Also there are other dimensions of emotion and sense, such as the anticipation of the tea and its taste. The cups are very beautiful and feel wonderful. The teahouse has its own aesthetic and doubtless there will be flowers with their fragrant aroma.

Whether we like it or not we are less aware of our senses than we should be. A person who is blind will point this out to us, and so indeed will our friends who are deaf. An environment, as we generally know it, has a real and reactive form involving all senses. Part of the reason for ignoring our senses is social. As we have said, expressions such as 'do not touch, please be quiet, and do not mention the smell', were certainly part of our childhood and the social ambience that we were brought up with and perhaps with you as well.

One might ask if the other senses than sight are really necessary. If we step back and consider matters, all senses are in themselves important but put them together and it adds up to an awareness which is to our mind a higher state. There is a very interesting quote by the 18th century philosopher Bishop George Berkeley which illustrates their importance:

Thus, for example, a certain colour, taste, smell, figure, and consistence having been observed to go together, are accounted one distinct thing, signified by the name apple. Other collections of ideas constitute a stone, a tree, a book and the like sensible things; which, as they are pleasing or disagreeable, excite the passions of love, hatred, grief, and so forth. [2]

Of course there are deeper meanings in much of the Bishop's work, and we would not subscribe to some of Berkeley's philosophy, but as it stands this quote does show how much we rely on our senses for absolutely everything.

As a general principle if more than one sense is used in communication or design then it will reach more people and perhaps almost everyone. We will illustrate what we mean. Going back to basics it is said that we have five senses and you can recite these as well as we can:

SIGHT
HEARING
TOUCH
TASTE
SMELL

In all probability these words came from the Greek philosophers where five was seen to be a good number. The real number and combination of senses is an interesting subject. However, five is convenient and is reasonably accurate in its general idea and is useful until we examine the situation in close detail.

To illustrate the point, let us think for a moment that we are all profoundly deaf. We will have other senses that we can use and these are what our deaf friends will use. Let us recite the senses we still have.

SIGHT
TOUCH
TASTE
SMELL

If we only communicate in sound then we will not be able to communicate at all. However, if we use all the remaining senses then there is less of a problem.

So now let us think for a moment that we are totally blind. Again there are many people who are blind or visually impaired. The senses we are left with are:

HEARING
TOUCH
TASTE
SMELL

If we communicate using these senses then it is a great help and much of the content and enjoyment of the communication will be retained.

If what we are communicating has only one sensory dimension then we have to deal with this differently. Because of the history of the senses this is frequently related to the use of sight but of course, it can apply to any sense. A painting for example is designed to be seen and while it has a texture and haptic form, a smell, and sound when touched the communication issue is the graphic form expressed on the front of the painting. If I cannot see then there is a problem. In this situation it is necessary to describe the painting using another sense, this is known as transcription. It is not possible to communicate the graphic form except in an analogous form. This can take the form of raised diagrams, audio description and so on. However, on analysis much information that needs to be communicated about a particular painting does not relate to graphics at all and can be communicated readily through other senses. Similarly, such thinking can be applied to anything designed primarily for any one sense. This illustration also demonstrates the main disadvantage of mono-sensory design or communication.

### The development of multi-sensory design

At this point we need to discuss the future and tell you where we are going. Based on what appears to be happening in the real design world, we need to be looking towards a new concept that will be inclusive. Further to this the world of technology is opening up a whole new set of opportunities that will help us achieve this more universal approach.

In order to illustrate the new concept that I am suggesting I would like to again quote Professor Juhani Pallasmaa, from Helsinki from his wonderful book entitled <u>The Eyes of the Skin</u>:

> Various architectures can be distinguished on the basis of the sense modality that they tend to emphasise. In addition to the prevailing architecture of the eye, there is the haptic architecture of the muscle and the skin. There is an architecture that also recognises the realms of hearing, smell and taste.[3]

The significance of this statement is considerable and to hear this from someone who is well-known in the architectural world is important.

Most design work is still based in thought on the drawing board with all the limitations that this implies. Design must move forward! Not only architecture but also all arts, we suggest, need to start again using this premise. Given good multi-sensory design for everyone many of the traditional communication barriers will disappear. Given good multi-sensory design the Trust believes that many of the barriers between so-called able and so-called disabled will also disappear!

Architecture is not alone in looking to a broader approach. In a fascinating essay entitled <u>Sound Symbols and the Landscape</u>, Trevor Wishart, who is a very interesting composer of music and sound, works his way through the morphology of sound and says:

> The sophisticated control of this dimension of our sonic experience has become possible with the development of sound recording and the control of virtual acoustic space via sound projection from loudspeakers. It would certainly be foolish to dismiss this new world of possibilities on some a priori assumption that they are not of musical concern. In fact, any definition of musical activity which does not take them into account must, from here on, be regarded as inadequate.[4]

There was even a BBC radio programme that went as far as relating music to paintings and a V&A exhibition did the same. That is moving convention along. It is good to know that sound and vision together are now acceptable. It is interesting to read the arguments put forward when 'movies' first got sound in the 1930s.

If we now look at the developments in technology much is happening and much could happen particularly if the logic of multi-sensory design is well stated and accepted. Clearly those computer programmes that deal with Computer Aided Design are in the forefront. Now with the development of more intuitive controls the programmes are becoming more useful. These programmes can manipulate solid objects, sound, acoustics and so on, all of which took a considerable amount of design time in the past; it is all speeding up. Programmes to check the universality of a design are another significant feature.

Whatever the status quo of the senses I have to tell you that other senses than sight are also important but are hardly noticed. However, let me remind you of my example of the Japanese Tea Ceremony. This is just a random example but it is a situation where every sense is used and no one can deny how good it is. If you think about it, most of life relies on the use of all, rather than one sense, even if the use is subconscious.

The history of technology also has a strong influence on our habits. Printing on paper is a good example. Books do in fact have a component of touch and smell but they are essentially graphic forms. Many traditional crafts still have their multi-sensory base such as pottery, furniture making and deserve a proper understanding through the senses. Many of us watch television, which also has something to listen to and so uses sight and hearing. We can now play music and derive images from all sorts of carriers such as tape, CDs, DVDs, Mini-discs flash cards - all using digital information that can deal with material for sight and hearing without difficulty. There is evidence that commerce is not unaware of the possibilities of making a 'fast buck' out of new technical developments. We should be considering the potential development of the technology of a multi-sensory environment before commerce does, to make sure it is developed on an inclusive basis.

However, whatever we think, technical changes are now upon us and need to be dealt with. It does not take a great amount of imagination to see that present technical barriers can be pressed back and environments for all senses can be provided as part of the normal world. Design of a Real and Virtual form can now be considered by the manipulation of sensory provision often by digital means. The future is very exciting and in this 'New World' of design we want you to consider those of our community with sensory problems. If we are now going to design in proper sensory ways I know that you will agree that it would be good if everyone were included.

From what we have said you will see why multi-sensory communication and design, which are relatively new ideas, are used by The Dog Rose Trust wherever possible. Experience has shown that by using various techniques and senses, it is possible to communicate with almost anyone. Perhaps we have oversimplified the concept of multi-sensory communication and design. Alongside this we are not unaware of the problems that we face in terms of transcription. Peter spent four years as Chair of the National Confederation of Transcription Information Services (COTIS) and so we do know the problems.

In summary we suggest it follows that it is of advantage to those of us dealing with sensory design problems to use a multi-sensory approach to design and communication. Where necessary we have to, but emphatically, it is also a good idea for all of us.

[1]K. Okakura, The Book of Tea, Sydney, Australia 1935, page 43.

[2] George Berkley, A New Theory of Vision, London (first published 1709) 1950. He may also have written:

> Take away the sensation of softness, moisture, redness, tartness, and you take away the cherry. Since it is not a being distinct from these sensations; a cherry, I say, is nothing but a congeries of sensible impressions or ideas perceived by various senses; which ideas are united into one thing…

However, we cannot find it in the edition we have of his book.

[3] J. Pallasmaa, The Eyes of the Skin, Architecture and the Senses, Academy Editions, London 1994, ISBN 1-85490-439-6, page 48.

[4] T. Wishart, Sound Symbols and Landscapes.

# *Psychophysics and Cognition*

The concept of psychophysics and cognition is an interesting one and some understanding of this is important for the designer. For us this is an area of interest rather than specialisation; nevertheless, it is of considerable importance. These are the first steps in the whole of psychological thinking. In crude terms psychophysics is the interface between an animal and its environment and cognition the first step in the processing that takes place in the brain that initiates action.

Within this overall, and somewhat oversimplified, picture there are other areas and words that need to be mentioned. Sensation refers to the process of detecting a signal in the environment. It is the necessary collection of information about the environment. Perception refers to that in which we interpret the information gathered by the senses. Psychophysics is the study of the way we detect and sense signals. Cognitive science is concerned with the way the mind works. Cognitive scientists try to understand perceiving, thinking and other mental phenomena.

Cognitive psychology has been referred to as the 'architecture of the mind'. As we are already aware, senses from different organs work together in the mind to produce an enhanced result that is more useful than from one single set of signals. In Cross Modal Space and Cross Modal Attention, edited by Charles Spence and Jon Driver there are a series of essays on the results of cross modal perception as for example with sight and hearing.[1] Recently, the way that the mind works and its physiology has been studied in detail and the results are very interesting and significant. A recent book entitled The Hippocampal and Parietal Foundations of Spatial Cognition, edited by Burgess, Jeffery and O'Keefe contains essays referring to the function of parts of the brain and indeed multi-modal processing.[2]

There are also books that deal specifically with cognition. For example Cognition – Exploring the Science of the Mind, by Daniel Reisberg.[3] Various subjects are covered in this book which have some importance to what we are trying to do. Sadly, the designer has very little help from the world of psychology. There is so much that could be done especially where the design is being made for those with special disabilities.

Because of the importance of sensation and perception we seem to have quite a few books on our shelves covering this subject and that focus on this particular aspect. Most of these books tend to be teaching books from the United States although Oxford are publishing some startlingly good books. The three books we refer to are: <u>Fundamentals of Sensation and Perception</u>, <u>Sensation and Perception</u> and another <u>Sensation and Perception</u>,[4]

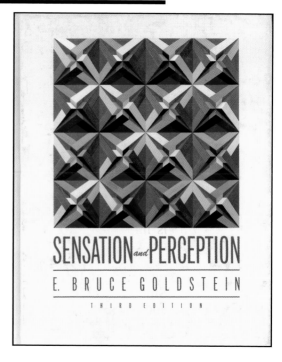

In each of these books the senses are divided into the more obvious ones: Sight, Hearing, Touch, Smell and Taste. This is probably the point to mention that the senses are related to each other and as science moves forward this seems to be appreciated. It is worth mentioning that some non-scientists have caught up with this.

Two recent books remind us that the world of psychology is an active one. The first is <u>Ways of Seeing – The Scope and Limits of Visual Cognition</u> by Pierre Jacob and Marc Jeannerod which covers a new approach and is written by a philosopher and a neurologist. The other book is <u>Active Vision</u> by John Findlay and Iain Gilchrist, which deals with the dynamic process of gathering information by the eyes as they continually sample the world around. Both are published by Oxford. We are particularly interested in the sense of hearing and touch, but it is these approaches that explore new avenues of thought that get us closer to an understanding of a very complex subject.

Cognition and hearing as a subject have moved forward from the past very quickly. There are three books that we need to mention here. <u>Listening</u> by Stephen Handel is in many ways an old-fashioned book but it has much of interest. <u>Auditory Scene Analysis</u>, by Albert S. Bregman is a classic that had been mentioned several times and needs to be read through carefully. <u>Thinking in Sound</u>, edited by Stephen McAdams and Emmanual Bigand, is particularly important. From this one can adopt models that are useful.

Sight has been understood as the most important sense and it is true that sight is a very useful sense in that information can be accurately registered very quickly. However, other senses have different qualities and content. The result of this preference for sight is that we know more about the use of sight in psychophysical and cognitive terms than any other sense. This uneven development of research has further unbalanced the general appreciation of the necessary consideration of inter-sense modality. However, this situation appears to be changing.

In a brilliant intuitive book entitled <u>Blindness: What is it, What it does, and How to live with it</u>, the Reverend Thomas J. Carroll discusses the use of the senses:

> Scientific studies of the last century have demonstrated that the number of human senses is far more than the classical five. No listing now seems possible which would be satisfactory for every branch of study; the number in each case depends on the particular emphasis and purpose of the study. Here ... we are concerned, not so much with the separate senses from the physiological point of view, as with the sense activities that appear to be particularly important when sight is gone.

Carroll gives a list of factors that are worth consideration. It is important to realise that this list relates mostly to mobility, but it is nevertheless a useful illustration. He talks of Hearing and within this he defines the discrimination of sounds, localisation of sounds and sound reflection (in echoes, in change of timbre and 'facial vision'). He talks of Smell and Taste that are very similar, and Touch with its sense of pressure and pain, and of temperature. He goes on to talk of the sense of balance, kinaesthesia and stereognosis. Further he defines motor memory, spatial relations, integration of sensations and visualisation. There are several studies by psychologists on the inter-relationship between senses but there is an interesting intuitive understanding of senses in what he says. Here then is a pragmatic approach to inter-modal understanding which we think is very important.

We found in a study that we did for the University of Leicester entitled <u>The Consideration of the World of Music and the Deaf Person</u> that the part that sound played in the comprehension and practice of music is relatively small. A large proportion of the field is intellectual and not directly sense-based, and a considerable amount is visual. This does not mean that the experience of sound is not important but it is not complete in itself. Carroll, and other writers, particularly over the last ten years, remind us of the connection between the senses. These are not entirely new ideas, similar thoughts can be found in the design and teaching of the late twenties and early thirties in the writings of such teachers as Moholy-Nagy. In truth if we go back to the 1920s the perspective of design was beginning to break through but matters were not clear although the Gestalt (literally translated 'shape') psychologists of that period seemed to see things as a totality. Maybe there was a connection. This might make a good interdisciplinary Ph.D subject.

[1] Edited by Charles Spence and Jon Driver, <u>Crossmodal space and Crossmodal Attention</u>, Oxford 2004, ISBN 0-19-852486-2.

[2] Eited by N.Burgess, K.J.Jeffery and J.O.O'Keefe, <u>The Hippocampal and Parietal Foundation of Spatial Cognition</u>, Oxford 1999, ISBN 0-19-852453-6

[3] Daniel Reisberg, <u>Cognition, Exploring the Science of the Mind</u>, New York 1997, ISBN 0-393-96925-8.

[4] Fundamentals of Sesnation and Perception, Michael W Levine, Oxford, 2000, ISBN 0-19-852466-8; E Bruce Goldstein, <u>Sensation and Perception</u>, California 1989, ISBN 0-534-09672-7; Stanley Coren, Lawrence M Ward and James T Enns, <u>Sensation and Perception</u>, Orlando 1994, ISBN 0-15-500103-5;

## *General Concept of Place*

The concept of place has to be an ultimate key issue. The concept is not a new one. Edward S. Casey in his book <u>The Fate of Place, A Philosophical History</u>[1] takes us back to ancient Greece and we would guess that thoughts on place might go back even further. This history is important but essentially philosophical. Here we need to attempt to consider what the characteristics of place actually are. We are designing around these issues and they are our whole gamut of variability. In simple terms, space is a vital issue and it is the placing of objects in space and their significance that give us a point of departure.

The history of the psychology of place goes back a long way. In his interesting book <u>The Psychology of Place,</u> David Canter gives a history of Places and Cognition and its theoretical origin.[2] Clearly, there was an awareness of place back in the 19th century but it was the 'image geography' that became a focus. Indeed many geographers took an interest. Before this, psychologists had taken a very significant stance in relation to conceptual systems, but it was the spread of these ideas into the world of planning and geography that was to be of significance to the designer.

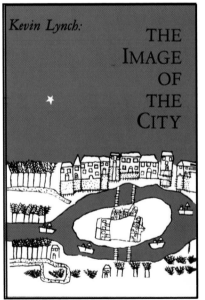

Kevin Lynch's book, <u>Image of the City,</u> had the greatest impact. [3] He wrote many useful books, such as <u>What Time is this Place,</u>[4] and <u>Managing the Sense of a Region</u>[5] which address broader issues. One of the ways that he measured the city was through the minds and mental images of the people who lived there. The overall impact of his thinking is rounded off in a book entitled <u>City Sense and City Design – Writings and Projects of Kevin Lynch.</u>[6] The essential issue that he recognised, working in conjunction with Gyorgy Kepes, was the symbolic nature of buildings, streets and traffic. The five useful elements that Lynch put forward on the basis of his experience are:

> Paths
> Edges
> Districts
> Nodes
> Landmarks

The exact extended definitions need to be read in the book, but we have found that these practical concepts can be used for analysis or design but by no means cover the whole subject.

However, one problem that we are frequently faced with is the appropriate concept of cognitive maps and their translation into a practical form. In this respect Canter's comments on cognitive cartography have proved to be very useful.

In the above we have discussed place in terms of essentially visual forms. There are many situations that depend on other senses. Sense of Place,[7] a series of essays edited by Steven Feld and Keith Basso, includes an essay by Feld, called *An Acoustemology of Place Resounding in Bosavi, Papua New Guinea* which describes Bosavi culture. In essence he describes an environment in a tropical rainforest where seeing is not so valuable as hearing. One spin-off from this is the development of a verbal culture that is very impressive. Using Maurice Merleau-Ponty's concepts presented in Phenomenology of Perception,[8] Feld in his book describes this environment and the essay is worthy of careful study. He wrote:

> At its broadest, the multi sensory character of Bosavi acoustemology is suggested by the complexities of everyday practices linking sensory experience of the rainforest to artistic processes in visual, verbal, musical and choreographic media

Compared with our environment which is driven by curious economic forces with its sound obliterated by the internal combustion engine, we really have to think carefully about what we need to achieve and how and to consider what happens in other places.

Joy Monice Malnar and Frank Vodvarka wrote in Sensory Design:[9]

> Suppose for a moment, that sound, touch, and odor were treated as the equals of sight, and that emotion was an important part of cognition. What would our built environment be like if sensory response, sentiment, and memory were critical factors, more vital even than structure and program?

There follows a full book of information on this concept. It has been criticised as being too architectural for general use, but after all architecture is an ancient craft and notes on past thoughts are very useful. However, the mixing of emotion into the equation make the subject difficult to handle and thus difficult to understand but the exercise is nevertheless useful and contains much of interest.

### Ambience And Location
A recent conference organised by the Sensory Trust focussed on the effect on design of thinking about the use of the senses. While this

was proven it was interesting that there were additional views on such matters as the use of wild flowers in the environment. The point made is not immediate but we live in an environment that, while we try to defeat botanical succession with monocultures, succession is part of our ecology. In another paper the dynamics of development become an important aspect of the environment. Both of these papers demonstrate that there are facets to every environment that need careful study even though they do not seem to be of importance at first examination. An overall awareness is important and an essential tool for us to use.

[1] Edward S Casey, <u>The Fate of Place A Philosophical History</u>, USA 1997, ISBN 0-520-21649-0.

[2] David Canter, <u>The Psychology of Place</u>, UK 1977, ISBN 0-85139-532-5.

[3] Kevin Lynch, <u>The Image of the City</u>, Cambridge USA 1994, ISBN 0-262-12004-6

[4] Kevin Lynch, <u>What Time is this Place?</u> Cambridge USA 1993, ISBN 0-262-62032-4

[5] Kevin Lynch, <u>Managing the Sense of a Region,</u>, Cambridge USA 1991, ISBN 0-262-12072-0

[6] Edited by Tridib Banerjee, <u>City Sense and City Design, Writings and Projects of Kevin Lynch</u>, Cambridge USA 1996, ISBN 0-262-12143-3

[7] Edited by Feld and Basso, <u>Sense of Place</u>, Houston USA1996, ISBN 0-933452-94-2

[8] Maurice Merleau-Ponty, <u>Phenomenology of Perception</u>, Oxford, 1992.

[9] Joy Monice Malnar and Frank Vodvarka, <u>Sensory Design</u>, Minneapolis USA 2004, ISBN 0-8166-3959-0

*Places are often used for different activities. Here a place in Ludlow is host to street theatre during the Streets Alive Festival*

# *Wayfinding*

We have been thinking in terms of the senses except we are considering the broader implications of senses in its scientific interpretation. Wayfinding is precisely about what it says and is critical, particularly to blind people, and to everyone for that matter. However, the problem is not only one for those of us with sensory or cognitive problems but for just everyone. Strictly the problem of wayfinding comes within the category of cognition and is not directly a sensory matter.

The reality is that wayfinding results in a cognitive action after we are aware that the sensory signals are clear. One way to help in this situation is to use various devices in an analogous form, for example a three-dimensional model. However, sensory design solutions are various and include tactile floors and sound beacons which do have an effect on a person's appreciation of the space they are in, in addition to accessible signs, instructions and any other communication form. Everyone needs to be able to find their way around a building, a square or even a town. Again, as it is pointed out elsewhere, the aesthetic of even a city is made up of what one can sense, plus an appreciation of the broader aspects,

such as the wayfinding aspect of the situation. All of this is the same problem but the relevant solutions are different. It is important to remember that the solutions should be interesting and exciting!

Perhaps the definition by Paul Arthur and Romedi Passini in their book <u>Wayfinding, People, Signs, and Architecture</u>, will help:[1] 'Wayfinding is problem solving. Making a journey and reaching a destination are wayfinding goals. Attaining these goals requires action and behaviour , some quite obvious and some less so.' This book is a very useful one and refers to many of the problems that are faced in considering wayfinding. While we accept this direct approach as being extremely useful we sense that the whole needs a broader  appreciation and, perhaps, the choice of another word to head it up.

It would be wrong to think that we should only be considering sensory and cognitive action separately. There are situations where sensory signals can add to a cognitive situation with relevance. An example is where we realise that we are on a frozen pool from using our sight, which is also supported by our feeling of the temperature of the air. However, if we then hear a crack we know we have problems. If we were to hear the same crack when we knew previously from our senses and our cognitive formulation that we were on safe ground, it would be a matter of interest rather than concern.

There are quite a few 'fast buck' answers in the form of guidance systems for blind people. If there were a national standard then these might be acceptable but as closed systems they are not. The environment should be capable of providing information to everyone and this means unimpaired people together with those with sensory and cognitive problems. It is not satisfactory to provide an expensive gismo when the problem applies to everyone.

To go back to basics we need to grasp what this is all about. I referred to the very useful book by Paul Arthur and Romedi Passini. They start their book by listing the problems of wayfinding, which, with a little thought we can totally identify with. Some of the problems are quite clear, for example finding the entrance or where the lifts are. Others are not so clear, such as missing the signs or not being able to read them. And of course if you cannot see then there is no way you will 'see' a visual sign but you could hear a sound beacon or announcement. Here is another case for multi-sensory design. Thus what we are looking for is a clear statement as to what wayfinding is. In fact it is a small part of a total problem which is contained within the discipline of cognition and is a small part of what one might term decision-making. Clearly, from what Arthur and Passini write there is a need for awareness, not necessarily of wayfinding solutions as such, but of the parts of the area of cognitive study that make up the problem. In short there are real problems!

Cognitive mapping is a key issue here and is the basis on which we solve the problems of finding the way. This does not mean that we need to provide a map although in practice this is quite a good solution but that is jumping forward too fast. The cognitive map can be of various forms in words, pictures or tactile forms. There is also the issue of environmental perception.

The cognitive map in a person's mind could use any sense or set of senses in its construction. It could be of consecutive sounds; it could be a series of words or a series of smells. For example 'lavender, ten paces ahead until I smell lilac then turn right'. Smell in this case is somewhat transient and depends on the season and the weather. However, it could be a combination of all sorts of sensations. If you truly examine your own view of a place or path you will find that you use more than one sense and besides this most of the emotional connotations belong with other senses than seeing. Wayfinding should be part of an exciting multi-sensory design procedure rather than just a battle to find the public lavatory..

Reginald G Golledge edited a book entitled <u>Wayfinding Behaviour – cognitive mapping and other spatial processes.</u>[2] In this book there are a series of essays that highlight human, animal and insect navigation and it is a combination of these areas of study. In this book Golledge identifies the work by Tolman in 1948 in developing the concept of cognitive mapping. He states the process very clearly:

> The consensus is clear: humans acquire, code, store, decode, and use cognitive information as part of their navigation and wayfinding activities. Although over the centuries they have developed numerous ways of supplementing personally stored environmental information (e.g. maps. written descriptions, and various forms of image representations), it appears that humans rely on personal cognition to make many spatial decisions and to guide their movement behaviour.

The environment has to be expressed and designed in a multi-sensory manner. Tactile paving should be used correctly and with imagination. Sound beacons are useful but not to everyone. However, usually maps are about the interpretation of a poorly designed environment and this makes its expression very difficult. There could be maps or their equivalent for all environments and this would make life for everyone more enjoyable.

The cognitive map needs to be tried with various possible clients, some of whom have to have sensory problem. Some of the items that have to be taken into account are local reference systems, that is, roads and proximity of places. We check landmarks that may not be seen, but will be known about. Routes are important and so are the sounds that are alongside them. When considering the form of the map certain places have to be anchor points.

Clearly, it would not be satisfactory to base the map purely on sound or even provide a link that depended on sound alone. Similarly, visual clues alone will not help everyone. It has to communicate a multi-sensory representation. With the bronze model of part of the centre of York there is a carry round plan and an audio guide. A survey we made of the views of blind and visually impaired people in York came out with the fact that they liked the smell of pies being cooked at 'Thomas the Baker' in Lendal. It was no surprise to find that everyone, except vegetarians, enthusiastically recognised the street by the wonderful smell. While we were unable to simulate the smell of the pie shop we did mention it in the audio guide.

Wayfinding, or navigation, can also apply to objects; typically finding out how they work and what their purpose is. For example a hair dryer has a characteristic shape but for a blind person they might need indications of where the switch is and, somewhat more critically, where the hot air comes out. This guidance could be in sound or by touch. A door could be sculpted so that the hand is directed to the door handle or to some instruction point. Tactile sculpture has tremendous potential. One might be allowed to touch a piece of sculpture in a gallery but contrary to the Disability Discrimination Act one usually cannot touch. It would be interesting to work out whether one should be challenging the artist or the gallery under the Act.

Not every wayfinding problem consists of a space through which one has to pass, it can be a solid object which one needs to understand. A 'black box' that is a new device without an established image is a greater challenge but could quite easily have a tactile tracking from control to control and a Braille and/or image starting place. Such thinking can be useful to everyone. For example, there are many instances in our sound studio where we operate equipment in conjunction with looking at an editing screen which is in a different direction - but which button of the 57 on the control of the digital audio device is which? But come to think of it, a functionally sculpted operating front to one of these devices could be very exciting besides being very useful!

[1] Paul Arthur and Romedi Passini, Wayfinding, People, Signs, and Architecture, Ontario 1992, ISBN 0-07-551016-2
[2] Reginald G Golledge, Wayfinding Behaviour – cognitive mapping and other spatial processes, Baltimore 1999, ISBN 0-8018-55993-X.

# *Summary of Principles*

This is intended to be a summary and not a set of conclusions. Indeed we may make some suggestions but conclusions in a world that is a complete mess would show an optimism that we are not very sure about. However, two conclusions are fixed in our minds. They are:

1) Using all our senses in design is of advantage to all of us and this includes so-called normal people and so-called disabled people. It really is for everyone!

2) Using George Ashiotis's idea, (see what he has written about the *Theater by the Blind*) we support his concept that we should be looking for a common or shared aesthetic between ourselves and those with whom we communicate. This does not mean that we do not appreciate differences and in fact differences are very important but they are not matters of conflict but of excitement and understanding.

### Using our senses

Emphatically we need to use our senses more. In the past social mores governed what we thought in our own particular social group and culture. We need to break out and understand others by considering our sensory signals against a background of real living.

### The multi-sensory design approach

Here we can almost reach a conclusion. It is important that communication should use all sensory facilities. In this way we can communicate with as many people as possible.

### Design

The sequence of events that make up design will develop over the next few years and become more complex. However, this does not mean that it becomes the exclusive right of the designer but rather that everyone should take part in the event of design.

### Universal design

To make design universal is sound thinking and it should be more of the accepted standard in the design world in the UK. In the USA there are economic and political problems that impede its complete adoption but it is making good progress. Quite a few design schools and schools of architecture in the USA have adopted it and have gained much from doing so. In essence the quote we give sums up the present approach. 'The design of products and environments to be usable by all people to the greatest extent possible, without the need for adaption or specialized design'. Clearly, the concept will move forward and this is necessary for the development of design.

### Universal communication

While universal design must govern our physical design, universal communication needs to govern our world of communication. However, the two are closely related and maybe it is not good to think about them separately except in terms of design technique, as the concept has the same basis.

### Psychophysics and cognition

We have dealt with this carefully because it is a specialist field but it can be seen from what we have said that it is extremely important if we are going to understand how our senses, and of course the senses of other people work.

### General concept of space

This, of course, connects with the next item which is Wayfinding. However, wayfinding has been seen as the putting together in the mind cognitive maps, but there are other cognitive forms that need to be considered in terms of the totality of space. Space is a geometric form until thought about and then it can be clearly seen as a total sensory experience. Like most thoughts this needs organisation and in this it will overlap with other cognitive functions.

### Wayfinding

Although this is what might be seen as an 'add-on', it really is part of the complex world picture. In places there are glimmers of hope. We have done many things in the interests of disability, but what we need to do is work in terms of real people where being disabled, white or black, British or American or any contrast one can think of adds up to an identity rather than a conflict. We hope that the principles that we have outlined might be of use in the coming sections of the book. These sections contain tools to use.

We return to the quote from the New York company, Theater by the Blind and George Ashiotis who says 'Our goal is to unite performers and audiences of all abilities in a shared aesthetic.'

We feel very much the same!

# *The Nature of Sight, Smell and Taste*

The parts of the book that follow cover primarily two senses. They are, in the order of the book, Hearing then Touch in Chapter 3. However, it is not possible to consider these two senses as totally independant and so we discuss very briefly in this section the other senses: that is Sight, Smell and Taste. In the end all the senses have to be together because nothing is wholly complete without all the senses.

As we have said above the three senses, Sight, Smell and Taste are not part of the main plot for this book, but as you may have noticed, we are vitally interested in all the senses, but we do not have room to deal with them all. Sight is the most significant sense and more is written about it than any other sense. In fact we have reached the stage where everything is assumed to be seen, but not touched or smelled or tasted. We need to return to a more wholesome view of the senses. Before you laugh at the thought of taste being used remember that this book is being written in Ludlow, the regional 'foodie' capital of the UK.

### Sight

We are well aware of the importance of sight and as elsewhere, we would refer you to the psychophysics of the situation. The theories of sight are particularly well developed and readily available. Since we are concerned with printing books and other documentation, the theories of colour are particularly fascinating.

It is worth remembering that sight is important to many blind people. Many blind people can see something and the use of very large print and colour are useful and should be considered in your design. Sight is very important and in the context of universal communication and needs to be considered carefully.

### Smell

It is as if the world wants to get rid of any sense of smell completely since it hardly ever thought of. This would be a great mistake since the potential contribution to the environment by smell is considerable. The basic problem is that we cannot handle the sense or the situation. We cannot design in smell because it is not easy, at the present time, to digitise. Digitised forms have been discussed and to an extent been developed for use by computers. It does not need great thought to see that if smells could be embodied in a set of oils, somewhat like an inkjet printer, they could be released from capsules in digitised quantities and combined to make a 'smell station' around your computer. However, a new form of virus could not only make your smell station uninhabitable but also your home or office! In her book <u>A Natural History of the Senses</u>,[1] Diane Ackerman mentions a system of classification in the section of the book on smell that seems to be of use to those computing perfume.

**MAGICAL MONKEYS, MANGOES AND MUSIC**

While we have given a warning about using smell we have had one great success with smell. It was in a superb presentation by Richard Hayhow, who directed The Open Theatre Company in a performance of <u>The Monkey King</u> and we were the communications consultants. Between us we arranged for the smell of the mango, a key fruit in the plot, to permeate the theatre at the correct moment. It was very effective.

If we look at books on the subject of smell, or better and more acceptable, the word aroma, we find that it is a particular characteristic of 'modern' civilisations that smell has to be eliminated. On the other hand in more aware civilisations smell is a vital part of the language and the culture. In an important book entitled <u>Aroma</u> there is a chapter entitled Universes of Odour in which several civilisations are compared and all those illustrated, unlike us, depend on smell as an essential part of their lives.[2]

Also in this book there is a history of the culture of smell and this should be looked at. Essentially, it is fundamental to animals, but became very sophisticated during the Roman period. During this period there was a distinct connection between religion and smell which continues to this day in the form of incense. It seemed to have reached a high point where it was almost an effete part of the culture. This was overtaken by the fall of the Roman Empire when other tribes became predominant. They had their own smell values and culture which appears to have been much more basic than the Roman appreciation of smell.

In the middle ages there was a simpler appreciation of smell. However, some of the ideas carried forward from the Roman culture. Because of the need to create towns and particularly cities there was a very great problem of smell because of the lack of ways to deal with sewerage and rubbish generally. In fact it was not until the 19th century that this country was sufficiently organised to deal with sewerage. It was the revolution brought about by Victorian engineers that began to reduce the smell. Houses in the middle ages were a mixture of fragrance from, for example, herbs spread on the floor, and the foul smell of inadequate drainage. Nevertheless, there was always the smell of food that has been a thread of hope right through history.

Although we have looked through our heap of text books on perception we have not come across mention of Jacobson's Organ. This is discussed in a fascinating book by Lyall Watson entitled Jacobson's Organ and the remarkable nature of smell.[3] Besides the description of this organ, which is situated in the nose, he writes about smell. He gives a very useful definition of smell which is so neat it is worth quoting;

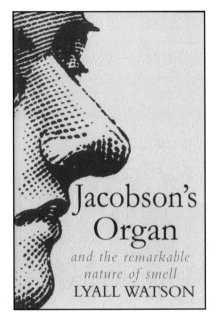

Smell is a chemical sense. What the receptor cells in the nose do is translate chemical information into electrical signals. These travel along olfactory nerves into the cranial cavity, where they gather in the olfactory bulbs. These, in turn, feed the cerebral cortex, where association takes place and nameless signals become transformed into the fragrance of a favourite rose or the musky warning of an irritable skunk.

In a section of the book related to the self he talks of the fascinating, but complex pheromonal communication of the body. Perhaps we should call human smell 'pheromonal communication' to take away the stigma of the word 'smell'; we need a new vocabulary to describe what was 'smell'.

While we pay money to 'silence' the communication from our armpits this is a place where part of the communication on a sexual level emanates. It is hard, until we all get further with our experience of design for smell, to imagine which way we are going. However, using design concepts that conform with our old-fashioned views on design Lyall does point out a Victorian design success related to smell, although it was not meant to be so. It is the 'S' shaped love seat where the couple sit facing in opposite directions with a solid arm between the couple that prevents actual contact. However, the armpits that contain the organs that communicate sexual attraction are, because of the seat's shape, closer to the nose of the other person than if they sat side by side. Perhaps this is why the love seats were such a success!

In her book Worlds of Sense,[4] Constance Classen writes of the odour of others which serves to point out that it is not only sex that is communicated. She outlines the extent and significance of smell to various cultures:

> While there is an apparent bar on smell it is nevertheless very much part of our personal lives. Most of know or remember the smell of our children. In a more complex way we know the smell of our partners and the parts of their bodies and their changing moods and quite rightly can tell when they are not well from a change in smell. Our animals do not know about our curious need to eliminate smells and so few of us are unable to bring immediately to mind such smells as 'wet dog' and 'over-friendly cat'.
>
> Insects are curiously similar to human beings although the actual organs of sense are perhaps less evolved than ours, but in other ways they are often more sensitive. Since we are mammals it follows that animals in general are similar to human beings. To the insect, smell is of prime importance and because it can be sensed from a very small number of molecules it is a very efficient method

of communication. The bee has ways of communicating by the use of two organs on its body, one close to its mandibles and the other close to its sting. In his book <u>The Dance Language and Orientation of Bees</u>, [5] Karl von Frisch writes about the Danceless Communication by Means of Sounds and Smells which describes how the bee picks up vibration and is very much aware of the smells. Von Frish wrote that the 'olfactory stimuli are of extraordinary significance for mutual communication among the bees as is already evident from several examples'. If you keep bees, then 'alarm fanning' is a bad sign and this is where the bee pushes its tail into the air and whirs its wings and this fans air across the bulb of the stylet adjacent to the sting. In moments the whole hive is on the offensive against intruders which, of course, includes the bee keeper. Bees will also fan on the landing board of the hive to bring home lost members of the colony and the smell is picked up at some considerable distance from the hive.

There is reference to the olfactory ability of insects in <u>An Introduction to the Behaviour of Invertebrates</u> by J. D. Carthy.[6] This book seems to be one of the first to look at the total sensory world of insects and contains interesting information that shows a certain parallel sensory form to the human being.

In the modern period we seem to have negated the whole culture of smell so that it is seen to be a bad thing. On the other hand we have come to the point where quite artificial tastes are included in foods and made into a brand form and sold. Perfume has a long tradition and is still part of a large industry. Many of these tastes and smells have become fashionable. Fortunately the thread of the smell of real food continues and does not change.

It may not seem to be a design subject but it certainly is. Remember that sensory garden that you saw a little while ago that was certainly by design. Talk to a gardener and he or she will describe their garden in terms of smell besides the colour of flowers. Wherever one goes there are exciting smells. There are so many examples the sea shore, the hay field, and so on. But quite simply, at present, there is no way to measure smells; but there are increasingly ways of simulating it.

Smell, or should we say aroma, has become the subject of much contemporary thought and this is promising for the environment. The sensation and cognition resulting from smell has been carried forward as with the other senses. However, cognition of smell is less well researched than for other senses since these are seen as more essential. However, the U.S.A. Society for Neuroscience is currently researching smell by looking at:

> Processes thought to underlie odor recognition
> Ways odors may affect human behaviour
> Strategies for helping people whose sense of smell
> is diminished or lost.[7]

This coupled with much other research indicates that we should be aware that this is not a sense to be ignored.

We now need to look at how smell can be used in interpretation. We advise using caution because it can be very invasive and hard to control.

Rone Weekes from Quest International looked at 'How smells can enhance a place' in a paper given in July 2004 at the conference, <u>A Sense of Place</u>.[8] This company creates special smells for specific places and occasions.[9] Dale Air - 'Aroma by design' - produce smells and scents to fit in with displays and exhibitions.[10] Their wide range of smells can be used with a unit that will dispense them to large or small areas. Their website reports on the Virtual Holidays they are developing with Thomson and Remote Media. This is a multi-sensory advertisement for holiday destination with smells, sight in the form of 3-D video, and sound. Thomson's sales director commented: 'This is a real taste of how holidays could be sold in the future'. Why not museums also?[11]

Eric Sayce has written about the 'Scratch and Sniff' cards used in the Belgrade Pantomime. These were also used in the cinema:

Speaking of previous eras, I was happy to learn that theaters are still providing those scratch-and-sniff cards for the viewing of John Waters' film Polyesterhttp://www.netcatchers.com/waters/water4.htm. For anyone who hasn't seen the film, there are ten numbered scents on the card. Throughout the film, whenever a signal is given, you're supposed to scratch that scent and sniff it, creating a sort of Smell-O-Vision effect. The scents range from pepperoni pizza and air freshener to dirty socks and skunk. It's been years since I saw Polyester in a theater, and my scratch-and-sniff card is pretty much warn out. So I was happy to know I can obtain a new card if I want.[12]

For years we have taken around to seminars and talks a pack of impregnated cards from Celessence.[13] Some of these are produced for the travel trade, such as coconut oil and exotic flowers (actually many of them have no discernible scent); these could have a place in your displays.

We saw one of the most practical and elegant ways of conveying smells for an exhibition in Elche, Spain. The touring exhibition, Los Aromas de al-Andalus, was a splendid multi-sensory experience housed in an elegant marquee. All around the exhibition were containers with the aromas that can be found around Andalusia such as mint, rosemary, lemon and sandalwood. We wrote about this for Barrierfree:

They are in cylindrical Perspex containers with a phial of essential oil in the bottom. A fan of absorbent paper stands in the oil and draws up the scent. In the center of the container is a Perspex disc which can be turned and moves the air within the space to direct the scent towards the holes at the top. Each container has a Braille label.[14]

A cheaper version of this can be made with sugar or flour sifters which will convey their smell through the holes at the top when shaken. Any round container with a lid could be used, as long as small holes can be made in the lid.

The right smells can also be good for you. 'In the hospital of the future, patients will recover quicker because of the colour of the walls, the view from their bed or the scents vented through their ward.'[15] Architect Mike Nightingale claimed that people could be distressed through the use of particular odours. Experiments had shown that aggressive behaviour in A&E departments 'could be disarmed by the use of baby smells.'

In the future are on-line smells and virtual smell technology. A newspaper article a few years ago reported that France Telecom 'is looking at taking the idea of e-scents well beyond fragrances of the cosmetic kind ... and is hoping to deliver not just sight and sound over the internet, but also smell.'[16] One idea was for a computer bolt-on with a 'series of impregnated solid polymer discs with a fan to propel up to a dozen fragrances into the atmosphere'. The other idea was for a device to be worn around the user's neck which contained about 30 different fragrances, not smells you note – which could be used in conjunction with interactive television. Lingering scents was one of the problems they would have to solve.

The Indians were also involved in this research; 'Indian gets patent for virtual smell technology'.[17] 'You can smell through your hi-fi system, computer, telephone and television – any mode of two-way interaction,' said Sandeep Jaidka, who obtained the world's first patent on the creation of smell and sensation through multimedia from the US Patent Office. His idea relied on digitally encoded signals to produce a variety of sensations not specific to an enclosed or open space, but in order to put this into practice they needed $10 million and this does not seem to have progressed much further as no current information could be found on the internet. Before anyone thinks this is a hoax, which it might well be, nothing should be discounted in the world of technology today – after all someone considered that the computer would not catch on.

### Taste

As we have said, Ludlow is a good place to write about taste. The food we all eat is related to taste. It is possible to taste other things: we have mentioned the friend who is a geologist who will taste stone and from the taste he can tell more about its origin.

Taste is quite another sense to smell but it is related because the nose is situated above the mouth and as one eats the smell of the food is picked up by the nose. It is also related to sight: simply try mentioning blue potatoes. In Sensation and Perception,[18] E. Bruce Goldstein mentions the work by Cabanac on a phenomenon called 'alliesthesia'. In short, this is about the set of desires and pleasure related to taste and eating and drinking. He cites a situation very familiar to any of us who think about food. A special banana cream pie is wonderful – and we can believe it – except that after eating a good helping one does not want any more. It seems so obvious that the body has had enough. Perhaps we could look for a common law that applies to all senses. We know that good loud music reduces the sensitivity of the ear over time. Is this the same principle? The mechanism of taste is as fascinating as the other sensory mechanisms.

The aesthetics of food relate sight to taste very easily and have a history that goes back to the caves. As carnivores who respect their vegetarian friends we will not go into details, but a roasted leg of deer must have had the same visual, aroma and taste appeal then as now. We should add into this the texture of the meat in the mouth. There is a rich history of the dressing of tables with food which implies a connection again between sight and taste. See the book The Art of Dining by Sara

Paston-Williams which gives many examples.[19] When we take people to historic buildings we try to provide suitable historic music and food. In this way everyone can begin to understand the sensual events of the time. Taste is definitely to be taken into account!

**See you at the Ludlow Food Fair!**

[1] Diane Ackerman, <u>A Natural History of the Senses</u>, London, 1990, ISBN 1-85799-403-5

[2] Contance Classen, David Howes and Anthony Synnott, <u>Aroma</u>, London, 1994. ISBN 0-415-11473-1

[3] Lyall Watson, <u>Jacobson's Organ and the remarkable nature of smell</u>, London, 1999, ISBN 0-713-99347-2.

[4] Constance Classen, <u>World of Sense</u>, London, 1993, ISBN 0-415-09595-6

[5] Karl von Frisch, <u>The Dance Language and Orientation of Bees</u>, London, 1967

[6] J. D. Carthy, <u>An Introduction to the Behaviour of Invertebrates</u>, London, 1958

[7] Society for Neuroscience, http://apu.sfn.org/

[8] A conference report on <u>A Sense of Place</u>, can be downloaded from the website of the Sensory Trust who organised it; there is a modest charge for it. <u>www.sensorytrust.org.uk</u>.

[9] <u>www.questintl.com</u>.

[10] <u>www.daleair.com</u>.

[11] For those interested in odd facts, Dale Air provided the smell of Kylie Minogue's breath for her model at Madame Tussauds.

[12] From <u>www.coffeebeer.co.uk</u>., a wonderfully eccentric eclectic site by J C Mitchell. For an explanation of how these fragrances work, see <u>http://www.straightdope.com/classics/a1_246.html</u>.

[13] <u>www.celessence.co.uk</u>.

[14] <u>Barrierfree</u>, Issue 8, Spring 2001.

[15] <u>Building Design</u>, March 14, 2003.

[16] Mark Milner, <u>The Guardian</u>.

[17] Article by Deepshikha Ghosh, India Abroad News Service, 15/02/01.

[18] E Bruce Goldstein, <u>Sensation and Perception</u>, USA 1977, ISBN 0-534-09672-7.

[19] Sara Paston-Williams, <u>The Art of Dining, A History of Cooking and Eating</u>, UK 1993, ISBN 0-7078-0173-7.

# *The Nature of Sound*

Most of us hear but do not know all about sound. This section is purposely entitled the Study of Sound simply because we believe that we do not know enough about sound and hearing and its meaning. The evidence in the world around us supports this view We are also dealing with people who have a range of hearing ability from so-called seriously impaired to so-called normal so that we need to understand how the human being operates. Often we should be considering sound alongside the use of other senses in our communication.

In this section of the book we are looking only at sound. With this is mind we must first define what sound is, then what is noise, and to continue this traditional way of thinking; what is music? Most important we need to understand how the ear and the brain work.

**Sound is what we hear with our ears and it has meaning!**
**Noise is unwanted sound or sound without meaning!**
**Music is organised sound which follows a cultural pattern!**

All of these definitions are pretty crude and have pit-falls but we need to think about these expressions carefully because they are part of normal culture. Noise amounts to a personal view because all sound communicates something even if it masks other messages.

As with any piece of machinery it is worth putting the parts together and then taking them apart. We must reconsider in outline the psychological substance of sound. If we take any of the books that we have referred to in our previous section on psychophysics and cognition there are very useful descriptions of how the system works. Apart from being interesting it is also pretty amazing. Essentially, the mechanism can sense the compression and rarefaction of the air around the ear which is then analysed against various criteria. We need to remember that the ear is very sensitive and can be damaged; in fact much information comes from the variation in amplitude that the ear measures so accurately. Such changes in amplitude will tell us if the object making the sound that we can hear is advancing or retreating. What is heard is sequenced in time which gives the frequency of the sound, which is usually complex and in this complexity there is both a pitch and a timbre. There is a limit to the frequency response of the ear and this is usually quoted at 20-20, that is 20Hz to 20,000 Hz. Although these are not the limits they are taken as the practical limits. The way in which the ear functions is complex and this is not the place to reiterate what the books on psychophysics say. However, we must appreciate the response of the ear. Such matters as loudness, musical pitch, sound quality, frequency range and so on are critical to our design.

The complex 'readings' of the ear are interpreted by the brain. The study of this relates to cognition. Research on this continues and useful hypotheses are being developed. For example, Thinking in Sound, Stephen McAdams describes a possible, and indeed probable, sequence of events.[1] The diagram follows the following steps. (For details of this then we refer you to this interesting book)

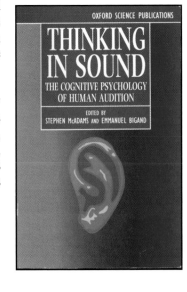

Sound

Sensory grouping

Auditory grouping

Analysis of
auditory properties and/or features

Matching with
auditory lexican

Acess to
lexicon of names

Access to
meaning
and evaluation of
significance with
respect to current
context

Recognition

### Recognition

In the above McAdams refers back from recognition to 'auditory grouping and 'analysis auditory properties and/or features'.

Clearly, the process is involved but of great significance to the sound designer. In this book Albert Bregman outlines his thoughts on the subject. As we have mentioned earlier, Bregman's own book, Auditory Scene Analysis is of great importance.[2]

We must also consider the physics of sound since much of what we may do will follow the rules that have been discovered. The frequency of the waves of compression, and rarefaction of the air that is sound, have various frequencies and to an extent the behaviour of the sound will relate to this. The diffraction of sound around objects is also related to frequency.  The velocity of the sound as it passes through a material is relevant in various environments. Reflections of sound are vital in our appreciation of space.

[1] Edited by Stephen McAdams and Emmanuel Bigand, Thinking in Sound, Oxford 1993, ISBN 0-19-852257-6.

[2] Albert S Bregman, Auditory Scene Analysis, USA 1990 ISBN 0-262- 02297-4

# *Sound Engineering*

Having referred to the mechanism of sound and the body and to the way it functions, we need now to look at the overall sound situation in order to get some appreciation of what our sound world is like. Following from this we must consider how we might engineer it or more usefully see the whole as a soundscape. In this consideration we should be aware of the way sound is generated and read by the ear and the mind, and the characteristics of the environment in which it is found. As an intellectual exercise we can basically divide our overall sound environment into three.

> The natural environment
> The built environment
> The enclosed environment

We might then further recognise in each of these sections three categories. These artificial secondary characteristics might be:

> Natural communication
> Acoustic character
> Human communication

And there are many more.

Each of the sections of our overall spectrum have particular characteristics. Sounds of natural communication are most developed in the natural environment and the origins of the sounds tend to be from natural and meaningful sources. Human communication is not of great significance in this situation. The built environment usually has a clearly defined acoustic character and, because of its regularity, very positive acoustic forms. The natural communication matrix is less complex in the built environment than in a natural situation, but the human communication matrix is of greater significance. The enclosed environment has a very positive acoustic character and little natural communication content. In the last category human communication is of prime importance.

It is possible to engineer sound physically in open environments and there are various ways of doing this. Mostly this engineering is about specific situations, such as reducing the sound that escapes from a major highway. Interior sound engineering on the other hand is more direct and we have more experience with this than out in the natural environment. For example there are ways of allowing the visitor in the back seats of a concert hall hear enough to feel that they have not wasted their money buying tickets.

There is much more that can be done, especially with the help of electronics. One example that relates to our own work is that we have recorded the sound of aquatic insects in ponds so that blind children can listen to them. It is also possible at the other end of the scale to 'build' an auditorium in an open field using speaker systems and mobile stages.

The design of sound in restricted environments is particularly important in human communication. Much of what we have written is about this, but here we are making sure that we see this work as part of a total environment of sound rather than the only thing that we are considering. We should also be aware of the ways that we can extend what we do through induction systems and maybe transmission systems.

We need to grasp the overall concepts of sound design at this point. Perhaps a concept of soundscaping is what we are looking for. Soundscaping has not been quite defined yet, but it is something that could be applied to all environments to a greater or lesser degree. We would see this as applicable to a complete environment in the same way as a seventeenth century landscape. The schemes of *Son et Lumiere* that have been applied to buildings are perhaps a good example of sound design being applied to a built environment. Another example of sound in the environment at about the same scale is the open air concert; the concerts at Kenwood House in London are a case in point.

# *The Existing Sound Environment*

But while we can talk of sound-scaping and designing sound in an environment, what of the environment around us as it currently exists or as it existed in the past? We should say at this point that one must take great care in altering a sound environment but nevertheless we need to see the sound environment as a whole before we even consider change in the form of sound design.

We vibrate with a thousand sounds and movements. There is no escape any more, and maybe there never was! However, much of the sound needs to be carefully considered because it is quite wonderful. But sadly some, in fact quite a lot, is not.

If we stand in the middle of a field in the United Kingdom we know that we will hear a motor vehicle. There are perhaps a few places where we may not, but we have recorded in many wild places and it is always there. In other countries such as central Russia and South Africa it is still possible to hear the natural sounds. Not only do we hear the motor vehicle, but we hear aircraft passing overhead fairly frequently during the day. Often they are quite quiet, but in many cases we hear the heavy intrusion of military aircraft. In addition, there are sounds of other mechanical equipment. All of these sounds mask the real and more interesting messages of both town and countryside.

*Rush hour in Hydra*

One spring we were on the Greek island of Hydra. On this island there are only two motor vehicles. One is the town dust cart and the other a heavy refuse collecting lorry. The result is that when one stands at the top of the hill above the town it is possible to hear what the town has to say about itself. Standing within the town itself the observer, and in fact everyone, becomes part of the internal conversation between activities that make up the town. One hears children playing, workmen working and babies crying, dogs barking and many many other sounds. There are also evocative sounds such as the bells of the goats grazing and the sound of wild birds singing. But of course people also live in this little town as they do in all towns and what we hear is a by-product of their living. Not all the sounds are beautiful sounds but they communicate more than the constant roar of the internal combustion engine, although the rhythm of the day is punctuated by the noisy arrival of the ferries bringing fresh loads of tourists; they themselves bring a new set of sounds: different European and far Eastern accents and American twangs. It is in situations such as this where one becomes aware of the importance of sound and its real meaning. It is important to us also for sounds that do not normally get through to us. Contrast the peace of Hydra with the raucous, medieval sound of the Istanbul bazaar on the sound examples.

Even the oceans are not quiet. At a recent conference on whales, Dr Christopher Clarke of Cornell University is reported to have said that over the last 20 years the acoustic communication distance of the whales of 1,600 km has been reduced to 400 km due to noise. This limits the range over which animals can navigate and find food or mates. He said, 'We are slowly, inexorably, raising the tide of ambient noise in the sea so that their worlds are shrinking just to the point where they're dysfunctional.'

It is possible to control sounds both in the eradication of sounds and the enhancement of sounds. In simple terms we can ban motor cars and encourage red kites on the basis that we do not like the sound of cars and we do like the sound of the kites. In absolute terms roads could be designed with sound absorbent shoulders and cars banned from other places. Kites could be encouraged to breed, as indeed has been done. We then face the problem that we cannot travel because there are no suitable roads, or they cannot get to where we want to go. On the other hand the kites could return to the state of scavengers which is where they were before and become a dangerous nuisance.

The moral and planning issues are complex and are further complicated by the fact that people are on the whole a greedy, unpleasant and a pretty inferior species. Nevertheless, we need to understand and have real values for the world of sound. Whether we can persuade people to change and do what we suggest is quite another matter.

Thus, putting on one side the moral issues, we need to appreciate that much can be done, often in other ways than the obvious and clearly unacceptable ones. First we need to develop an awareness of our world before we ever think of altering it. While there is a long way to go there are people out there who have thought about it and we should note carefully what they say.

There are several very significant books on the subject that we recommend. The first has to be <u>Our Sonic Environment and The Soundscape – the Tuning of the World</u>, by R. Murray

Shafer. [1] In Chapter Three he talks of the rural sound-scape which he develops through town and city. However, it is likely that the rural sound-scape is the oldest form that is affected by human habits. Thus it is historically important and when considering the sound-scape of, say, the medieval period we should take it into account. Similarly, when we look at other periods we should be aware of this evolution in sound-scape. In his fascinating book, <u>The Acoustic World of Early Modern England</u>, Bruce R. Smith looks at the sound-scape of the early renaissance world and describes it with care and in considerable detail.[2] As we continue to develop our understanding of the past we must take this way of thinking into account.

There is a growing awareness of the world problems that we have with sound and also its fascinating potential. The University of Oregon hosts the World Forum for Acoustic Ecology; it is worth looking at their website.[3] Another book of interest is <u>Wild Sound-Scapes</u> by Bernie Krause in which he takes a critical look at the natural sound-scape and makes comment on the intrusion of man-made sound into this complex environment.[4] And while these are two significant figures in a world that does consider a proper world of sound we suggest that you look at <u>The Book of Music and Nature</u>, edited by David Rothenberg and Marta Ulvaeus where there are many interesting essays about this subject. [5]

If we were able to listen then we would find that there are many sounds to hear. Many of these sounds have meaning and in certain circumstances our methods of communication would be very much affected. We have mentioned elsewhere the ideas recorded by Feld about communication in the jungle. Where noise is not allowed then other forms of communication are evolved; for instance during a recording session where something has to stop then a symbolic sweep of the hand across the throat, as though cutting it, signifies stop without any sound. Braille evolved in much the same way: you can read about its history in the section on Braille.

It is possible to engineer sounds in various ways. The obvious and seemingly up-to-date way is to use electronics but this is not the only way. Barriers at ground level can reduce noise. An example is on motorways where a simple imperforate fence is used to shield housing areas. Isolation of noise in housing is another example.

Noise can also have uses. When we made a survey of the campus of the University of Birmingham we found it was possible to navigate by the noise made by equipment on the site. Each faculty had a different sound, mostly from the air conditioning units. We were able to identify these on a guide tape which helped blind and partially sighted students around the campus. There are pleasanter ways of providing sound beacons, but it certainly seemed to work.

We are used to virtual sound and also computer generated sound. In our living room we have a virtual orchestra which is currently playing The Symphony in E flat by Joseph Kraus and in my black boxes in the corner of the room we have the Swedish Chamber Orchestra playing this piece for us. Clearly, it is not the real thing; it is a virtual image created electronically. In fact it comes from what used to be known as a gramophone record. We accept, and indeed enjoy, this facility and therefore it is important that we realise that it is virtual and consider the potential of these techniques.

With the early music movement we accept the use of original instruments and indeed pieces of music do sound different. Recording engineers and producers are able to alter the acoustics to what is commercially appropriate. In fact the acoustic environment has much to tell us and we should look carefully at this aspect of virtual sound. If we are going to listen to recorded music we should learn about the place from the character of the acoustics. The reverse is now possible since we can now recreate the acoustics of a specific place. The music of Kraus played in the Drottningholm Theatre in Sweden as it would have been for King Gustav III would have sounded very different. This theatre is part of the palace but it is made of wood and the piece I am listening to would have sounded as if it was being played in a wooden enclosure rather than a concert hall.

Recently, with Dr Damian Murphy of the University of York, we have been working on the acoustics of buildings that no longer exist. One exercise in particular was to reconstruct the acoustics of the bombed Coventry Cathedral in the computer. Sound, in particular a celebration of mass from 1522, was fed into the computer and the sound that came out was that as though the mass was being sung in the cathedral (then a Parish Church) in 1522.

There are many situations where historic performances or events could be reconstructed in sound with advantage particularly to blind people. Of course, it is also possible to reconstruct the visual form of buildings in the past but now it is possible to reconstruct their sound. The world of our perception can be virtual rather than real. That is provided we see this virtual world as a useful tool rather than a substitute. In fact substitution is one of the most sophisticated and misplaced human arts.

The management of sound and noise is something that should be aimed at in a way that is best for all. This is common sense but is not always achieved. However, there are positive ways that noise, or rather

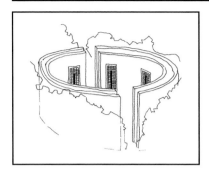

sound, can be organised. There are many sound designers who could pick up the threads of this and produce something positive. This might be in an architectural way by sound designers such as Bernhard Leitner. An example of his work is *Le Cylindre Sonore* at the Parc de la Villette in Paris, but he has done some very interesting work all over Europe. There is a very useful book on his work entitled <u>Sound Space</u>. [6]

If it is a question of transmitted media then look at the work of Ben Rubin and his EAR (Electronic Audio Research) Studio in New York.[7] There are people about who can do things but no one seems prepared to find any money to make any steps forward. There is plenty of room for interesting work by everyone! Both of these sound designers work with physical acoustics of the environment and that is particularly important. In a world that has virtual sound which is electronic, physical acoustics, architectural environments and townscapes there is lots of room for ideas and action. That is if someone were to come up with the money!

Thus, it has to be agreed, there is a very strong case for the importance of sound in our environment. Also we should think carefully about how we introduce more sound into our environment. In many situations it is more important to encourage understanding of the sound that does still exist than to introduce more. However, we do need to carefully design the introduction of sound in certain situations. If we are providing an environment that is about communication of some message to people then there has to be carefully designed sound. In fact the provision of engineered sound is relatively new and it is worth looking at the way it has come about before we commit ourselves to the provision of even more thoughtless sound.

We live in a world in which sound is becoming emancipated. It no longer needs to be confined to a small disc and a commercial playback device; it can be engineered in many sophisticated ways. Our environment can contain sounds as they would have been in the past. It can contain sounds carefully designed to express the space. It can have sound that connects with large moving pictures. For a 'few pennies' almost anything can be done. In order to understand the present we should go over the history of the modulation of sound.

# The Existing Sound Environment

[1] R Murray Schaffer, <u>Our Sonic Environment and the Sound-Scape, the Tuning of the World</u>, Rochester, Vermont 1977, ISBN 0-89281-455-1.

[2] Bruce R Smith, <u>The Acoustic World of Early Modern England</u>, Chicago 1999, ISBN 0-226-76376-5.

[3] http://interact.uoregon.edu/MediaLit/wfae/home/

[4] Bernie Krause, <u>Wild Sound-Scape,</u>,Berkley, California 2002, ISBN 0-89997-296-9.

[5] David Rothenberg and Marta Ulvaeus, <u>The Book of Music and Nature</u>, USA 1997, ISBN 0-8195-6407-9.

[6] Bernhard Leitner and others, <u>Sound;Space</u>, Vienna 1992.

[7] www.earstudio.com

# *History of Transmission and Recording*

First we must take the broad view and look particularly at the history of sound transmission and recording. However, the experiments with transmission come first. After one or two technical breakthroughs in the world of transmission of sound this was followed by the recording of sound. For us the significant aspect is that of recording sound but the two are closely related. Another dichotomy that one needs to be aware of is that of the technical history and the economic history. Clearly these are inter-related but the driving force has to be that of economic advantage or what we have called the 'fast buck' philosophy.

In order to find a time-scale it is worth saying that in December of 1877, Thomas Alva Edison, with the help of his assistant John Kreusi, completed the first 'phonograph' which used a wax cylinder to record on. This device was to be overtaken by the work of Emile Berliner who developed the disc that was to become the basis of future development. The 'gramophone' as Berliner's device was called was first demonstrated in 1888. There were many technical developments that took place before and after this date because the time was right, but from the commercial point of view the phonograph and subsequently the gramophone were of the greatest overall significance. Discs are still popular and Vinyl LPs are still being made!

It was all a great breakthrough from the point of view of the anthropologist and ethnomusicologists. Dr Jesse Fewkes of Harvard University, in 1890, recorded the songs and stories of the Passamaquoddy Indians of Maine, US; they are now, sadly, an extinct race. This was reissued as an LP in 1977 by the US Library of Congress. On the other hand the history of commercial recording tells of a world which has been over-run by recording companies each colonising ever-new areas. The impact was culture-splitting and continues to be so today. For example in 1902 the Gramophone Company of London sent Fred Gaisberg to India, China and Japan to record music of the orient. In 1909 they sent Franz Hampe to record in places from the Caucasus to Central Asia. Partly due to the effect of sound recording and to the unstoppable march of history everything has changed. Some of these recordings have been issued as a CD which contains 23 tracks from the 1200 that he recorded and represents almost everything that Hampe thought might be a commercial possibility from Georgia, Armenia, Azerbaijan through to Xinjang. It has been published by Topic for the British Library National Sound Archive.

Big sounds from small peoples

The music industry in small countries

Roger Wallis and Krister Malm

Communication & Society series

Coming forward in time the music industry as a whole continues to have a contentious impact. Roger Wallis and Krister Malm's book <u>Big Sounds from Small People</u> examines the impact of the industry on small countries.[1] Clearly, it is of financial advantage to the large music industry companies to impose already recorded culture onto the smaller countries. To be sure it is not only a one-way influence but nevertheless the impact is considerable. World music is an example of the reverse influence where ideas from the field are going back to the economic centres of the music industry. Nevertheless, music is part of a flexible cultural reaction and can be readily influenced by examples and the movement of money.

Audio engineering covers the whole of this field in engineering terms. Over time the technology has formed into a coherent body of knowledge. However, there is some fluidity and the edges of technology become blurred. The economics of scale and protected areas shows in our field in the scale of computer parts and programmes versus the manufacture of specialist audio equipment; the result is that more sound work is being done on computers than in the past. A recent example of this fluidity is that of the crossover from the audio industry into the computer industry. In the past the process was a specialist function of audio equipment but is now a function of quite inexpensive computer programmes. This is partly why we are able to make the suggestions we are making about access to equipment. A short while ago it was only possible to do what we can do now with very expensive equipment. A future example could well be the amalgamation of sound and vision with cross-platform files on computers so that 'video' will become a normal way of expression.

[1] Roger Wallis and Krister Malm, <u>Big Sounds from Small Peoples</u>, UK, 1984, ISBN 0-09-465300-3.

## *The Current Situation*

Over the last few years the world of audio-visual design has taken big steps forward. Coupled with this the development of ideas over the last few year on 'disability' and 'universal design' have moved us forward. The concepts of disability have now been highlighted by the 1995 Disability Discrimination Act which came into force over time, with the final sections of the current legislation in October 2004. There is little doubt that further disability legislation will find its way onto the statute book over the next few years. Similarly we could well see legislation that begins to break down ethnic and cultural barriers to an even greater degree, which will enrich all our lives. However, the essential part of our brief has to be to interest as many people in our communication as possible and this has to include everyone.

Our introductory ideas concentrate on audio as a communication technique. Sound has to be designed in such a way that it will work with designs for other senses. The use of audio stretches from the grand scheme for a whole environment to messages repeated on the tripping of a Passive Infra-Red sensor (PIR) to give a ten second message to warn everyone that there are stairs ahead.

We are suggesting that much of the work on audio can be done 'in house'. With experience the work could be quite extensive and relatively inexpensive. However, there comes a point where the project is so large that an organisation could not cope with it. The obvious step is to employ a specialist sub-contractor. This is what happens with the design of exhibitions at the present time. The fact that the contractural basis of most of these sub-contracts is questionable seems obvious to us.

The manner in which exhibition designs are evolved and the contractual procedure that is in use at the present time leave a lot to be desired. If you are going to commission any of these ideas from grand and impressive to small and useful then you must understand the design and how the work is to be done and then one needs to consider the procedure to adopt.

As a sketch procedure we would suggest the following. There is nothing absolute about this suggestion but one way or another it does cover the sort of thing that will happen or rather should happen. It is important to have an overall view of this or your own procedure in order to organise the work.

A. Overall design – this has to take into account all senses. However, here in this section of the book we are dealing only with sound.

B. Sound or audio design – there are some professionals who do this work but much can be done by the establishment itself. Clearly, if there is a lot to do then it would be appropriate to sub-contract the work to an experienced sound designer.

C. Equipment design and supply – as soon as a clear performance specification is drawn up by the designer, tenders can be obtained from specialist firms. When a firm is selected the details of the system design can be finalised. It goes without saying that the contractor has to be experienced in this sort of work. You may choose to rely on the system specialist contractor but take great care because he will see the situation from his point of view and you cannot expect him to do otherwise. It is possible that other sub-contractors will need to be employed to cover such items as joinery and building work. Again it is better if the design can be completed before the other sub-contractors are selected.

D. Overall requirements of the design – sound has many advantages but also it presents certain problems. To start with there is public and private sound. Public sound comes from loudspeakers and is heard by everyone. Private sound can be provided on special playback machines that are given as part of the entrance package or are rented separately.

Much of the following is based on research done by the Trust on the basis of experience gained in making a large number of audio guides for people who are blind or have some visual impairment. However, on reading these through you will note that it gives guidance that can reasonably be applied for everyone's benefit. With care none of the recommendations stand in the way of creative exposition.

There are several fundamental rules that need to be taken into account for any additional information that is fed into a communication system that might be applied to an exhibition or a museum, or most other situations.

If we are going to lead someone along a path and add explanation on the way then the path must be clear and understandable. It is possible to provide random access to any number of points but even so paths have to be defined. Whether our visitor can see or not the mental map has to be defined and will be used by the visitor. This can be done in words but in fact plans and tactile models are much better. As with most ways of exposition, 'see it, hear it and touch it then everyone will get it'. However the way it is described has to be accurate. Care should be taken to set out the rules and limits at the beginning to cover any legal action. However, no words can cover for a badly designed wayfinding system.

Whatever is described can be explained with advantage at various levels. One level might be quick and another slow and elaborate. Another level might be expert and another introductory. And so on. These can be built into  tripping devices for the sound. In wand-type guides using MP3, where there is plenty of file space on the machine  several levels of information can be accommodated.

Space is defined in our perception in several ways. One of these ways is in sound which we will refer to in detail elsewhere. In the case of the guide there is a lot to be said for using two channels to imply stereo. Many of the sounds around us are occasional but of significance. Sounds in the environment reflect and tell you about the space. In any dramatisation it is vital to get the sounds right. Many guides with their 'rent a lute' approach are totally incorrect; the correct recording of an environment is relatively simple.

As time goes by the time that one can keep the attention of those listening gets less. It is critical to determine the amount of time for a guide or a frame of sound that will take this into account. A guide that is more than 30 minutes in length will probably lose listeners towards the end. A frame of sound, for example, a description of some part of a building or a piece of art will probably not be listened to in its entirety for more than 4 minutes. A whole popular song, as on Radio 2, lasts only four minutes and probably always has done although some folk songs contain interesting narrative and last for verse after verse as the story is unfolded.

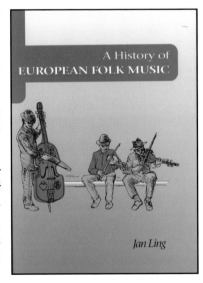

Jan Ling's book, <u>A History of European Folk Music</u> describes the function of folk music which related to tasks and took their length from the operation in hand.[1] However, in India a Raag can last for a long time and a popular Syrian singer talked about  the length of time the songs would last for in their native setting; they had been shortened for Western culture. Many European folk songs are short so perhaps human attention has always been limited and perhaps we should be looking at the way we communicate in the light of history rather than starting all over again. Killing time and making money is no way to structure a

sound communication system, and we could look at history for some clues with life as it is now as our basis.

In sound engineering there are quite few rules that need to be understood if everything is going to work. There is no need, but it would be an advantage to have a degree in electronics, but you should know something of the rules. There is a very useful book entitled <u>Sound Engineering Explained</u> by Michael Talbot-Smith.[2] We do suggest that you get yourself a copy. Beyond this ask a good engineer!

[1] Jan Ling, <u>A History of European Folk Music</u>, Rochester, NY 1997, ISBN 1-878822-77-2.
[2] Michael Talbot-Smith, <u>Sound Engineering Explained</u>, Oxford 2002, ISBN 0-240-51667-2

# *Soundscaping*

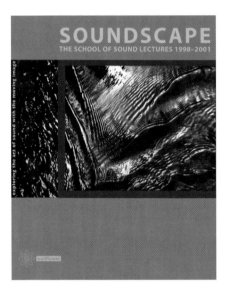

We are not quite sure of the real definition of soundscaping. Right now it is what we think it should be and it is not in the standard dictionaries. If you want to see how broad the definition is then look at <u>Soundscape; the School of Sound Lectures 1998-2001</u>;[1] these are a selection of essays by well-known practitioners of sound and soundscaping in cinema, given at the *School of Sound*, a lively conference held in London and organised mostly by Larry Sider. We hope that one day those involved in this conference will appreciate that the cinema is not the only place for soundscaping.

In thinking about soundscaping, we need to have a different view of what we are recording. In traditional consideration of sound in film and in theatre sound is divided into four categories. It is worth thinking of the sound under these categories:

**Voices**
**FXs**
**Silence**
**Music**

An additional category in films is synchronised sound, but this is especially for film.

This list of headings, and they cannot be more than a convenience, we will apply to our initial thoughts on soundscaping.

**Voices**

Dialogue is about words but is something of a hybrid. It is natural but it does cut across our classification. Dialogue has two aspects, first its meaning and its inherent sound. This sound is easier to recognise when one cannot understand the language being used. Personality and the language make fascinating listening.

There are important differences within sound. Different genders have different voices as indeed do younger humans. In fact young, adult, and elderly have significant differences in their voices and each individual has rich messages in his or her voice that are independent of words. In terms of sound, as opposed to literal meaning as in words, voices have special sounds. These sounds are very interesting and can communicate all sorts of meanings without words. The acoustic ambience of the voice is another matter which is important in space but is not strictly relevant at this point.

### FXs

A 'sound effect' is something that we all know about but have rarely thought about. Life is full of FXs: for example few of us will not recognise the sound of a beer pump or the clink of a tea cup. In a film or an audio piece or for that matter any media that contains sound, an FX is a sound that we add to something else to do something, but then, what and why?

In a very useful article published on the internet entitled *Designing a Movie for Sound*, Randy Thom suggests some things that sound can do. He is, as the title implies, talking about movies but the list is worth mentioning as is it very perceptive. He says that 'music, dialogue and sound effects can do any of the following jobs and many more':

> Suggest a mood, evoke a feeling
> Set a pace
> Indicate a geographical locale
> Indicate an historical period
> Clarify the plot
> Define a character
> Connect otherwise unconnected ideas, characters, places, images, or moments
> Heighten realism or diminish it
> Heighten ambiguity or diminish it
> Draw attention to a detail, or away from it
> Indicate changes in time
> Smooth otherwise abrupt changes between shots or scenes
> Emphasise a transition for dramatic effect
> Describe an acoustic space
> Startle or soothe, exaggerate action or mediate it.

With a little thought more items can be added to the list but it does set us off in the right direction. It is necessary to analyse the situation and to propose a solution to the problem or an addition to the situation. This solution then needs to be tried out and played back a few times with adjustments in levels to see how it works.

As we have said, is possible to buy CDs with effects for all occasions on them. There is even a very amusing American web-site by

*Yuckles Pet Store, Sound Effects for your Dog.* This contains such effects as Can Opening, Howling and a Doorbell. Perhaps we should put together a site for Guide Dogs especially for those who are part of our team!

### Silence

In a fascinating essay in a book entitled <u>Wireless Imagination,</u> Francis Dyson writes about John Cage: 'Using silence as a structural device for organising sonic material, Cage was able to expand his musical domain to include what lies beyond the consideration of music as an art form; the world of noise.' [2] This is not the place to discuss the fascinating sounds produced.

There is a theoretical silence and real silence. This is not an empty comment. The moving sensitivity of the ear will always find something. In recording this is also true. All electronic circuits make noise. In fact audio engineers hear 'mains hum' even in the bath! The better the quality of the electronics the lower the noise level but nevertheless it can be heard. There has been discussion about the aesthetics of random digital noise, but we do not want our audience to go down that path. Thus, if we make a space that we imagine is silence it will be appreciated quite quickly by the listener that it is not really silence. Not only is there the distracting silence of the equipment but over a short period of time the listener will become more sensitive to sound and hear the environment and their fellow humans with their constant movement and personal activities. The time it takes for a person to become aware of other sounds is quite short and this should be taken into account where silence is being used. It is perfectly reasonable to maintain, during a theoretical silence, a sound that represents silence as a cover but the choice has to be carefully made.

### Music

We have over 1000 books on the shelves that relate to music and many CDs of our own recordings and others. Yes, we are interested in music. The following is not a summary of these books but an attempt to put together a working concept that will help in the consideration of music as an element in recorded sound communication. In other words in soundscaping.

Try listening to the voice music of Trevor Wishart. These pieces are quite stunning especially on film. Or the poems of Kurt Schwiters. These Schwiters poems are half soundscape shock and half-meaningful words shock!

We came across a 'talking holdall' in a Copenhagen park. We walked through a copse where the trees were making weird and strange noises, almost like wild animals but not quite. Then we heard voices singing from a holdall on the grass near the Chinese Pavilion. We stood over this holdall, listening to it while admiring the Pavilion and the tame herons that were perched on the bridge nearby. A good example of soundscaping of an unexpected nature – a staid park and abstract sound.

If we give the matter some thought then there are some clear-cut elementary reasons for using music. However, it is not essential and in certain instances natural sounds can be used or none at all. A simple commentary does not need the sound of a symphony orchestra. Perhaps the simple reasons might be:

> The signature of the piece
> The joining sequences
> Crisp inserts for various reasons – for example a 'sting' to highlight a dramatic point
> The end of the audio piece – a cadence in musical terms.

The connection between people and music is complex as is the connection between people and sound. The above is a brief list of uses for music and it can have much more complex connections. It is not difficult to imagine situations where music has an almost terrifying effect. The brass instruments used by the Vikings in battle is at one end of the scale and a lullaby for a child at the other. Groups can be affected by music, take a military band for example. Groups of people can relate to each other through music in strange ways.

It is essential that we are aware of the various periods of music and their characteristics because of the historic connotations. Since we are often communicating information about the past and those who cannot see will pick up their information and atmosphere by listening, it becomes very important. Some music would clash unbearably with certain situations or at least bring up strange connections. Bach at a rock festival might work, but probably not.

David Sonneschein in <u>Sound Design</u> has a section on music written from the point of view of a sound designer. A musician would have a very different approach possible on the basis of composing a whole piece of sound rather than a piece of music for performance in a concert.[3]

It seems to us that the human race and music have been together since the beginning of time. In fact evidence of very early music is rare: we have given two examples. The civilisation of Greece is ancient and complex but we have only a small amount of written evidence of music. The form of music is important in that it gives us a clue as to what it was used for. There have been efforts to reconstruct Roman music in a similar manner.

There is little evidence as to the use of very early music. We can be sure that people made music and enjoyed music but it is hard to find evidence. One thing is certain and that is that it was not commercial. Musicians and performers would have moved from place to place but certainly almost everyone made music and did so in our civilisation until recently. The closest to the function of very early music is folk music. There is much evidence of Royal music and liturgical music from the middle of the first millennium but little evidence of folk music. It is hard to imagine a world without music but we do not really know how musicians and people related to music. It would be difficult to isolate music from other activities. We learn about what African 'musicians' did and still do in a useful book, <u>Griots and Griottes</u>[4], which describes the history and function of the sub-Saharan Griot, which was certainly not only music.

Currently with the development of communication music has been freed from at least part of the 'traditional' commercial structure. Radio and now digital radio via the ether and via the web has allowed much greater flexibility of access. The war around the delivery of MP3 files via the internet will eventually be sorted out. Traditional instruments have been carefully considered and now we can obtain copies of earlier forms of instruments and high standard modern instruments. Whatever the quality of instrument they do need to be played by highly skilled musicians. The development of electronic music has a history of success and is generally easier to manipulate than the traditional instrument and has fewer problems in transmission.

Popular music, to use a misguided term, has grown in volume and standing. The cultural spread of this has been presented in the BBC 3 programme *Late Junction* and the 'backroom', mostly electronic music, played on the BBC programme *Mixing It*. MP3 down-loads can be obtained from the internet and CDs can now be ordered in the same way. CDs mastering has been revolutionised and the result is a broader spread of music than ever before and a complex culture, only some of which is to be found on public radio and generally-available CDs. There is an underground that is vast and mostly uncharted. However, the American scene appears on the internet as indeed does the Finnish scene. One reason that it is not 'household information' is that the work is as outspoken as the now-acceptable 'avant garde' used to be before it became a commercial success.

Although much is below the immediately visible surface, it is possible to find about it in magazines and on the internet. One website worth visiting is *Ishkurs Electronic Music*. This shows a pattern of relationships of the various types of music and will play from MP3 downloaded examples of the various types. Watch out! Our speakers gave us the music at 110dB which is very loud, so turn it down before you start. Many sources on the internet are able to supply CDs of lesser known groups in the normal manner.

An awareness of early music has to be credited to David Munrow. Both of us listened to the BBC programme *Pied Piper* in which David presented early music with a freshness and authority that bowled us over. He worked very hard and recorded 50 albums and much more. Sadly, in a fit of depression in 1976 he committed suicide. Look on the internet for details of his recordings and where to obtain them. They are very worthwhile!

Access to early music was like opening a window; it was no longer some distant paragraph from a dusty book but accessible at last. Part of its success lies in the smaller, and therefore achievable forces, required to perform the music and a more general appreciation of music in a context that is not the concert hall. We were part of the *Border Marches Early Music Forum* which was one of many fora throughout the country. These small organisations provide workshops for amateur musicians and spread an awareness of early music.

Classical music has been very much influenced by the approach developed for early music. The definition is more complex than the standard one where it is a period of music that comes between High Baroque and Romantic. With the downturn of sales of classical music there was a move to pull the early music approach into the classical view. The result of this was a better understanding of authenticity and accuracy. Essentially this move was part of the world of concert and music publishing to achieve economic rehabilitation.

World music, again supported by the BBC, has had a considerable effect on the music scene and its programme *World Routes* is worth hearing. It acts as a counter to our view of music as being essentially European. Each area has its own music. There is also an Asian programme entitled 'Asian Network' that gives some clues as to what Asian music is being produced in this country. We have recorded Zulu music in South Africa and we are looking at the possibility of producing a CD of the music put together by children from the shelters in Durban. If this music is not attractive to other people then the aim of raising money to help them will not work.

Without exception music relates to social groups often with particular characteristics. In Modulations; A History of Electronic Music; Throbbing Words on Sound there are descriptions and disc references to various groups of producers and composers of electronic music.[5] In his introduction, Peter Shapiro puts his finger on the ability to move sections of sound around as essential to all modern electronic music. The breadth of music and the people it is intended for, is very wide and seems to be reaching out much further than earlier histories of electronic music. For example there is an examination of *House* music and its reinvention. Again with *Krautrock* the character of the audience is discussed.

As you put together your sound presentation you will be aware of the group to whom you are presenting. That group will have its own musical customs and indeed it will have other cultural and sociological characteristics. Try to sort this out before you consider the insertion of music into your work.

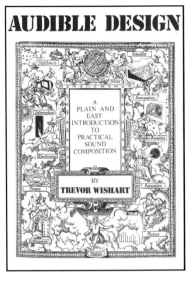

In terms of a cross-over between music and sound then one is looking for some very clear thinking by people like Trevor Wishart. He has written two books with similar contents. First, <u>Audible Design</u>,[6] which he describes as 'A plain and easy introduction to practical sound composition' and that is what it is. Small type and hard work but very worthwhile. In 1996 under the editorship of Simon Emmerson, Trevor Wishart wrote <u>On Sonic Art</u>.[7] This book is particularly interesting to those who are thinking in terms of soundscaping.

.

[1] Edited by Larry Sider, Diane Freeman and Jerry Sider, <u>Soundscape; the School of Sound Lectures 1998-2001</u>, UK, 2003, ISBN 1-903364-68-X.
[2] Edied by Douglas Kahn and Gregory Whitehead, <u>Wireless Imagination, Sound and the Radio Avant-Garde,</u> London, 1992, ISBN 0-262-11168-3
[3] David Sonnenschein, <u>Sound Design</u>, USA 2001, ISBN 0-941188-26-4.
[4] Thomas A Hale, <u>Griots and Griottes</u>, Indiana. 1998, ISBN 0-253-33458-6
[5] Jan Ling, <u>A History of European Folk Music,</u> New York 1997, ISBN 1-878822-77-2
[6] Trevor Wishart, <u>Audible Design,</u> U 1994,
[7] Trevor Wishart, <u>On Sonic Art,</u> Netherlands, 1996, ISBN 3-7186-5546-1.

# Soundscaping

*Soundscape often has to be added to an existing situation. Here we are examining the sound environment with the Telinga field microphone on the Stiperstones in South Shropshire*

## *Theory of Film Sound*

One of the sources for ideas for creative sound has to be the cinema. Immense amounts of money have been made with film, and one has to say, also lost. As a consequence much time and money has been invested in the work on film sound. Partly because of this, much thought has gone into the making of films and their sound and it is worth going over this work to see what might be applicable to our work. Academic thinking about film has become a reasonable field and for us this is particularly important although it covers a slightly different field from ours.

A notable characteristic of Holywood films is the ease with which they are edited so that it is hard to notice when a cut occurs. This is a skill but the greater skill is the manufacture of emotion by the cutting of one shot against another. To simplify matters we can call this montage and this is a concept that comes from film and we should note how it is done.

Essentially the sound on a film is made up from various sources, such as synchronised sound and sound effects. These are dealt with in more detail in the next section.

Recently another component has been added and that is Sound Design which is an overall concept. Most of the parts run very much together, but as a general rule music tends to run parallel rather than being an integral part of the sound track. It is worth remembering these components as we run through some of the theory of film.

While these components will be expanded in the next section this is a useful start as all of these components will apply to the production of other audio forms. They need to be carefully considered and indeed in a good film they certainly are and it is worth watching and listening to a good film to analyse how it is put together. The human voice has to fit the subject and is generally synchronised to the image. The sound effects need to be suitable and are either straight recordings or made up to sound like what the effect is imagined to be. Music can be used as a signature or an underwriting emotional addition and is very complex.

Technology has advanced since the time when Paul Rotha wrote his book <u>Documentary Film</u>[1] in 1936; he has the sort of clear-cut ideas that one would expect from the documentary film makers of that period.

A point he makes, which has only recently become acceptable, is to use the voices of real people and the voice of poets. He says:

> Let the smith in charge of the steam-hammer tell us in his own language what he is doing. Let the shot firer in the mine speak of his own job. They do it better than the professional commentator at three guineas a time; in simpler, more humble and more honest speech. Yet another line that might be developed is that of the poet as narrator.

There are severe restrictions when working with film such as the small screen and, until recently, poor sound. A further limitation is the fact that in order to collect the money the large audience has to be fixed in rows of seats. The same restriction applies to television although it is one small box and living room seating.

One has to take care in reading about film theory not to fall over this and to recognise when this restriction has been enforced because it is often not mentioned or even admitted. With digital multi-track audio and vision the only need to pin people down is to catch their attention and hold it for a while and certainly not for the length of an 'A' category film. We have to remember that for us there could be several separate, but related screens and multi-track sound; an example that showed this potential was the *Radical Fashion* show at the V&A a few years ago.

A recent edition of <u>AV Communication for Business</u> magazine carried an article headed 'Plasma and LCD Sales Through the Roof', which suggests that we are not alone in seeing a future for multiple large moving images. The single story of the single film is nothing like the multi-path story that has to take place in a museum or exhibition for example. We can learn from it, but it is quite different. However, it is worth noting that sound film uses both vision and sound and is therefore multi-sensory.

Within the theory of film sound there is the strange concept of 'diegetic sound'. This means that the voices of the actors and sounds and the resulting space created in the story space are 'diegetic'. Sound outside the story space is called 'nondiegtic'. Perhaps this is necessary because of the small single visual frame of the cinema or television. However, it is a useful concept and the psychology of having inside and outside sound and space is very useful and we should also consider its use.

To simplify this concept even further, the on-screen sounds might be the voices of the characters or sounds made by objects in the story. However, the space can be extended by having the voice of the characters off-screen although clearly they belong on-screen.

The off-screen sounds might be a narrator's commentary or sound effects to add drama.

The book by the French author Michel Chion, <u>Audio-Vision,</u> gives a useful description of the concept of 'off-screen space'.[2] He has to accept the limitations of cinema sound but in a section entitled, 'The Question of Off-Screen Space' he discusses the segregation of sound and space in useful detail. There is also a measure of linkage to elsewhere. The word 'acousmatic' which means 'sounds one hears without seeing their originating causes' comes from Pierre Schaefer. He is an important person who theorised about *musique concrete* some years ago.

In retrospect the theory of film and in particular the concepts that were brought up when films absorbed sound are very interesting to us. Reading about it now, it seems a very clear change from silent movies to talkies, but the truth is that it was terrible revolution. We have one book on our shelves that presents this very well: <u>The Speed of Sound</u> by Scott Eyman.[3] It is an excellent story of Hollywood and the Talkie Revolution from 1926-930. One wonders if this takes the same path that other industries take when there is a radical change in product. There are, of course, more straightforward and simpler histories of this change. There are more analytical reviews of this piece of history in the book <u>Film Sound Theory and Practice</u>, edited by Weis and Belton.[4]

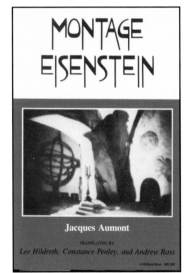

If we now step aside from the over-aweing history of the change from silent film to talkie and look at what was actually written about the theory of the change, we find some revolutionary thoughts came up, but in the end the solutions adopted were fairly mundane. Nevertheless it did offer the opportunity to think and to express these revolutionary views. While thinking does not necessarily make money, it does pass on useful ideas and we should be grateful for this.

Historically, one of the most important thinkers on film was Sergei Eisenstein who was Russian rather than American. There was already a 'cold war' between the US and USSR even in the 1930s. It is worth mentioning here that many other countries were making films for national and economic purposes, although not to the extent of the big powers. Britain was one of these. There is a lot about Eisenstein's concept of visual montage in his writing but not very much on sound; montage is the art of putting one sequence of film against another. Eisenstein defined various categories of montage which we suggest could be applied to sound in a parallel manner. Jacque Aumont in <u>Montage Eisenstein</u> points out that it is not easy to pin down the thoughts of Eisenstein from his writing.[5] Again, Rudolf Arnheim in <u>Film as Art</u> writes what he considered to be the principles of montage and these could well be examined for their possibilities in cutting sound; he also lists the ways of montage that Timoshenko has given.[6] For us the issue is not one of academic film making, but sound communication and so we can take from these lists what is useful to us.

Timoshenko lists:

| | |
|---|---|
| 1) | Change of place |
| 2) | Change of camera position |
| 3) | Change of range of image |
| 4) | Stressing of details |
| 5) | Analytical montage |
| 6) | Return to past time |
| 7) | Anticipation of the future |
| 8) | Parallel events |
| 9) | Contrast |
| 10) | Association |
| 11) | Concentration |
| 12) | Enlargement |
| 13) | Monodramatic montage |
| 14) | Refrain |
| 15) | Montage |

Looking at the list not so many items are translatable into pure sound concepts.

Eisenstein talks about montage in many ways and his thinking, as we have already said, has to be interpreted carefully. Montage, he says, is 'conflict'. While he writes about montage in the abstract at one point, he actually defines graphic montage, that is conflict, as follows:

Conflict of graphic direction
Conflict of scales
Conflict of volumes
Conflict of masses
Conflict of depths

All of these definitions have an equivalent in sound. In stereo sound it can also come from different directions; there can be a large sound and a small sound. One sound can be spatially bigger than another and there can be differences of frequency. Although this is stretching the concept, the general idea is still valid when we consider a montage of sound.

Dziga Vertov was an interesting person who seemed from his writings to be a much more pragmatic film-maker. He made comment on sound but mainly that the equipment was not as mobile as he and other 'documentary' makers would wish. He

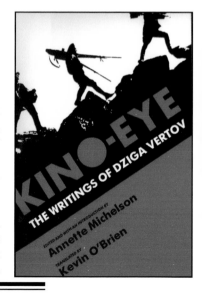

and his fellow *Kino-Eye* operators had an interesting immediate approach to film and sound and are worth reading. The book edited by Annette Michelson and translated by Kevin O'Brien is <u>Kino-Eye, The Writings of Dziga Vertov.</u>[7]

For us, the issue is that of placing one sound against another, although with the trend towards visual work we do need to look at montage as a whole. Already we face the problem of having fixed images against which we need to pitch sound.

With the addition of high definition video we may find that we are dealing with moving images quite soon and already still images are part of what we should be doing. With new computers and programmes there could be several sound tracks and several moving images. However, right now we have to look at the lists of montage techniques and take from them what we need.

Siegfried Kracauer wrote <u>Theory of Film</u>[8] in 1960; it has been recently republished. Much of his consideration of sound hinges around the importance of dialogue but always in relation to the image. Naturally he is concerned with the synchronisation of the sound with the image.

Our image is essentially in the mind but it might also be related to real images where subtitles and signing are part of the frame. We might also have more than one frame. He writes also about 'Sound Proper' and its characteristics as well as music. The three categories of sound in film that he mentions are 'voice, sound and music'.

Kracauer begins to examine the form of sound but not in sufficient detail to help us. He discusses dialogue, which has a tradition that is very historic and has come down to us from ancient Greek culture through theatre to the present time. He does mention 'Speech de-emphasised' but this does not answer all the questions of how to use the voice.

Kracauer says that there is a continuum of forms of sound from the unidentifiable to the obvious. We would make the point that the meaning of sound is critical. For example, to us in the UK sound of walking on snow is unusual but just recognisable; our Finnish friends are able to tell what type of snow it is and the current temperature at the time of the recording. Individually we have varied understanding.

Raymond Spotiswoode in <u>A Grammar of Film</u>, first published in 1935, extends ideas of sound by various definitions.[9] By defining the type of sound, we can get a better understanding of what we are using. He lists under *The Sound Factor*:

Speech
 Realistic Use
 Selective Use
 Combinative Use
 Tonal use

Natural Sound
 Realistic Use
 Selective Use

Music
 Imitative Use
 Commentative Use
 Evocative Use
 Contrastive Use
 Dynamic Use

While he writes about film in a general way and makes points on sound in this text, he does not expand on this list by way of explanation. However, any way to define the gamut of sound that we are dealing with is useful.

Kracauer looks at music systematically but not from the point of view of the present situation as the text is historical. Current popular classification groups music into background music and main theme music. However, if we look at the classic book on film sound by Adorno and Eisler, <u>Composing for the Films</u> we begin to get a more focussed view of film music.[10] This was first published in 1947.

It should be noted that while we are taking an oblique view of the texts in this paragraph, that Kracauer, Adorno and Eisler all came from Germany in the 1930s and went to US as a result of political pressure. Inevitably, their view of the situation is not at all that of the established American view and in many cases problems arose from this. Nevertheless, their thoughts form a cornerstone in the theory of film. The issue here is that we are taking a different view, but there is much to learn from all writers on film and indeed those who deal with sound.

Another person interested in film was Lazlo Moholy-Nagy; he said that there had to be a new approach to sound as there had been a new approach to cinema, which at that point was silent cinema. He said:

 In regard to the second series it will not be possible to develop the creative possibilities of the talking film to the full until the acoustic alphabet of soundwriting will have been mastered.[11]

In other words he is saying that until we can write acoustic sequences on the sound track onto the film without having to record any real sound we will not be able to adequately edit sound on film. Once this is achieved the sound film composer will be able to create music from a counterpoint of unheard or even nonexistent sound values by means of opto-acoustic notation. In fact Moholy-Nagy was working with drawing the wave forms and other images directly onto film and using this as a basis of sound design.

Moholy-Nagy was referring to the actual optical track on the film but more broadly it is prophetic in that it is only since the tracks could be seen in digital editing in wave-form on a time line that the scope of creative sound has been released. One feels that it would have been a natural step for him to open up a digital editing programme and to start work. His tactile machines, developed when he was teaching at the Bauhaus, are also amazing and point to his understanding of multi-sensory design.

Much thought has been given recently to the history of film sound especially in the US. Two books are of special note:

Sound Theory and Practice edited by Rick Altman

and Theory and Practice Film Sound, edited by Elisabeth Weiss and John Belton. Both books have significant essays on sound in relation to film but are also useful in the consideration of sound alone.

In summary, there is a much to be gleaned from work that has been done on sound for films and this warrants more research. However, there are limitations in the study of film sound that seem to come from the unpromising format which presupposes a single screen and finite time and the form that the industry needs. We do not have the same problems as the film maker; our problems are different, but we can learn from what has been written in this field.

[1] Paul Rotha, <u>Documentary Film</u>, London (originally 1936) 1952.
[2] Michel Chion, <u>Audio-Vision, Sound on Screen</u>, New York, 1994, ISBN 0-231-07898-6
[3] Scott Eyman, <u>The Speed of Sound, Hollywood and the Talkies Revolution 1926-1930</u>, USA, 1997, ISBN 0-8018-5192-6
[4] Edied by Elisabeth Weis and John Belton, <u>Film Sound, Theory and Practice</u>, New York, 1985, ISBN 0-231-05636-2
[5] Jacques Aumont, <u>Montage Eisenstein</u>, UK 1987, ISBN 0-81570-187-6
[6] Rudolf Arnheim, <u>Film as Art</u>, UK, 1958.
[7] Edited by Annette Michelson, <u>Kino-Eye, The writings of Dziga Vertov</u>, California, 1984, ISBN 0-520-05630-2.
[8] Seigfried Kracauer, <u>Theory of Film</u>, USA, 1997, ISBN 0-691-03704-3
[9] Raymond Spotiswoode, <u>A Grammar of Film</u>, London 1935.
[10] Theodor Adorno and Hanns Eisler, <u>Composing for the Films</u>, New Jersey, 1994.
[11] Richard Kostelanetz, <u>Lazlo Moholy-Nagy</u>, UK 1970, ISBN 0-71390760-6.

# *Making Sound for Films*

The actual way of making sound for film is also of interest to us and has to be understood if we are to make the most of the vast amount of information that is available on sound for films.

As we have said, generally film sound is made in three quite separate sections, or even five sections, in the manufacture of the film. Of course, scripts and schedules are made and the work follows these quite closely. These sections generally are:

1. Synchronised (synch.) sound – usually speech
2. FXs = sound effects
3. Foley Sound
4. Sound design
5. Music

It is worth understanding the reasons for these three sections which we will deal with separately. These various forms of sound are critical issues in the film industry so that it is not sufficient just to imagine the character sound of the cartoon films. There is always something to learn.

**1. Synchronised sound**
This is essential in film so that the characters are seen to speak and the sound appears to come from the mouths of the characters or from the events that take place. Of course the characters might be animals or cartoons or even an inanimate object. Insofar as we might have similar situations we would have to do the same. In some cases the sound is recorded on the vision cassette, but with larger commercial equipment there have to be devices that allow the vision to run at the same speed as the sound and a pulse needs to be printed onto both at the same time so that they can be matched in the editing. Such systems run under SMPTE system.

Both <u>Audio in Media</u>  by Stanley R Alten and <u>Sound for Film and Television</u> by Tomlinson Holman contain useful chapters on synchronisation and you should refer to these if you need more information

When synchronised sound is recorded the microphone is often close to the person and it is recorded on a boom or similar device. In fact on television the microphones suspended from the boom are sometimes seen by accident. It is worth being aware of the techniques used.

On one occasion we were recording fish laying eggs in the reeds and to use a boom was the only way to get the microphones close enough to keep the signal-to-noise ratio down sufficiently to hear the fish. A bird in a nest in a tree, or a politician on the other side of a crowd, present the same problems and generally the solution might be the same.

We have referred to speech already but it is worth mentioning again that this is a particular type of sound. It has to be considered in terms of the history of drama. Rhetoric is a curious habit and has a particular relationship with recorded voices that needs to be carefully thought-out so that the voice is not only rhetoric, but meaningful action.

### 2. FXs

Sound effects (known as FXs) are a vital part of putting together a dramatic sound presentation. Of course it is possible to put a film together without sound effects but if the sync. recording is made clean and without ambience then the rest has to be added afterwards. This is an obvious recording problem and for this reason there are things to be learned from the film world. As part of the assembly, since the sync. recording is dry, that is, has little reflected sound, a recording of an ambience has to be selected and included. The correct ambience is so important that is often carefully selected by specialists. The continuity between the ambiences is critical as well with long cross-fades and engineered changes. Often the ambience has a special content into which the sync. sound can be placed.

Libraries of sound can be bought on CD and these come with a copyright arrangement for you so that you can use them freely. Effects can be obtained from sites on the internet. Sometimes, as with selecting existing photographs to fit a new situation, the library sound does not fit and the sound has to be recorded. In many cases the library sound is of something that would be impossible to record for oneself. An example might be the erupting of a volcano; in our town this very rarely happens!

### 3. Foley Sound

This is a very specific way of producing sound effects often in sync. with the image. It was named after Jack Foley of Universal Studios. Generally the Foley artists, probably two or three of them, work on a specific sound stage in front of a projection screen so that the artists can create the appropriate sound at the right time in sync. with the picture.

The movement of a garment and the sound of a cigarette lighter have to be present in close up and if you miss them in your recording you might have to be your own Foley artist. On occasions these recordings are multi-tracked and rehearsed time and again.

In certain cases the use of the Foley artist is warranted and almost inevitable. In fact these incidental sounds are very important and very difficult to record on the same track as the speech. Not only would the leading actor in a drama not wish to do two takes of a punch on his jaw, but convention says that the reality is not the acceptable sound. We are told that a fist into raw liver sounds more realistic. Personally, we like our liver fried and on a plate. However, some of the techniques are of use and this is a useful way of thinking. Some simple examples are:

> Rain = salt sprinkled onto paper
> Hail = rice sprinkled onto paper
> Walking in mud = hands on soggy paper

And there have to be many more procedures and experiments that can be rewarding. It is a debatable point whether people recognise the real sound unless they have heard it before. Care must be taken in the provision of sound for those who depend on it, because they might well remember what the original was like. In certain instances the symbolic Foley sound is so far from reality that it is of no help to someone who cannot see.

### 4. Sound design

In film the evolution of the Sound Designer is fairly recent and is specific. However, while film is always changing so does the broader view of the Sound Designer and this broader view is discussed elsewhere. In film the role is the inevitable integration of various jobs. Nevertheless, what is achieved by Sound Designers is of significance and should be taken

into account. To quote Walter Murch: 'So if you have a sound that you can't get from a library, that you can't go out and record yourself, but that you have to concoct out of a different number of contributing sounds, then that becomes what the sound designer does'. This seems a rather limited approach.

One book that gives more ideas per page than most is <u>Sound Design – The Expressive Power of Music, Voice, and Sound Effects in Cinema</u> by David Sonnenschein. It is full of ideas as well as a good number of very real points. It is not appropriate to follow the exact schedules and sound maps that one might make for a film, but there is much to learn from the sequence of events in making a film and the agreements that have to be reached. Also, is goes without saying that the file organisation in one's computer needs to be very carefully thought through.

## 5. Music

Many films and television pieces have music. The tradition of music and film was in operation before the 'talkies'. Music is not obligatory but is very useful. We have run community music workshops and we have employed composers to produce music for us. However, it is quite expensive and you will need some skill if the music needs to be recorded. We have done various deals with musicians and singers where we produced a CD from our recording and they gave us the reccording to use, but you need more than a mini-disc to do that sort of thing, as well as a fair amount of expertise. A composer working on an electronic keyboard is perhaps the most economic. There are many amateur musicians working in the electronic idiom that might be able to help in exchange for a copy of the final result. But remember that musicians need to earn enough money to live on. Films do not have quite the same problem and use orchestras and have sound stages, which are effectively large recording studios with a cinema screen. Low budget television is closest to our situation and so it is worth being aware of the music that is used at this level.

David Sonnenschein outlines the function of film music. Of course there is a large area of musical history in the development of film music but for us it is a bit academic. David suggests the following heads.

Emotional signifier - gives a sense of place

Continuity - bridges the gaps

Narrative cueing - helps orient the audience

Narrative unity - provides unity

Programmatic music - represents action called 'micky mousing'

Anempathetic music - ironic use of a theme

This a very much over-simplified version, essentially because while we have similar problems we need to deal with them in other ways. Clearly, much of the above can be dealt with by FXs and sound textures.

# Radio Sound

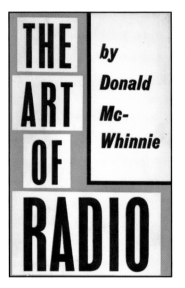

Radio is a medium that deals only with sound. However, there are very few references to radio sound as compared with cinema sound. One classic book which deals with radio as an art form – which of course it is – is <u>The Art of Radio</u> by Donald McWhinnie.[1] This is a key book and contains much that needs to be thought through. He talks of the experience of radio and in particular 'The Raw Material' of radio. His breakdown is similar to, and may have been the origin of, the classification of sound found elsewhere. He talks of the Word, Sound, Music, Natural Sounds, *Musique Concrete* and Radiophonic effects, and silence. He is aware of the communal experience of radio which is not simply the consideration of radio for one person. Of silence, he writes:

During silence, things happen invisibly, in the minds of the players and in our imagination; we are drawn through the shimmer of words into a world in which there is another level of existence apart from what is merely said. In fact, silence adds a dimension; sound comes from it, sound returns to it, words have been surrounded by it, it is the cloth on which the pattern is woven.

At the present time radio is seen more as a vehicle for news and comment than as an art form. Nevertheless, the BBC produces a very impressive number of programmes which include a high proportion of drama. The quality of production in the BBC, in drama particularly, is very high. However, it is seen as an important communication media and books such as <u>Media and Meaning</u> give sets of principles that are worth consideration not only for radio but for other media.[2]

It seems very likely that the form of radio will change over the next few years. In the past, on the basis that there are very few suitable slots in the 'airwaves', transmission has been limited by licence in most countries. It could be argued that this is also a way of control of communication. However, the classic 'freedom of the press', and other media, really applies only to the owner of the press or other controlling influences.

Now, it is possible to transmit via the internet and the Dog Rose Trust has its own internet radio station: www.dogrosesound. org. It is aimed at the provision of interesting guides to buildings and news items that can be down loaded in various ways. We aim to provide archived guides and programmes that can be accessed 24 hours a day.

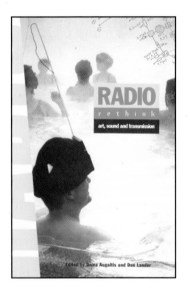

The freer situation of broadcasting on the internet does not mean that standards have to be lowered, but rather they should be higher than in the past because of the extended international audience. However, while the effort to produce a programme remains the same, the 'on costs' of running the internet station is considerably less than the traditional radio station and this is also helped by the new technology that is available.

McWhinnie cites various works which have been written for radio such as *The Dark Tower* by Louis MacNeice, and *Under Milk Wood* by Dylan Thomas. These works belong to a special historic group from the 1950s and are considered as significant examples.

*VIP ON AIR*, is Europe's first radio station for blind and visually impaired people. It is an internet radio station put together by our good friends in Glasgow. 'It produces four hours of original programming Monday to Friday with an aim to provide information that its audience would otherwise struggle to access elsewhere.' They have been given some useful support by many organisations, not least Glasgow Council who put in £200,000 to build what must one of the few accessible studios in the world.

With the above in mind there was a movement to reach more people that seemed to start in Canada. It was a sort of revolution. There are three key books that express this revolution and it is worth mentioning them right now.

1)    Radiotext(e),[3] this book contains chapters such as, Alternative Histories, Perpetrators, Listeners and Cranks.

2) <u>Radio Rethink</u>,[4] published by the Walter Phillips Gallery at Banff, Canada, contains essays on various related subjects and the interesting experiments carried out there.

3) <u>Wireless Imagination Sound Radio and the Avant-Garde</u>, This book is more or less what its title says.[5]

While the abstract concepts are important there is a lot to be considered in the production of programmes for radio. Perhaps the most useful and standard book, now in its fourth edition, is <u>Radio Production</u> by Robert McLeish which systematically goes through the process. [6] In the Preface to the fourth edition he says:

Digital technologies continue to make equipment not only smaller but immensely more versatile so that the facilities of the whole studio – sourcing, presenting, interviewing, mixing, multi-track recording and editing – can be compressed into a portable package for automated playout. Create the same techniques for pictures as for sounds, and there is no technical reason why they should not be crafted by the same people.

This is an interesting and relevant comment. McLeish covers most of the types of programme that one might wish to make and much of this would also be relevant for vision. There are many useful ideas under the various headings.

# *Radio Sound*

[1] Donald McWhinnie, The Art of Radio, London, 1959

[2] Colin Stewart, Marc Lavelle and Adam Kowltzke, Media and Meaning, London, 2001, ISBN 0-85170-844-7.

[3] Edited by Neil Straus, Radiotext(e), New York, 1992, ISBN 0-093-95779

[4] Edited by Daina Augaitis and Dan Lander, Radio Rethink, Walter Phillips Gallery, Banff, Canada, 1994, ISBN 0-920159-66-4.

[5] Edited by Douglas Kahn and Gregory Whitehead, Wireless Imagination, Sound Radio and the Avant-Garde, Cambridge, USA, ISBN 0-262-11168-3.

[6] Robert McLleish, Radio Production, Focal Press 1999, ISBN 0-24051554-4

# *Internet Radio*

We talk about internet radio, but we should also be talking about a broader approach where vision is also streamed at the same time or independently. In addition we can think about any other streaming and storage concept and the same general principals and issue will apply. Thus, for the first part of this section we refer to radio but imply a broader concept. There will no longer be a simple historical concept of a radio programme.

Internet radio has special characteristics that are very useful in the area of disability. Not only can it transmit programmes as traditional radio, but it can supply, from its server, archive programmes which are kept there for the convenience of those interested. Radio has its own character and we need to think how it will fit into the new world of multi-sensory design and communication. Couple this with its ability to create communities, as with local radio, then there is a future for internet radio that is beyond the simple entertainment machine.

The computer has been with us for a while but not that long. With the computer came the internet which was initially developed to make communication between certain scientists possible, even if there was a breakdown in a particular landline. From this there developed the internet as we know it now. With the advent of broadband the speed at which information can travel from the server to the personal computer is increased to the point where sound files can be streamed from the server to the computer. Thus the computer can receive transmissions from a radio station  and this can be listened to or stored and listened to later.

If we look at the history of radio in this country and Europe and also in the United States there are differences, but mostly in the attitude of the politics behind radio. Both the free system of the United States and the more governmental approach of Europe, including ourselves, quite quickly saw that unless control of the air waves was achieved then interference and technical problems would upset the whole structure. Thus everywhere broadcasting licences were established. With this came other controls and the use of the radio in the 'national interest'.

There was a time when everyone sat round in the same room around a large radio, but this soon was overtaken. In the 1970 there evolved the commercial product of the small radio brought about technically by the advent of the cheap transistor so that everyone could have their own radio. Soon there were inexpensive playback systems for recorded sound; the workman on the roof of a building to the housewife working in the kitchen could then tune into their favourite programmes. Although this produced diversity, it was only to the extent of the programmes provided.

We are well aware that the limited airways carried the programmes but the recorded sound had to be purchased, initially in the form of Phillips Cassettes and later CDs. The way that the CDs were duplicated was kept within the industry until recently. In this way the music industry retianed control of what was being produced and this was in some ways parallel to the limited programmes on the radio.

Occasional 'breakouts' occurred in the form of pirate radio stations and for that matter pirate duplication of recordings. *Radio Caroline* was possibly the first and this was transmitted from a ship in the channel which made it difficult to control. This was followed by a wave of small pirate radio stations that were fairly elusive and indeed popular.

The current picture in this country compared with the US is interesting in that the BBC puts on programmes that are of general cultural interest whereas in the United States the 'public service stations' spend a lot of their air-time begging for money in order to broadcast what the BBC does as a matter of course. The BBC has now developed internet sites and replay systems so that past programmes can be heard. It has also developed cross-cultural programmes which plays 'popular' music from all over the world.

We put 'popular' in inverted comas because herein lies one of the problems of radio and any other mass communication system. At a point where the recipients number millions (and there are occasions when they do) then the efficiency of the large controlled system is proven. But what about the very special tastes of people and without doubt, given encouragement people will develop very individual tastes, then what is the best system? If we look at Mark Slobin's book, Subcultural Sounds – Micromusics of the West we can see how a very aware ethnomusicologist has tried to classify groups of music and failed. Certainly he comes out with very interesting observations but he proves that there is no simple system that might be applied.

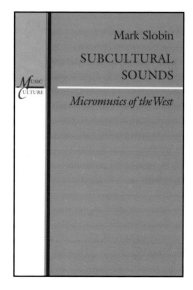

At this point we asked one of our consultants, Keith Bramich to add his thoughts to this interesting subject.

### New Media in New Places - anything anywhere?
### by Keith Bramich

The vision of any type of media being available anywhere is tantalisingly close. If your material can be stored in computer-readable form, the communications technology of the 21st century can make it available in a wide variety of ways.

The computer made its mark on the 20th century, but it looks certain that the next few years will see our liberation from the computer and various new ways of accessing media. The most obvious contenders are currently the mobile phone and 'palm-top' devices, but we're already seeing different devices, such as internet radio players in the home and information points in public places.

Traditional media are being adapted and merged into the new. Radio, and audio in general, for example are being given a new lease of life by the new ways in which programme material can be prepared, stored, distributed and presented.

A museum, tourist attraction or public service can use its website to disseminate material online, either free, revenue-producing or a mixture of both. Familiar services such as audio guides can be distributed in new ways. Via the internet, for example, potential visitors can experience something of your facility before their visit. On arrival, using various kinds of new technology, including hand-held devices and wireless networking, they can tap into as wide a variety of material as you are able to make available, at transfer rates that make high quality audio and video a doddle. On leaving they can be invited to buy personal copies of some your material, in whatever form.

One of the most important advantages of all this is that providers and distributors of media need only make it available in one electronic location. If something needs updating or changing, a simple edit will bring things up to date; there's no longer the need to copy your changes onto replacement tapes, CDs, flash cards etc. or to redistribute.

As you'll have already discovered from other sections of this book, new technology is also making the production and editing of audio and visual material much easier. With a bit of practice, the work required to produce a new audio presentation can be fairly minimal. Switch on a microphone, record your presentation and upload to the webserver. Or send it out live. Traditional broadcasters have been doing this for decades, of course, providing live and recorded coverage of news and current events.

The effort and experience required to broadcast or webcast audio, live, 24 hours each day, and to keep it interesting is, of course, phenomenal.

Pre-recorded material tends to be of higher quality because the efforts of many hours' work can be concentrated into a programme lasting just a few minutes. Something else the new technology gives us is the storage capacity allowing online access to huge amounts of recorded material. The small organisation can use this to powerful advantage, gradually preparing short, high quality programmes, and building an online library of material, which can be listened to on demand.

One of the secrets of gaining attention on the internet (or indeed anywhere) is to continually provide something new. An online radio station doesn't have to broadcast live continually, but if your listeners know that what you provide is interesting and worthwhile and if you provide this for them regularly, they will return (and tell all their friends).

As a charity providing help to people with visual impairments, the Dog Rose Trust has a keen interest in audio media, which gives people a common experience regardless of the power of their eyesight. This is one of the reasons why we've set up *Dog Rose Sound*, an on-demand internet radio station based on the many cathedral audio guides produced by the Dog Rose Trust over a number of years. These guides are gradually being made available, in forms suitable for listening online or downloading for personal use, but we're also recording new material especially for *Dog Rose Sound*, and will be inviting other groups and individuals to make programmes for us. Come and listen: we're at www.dogrosesound.org

Keith Bramich is managing director of Orion Computer Consultants Ltd, a web design firm working with the arts and public sectors to empower clients to build their own online content. He is also one of the founders of *Music & Vision*, a daily online music magazine which makes creative use of audio and video to illustrate its authors' comments about new CDs and DVDs.

# *The Use of Sound in Interpretation*

> *Ralph Richardson found the theatre was entirely made of wood – acting there was like playing a violin: the best setting he had ever spoken in.*

### Introduction

Sound can be used in many ways to interpret sites and exhibitions. Sound is a useful medium for a wide range of users and therefore should be used more often in a creative way. The word creative is stressed because there seems to be a fear of using sound as it might annoy visitors, staff or disturb the peace of the exhibition areas. There are places where sound is not appropriate, but if creative use is made of it then it can enhance the experience of visitors and become an integral part of a display.

The Trust has worked on many sound projects and has always tried to look at methods of making them different or more interesting and exciting. You want your visitor to keep listening, just as you want them to explore all areas of your site, so it is up to you to make it engrossing and alluring. You know your site better than anyone else and are in the best position to interpret it.

All buildings have their own sound, as Ralph Richardson points out. This has been recognised by many who have thought about design. Richard Neutra wrote in his book <u>Survival through Design</u>, 'Architecture is illuminated not only by light but by sound as well, in fact it is brought into relief through all our senses.'[2] He is not alone in this as Goethe had similar thoughts in respect to sound and so have several other respected writers on architecture.

Our approach to the design of cathedrals was brought about by the research work that we did on the recordings of the reconstruction of the late medieval mass put together by the post-graduate music students from the University of Exeter. Their interest was in recreating the music from the original documents, but ours was to record the real sound of the churches in which the reconstructions took place. In acting out the mass they also illustrated what changes had taken place in the layout of the chancels since medieval times. Neutra also realised how important the acoustics of the mass were and wrote in his book,

# The Use of Sound in Interpretation

As an auditory performance, the ritual during Mass actually reveals the interior of the church to us. It is an error to think of the cathedral as only containing or housing candles, singing people, a sounding organ. The choral modulations, the booming of the basses, the diminishing pianissimos illuminate the grand interior acoustically just as the candles do visually.[3]

It was with this background that we developed the binaural techniques that give such good 'stereo' and portray the shape of the buildings.

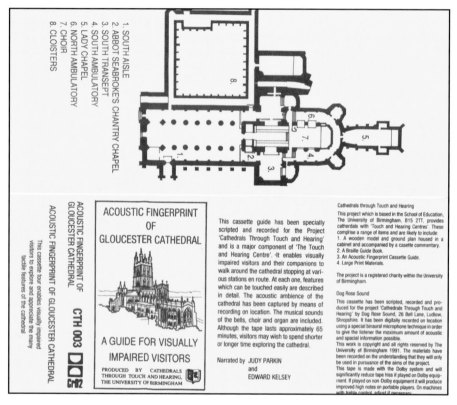

## The Use of Sound for describing and explaining buildings and architecture

This rather unwieldy heading was one we used for a Powerpoint presentation on the Use of Sound, given at an American Association of Museums Conference in St. Louis. We could not afford the fares to go there at the time and so sent this presentation and afterwards we had a link up by telephone to answer questions. We have never been good at realising our limitations and so we put sound, pictures and text on the presentation, thereby stretching it to the limit. We also attempted, and partially succeeded, in making the presentation fully accessible on Universal Design guidelines: the pictures had a brief audio description and the sound had text and all this in fifteen minutes; the new Powerpoint makes this much easier now. The audience must have been left breathless and wondering what was going on. It is hoped that what follows is more coherent.

*The Acoustic Fingerprint Guides of Cathedrals* may have already been mentioned but this seems to be the place to talk about them in more detail. The Guides were part of the Touch and Hearing Centres of Cathedrals which were set up by Dr. John Hull of the University of Birmingham. Dr Hull, a distinguished theologian who is blind, felt that these wonderful buildings did not mean much to him and looked at way of presenting them to people who could not see them.

The Touch and Hearing Centres comprised a model with a spoken commentary, a large print and Braille Guide and an audio guide. At first Dog Rose Sound, as it then was, only worked on the audio guides, but latterly wrote the large print and Braille guides and then managed the whole project for Winchester Cathedral.

The Guides were recorded in the Cathedrals at night. The many years of recording liturgical music in churches had convinced us that the sound of the building would help a blind person to understand its form and architectural detail. When Dr. Hull set up his project we sent him a paper about these ideas and he said, in his forthright Australian way, 'come and do it'. So we did and for several years worked in these remarkable buildings around England.

The script was written as a series of stations or stopping points. These were chosen so they would take advantage of the structure of the building. Each area has its own story and individual style that indicates its function and period of history and much of this can be told through touch.

The key aspect of the Guides was pointing out the acoustic differences in each area. The stereo microphones were moved to the point being described and the recording took place there. This enabled the acoustics and reflections of sound of that space to be fully captured and so enabled the listener to build up an audio picture. For extra large buildings such as York Minster long lengths of cable were purchased and run out from a vestry around a building that is nearly one tenth of a mile long. The results were worth it; you can hear the differences between the high roof of the Chapter House and the low roof of the crypt.

The scripting section talks about the descriptions of acoustic spaces and how to make use of these to explain the structure of the building to people who cannot see. A parallel guide for sighted visitors was written for Winchester Cathedral and we insisted that these descriptions were left

# The Use of Sound in Interpretation

in so that it would make people take in their surroundings in a different way. People with sight are so vision-focussed that they often forget to use their ears properly.

The on-site recording techniques and descriptions of the sound of spaces can be applied to any environment, indoor or outdoor. It is harder work and more time consuming doing it this way, but it is worth it. The hard work comes from having to take the recording equipment to the site, but this, as detailed in the audio sections, is getting smaller and lighter very fast. It takes more time because of having to stop for intrusive sounds such as helicopters and aeroplanes, noisy motorcycles and barking dogs and the weather, if recording outside.

Most environments are noisy and obscure the real sound of a space, but we suspect that this has always been so during the daylight hours. In the past it would have been creaking wooden wagons lumbering past, street vendors shouting and horses hooves on cobbled streets. When it is really quiet somewhere, you can hear the silence.

*Judy Parkin and Edward Kelsey recording in a cathedral*

Characteristic sounds and music help to enhance the building or environment. Obviously the choir is the choice for a Cathedral, but for Bolsover Castle in Derbyshire we arranged for some friends to sing music written by John Wilbye for his patron, Charles Cavendish, who built the Little Castle. They came to Bolsover and sang the beautiful madrigal, Adieu, sweet Amaryllis in the Little Castle; visitors were surprised and delighted to have an unexpected concert that day.

*Patricia Greene and Timothy Mowl recording at Bolsover*

At the top of the Little Castle is the lantern 'of eternal sunlight', as it was called in the script, a lutenist played more of Wilbye's music - it floated around the lantern and down the stairs, reinforcing the ghostly message of the narrative.

The script for Bolsover Castle was a dialogue between Patricia Greene, the narrator, and Dr Timothy Mowl, a distinguished architectural historian who had written about the period. Both of them added their own personalities to the recording, which was all done on site on a cold, wet and windy day; at one point some of the equipment, covered by polythene, caught fire. Fortunately this was outside and so no real damage was done. We would not like to have been responsible for the destruction of the wonderful Little Castle.

*Peter Bull at Hardwick Hall*

*Emilie Fane at Highbury*

For Hardwick Hall, two guides were made. One was a straight narration was recorded in the house, again with Patricia Greene, together with actor Gil Sutherland. To help bring this grand 'prodigy' house to life Peter Bull, psychologist and period musician, played a range of instruments and performed songs suitable to the different rooms. A song in praise of tobacco was particularly apt for the ante-room to the dining chamber.

The other guide was about the park and garden and the people that worked there. The stonemasons, head gardener and other people involved in the maintenance of the great house were all recorded talking about their work. This was then mixed together with actual recordings of the activities associated with their jobs, such as a chainsaw for the gardener and a chisel for the masons.

Joseph Chamberlain's house Highbury, in Birmingham, needed different treatment. A Victorian Arts and Crafts house, there was little to touch and few acoustic changes in the rooms. It was decided to 'people' it with the characters who would have lived there.

An old book about the life of Chamberlain and his marriage to his American third wife, Mary Endicott, was found by chance in a second-hand bookshop and this provided the raw material for the script. The letters between the two, before and after their marriage, enabled much of the script to almost write itself.

As the listener toured the house, they were greeted in each room by a different character: Chamberlain himself, his wife, Lily the maid and William the butler. The same script was written for both sighted and visually impaired visitors with the latter having extra directions and some tactile information. Appropriate sound effects were added.

In addition, a short outreach recording was made with Emilie Fane talking to the manager of Highbury. Her fact sheet for the interview had been Brailled and on the recording you can hear her fingers speeding along the dots.

# The Use of Sound in Interpretation

The recording for the Palace of Westminster, better known as the Houses of Parliament, was made to accompany the tactile model. The script described the function, architecture and appearance of each area. Each track had to be kept short but concise as the listener explored the tactile model and plan.

The recording was made on a Saturday when this amazing building had a very different appearance from the weekday bustle; the only disturbance was from the workmen on the roof doing necessary repairs when the occupants were absent.

*Edward Kelsey at the Palace of Westminster*

## The Use of Sound to enhance displays and collections

Guides of buildings are usually for private listening whereas sound for displays can often be public sound. It can be exciting to create sound for a display, gathering suggestions as to what might be suitable, collecting the sounds, writing the narrative and choosing voices for the recording.

You might decide that you do not want any narrative, only evocative sounds that will stimulate the imagination of visitors. The exhibition might be enhanced by specially written music – the choice is endless and rewarding for both you and your visitors.

A tactile representation of a picture was created for Wolverhampton Art Gallery by Ludlow artist James O'Hanlon. The picture chosen was The Wall Street Journal by Conrad Atkinson.

This was a fun multi-sensory piece to work on. James created a cabinet in which he placed both fixed and loose objects as painted in the original. Fortuitously, the original picture has written text on it, albeit nonsense lines. To create the sound, some of these lines were recorded by an American living in Ludlow and some by a friend who worked for Sotheby's at the time; he appropriately recorded the lines about the British Foreign Secretary.

Shortage of funding often means that friends are co-opted to help with projects or work with us on an exchange basis. Sound effects were added and Adrian Williams, an international composer, then wove music around the words and sounds. For the lines about 'window shopping', three cash registers were found in Ludlow that went 'ping' and their sound was recorded.

The sound track was accessed in a variety of ways:

1.      By opening the door of the cabinet to set off the sound for the introduction

2.      Pressing brass buttons alongside tactile objects

3.      By pulling out a draw which had a tactile object inside. A good example of this was the line about the '5-star general'; inside the drawer was a five-pointed star and the music entwined the Star-Spangled Banner with the words.

The talking picture was popular with children as well as people with visual impairments, but was consigned to the basement to make way for an exhibition and has never been out again.

Changes to a gallery soon make an audio guide or information about the gallery out of date, hence the need to be able to continually update in-house. At the same time as the Wall Street Journal was being created, we were working on an outreach guide to encourage people with visual impairments to come and visit Wolverhampton Art Gallery; it could also be used in the Gallery.

Staff at the Gallery took part in the recording, talking about their particular expertise. This was packaged together with tactile plans of the building and tactile images of keys works described on the guide. Changes to the Gallery soon made this obsolete.

*Trinity Hospital Clun*

Scripting for the audio guide for Coventry Transport Museum, formerly the Museum of British Road Transport in Coventry, is described in more detail at the end of this section. It was planned to take this further and put more sound around the Museum. Some of the models, representing a car of that decade of motoring, would have a sensor by them or the tactile track have a pad on it, so that when someone stepped on it the sound would be activated. The sound in this case would be the signature tune for that decade of motoring. This would alert the visitor that there was a model to touch and a car nearby to explore.

When some of the cars on the audio guide route were moved into the Boomtown Gallery, sound to accompany the printed panels was needed for visitors with visual impairments. We wrote a script which reflected the information on the panels told from the point of view of the owner of the car so that each one had a different character. This was to be recorded by the members of the Amateur Dramatic Society, including the actress who represents Lady Godiva in the Coventry events. The sound would be activated by a sensor when the car was approached.

# The Use of Sound in Interpretation

This project was never carried out so we did not get the opportunity to see how it would work in practice.

### The Use of Sound for Wayfinding

The theory of wayfinding has been written about in more detail already, but this seemed to be the place to give examples of sound, and touch, as wayfinding tools. The Lottery Awards for All funded the Trust to produce audio walks and tactile plans of two South Shropshire towns, Clun and Craven Arms. There were produced together with visually impaired colleagues, Eric Sayce and Denise Collier. Additionally, Leader II funded the Trust to produce the <u>Accessible Marches</u>, a 'colour brochure' in sound of the border area of Shropshire. This is also included as Case Study at the end of this section.

Eric and Denise acted as consultants on the subjects covered, checked the directions and interviewed people about different aspects of the towns and area concerned. Denise is also hearing impaired, so making a recording was a big step for her and one she was at first reluctant to take on. She was persuaded that she could do this and in the end she enjoyed herself.

Tactile A4 plans were drawn, white on black, checked with Eric and Denise with swell paper copies and then produced by raised silk-screen printing. The audio described the plan at the beginning of the recording so that listeners had a good idea of where they would be going. The walks that followed included the main sights of the towns, such as the churches, Craven Arms auction market (now closed down), Clun Museum and not forgetting to mention places to eat.

At various points Eric and Denise talked to people who had a good knowledge of that part of the town; the Vicar in Clun Church for instance, local historian Chris Train on the Craven Arms sheep sales and Big Nev, the brewer at the Six Bells in Bishop's Castle. The variety of voices makes the recording more interesting and lively.

*Recording at Clun Castle*

The Accessible Marches covered information in a more general way, describing visitor attractions, walks, accommodation, pubs and local events such as festivals. Wayfinding was also helped by the mention of sound in the towns.

For Clun, the 'sound icons' are the chiming clocks: the ting-tang one on Trinity Hospital and the deeper one on the Parish Church. These help to give spacial information and direction to a small town which is in a hollow. In Craven Arms, the River Onny acted as a sound icon and local historian and naturalist, Bob Milner, graphically described the leaves of the trees growing alongside it. The narrator was John Kirkpatrick, a well known musician in the folk world.

It is important not to forget people who cannot hear that sound. Provide printed scripts for them and remember to include the sound effects. This helps to bring the script to life, a fact we were reminded of when giving a talk at the second Universal Design conference. A hearing impaired member of the audience stressed that we should include mention of the sound effects in the text and we have always done this since then.

*Denise Collier and Bob Milner*
*recording in Craven Arms by*
*the River Onny*

**Summary**

Sound can be used effectively everywhere, indoors and outdoors and the important thing is not to be afraid to use it. The use of sound can enhance the visitor experience for a wide range of people. A few words can build up a sound picture of a place. Sir Christopher Wren frequented Man's Coffee House in London, where pipe-smoking was discouraged; instead the customers took snuff. One customer wrote:

> the clashing of their snuff-box lids, in opening and shutting, made more noise than their tongues [and] sounded as terrible ... as the melancholy Tick of so many Death-watch beetles.[1]

This is not, perhaps, a description many people would want of their venue, but it does conjure up a wonderful picture of the unexpected sound of this Coffee House in the 17th century.

---

[1] Quoted in Adrian Tinniswood's life of Wren, <u>His Invention So Fertile</u>, London, 2002, ISBN 0-7126-7364-4, p. 228.

# Scripting for Audio

*'Begin at the beginning,' said the King gravely, 'and go on till you come to the end: then stop.'*

From <u>Alice in Wonderland</u> by Lewis Carroll

### Introduction

The Trust's audio work has been principally concerned with indoor and outdoor environments, historic buildings and museums and their collections. The scripting guidelines are based on this experience over many years.

There are many reasons of conveying information in audio, such as outreach. Some people prefer to have their information before they visit and for people with visual impairments this needs to be in large print, Braille as well as audio. Audio can be used for a special exhibition or display or for use on a site.

This section will cover writing a script for different purposes, as well as keeping your script in order and logging the recordings.

### Scripting for outreach information

Without outreach and publicity, blind and visually impaired people will not know that your site has something to offer them. If you want them to come and see what marvellous things you have done, then a positive outreach effort has to be made.

A target audience of visitors with visual impairments is not easy to define. As with any other audience the information needs to appeal to a wide range, from those who have never visited a heritage or other site when they were sighted but are looking for places that can offer something to those who were regular visitors when they were sighted and wish to keep up that activity.

Usually less attention is paid to writing and recording outreach audio information than for an audio guide around the site, for instance. Part of the reason for this is that the information changes and this is where the advantage of doing your own audio comes in; you can change it as your site and exhibitions change and develop.

Some enticing information needs to be included; you have to convince visitors to visit you rather than go to another activity. Snippets from an on-site audio guide and input from staff could be included. If the guide is recorded in the actual building, acoustic clues, 'sound icons', the sound of each space will help people recognise it when they arrive there. Even if the guide is not recorded in the building, these 'sound icons' should still be included in the script. These are particularly useful for people to listen to before they visit the gallery.

Audio information for outreach purposes should be considered as a sound picture audio, a colour brochure. It should include information about:

- A contact number; if it is at the beginning it is easier to find again

- Opening times and entry charges

- Directions for public transport as well as car for the benefit of family and friends

- The distance of the site from public transpor

- Facilities offered such as accessible toilets (necessary for those with Guide Dogs as regular cubicles are too small)

- Menus in Braille and audio

- What interpretation your site can offer to people with visual impairments and other disabilities

- Mention seating, if any, on the site. Some galleries have fold-up stools that people can borrow and take around with them. This not only gives them a place to rest when they need it but also allows someone with partial sight to sit down near a work of art and really study it.

Eric Sayce has written about this subject in more detail in *Access to Leisure* in this Chapter.

### Scripting for on-site audio guides

The advice given by the King in <u>Alice in Wonderland</u> is good advice when writing a script, especially for an audio guide to be used on site. The on-site tour can be linear or random access, although it is more difficult for people with visual impairments to get a whole picture of the site, if the description is not sequential.

Scripting for this purpose is challenging and needs thought and consultation with end users. Eric Sayce and his Guide Dogs, first Dorcas, then Harry and now Wills, have been advisers for many of the Acoustic Fingerprint Guides of Cathedrals and other audio guides written by the Trust. Other blind friends, Emilie Fane, Cambray Jones, Liz Matthews and Denise Collier have given the Trust advice over the years.

'Begin at the beginning'. Good advice, but easier said than done, as the most problematic part is the beginning; get that right and the rest will tend to follow. It is usual to start with instructions for using the audio machine and the work we have done is no exception. It is unfortunate that the playback machines are not better designed for users who are visually impaired and more self-explanatory. In many cases, the models often change. Guidelines for audio guides by Peter Bosher can be found in the Appendix. He wrote these for the Talking Images project.[1] These were subsequently published in <u>Barrierfree</u>[2] and Peter has kindly allowed us to include them in this book. Also we have written a run-down of hi- and low-tech playback equipment. More testing of this will be done and we will post the results on the website – www.dogrose-trust.org.uk.

This the point where staff training is particularly important. The reception staff, who will probably give out the guide, are the front line and need to be well briefed on its use so that they can show visually impaired visitors how it use it. With a multi-selection 'wand-type' of machine, a dedicated, easy-to-find button, is usually given for accessing the instructions. A tactile plan of the controls of the machine is useful; this could be produced in 'swell paper' at low cost. In some cases, tactile markings could be put on the machine. Whatever course you provide, make sure that all the staff know all about it.

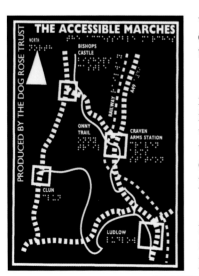

For a CD player, preface each track with a number and where you are. As the listener might not be able to see the LCD display screen with the number of the track, the announcement of the track and place number is reassuring.

Having sorted out instructions for use, the next decision to make is where to start the tour. Much will depend on the venue and its layout. Being able to sit somewhere out of the mainstream of the visitor flow is helpful; this gives a chance to listen to an introduction which includes the content of the guide, an approximate length of the tour and any other useful information, such as an overall picture of the building, gallery or environment the listener is in.

This overall description is critical and should be referred to and underlined subsequently in the script. Without a cognitive shape the building or site, since it cannot be seen, means little to a person with sight problems. For this reason a tactile plan is a very useful adjunct whether this is a single plan, a booklet of plans, a repeated plan or a 'give away' A4 plan. If there is an interactive sound component to the plan, it can provide blocks of information about specific parts of the site.

The same principles apply to describing the construction of the building. This can, in general, be described as an abstract form but it needs to be illustrated in physical perceivable examples. For example, touching a buttress or the outline of a window and then referring back to the overall cognitive form is a typical cycle in the scripting. It is probably still useful to give measurements in imperial and metric but gradually this will become redundant. Comparisons of size should relate to something that is known, the size of one's hand for instance or length of your arm.

Directions for the start of the tour or the next point of interest need to be given with the visually impaired listener 'fixed' to a place. It is not useful to give directions from a particular point unless you have made sure which way the listener is facing.

Discussion centred on this when working out the directions with Denise Collier for the Uturn Wind-up audio units on Stiperstones, the wild upland area of South Shropshire. Directions had been given for east and west, left and right, ahead and behind assuming that the person listening

*Scripting discussion on Stiperstones in winter*

was also turning the handle of the audio unit. This may be the case, but it also may not be. It is more reliable to write into the directions 'as you face the audio unit' and then you know which way the listener is facing. And don't forget to include the sound icons.

Points of the compass for directions are even more unreliable but once a person's position is fixed, then these can be used for orientation. 'Ahead of you is north' then makes sense.

The introduction to the guide should cover any legal action against the provider of the information in case of accident.

Keep sentences clear and simple and not too long and involved, without talking down, then the audio will appeal to a wider range of visitors. Art, architecture and allied subjects are complex for many people and a good clear explanation, with imagery that relates to things that people know, is a very useful tool.

### The use of colour

Emilie Fane insisted on the use of colour in descriptions. She has never seen colour clearly but has a vivid idea of what she likes and does not like, green being a particular dislike. She explained that 'colour divides things up'. When a Tudor monument in Hereford Cathedral was described to her, the information that the lady wore a red cloak, and blue dress with black shoes, meant she was able to build up a picture of the statue in her mind.

Perhaps none of us see the same colours so what Emilie sees and what we see are quite different. Does it really matter? Once we gave this example at a seminar and said, 'I am wearing black trousers and a blue jersey' and some of the students said, 'You are wearing a purple jersey'. We are still sure it is blue but that's the way we see it and it is different from the way they saw it. The important thing is to include colour so that the picture can be built up. For some people temperature analogies, used in a multi-sensory context, will help conjure up colours.

### Look and see

It is not necessary to avoid works like look and see. Trying to avoid them often causes the writing to be forced and unnatural, but it is preferable not to say things like 'as far as the eye can see' as many blind people will have little or no concept of perspective. If you are describing a picture placing sounds in space can help to give an idea of its spacial nature, but this is a technique which has been used little in art galleries although it is used on radio and by sound artists. Always keep in mind the need to build up a picture in sound.

Some years ago Erica Othman of the Finnish National Gallery created a brilliant piece of audio to describe one of their pictures. This showed a woman going across the snow-covered ice to collect water from a hole. In the background was a forest. You could hear the feet moving across the snow and a spacial effect came from a dog barking in the distance. It also has to be the right sort of snow; in this country we get so little now that we would hardly know one sort of snow from another but in the Nordic countries it is important to get this right.

Rain can define a space as it drips onto buildings, cars or trees; each one sounds different. Open your ears and listen and then include that information in your script.

Writing audio description for paintings and works of art for people with visual impairments is a specialised task and needs a different approach. For more information see the website for *Art Education for the Blind* in New York.[3]

### Important features

Always include brief descriptions of important features even if they cannot be seen by a person who is visually impaired or are too far away to touch. It is often assumed that a person who cannot see only wants to know about something that is within reach so that it can be touched.

Eric Sayce, with no sight at all, could walk in and out of York Minster without knowing that there is a famous Yorkshire Heart window there if it was not included in the audio tour. He may not be able to see anything of it, but he will know it is there so when someone mentions it, he will not feel that he has missed something. However, minor features should be left out or just mentioned in passing as there is usually too much else to say to spend time on them.

### Scripting in a multi-sensory way

For someone who cannot see, it is important to bring all the senses into play in describing items that cannot either been seen or be touched. An example given in a report for Manchester Art Gallery was for John Everett Millais' painting *Autumn Leaves* where the crackle and smell of leaves could be very evocative. Smell, taste, sound and texture are all important in building up a picture in sound.

Try as far as possible to tell the story of a building or historic place in touch and sound. Look at the venue in a multi-sensory way: how does it sound, what can you smell, is there a temperature difference, how does the feel of carved medieval stonework differ from the 19th century restoration? What can you get close up to see if you have some sight?

### Sound

Hearing is a very evocative sense; we talk about 'seeing with the mind's eye' but we do not say 'listening with the mind's hearing'. Why not? We can often hear someone's voice long after we have forgotten what they looked like or their faces have faded from our memories. It follows that the narrators on audio should have, if possible, distinctive voices that the listeners, especially if they are blind, can associate with your site.

Dealing with each point at a time, starting with how a building sounds, it has been the practice of the Trust to record on site where possible. This means that each area that is described has to be analysed for its acoustic characteristics and explained to the listener. Hard stone walls are more reflective than wood or fabric hangings which make the sound softer and absorb it more; sound bounces off glass, the famous example being Ely Cathedral's Lady Chapel which has a nine second reverberation time, that is the time before the sound returns to you.

**ACOUSTIC FINGERPRINT OF YORK MINSTER**

CTH 008

ACOUSTIC FINGERPRINT OF YORK MINSTER

This cassette tour enables visually impaired visitors to explore and appreciate the many acoustic and tactile features of the cathedral

**ACOUSTIC FINGERPRINT OF YORK MINSTER**

A GUIDE FOR VISUALLY IMPAIRED VISITORS

PRODUCED BY CATHEDRALS THROUGH TOUCH AND HEARING, THE UNIVERSITY OF BIRMINGHAM

This cassette guide has been specially scripted and recorded for the Project 'Cathedrals Through Touch and Hearing' and is a major component of 'The Touch and Hearing Centre'. It enables visually impaired visitors and their companions to walk around the cathedral stopping at various places en route. At each one, features which can be touched easily are described in detail. The acoustic ambience of the cathedral has been captured by means of recording on location. The musical sounds of the bells, choir and organ are included. Although the tape lasts approximately 75 minutes, visitors may wish to spend shorter or longer time exploring the cathedral.

Narrated by PATRICIA GREENE and NORMAN PAINTING

Cathedrals through Touch and Hearing

This project which is based in the School of Education, The University of Birmingham, B15 2TT, provides cathedrals with 'Touch and Hearing Centres'. These comprise a range of items and are likely to include:
1. A wooden model and ground plan housed in a cabinet and accompanied by a cassette commentary.
2. A Braille Guide Book.
3. An Acoustic Fingerprint Cassette Guide.
4. Large Print Materials.

The project is a registered charity within the University of Birmingham.

Dog Rose Sound

This cassette has been scripted, recorded and produced for the project 'Cathedrals Through Touch and Hearing' by Dog Rose Sound, 26 Bell Lane, Ludlow, Shropshire. It has been digitally recorded on location using a special binaural microphone technique in order to give the listener the maximum amount of acoustic and spacial information possible.
This work is copyright and all rights reserved by The University of Birmingham 1992. The materials have been recorded on the understanding that they will only be used in pursuance of the aims of the project.
This tape is made with the Dolby system and will significantly reduce tape hiss if played on Dolby equipment. If played on non-Dolby equipment it will produce improved high notes on portable players. On machines with treble control, adjust if necessary.

A high ceiling produces a more resonant tone than a low one which has a more enclosed sound. This information helps to build up a sound picture for the listener, but will really only be effective if the narration is recorded in the places being described. The sound example from the *Acoustic Fingerprint Guide of York Minster* contrasts the chapter house and the undercroft.

Listen to Track 2 of the Examples CD - the Chapter House and Crypt of York Minster. There is nothing like a quote from a contemporary source to give veracity! The description of the Chapter House at York from Pope Pius was gift. Similarly William Camden's description of Hardwick Hall, sums up Bess of Hardwick's prodigy house perfectly and sets the scene immediately.

To build up a sound picture, include things that characterise the place; choirs and bells for cathedrals and churches, ducks and geese for public parks and ponds, machinery for industrial venues and so on. Try and make sure these are as authentic as possible and are not always stereotype downloadables from the internet, although these have their place too.[4]

Gather up a collection of sound effects to use for different occasions. Although collecting sound effects can be time consuming, it can also be entertaining, interesting and unique. The Trust has recorded stone, flint and bronze axes chopping posts for a recording of audio information on the Somerset Levels. The crowing cockerel was only included for the Bronze Age recording not the Neolithic, as chickens were not introduced until later than that date.

### Smell

Smell is more prevalent that you might realise or notice in a building. An undercroft or underground area often smells damp or musty, although the owners will not always be pleased if this is said. Old tapestries have a distinctive smell and so does the beeswax polish for furniture. Be aware of what smells your venue or environment has and make use of them in a positive and also practical way.

A remark about the smell from the cafe might remind people that they are hungry and could be tempted to have lunch there. The supermarkets know how powerful this sense is and for that reason the smell of 'fresh' baked bread wafts through their shops.

### Temperature

Certainly the temperature is usually different in an underground area; the crypt at Worcester Cathedral, with its marvellous 'forest of columns', was refreshingly cool after a hot summer day outside. Different types of stone have a range of temperatures; compare cool marble to the warmer sandstones. The down-draught from an old stone staircase will give a listener an orientation clue as to where they are.

### Taste

Taste is not easy; health and safety have made sure of this. A 'petrographer' (a sort of geologist) friend identifies stones by licking them, but this is not advisable. Taste by implication has been mentioned in connection with gardens and outdoor sites and the same can be done at other venues. For instance monks ate porridge ('yuk' to some people) and kept bees so they had honey (yummy to most people). If honey is sold in the shop, then link it up and you might sell some.

### Sight

Sight is very important to people with some vision. Clear print cannot be stressed too much. Include items in a display or exhibition that can be seen clearly, that are within visual range and have good lighting on them. Hereford Art Gallery, with advice from the students at Hereford National College, have put yellow card behind described items to emphasise them visually. If labels, or written information, are referred to in the audio guide, then make sure they are easy to find and read.

Write about the spaces and the wayfinding so that people with a little sight can make use of it. If the directions are to walk towards a window, or natural light from another source, then include this information. Similarly, mention if the route goes to somewhere that is darker. Pick out the predominant colours in a stained glass window, tapestry, painting or whatever you are describing.

*Patricia Greene*
*at Hardwick Hall*

For pictures that cannot be closely studied for security reasons, a coloured digital image of the painting, perhaps hanging on a chain nearby would assist the appreciation of the work by people with partial sight. To be able hold it close to the eye at an angle that suits greatly assists being able to see the detail in paintings.

### Touch
Being able to explore by touch something that relates to what is being described will greatly help the image of it that is being conveyed. The possibility of being able to place a tactile artefact near the actual place would be very helpful for those with no sight.

Touch can be the most important sense of all to people with no sight, but it can also be very informative to everyone. Decide what can be touched in consultation with curators and conservators and write much of the script about these items. Other points will follow but if something can be touched then it will be more satisfying to the listener. For example, the door furniture can convey the quality and age of a building; there are some amazing examples at Hardwick Hall.

Even better, put out items that can be handled at each section or area round the venue for everyone. Nearly everybody likes to touch objects so provide something. Put a sample of fabric near a fragile tapestry or some material that resembles a costume in a painting. This is often done in the children's galleries, but not for adults. Why not? It would be more fun all round.

The same principles of touch apply to describing the construction of the building. This can, in general, be described as an abstract form but it can be illustrated in physical perceivable examples where the items are of a more sturdy nature. For example, touching a buttress or the outline of a window and then referring back to the overall cognitive form is a typical cycle in the scripting.

Hereford Cathedral has a Norman font where statues of the apostles stand under vaulted niches. This gave an opportunity to compare these with the vaulting overhead, something that is hard to explain without a tactile example.

Background 'noises' or FXs should be an intrinsic part of the text and not just there for the sake of sound. It should also not be assumed that because people cannot see they also cannot hear and they are often very interested in music and historically correct sound.

### Wayfinding and directions
Unlike sighted visitors, the experience of a building is not overall, but linear. This is why the overall description is vital and should be referred to in order to place experiences in context.

The principles of wayfinding need to be applied to script writing as well. Use the building itself to help with this; point out how the acoustics change in different areas and give tactile indicators that will verify that the listener is in the right place.

The tour information should follow the logical linear sequence of movement of the visitor who is blind or visually impaired because their range of perception is limited to a few feet around them, except in terms of sound. Unlike sighted visitors, experience of a building is not overall but linear. This is why the overall description is VITAL and should be continually referred to in order to place experiences in context.

### Directions
The directions for starting the tour have already been referred to and after that it is a matter of making a decision as to how much information should be included in telling people how to go around the site. The aim is to give people as much independent mobility as possible without overloading the script with directions and compatible with safety.

Analysis of the scripts written for the *Acoustic Fingerprint Guides* of the Cathedrals showed that 25% of the text could be taken up with directions. This is probably too high a proportion, although it did enable listeners to navigate around these complex buildings. Copies of these guides were circulated through Calibre, the audio library, and comments on the directions were received from people listening at home. Some said it really made them 'feel as if they were there' as they followed the directions around the building, up and down steps and into side chapels.

We have already mentioned the use of compass points as references alongside right and left; it can never be certain which way the listener might be facing if only right and left are given. Give reminders of levels, sound 'icons' along the way and the surface underfoot as a tactile clue; this confirms where you are during the tour and that it is the right way.

Mobility instructions between points of interest on the route should be checked with a visually impaired person, both with a Guide Dog and long cane during the scripting stages; a Guide Dog to make sure there is enough space and long cane to check that it does not get stuck under chairs or in gratings. Remember, as we have already said, to start each track with a number and place name; this is particularly important if using a CD and the display screen cannot be seen.

If the site is a large complex one then the directions may have to be concise and to the point rather than comprehensive. Whatever detail is decided on, steps, thresholds and uneven floor surfaces should always be mentioned even if the blind or visually impaired visitor is accompanied by a sighted companion. In practice we have found that the companion may not always be concentrating and it alerts the blind person to a hazard. For this reason we have often linked up both headsets to one machine with a line splitter.

It cannot be emphasised strongly enough that this information should be worked out with blind and visually impaired groups.

If there are problems of access to a place, decisions need to be made about what to include. Is the experience gained by visiting a lower or upper room worth the struggle down or up the stairs? What is there when you get there? In many instances there is little that could not be described in the narrative elsewhere or features that cannot be found in other parts of a building. Provide an option to sit and listen rather than struggle with difficult access. The same applies to providing photographs, video or CCTV for people with mobility problems who cannot access somewhere that has no lift or ramp. For an outdoor site, an indication of the distance of paths and trails and the type of terrain is important so that people can judge for themselves how far they want to go.

---

**01/11/96/Bolscrip2a.**      page 15

*again*

5.11    P.G: Now go into the Little Castle, ~~down the small~~ *over the threshold* step, through the open door; pause to explore the panelled and studded door with its original ironwork. Switch off while you do this.

FX MUSIC LINK
10 SECONDS PAUSE FOR SWITCH OFF

5.11    Next go straight ahead - the open doorway into the Ante-Room is to your left but we won't be visiting it - to find the open doorway into the Hall on your right. (PAUSE - Number 6 on the plan - PAUSE) You will recognise it by its reverberant sound. Watch out for projecting steps. Switch off now and on again when you are in the hall.

10 SECONDS PAUSE FOR SWITCH OFF

**MIC CHANGE 11**

**6.**     **THE HALL**

6.1    P.G:   The hall is a large and almost square with high stone vaulted ceiling and tall diamond paned windows so the sound is very resonant. It deliberately looks like a medieval great hall and was probably used for the entertainment of guests. Tables, chairs and stools are listed in an inventory of the building made in 1676. Keep to the left here and follow the dark grey wood panelling along to find the recess of the fireplace with the stone chimney piece jutting out into the room at about head height.

---

### Length
The length of the recording is always a difficult question; for sighted listeners the recommended 30-40 minutes is probably long enough. For visually impaired visitors, who require tactile explanations of layout, and information about steps etc., 40 minutes narration is probably about right, plus some extras such as special sounds or music related to the site. For those listening at home and learning about the building, either before a visit or as 'armchair' visitors, then an hour or even more is probably acceptable. There is a lack of informative material available to visually impaired visitors so that the more one can give in sound, while the research is being done, the better.

### Narration
In his demonstration CD, Richard Derrington says that when he is recording narration he talks to the photo of his wife. The same goes for writing the script. Above all, write the script in a natural way as if you are writing a letter to a good friend and explaining to them about the site.

Richard also says to read the script out loud and this is a very sensible point. This will, at an elementary level, eliminate any typing errors; for some reason when a script is being read, the eye dwells on the 'typos' and inevitably stumbles on the next words. It also eliminates grammatical mistakes, sentences that do not leave enough time to breathe and combinations of words that are hard or problematic to say. When the Trust was working on the Cathedrals Guides, we avoided the word 'bishopric'; say it as two words and you will understand why. These sort of words can set a narrator off laughing and once started, it is hard to get over that word without 'corpsing' as it is known in the theatre trade.[5]

So reading it out aloud yourself gets over some of these problems, but not all. If a narrator is tired, then words will fall over themselves. The narrator on one of the Cathedral guides was so weary that she could not get a composer's name straight; every variation came out until no one was sure what it should be. But it was well into the wee small hours so there was an excuse. The guides were recorded at night when the buildings were empty; these were amazing experiences when the buildings 'spoke' to us and revealed parts of them not noticed during the day. Standing alone in the Nave of York Minster at midnight is an awe-inspiring moment and one that has been a bonus of the work that the Trust has done over the years.

For a straightforward audio tour, it is probably best to have only two voices, one for the narrative and one for the directions. The listener has much to concentrate on and so a pattern of the 'division of labour' – male voice for the narrative and female for the directions for instance – helps him or her to know what to expect and rely on during the tour. It is hard work taking in the information through your ears and it is the job of the script writers and narrators to make it easier. Contributions from other people, beside a welcome from the director or similar person, could be distracting in a guide, but enlivening for outreach information.

Print out the script in one and a half or double spacing. This makes it easier to read but also slows the reader down; inexperienced or amateur readers usually tend to go too fast. If you are recording on site, then print out the script in larger point size – about 16 – as this will make it easier to read in dark corners. Take a torch; you never know when you might need it. Always have a pencil to hand for alterations to the script on the spot, such as when you suddenly notice that a feature you have said is on the right, is actually on the left.

### Source of information
A photographic record of the site for writing the script is also invaluable. This way you can check details of items. For the Cathedrals guides we put together a 'skeleton' which was based on the route to be taken and the features to be described. These were put into numbered

sections with a brief description of each place, why it has been included and a photograph alongside it to illustrate the point being made about acoustic and tactile features. This can be used to make sure that everyone is certain what is being included in the guide. You are probably thinking 'Why do this? Everyone knows their own site'. You would be surprised how few people really look at their site properly, and especially in a multi-sensory way. Opinions often differ about the history of a building, especially one as complex as a Cathedral. One Cathedral asked for comments on our script and forty four pages of fax came back with conflicting comments from different sources written on them. This was in the days before e-mail became common.

Specify the source you will be using for the information, or ask the venue to suggest one and stick to it. Too much background reading and you will get conflicting stories. You will also find bits of enticing information and want to include them making the script much too long. This happened at Exeter Cathedral where they have the wonderful accounts preserved from early Medieval times and we longed to include many of the details which made the people who had worked on and at the Cathedral come to life. We did manage to include the item about the money paid out for the Cathedral cat and the fact that it has a cat door to come into the building!

A multi-layered playback machine gives more scope for including extra information by pressing additional numbers as instructed. This means, for instance, that tactile information can be on a separate track, that might only be programmed on to machines given out to visually impaired visitors.

**Writing for specific playback machines**

Some playback machines need a particular writing style; for instance the Uturn audio units. As it takes human power and energy, the two minutes of handle turning is probably more than enough for most people, although the sound can be made to go for longer.

Writing for this length and keeping the material interesting takes skill and practice. We have compared this to the Japanese Haiku, the short poems which are valued for:

- Their lightness

- Their simplicity

- Their openness

- Their depth

It is better not to write up to what you think is the absolute two minutes as reading and speaking voices vary in speed. Be prepared to cut the text or recording; make it modular so that sections can be taken out without losing its meaning and impact. Remind the listener at the beginning to turn the handle and keep turning and remind them again half way through. Entice them on with 'turn the handle to hear what happens next' or with a 'trailer' for the next item.

For the Uturn sound for a tactile panel in Old St Chad's Churchyard, Shrewsbury, we were given an ambitious script to record; one side about history of the church of St Chad's and the other

*Panel with Uturn wind-up audio unit in Shrewsbury*

about the fall of the tower which was in the form of a mini-drama with several characters. The writer assured us that it was the correct length, but during the recording we were cutting all the time as we timed complete runs with a stop-watch. The end result worked well and the different voices are effective.

Generally speaking, because of the frequency at which the sound is relayed, lower voices work better than higher ones and the same applies to choosing sound effects. Keep these to a minimum as people are usually listening outside where there are already sounds, both natural and man-made.

## Organising the script and its contents

Give each paragraph of the script an identity number or reference and make sure the reader announces it before starting to read the text. The order is:

Paragraph - identity and reference – 5 second pause – narrative/text.

This is particularly important if the script is not recorded in order. Unless you have the references, it will be very difficult to get it into the right place.

And this is where logging is crucial.

Write down what is said and at what number on the counter on the machine, which may be revolutions or time. The easiest way of doing this is by having someone sit beside you during the recording and write down the numbers. You will not find it possible to do this yourself; you will be busy watching the machine and keeping an eye on other practical matters such as the distance the reader is from the microphone and making sure they maintain that distance. We put a carpet square on the ground and tell people to stand on it.

As the script is recorded, mark down each paragraph or even sentence; it is easy to leave something out. Everyone has their own methods, but we use a tick. When there is a mistake, 'fluff' or interruption, then we put a line across that tick to indicate that it was not a clean take and underline or mark the words that were wrong or were stumbled over. This makes it much easier when you come to editing, which may be some time after the recording when you have forgotten what actually happened. Also indicate which take you think should be used. In this way you are prepared when you start editing.

As equipment gets smaller, it is more difficult for someone else to log while the recording is in progress as the counter is so small. When the Trust bought its first DAT recorder it was large and the numbers on the front were easy to see. Now with the portable DAT or solid state machine this is not easy. But it is a job that has to be done and if need be after the recording. This means sitting down and listening to the recording and noting down the counter numbers of each section, of re-takes, mistakes, best take, intrusive noises and so on. Make sure you have labelled the DAT, mini-disc or whatever media you are using, with its own unique number plus the subject, place and date of the recording. Each track needs to be named with its own unique number plus the subject, place and date of the recording.

If the recording is fed straight into a computer via a USB lead, then it will a PCM (wav) file. This needs to be put in a separate folder with the title of the recording. The next step is to put it into your editing programme, which might be *Adobe Audition,* and then edit it into manageable size sections. These sections need to be given unique names, relating to the overall folder and also logged down with numbers and content so that you can easily find them for editing. Discard what you do not need from these sections, but always keep the original in case you need to go back to it.

### Further reading

Robert McLeish, <u>Radio Production</u>, Fourth Edition, Oxford, 1999, ISBN 0-240-51554-4

Rosemary Horstman, <u>Writing for Radio</u>, London 1991, ISBN 0-7136-3445-6

[1] The books from this project are <u>Talking Images Research</u> and <u>Talking Images Guide</u>, published by the RNIB in 2003 in conjunction with Vocaleyes. More information about Vocaleyes can be found on www.vocaleyes.co.uk

[2] In <u>Barrierfree</u> 15, Autumn, 2003. <u>Barrierfree</u> is the Journal of MAGDA, the Museums and Galleries Disability Association. See www.magda.org.uk

[3] <u>www.artseducation.info</u>. Their book, <u>Art Without Sight</u>, is useful in this respect.

[4] A good site is <u>www.sounddogs.com</u>. These are downloadabled in MP3 for a payment by credit card. The cost is quite small and varies according to the length of the piece and supplier.

[5] Theatrical term for getting a fit of giggles or laughing in a performance or reading.

# Principles of Sound Production
## by Dr Peter Windows

### Think of your audience

Think about who will be listening, where they will be listening, and how they will be listening. If the situation your listener is in is 'crude' - for example, there are competing noises - sophisticated, nuanced productions will be a waste of time. The setting will have implications for sound quality too. You may need a quality which 'cuts through' other sounds. Too much 'bassiness' will only muddy the sound.

### Plan carefully

Many producers work with sounds in their heads before going anywhere near a recorder or a studio. Imagine what might work well, and then compose accordingly. Listening to other people's work will help you to decide on the style and sound you want. Be systematic when it comes to gathering material. Prepare a 'shopping list' of ingredients.

### Less is more

The best starting point is to keep things simple. Sound production is usually most effective when it is not over-elaborated. Think about the minimum requirements for your production. Don't be tempted to throw everything in. It's likely to sound messy, and may confuse the listener. Some sequences may require layered and textured sounds. Pace is critical too. There's a great temptation to make things happen too quickly. Take it easy, and allow your listener breathing space.

### Practise with recorders and microphones

Modern recording equipment may seem simple to use, but to get the best out of it you need to practise. There are plenty of things that can go wrong, and it's only by practising that you can hope to avoid them. When you have made a recording, try to listen to it on decent equipment. That means proper loudspeakers. It's the only way to tell what the quality is like.

### Set high standards

At all stages don't put up with second best. If in doubt, do it again. And again if necessary. If you've made a journey to get a recording, you don't want to have to go back. Get it right the first time. Take trouble with editing and mixing too.

**Stand back**

It's very easy to get too involved in a production and lose perspective on it. A key part of the role of the producer is to stand back from their work and imagine what a listener will make of it. It's a skill you have to develop. You can - and should - always play the recording to a critical friend.

Dr Peter Windows is a lecturer in Radio Production at the School of Media Studies, UCE, Birmingham.

## *Access to Leisure*
## *by Eric Sayce*

Leisure means different things to different people. What does it mean to be a totally blind person? It doesn't mean that I cannot enjoy leisure, though my leisure activities and interests have changed from when I was sighted. Initially everything became a challenge but now I personally feel the richer for my experiences.

What does leisure mean to you? To be able to relax in a different environment? To experience fulfilment in creative activities? Experience physical exercise or enjoyment of the arts? All these are available to the blind and partially sighted, really they are! However, you may need to be determined in your quest because, sadly, information is not always accessible and access to buildings and services varies considerably. Where these needs have been recognised the marketing and public awareness is poor. Many of the providers of such activities lack marketing expertise, which is a shame when so much creativity has gone into producing an accessible product.

Having recognised the difficulties, I would like to illustrate, with examples, the pleasure and relaxation which I personally have experienced along with some of the difficulties encountered.

A sighted friend tells me, or I hear on the radio, about a heritage attraction which sounds interesting and one which I would like to experience for myself. It can be a castle, like Warwick or Kenilworth or a cathedral like Coventry.

### How do I get there?
Well, I have a guide dog who assists me but other blind and partially sighted people may prefer to use a long mobility cane. I visit the local library or the Tourist Information Centre. Sadly, all the available information is for sighted people: lovely, descriptive, well presented with colour photographs, but to me it feels just like a smooth piece of paper, as its information is not accessible. What should be provided is information in an accessible format: large print Braille, audio cassette, CD and computer diskette. The latter is particularly useful if used for outreach, which is so important when marketing the venue and yet so little attention is given to it. There are approximately 2 million blind and partially sighted people living in the UK;[1] we have around 2000 registered blind people living here in the West Midlands. They are all potential customers. So tell them

about your venue, use the local talking newspapers, clubs for the blind, radio etc. They won't come if they don't know about it.

Transport, how do I get there? Bus and train time tables are not generally available in accessible formats but telephone information usually is. If I travel by train I know that I can avail myself of the assistance service provided by the train companies. Where is the bus stop located in relation to the entrance of the venue? What bus services serve the venue and how frequently? How far is the venue from the rail station and what is the approximate cost of a taxi fare? All this information needs to be available and accessible.

When I arrive at the venue is the entrance accessible? I need a description; are there entrance steps, do they have tactile nosing and are they colour contrasted against the step itself, important for partially sighted people? Are the entrance doors automatic and sliding? How will I find the reception desk? Is there a tactile track which I can follow which will lead me to it? Walkway tiles designating the walkway against carpeting surrounds provides a good indicator.

Having reached the reception desk, have the staff there received disability awareness training? Will this have included training in the use of guiding techniques for the blind and partially sighted? Have they been advised how important it is to introduce themselves, by name and position in the organisation? Remember I am not able to see name badges.

If they are called away to deal with an emergency in the middle of a conversation, they should tell the blind person what is happening in order that the blind person doesn't continue to talk to an empty chair.

If they have to leave the blind person for any reason, please ensure that the blind person is positioned in a safe place and describe to them the environment where they are being left. Do not be afraid or feel embarrassed to ask the extent of the person's visual impairment. One needs to know in order to gauge the amount of assistance required. It should be noted that only a small percentage of registered blind people are totally blind, around 5%; 80% are over the age of 60, many of whom will have mobility difficulties.

### Different levels of competence

A person with a guide dog or using a long mobility cane will normally be a confident independent type person whereas a person using a thin cane, called a Symbol cane, indicates to the public at large I am blind. This cane is usually hanging from the wrist and will be used by either a partially sighted or a blind person accompanied by a sighted friend. If required, will there be a sighted guide who has received disability awareness training available to guide me around the venue? Above all it is important that the receptionist is able to generate a friendly, welcoming and competent atmosphere in order to put the blind or partially sighted person at ease. Hopefully they will want to return for another visit and recommend the venue to their friends.

Does the reception or information desk have a visitor's guide in an accessible format, such as large print minimum 14 font, Braille, audio cassette or CD which I can use during my tour, together with a tactile plan illustrating the layout of the building and exhibitions? Is the route around the building or exhibition tactile with different tactile floor surfaces used to differentiate between areas and rooms? Are there sound beacons which will assist my orientation, such as water fountains outside and infra-red triggers inside?

Are the exhibits labelled in such a manner that they are accessible to me in Braille, large print or using the latest 'barcoded' technology? Is the information positioned at a height accessible to wheel chair users? Is the glass used in the construction of the display cabinets non-reflective? This is particularly important for partially sighted people. Can I feel the exhibits? Are there displays which require a button to be pressed in order to activate them? If the button gives audio information about the exhibit, how do I find the button? There needs to be some form of tactile direction. Can I bring my guide dog and are there facilities for him such as a drinking bowl and an area for him to 'spend'?

Is there a cafeteria? Have the staff received disability awareness training in serving food and guiding? Do the toilets' entrance doors have clearly defined indicators such as tactile images or letters? Does the toilet furniture colour contrast with the walls and is the floor colour different to the walls? This is important for the partially sighted.

Remember if you are sighted these points are probably taken for granted and so they should be; chances are you never even think about them. For blind and partially sighted people however, they are crucial if one is to enjoy what the venue has to offer.

---

[1] There are about 2 million people with a visual impairment in the country but only about 300,000 are registered.

*Access to the countryside is important
for everybody. Here Eric Sayce and Harry
try out a stile with Nigel McDonald. They are
on the Onny Trail in Shropshire.*

## *Outreach*

Most exhibitions and museums are part of an educational system. For this reason the material needs to reach outside the site. This is known generally as outreach. The particular form and content of this material relates to the overall policy of the establishment. However, in the past the only way to contact people outside the site was by post and sending them cassettes or CDs and while this is still a good idea there are now other techniques. The material can be put on a web site and more easily transmitted by broad band. In fact we have set up our own 'radio station' that will be sent out on the internet. This may become the way to broadcast both sound and vision in the future and we know that many more systems will follow.

The policy for the whole needs careful consideration and should be set down complete with budget figures so that decisions can be made. While we are discussing sound it is essential that the overall policy should take into account every possible way to reach the intended audience.

It is as important to use every sense in the transmission of information as it is to put transcription into the process. All information should be transcribed into the appropriate form for everyone. This means that material should be in Braille, audio transcriptions, carefully written large print and so on. It is possible that an audio guide if properly written could be used as the basis of the audio transcription. COTIS, the Confederation of Transcription Services, has guidelines for producing audio for information purposes, as well as useful packing and labelling details. Their web site is www.cotis.org.uk.

A book on types of people and the types and forms of information that might apply to particular groups of people is The Informability Manual[1] by Wendy Gregory and published by HMSO. It is very much about the here and now and is therefore immediately useful and there should be a copy on your shelf.

Outreach information has already been discussed in connection with audio, but is a much wider subject altogether. An outreach strategy is essential in order to get your information out to as many people as possible. You can have the best exhibition in the world but if no one knows about it they will not come to see it. After all, outreach is only another word for advertising.

Lars Stenberg of the Sensory Trust said in a recent paper that 'the second most common reason preventing disabled people from visiting outdoor spaces is lack of information'.[2] For outdoor spaces, you can substitute almost any other venue. The first most common reason is probably accessible transport, but that is a big issue in itself and will only be dealt with here briefly. Lars went on to say that 'accessible information has three basic components: the message, the medium and the distribution.'

### The Message

It is important to think about your outreach material as a 'colour brochure'. There is no reason why someone who cannot see should have to put up with the 'black and white' version when everyone else has the colour one. Making sure that it is easy to read, access or listen to has to be the first priority.

A written leaflet, brochure or guide book recorded as a straight read will probably not be very exciting. This is where the 'colour' brochure comes in. Look at the important facts of what it contains. If it is a list of events of your venue, pick out the key components. Perhaps one of your events is for Africa 2005. You might like to include this information at the beginning, before the dates the event is on. It could go like this:

> Did you know that this year many museums are taking part in Africa 2005? Our Gallery is celebrating this by putting on an exciting exhibition by the South African artist, X. This will run from 3rd-20th May so make sure you don't miss it.

Try turning the information around or on its head and see what the facts are that will grip people's attention and make them want to come.

Your colour information will undoubtedly include pictures; then include pictures in sound by speaking to the artists or people involved in your exhibitions. Getting an interview with a South African artist may be more difficult owing to distance, but if your budget allows see if you can interview him over the telephone. We have a telephone recording device which we can link to the phone and record conversations.[3] This should only be done by arrangement with the other person who must be clear that the conversation is being recorded.

Or include information about the unseen part of an exhibition – the packing of awkward sized sculptures. We saw the Anthony Caro sculpture exhibition going into Tate Britain and it was like a construction site. The actual installation process may have been as interesting as the exhibition itself. The logistics of moving these large pieces is formidable; there is often a low-loader lorry outside the Museum of Modern Art in Edinburgh. People who cannot see this process might find it adds colour to the exhibition itself.

But back to the essentials. All advertising, whoever it is aimed at, should include details about access. At the very least details should be given about where to get further information about access for all disabilities, but it is preferable to include as many details as possible in your main brochure or advertising material.

Make sure your contact telephone number is given clearly and slowly early in the recording and if necessary repeated at the end. We are not good at taking down telephone numbers: one of us has unreadable writing and the other reverses numbers so this is something we are very aware of. We have all received telephone messages where the number is impossible to hear even though we listen repeatedly. This number is probably the key piece of information; if the listener can get that then they can find out all the other details.

Accessible transport is an important issue because without transport people may not be able to visit your venue. Find out about it and include in your literature such details as the distance to the nearest bus stop or tube or tram stop. Are the buses and these stops fully accessible? What about parking? Do you have disabled parking spaces? If so, say so.

The group travel organiser's first priority for an outing is 'tea and pee', so the same goes for giving access information. People who use wheel-chairs are not the only visitors who need an accessible toilet; Guide Dogs are big dogs and take up a lot of space in a cubicle so an accessible toilet is preferred by many Guide Dog owners. Many people have a relative or friend with a disability and they might see this information and then they will know that there is somewhere to take the whole family.

This prior knowledge, that you can find an accessible toilet and that there are lifts and ramps, will play a big part in making someone decide to visit your venue. It is hard to concentrate on even the most fascinating exhibition when you are desperate to go to the loo. So don't tuck these details away at the end on the back of the leaflet but make sure they are features that everyone knows about – after all they have been costly to install and you should be proud of them.

Now that 'pee' has been covered, 'tea' needs to be dealt with. Is the café accessible? Does it have large print menus and staff trained to help people with disabilities? Are they aware of what is in the food and are special diets catered for? Having a coeliac in our family has made everyone more aware of what is in food and asking about it. Cafés earn money and are often an important part of a venue's income.

If your visitors are assured that bodily requirements are taken care of, then the intellectual ones need to be appealed to.

### The Medium

Much time, effort and money is spent by museums, galleries and other similar venues putting out colourful and attractive advertising material in order to attract visitors. Unfortunately most of this material is useless to someone with a visual impairment, usually because the size of the print is too small, the type face is hard to read, the back-printing of images obscures the printed text and so on. If someone has no sight, then printed material is of no use at all. A flier received by the Trust from a national museum was almost impossible to read because of its small print in brown on a black background. This is not an usual occurrence but in this case the access officer, who has no sight, is making strenuous efforts to make the museum, its content and its information accessible to people with visual impairments. He cannot see how hard this flier is to read and probably does not even know about it.

If you have any doubts about clarity, make a copy of the design on a photocopier. If it does not come out clearly it is probably not easy to read, so back to the drawing board or in most cases, now the computer.

In recent years computers and the internet have become a valuable resource for gathering information. For people with visual and hearing impairments it has opened up a whole new world of information on your desktop. Reading programmes, in particular Jaws for Windows, have become more efficient and can cope with most sites on the internet as well as emails. This method of communication is much easier for blind computer-users than wondering what is on a leaflet or letter. Reading machines, such as the Kurzweil Reading Edge, have software that makes printed or electronic text accessible to people who are blind. It converts a PC and scanner into an advanced version of the revolutionary reading machine invented by Ray Kurzweil in 1976. Improvements are being made all the time with these machines but at present they cannot cope well with hand writing or Gothic and similar fonts.

Make sure your website is accessible to everyone. There are plenty of guidelines out there on the internet; look at www.rnib.org for their 'web accessibility' information.

### Distribution

If you have a focus or access group working with you on exhibitions then they will probably be the best people to spread the word of what you are doing. Word of mouth is one of the best ways of advertising, but it does take time and therefore exhibitions should be planned to run for a reasonable length of time and special events planned well in advance.

If money is being spent on advertising the venue generally and any special exhibitions, then money should also be allocated for getting the word out to people with disabilities. However, the good news is that many of the best sources are free. For many years the Trust has sent out information to Roland Myers of Soundings, the audio magazine which is widely listened to around the country.[4] Other audio magazines also have a countrywide audience, such as *Playback* from Glasgow. This comes from the Centre for Sensory Impairment in Partick which also runs an internet radio programme, *VIPonAir*[5] and of course our own radio station, Dog Rose Sound.[6]

Ask at your local disability resource centre for information about talking newspapers and magazines. As these are usually run by volunteers, a recorded contribution from you about your site, ready to slot in, would probably be welcome, but check first how they would like it and if there is a 'house style'.

Monthly magazines such as the RNIB's <u>New Beacon</u> and Scope's <u>Disability Now</u> are other useful resources, as well as interesting reading. As they only come out monthly the lead time for them has to be allowed for so plan well in advance. Build up a list of reliable sources that will help to spread your information, but do update it as editors, addresses and other details change.

**Other Outreach**

Philadelphia Museum of Art runs a programme called *Art Talk*. This is for people who cannot get to the museum because of disability or age-related issues. In a telephone conference a museum guide discusses objects from the collections. The individuals participate from their homes in a course which meets three times for one hour and follows a theme through thirty objects, ten each week. A booklet of colour reproductions is sent out before the start of the course.[7]

In September 2003 Equata ran *Above and Beyond, Celebrating a World of Disability* and the Arts and Culture.[8] This was a wonderful event which we were fortunate enough to attend. The comedy was marvellously 'unpolitically' correct and very very funny, the art inspiring and the mix of disabilities and nationalities made it truly inclusive.

Moya Harris, then director of Equata, asked the Trust to help with outreach. We designed and produced a tactile plan of Cheltenham Town Hall; fitting this building on to an A4 was not easy. Each large space was given a symbol – sun, moon and star – on the plan and these were reproduced on large brightly coloured signs to go over the appropriate doorways. We also produced a CD with information about some of the performers. We spoke to them over the telephone, or in the case of Anne Cunningham of The Nasty Girls, through Type-talk. Interviews ranged from David Roche in California to Matt Fraser in London. It was good to meet them all in person at the event.

The Nasty Girls gave us the music they were using in the show, thereby introducing us to Keith Alexander who has since run two of our community music workshops. This irrepressible trio also got a dig at us during their show by displaying our tactile plan and saying it was 'Cluedo for blind people'. We are linked to their website and we are described as:

> Working to improve access to the environment for blind and visually impaired people. Oh well, someone has to do it. More importantly they are fans of the Nasties!

Never act with children, animals or disabled cabaret artists![9]

[1] Wendy Gregory, The Informability Manual, London HMSO 1996, ISBN 0-11-702038-0.

[2] The Sensory Trust, Inclusive Action Group, Meeting 9, 23 November 2004.

[3] It came from Hagger Electronics UK– see www.hagger.co.uk

[4] www.soundings.org

[5] www.viponair.com

[6] www.dogrosesound.org

[7] For more information see www.philamuseum.org and an article by Street Thoma in Barrierfree 16, Winter 2003/4.

[8] http://www.equata.co.uk

[9] www. nasty-girls.co.uk. We advise you not to do a search for Nasty Girls on the internet as you can imagine what it will produce. Use this site.

# *Sound Recording*

### Introduction

Much of this information is the result of the papers we have put together for the audio courses we have run under the Innovative Actions project, building on our many years of experience. The CD of Recording the Voice with Richard Derrington should be listened to in conjunction with these sections about recording and editing.

Audio happens to be very useful for those who cannot see, cannot access written text, or cannot understand text easily. Our brief as a charity is 'to carry out research and development to help those with sensory and cognitive problems'[1] and audio fits with this very well. It is also, and this is important, very good for everyone. In fact the Trust follows a policy of multi-sensory communication and design which aims to give the maximum help to those who have problems with their senses and does not isolate them from others who also need information. And we have twenty five years of experience with this work - but this does not mean we have all the solutions. The real answer is simply to keep moving forward.

Another aspect of audio that has happened in the last few years is that prices have been forced down, partly by the computer industry, to which it is closely related, and the growing market of people who have become interested in audio. The mixer we bought some years ago cost £3000, but now you can get an adequate and useful little mixer for £75; not quite the same specification but perfectly usable for the work we are doing. The result of this is that many people are busy making their own sound, mostly music, at home and with considerable skill. In fact there has been nothing short of a revolution. There are now specialist magazines such as <u>Sound on Sound</u> on this subject that should be read. Professional quality sound can now be readily produced and manipulated with very inexpensive equipment.

The following is a first step into audio using current equipment. There are many alternatives to what we suggest and the possibilities change from day to day. This is strictly evolutionary but we make no apologies because life has to go on.

It is possible to spend less money than we suggest and certainly it is possible to spend more money so all we are saying is that this is the way we do it and this is more or less what it cost us. Development in the audio world takes place very quickly and in a haphazard way and in a way that is governed by the 'fast buck' economic principle. This outline covers a small but adequate beginning. Larger, but quieter audio computers can be used and larger storage units and grander equipment. Much equipment is sold to boost egos rather than do a job.

While we use recording equipment that is self-contained, that is records onto some media which can be anything from tape to solid state memory card, it is possible to record direct into a computer via the digitising pre-amp. This is quite possible and there are several advantages in recording this way. One obvious advantage is that it is possible to record direct onto a laptop computer and no time is wasted putting the information into the computer because it is already there. We have used computers for many years but we like the idea of having the sound stored on something outside the computer in case of failure. Sometimes computers simply 'die' which is sad, but if they have several months work on them it is very very sad. This is another good reason for using a separate hard disc or other independent storage system.

The whole area of recording audio is complex and constantly developing. Clearly the following description of equipment and procedure is just one way of processing audio with 'audio description' in mind.

Computers are developing all the time and are not priced in this brief description but audio equipment is a computer. Whether we like it or not we all seem to have a computer to do our work and these generally can be used to work with audio files besides other matters.

We have done much sound recording before the present systems which we describe came into use. These recordings can be of high quality and very valuable, but access is not straightforward. Much care must be taken to understand the technical background to the recordings. A useful book which contains information on past recording systems and how to deal with them is by Alan Gower and is <u>A Manual of Sound Archive Administration</u>. However, the moral is to take care and if in doubt find a specialist to look the job over.

The figures we have given are not absolute and generally indicate what we paid for items. A special microphone can cost up to £3000 and recording equipment can cost thousands, but for our purposes the following equipment produces very satisfactory results. You may wish to elaborate, or even simplify, your technique in the future with mixers and special recording and editing equipment or other magic boxes but here is a basic procedure.

We have chosen to take the standard CD as a usable quality. This has a sampling rate of 44.100 – that is 44.1 kHz-per second with a 16 bit depth. With stereo, that is two channels, the bit rate per second is

1,411,200. There is a standard for burning CDs, the so called the 'red book' which covers the overall specification and the start and stop of a 'normal' CD player and the rate of 44.1 kHz and the bit depth of 16; this is what we are using. The 'red book' standard was put together by the recording industry so that CDs to this specification can be played on any CD playback equipment.

In a recent article in the excellent journal <u>One to One - December 2004</u> which covers the duplication industry, Carl A. Snape writes about disc longevity of the CD (optical discs – they are read by a laser in your machines also therefore DVD, CD-RW, DVD-RAM and DVD-RW). There is no real answer to this because, as he points out, the polycarbonate CD has not been around long enough to find out. However, he does suggest several DOs and DON'Ts for CDs that you intend to keep.

- Do not write on the disc with a pen of any sort
- Do not put paper labels on the disc since the adhesive might affect the layers
- Do not play the archive CD or touch it
- Keep the CD dry since polycarbonate will absorb moisture
- Do not scratch them
- Keep away from UV light
- Store independently in a cool, dark and, stable place

We currently have problems with the playback equipment for Sony 'Beta' masters on which we have recordings that we need to make commercial CDs from. We say this to illustrate that there is a perpetual problem with archive material. Unless one is prepared to spend a considerable amount of time in updating masters to the latest equipment they are likely to be lost eventually. At present we pass archive copies of material to libraries on CD which may not be satisfactory but currently there is no reasonable alternative. However, we use CDs as working tools and, I am afraid, abuse them, but then most of them after the job is finished end up in neighbours' gardens hung up to scare birds. For immediate use care must be taken not to scratch them or leave them in the sun or put heavy objects on them; we have one that cracked in half.

With the research on compression of file formats many systems use less than the number of bits of information on a CD. While the 'red book' standard is in use we will stay with it since most CD players will accept it. Besides this mass-produced CD players are cheap as a result of the large market. We should be clear, however, that the CD-R can also be used for storing files of other types. Having mentioned storage on CD then one must remember that storage on the DVD is now possible and clearly more convenient because of the large size of audio files. Having said this we will also use a compression standard called MP3 for various devices and on our internet radio station we will use more standards so that everyone can hear what we are transmitting.

The Trust has microphones and recording equipment that will record at a sampling rate of 192,000 readings per second and a bit depth of 24 bits giving DVD quality of sound at a fantastic rate of bits per second. At the other end of the scale it must be remembered that many blind people still use Philips Cassettes and very few have DVD audio equipment. In fact the cassette and its related equipment was one of the most brilliant pieces of useful design that you can find. We have professional cassette recording equipment but many of the new cassette machines no longer have facilities to record. Equipment without recording facilities is cheaper and more profitable for the manufacturer.

We have taken the middle road and we are aware that it is possible to cut corners. For example the computer sound editing programme Audacity 1.5 can be downloaded free from the internet and adequate second hand recording equipment could be used. However, one is generally placed in a vicious and unpleasant market situation where computers are out of date in a year and half and the same is true for almost everything in this field. On the other hand it is reassuring to listen to the high quality of some old 78 rpm acoustic recordings played on good equipment built when these discs were the latest thing!

In this exercise we assume that your recording is put onto a master CD and then onto multiple CDs. Carefully selected simple portable CD players with good controls can then be used together with the duplicated CD to provide information for your visitors.

MP3 players can be used in a similar manner. The masters can be made for other playback machines using these programmes; often these have special programmes provided by the manufacturers of sound equipment.

Before we get too complacent about the use of sound we should be aware that developments in computer programmes and video camera technology run parallel with the developments in audio. With the current 'cross platform development' with computers it will be as easy to work with vision as it is with sound. Vision and sound together can be a very useful set of tools. The take-over by large companies of the audio programmes we use is an indication that there are changes in the wind!

### Getting started

If you need to have models for your work and wonder what it should be like, listen to the BBC and work out how they do things. There is a whole world of new and interesting work to be done which is not commercial but based on communication. Audio communication is important for everyone in museums, galleries and exhibitions where it is rare. Not only is sound useful in communication but in history. Oral history, that is recording people and their recollections, is a fundamental source for historical research. If you record people and their recollections make sure that they, and you, are clear as to how the material can be used.

There are also many other situations where audio could be introduced. BBC drama programmes are especially interesting as examples of audio technique. These programmes can now be accessed via the internet which makes listening easier. There is a whole interesting world out there which we want you to share with us!

### Scripting

The first stage is to put on paper a simple story line. This can be elaborated as necessary. A set of safety announcements might be one end of the scale and a full audio description of a building at the other. Brief notes are needed in one case and a full script in the other. However, a full script for everything is a good idea. Anyone with a reasonable voice can make the announcements, but it may need a professional to read an elaborate script efficiently so that you do not spend too much time editing. However, with practice anyone can do all these things. There is more information about scripting and the use of sound in other sections of this book.

### Recording Machines and Microphones

(Coding for the price brackets is at end of this section.)

For much of our field recording, we have used a Sony ECM 907 microphone, price code B. This is a useful little microphone at an affordable price. We have used it with a Sony Mini-disc MZ-800, price code D. Recently we bought some mini-disc machines which were 'end of line' for about price code B each - but take care to check if has a recording ability with a microphone input – some do not! There is some doubt if the mini-disc format will continue and presently it is difficult to find a machine that contains a suitable pre-amp and connection to take a microphone.

The successor of the mini-disc is the more universal MP3 compression system with a solid state file storage unit. Since there are no moving parts then the microphone could be part of the machine rather than being isolated, as it has to be when moving parts make a noise. The new recording machine by Edirol, the R-1, will make certain aspects of recording much easier. It records down onto a CompactFlash card and the amount depends on the capacity of the card and also the file type. A WAV file records every sound and an MP3 file compresses the file. The result is that WAV files take up more space than MP3.[2] A standard specification for a WAV file might be 16bit/44.1 kHz, and this is the same as a CD. A 256MB card will take 23 minutes of this specification of recording. This same card will hold an MP3 file at, say, 16bit/192kbps, to the extent of 170 minutes. It depends what you want to use the file for. The cards can generally be up to 2GB which will give a recording time of 188 minutes at the above WAV specification.

The size of the Edirol R-1 is around 25mm deep by 96mm wide and 130mm high and has a weight of approximately 310 grams with card and batteries. It has many other features that you will find interesting. The internal microphones are set in the body of the recorder without problems of vibration, other microphones can be added via a 3.5mm jack point. All of this makes it a handy portable tool. A few years ago such a device was not in anyone's mind.

### Making the recording

The recording is then ready to be made. You will have to learn how to use a microphone and a recorder but, again, practice and some reading through standard texts will get you there. You need to take into account the acoustics of the environment; for 'voice-overs' a dead acoustic is necessary. Normal acoustic ambience adds to an interview provided it does not overshadow the voice. Often the ambience in itself is of interest and importance.

Remember to announce what you are doing on each section of the recording otherwise at the editing stage you can easily get lost; in any event these announcements can be edited out at the near-final edit stage. Give the date, place and who is talking. Also, make a written log of what is happening. As you put the work onto the computer work out a clear file system and write it down so that when you pick up the job again after working on other jobs, you can find out what you did.

If you are using a mini-disc or solid state recorder such as the Edirol, you will now have a machine with several files on it. The next step is to put these into the computer for editing. In fact a certain amount of editing can be done on certain mini-discs but we find the extensive facilities on the computer more useful. You can delete superfluous files from the mini-disc while in the field, but we have found it safer to leave everything alone until you have returned to base. After downloading to the computer and editing, you can then burn a CD master with the edit on it.

### Equipment

Before you put any two pieces of equipment together you need to know a little about the engineering aspects. We suggest that you look at <u>Sound Engineering Explained</u>. [3]

### Computer

The computers we use at present are fairly standard and operate with Microsoft Windows XP Professional. They have a reasonable sound card, but for exact work we use monitors. Most commercial computers should prove satisfactory. We use standard office computers with the same programmes on each of our computers, but it is possible to purchase special audio computers for work on audio that are silent; for example one type of computer is water cooled, and this is good for music and fine editing because there is no sound of a fan to mask faults. However, care must be taken to make sure of compatibility of the computer with the programmes.

### Speakers

The monitors we use are Genelec 1029A active 'near-field' speakers - price code E a pair. These speakers have their own amplifiers and are very good indeed and we use them particularly for music. Already there are newer models. Simple speech editing can be done using the small speakers in the computer but better results come from using higher quality monitors and in a noisy environment a good pair of enclosed headsets can be used.

It is possible to buy quite reasonable speakers for as little as £50 each but they will need a power amplification system which might cost perhaps £100. We have recently purchased a pair of Edirol MA-10A active, analogue speakers with internal amplification. These are Price code B for the pair. The quality is very good for the price and worth considering since they are inexpensive and quite light to carry.

### Headsets

For headsets we use a pair of Beyer DT300 enclosed design which give isolation from the sound around you to the extent of 27dB Price code B. Also we use Beyer DT100 headsets for normal work. However, a headset costing very little which is designed for a portable CD player will do for checking tracks if you need to cut down the weight of gear that you are carrying. However, in the end, the real quality of the recording needs to be listened to on expensive amplifiers and speakers.

### Downloading the Sound

The mini-disc is played back from a mini-disc player deck, possibly a Tascam MD-359, price code D, through a digitising pre-amp. It is possible but less convenient to play the mini-discs onto the digitising pre-amp through the original recording machine. The MD 359 machine has various sampling rates which we could do without, since it is possible to accidentally turn them on. Sony are developing mini-disc recorders where the file may be transferred into the computer via a USB connection in future models, but this may not happen as mini-disc technology appears to be overtaken by solid state.

We are using audio transfer to the computer through an M Audio Audiosport Duo with separate power supply, price code C. We have seen these for price code B so shopping around is necessary, as with all items.

Separate connections can be used for microphones which also supply phantom power to the microphone if necessary. This has a USB connection to the computer. There will be many developments in this area over the next few years.

Another possibility is to use a Tascam 122 USB interface. Microphones can be connected directly to these interfaces and through a USB connection to the computer. The power for the Tascam comes from the USB lead. A programme is provided that presents many possibilities with connections for electric guitar and midi instruments. However, with modification of the windows audio in the computer the signal can be put into Cool Edit directly. The cost of the Tascam 122 USB is around price code C. However, we have found that because Windows does not recognise the driver for this piece of equipment it is possible that some computers will not accept the input signal from it. On the computer we use we had no problems but another did not operate until we had checked the designated input.

With both the M Audio Audiosport Duo and the Tascam 122 recordings can be made directly onto the computer which has something to be said for it. For example, it is possible to use a laptop on site as the recording machine. However, we feel it is best to record outside the computer and then put the material into the computer but in certain instances there are great advantages in recording direct to the computer.

In some cases it is necessary to mix the outputs of microphones and this is done in a device called a mixer. For simple work we use a very useful mixer called a Spirit Notepad which was designed by Soundcraft and manufactured in China. The cost is in the region of price code B. This allows for two pairs of stereo individual inputs; that is for four separate mics that can be stereo pairs or individual mics, and two stereo inputs. There are various combinations of inputs that can be mixed using this mixer and then sent as line-level out to the recording equipment or direct into the computer.

Another way to mix is to use a 'two in one out' microphone signal combiner which uses transformer isolation. The input can be adjusted by using line attenuators. However, watch out for hum. At the other end of the scale there are many excellent mixers that operate in digital form so that the signals can be fed direct into the computer, but these are typically £1000 each and well over.

### Storage

Audio files are large even when compressed and you will need more storage capacity. We use two Maxtors 160 gigabyte hard discs through a USB 2 connection; about price code E for the pair and the price is still going down. The Maxtors have USB2 and Firewire connections. We have just bought another Maxtor hard disc with 250 gig capacity for price code C. It is wise not to take your complete storage system on the road in case of loss or damage, so it is worth considering a separate storage unit to carry it around. It is hard to put a value on the files that are recorded on the hard discs and so think of this when writing the cheque for another storage device.

A 720 gigabyte Videoraid storage unit (£3000) might be appropriate for a large museum or gallery that is enlightened enough to use sound creatively, but it will store any sort of file and for an organisation it can be a very good idea. There is a whole world of electronic devices that can be used for storage of digital files. This is an area that has developed quickly and will expand as time goes by and is generally known as Digital Asset Management (DAM).

### Editing Programmes
The specific audio programmes we use are Cool Edit Pro and CD Architect 5.0. Both of these programmes have been bought out by large companies and now have different names. The Cool Edit programme we use for editing and CD Architect we use to set up CDs. Another suitable programme for editing is Sound Forge but Cool Edit has become a standard in the BBC and so we use it. The BBC has a tutorial web-site for this programme on. (www.bbctraining.com/radio.asp ). The BBC run other interesting training programmes so look at their website. However, Cool Edit has been taken over by Adobe and is now called Adobe Audition, price code D. For making the master CD we use CD Architect 5.0, about price code D, which uses audio files from other programmes. This has also been taken over but by Sony and is now called Sony CD Architect 5.0.

There is also a shareware editing programme called Audacity 1.2 which is available free from the net and with certain free CDs. Our limited experiments with this programme suggest it is good but not as elaborate as the programme we are using.

In the text we refer to equipment that has to be bought to do the work. The prices move down mostly, but certainly do not stay the same. With this is mind we have price coded the prices against a system of brackets. We have taken this from a useful little book that you should have if you are interested in making music on your computer, entitled The Illustrated Home Recording Handbook.[4] In fact we have extended it to upper levels.

It is:
A= free
B= £1 - 100
C= £100 - 200
D= £200 - 400
E= £400 - 600
F= £600 - 1000
G= £1000 - 1500

For further information about microphones and mixers, have a look at the following sections of this chapter.

## The future

What we have written could not have been written a few years ago and in a few years from now this in turn will be quite out of date – if it is not already! It is difficult to say what will happen in the future but some tendencies are quite clear.

Everything will be very small. Already it is almost impossible to use the buttons on certain equipment because it is so small. However, most professional equipment seems to be a reasonable size with controls that a human hand can operate.

With the advent of digital recording file storage became important and now we can store what could not even be dreamt of in the past. Solid state storage is coming of age and its direct fast feed into the computer saves hours of waiting before editing.

The cost of everything is now much less than it was. Or is it simply that the profit margins are smaller? Presently manufacturing in places like China are having a considerable effect on prices.

## References

There are many references available. Focal Press publish many useful and relevant books so watch their lists for new material. Such journals as <u>Sound on Sound</u> provide a useful connection with the almost secret world of computer audio enthusiasts.

<u>Audio Editing with Cool Edit</u> by Richard Riley, Focal Press, ISBN 1-870775-74-0

<u>PC Audio Editing</u> by Roger Derry, Focal Press, ISBN 0-240-51697-4

<u>Acoustics and Psychoacoustics</u> by David Howard and James Angus, Focal Press, 2000, ISBN 0-240-51428-9

<u>A Manual of Sound Archive Administration</u> by Alan Ward, Gower Publishing, ISBN 0-566-05571-6

<u>Sound Design: The Expressive Power of Music, Voice, and Sound Effects in Cinema</u> by David Sonnenschein, Michael Wiese Productions, 2001, ISBN 0-94118-26-4

<u>Audio in Media</u> by Stanley R Alten, published by Thomson Learning, ISBN 0-534-54804-0

[1] This was the wording required by the Charity Commissioners when the Trust was set up in 1995.

[2] Waveform audio files, developed by Microsoft and IBM as the standard format for sound on PCs. MP3 is short for MPEG 1, Layer 3. MPEG is an acronym for Moving Picture Experts Group.

[3] Michael Talbot-Smith, <u>Sound Engineering Explained</u> London 2002, ISBN 0-240-51667-2

[4] Ed Ronan MacDonald, <u>Illustrated Home Recording Handbook</u>, London 2004, ISBN 1-84451-179-0

# *Microphones*

In sound recording the microphone is the pencil with which we draw and like pencils they are different; the choice is very personal and some are sharper than others. After all it is the aim of the final edited piece to reflect reality with some accuracy where required and this demands a good microphone. In other ways sound can be created and modified electronically, but that is another subject.

The types of microphones and their characteristics can be considered in various ways:

sensitivity
way of working
directionality

Generally, the more sensitive and accurate the microphone is the more expensive it is. Some ways of working are better for certain types of situation. Directionality is of great importance since sound from only certain directions is useful.

Microphones are transducers that transfer sound energy into electrical energy. The amount of electricity is very small, perhaps 1/1000 of a volt, and is subject to interference, particularly when a long length of cable is used. The cable can act as a radio aerial and pick up radio stations and all sorts of electrical interference. It is particularly important that the impedance, or resistance, of the equipment matches, otherwise there are problems.

Professional equipment usually has balanced connections and non-professional equipment has un-balanced connections. In balanced cables there are three conductors; one is a screen or earth and the other two carry the electrical signal and should be identical so that any interference from outside will match in each cable. In unbalanced connections the outer screen is used as the return and can therefore acquire interference unevenly. Generally line two is 'hot' or carries the signal; do not make the mistake when an engineer says, holding a piece of cable, 'is this 'too hot? What he really means is, 'this 2 hot'.

It is sometimes worth putting a pre-amplifier in the line to raise the voltage to line level, usually the standard is -10dB (decibel) in domestic equipment or +4dB or +8dB in professional equipment. In certain situations, for example when recording wildlife, we use a variable plus 40dB line pre-amplifier to boost the signal from the microphone.

The following microphones, and most microphones in use at the present time, have an analogue physical function and the analogue reflected in the electrical message is the vibration of a diaphragm. Work continues with the use of the change in capacitance,[1] caused by the sound to change the instantaneous frequency of an oscillator operating around 10MHz. Inevitably the analogue pre-amplifier will be replaced by a digitising system which will eliminate many of the present problems, but no doubt produce its own problems. Radio connection should be much easier using a digital signal. However, right now there are some very simple but good microphones available, but it is as well to consider the future because of the rate of technical change.

### 1. By method of transduction

### Carbon granules and other earlier techniques
Earlier experiments and indeed practice using carbon granules and other techniques proved to have many problems and at the present time are not considered as an option. This system was used originally in telephone microphones.

### Moving coil microphone
The diaphragm and the connected coil moves with the sound to create electrical energy. The diaphragm has a light coil of wire placed so that it can move over a stationary permanent magnet. This produces a very slight electrical current that is an analogue of the diaphragm movement which in turn is moving in response to the sound that reaches it. Sometimes these are called dynamic microphones but moving coil is a better description. They provide a useful general purpose voice microphone.

This useful fairly robust type of microphone will cope with long cable runs. Our favourite in this category is the Shure SM57 LC.

### Ribbon microphone
This has a thin corrugated ribbon set between two poles of a permanent magnet. The movement backwards and forwards of the 'ribbon' produces an electrical current which again is an analogue of the sound pressure waves that hit the ribbon. Because of the shape of the magnet and direction of the ribbon this type of microphone has a particular pattern of response which is called a 'figure of eight' response.

These microphones are fragile but quite heavy. The fine results in recording voices was the basis of the early BBC broadcasts. Mention the STC 4038 to an audio engineer and he will dissolve into nostalgia. (I wish we had one!) They are very difficult, in other words impossible, to use outside because of the movement in the wind of the ribbon. However, do not forget that within the microphone there is a very large magnet that will eradicate an analogue signal on a tape without much effort – so watch out!

### Electrostatic or Condenser microphone

The diaphragm and the back plate form a capacitor and the unit formed by these two parts is known as a capsule. As the diaphragm moves it varies the capacitance between the diaphragm and back plate. A direct current of between 50 to 100 volts is passed through the capacitor formed by the diaphragm and the back plate. It is the variation of the voltage, due to the movement of the diaphragm, this generates the output of the microphone. For various reasons it is necessary to place a pre-amplifier close to the capsule and this has to be driven by an electrical current, as does the potential between the two parts of the capsule. This electrical supply is called 'phantom power', usually 48 volts, and passes to the microphone along the microphone cable. Most professional mixers and recording machines are designed to supply this.

These microphones produce fine results, but are troubled by damp, or to be exact are more troubled by damp than other microphones. Even on a humid day they may well produce intermittent noises. Some configurations of capsule are more sensitive to wind and handling than others.

Our favourite is the AKG 414 but then this is closely followed by the Russian Octava MK319. Both of these are large diaphragm microphones. Smaller diaphragm microphones have a slightly different feel and resulting sound and are used to obtain a presence at a higher frequency. We use somewhat temperamental AKG 421 mics but these are no longer manufactured.

A subsection of these microphones are the so called *Lavaliere* mics or lapel mics. These are very small and are used when recording people in difficult conditions such as where there is a lot of background noise; then the mic is put very close to the mouth. They are recommended by some for use in recording oral history. When pressed we will use them but we prefer at least some ambience to give the voice a place. Also we tend to work in stereo. They are small enough to place in positions where you need some 'effect' sound, such as on a vaulting horse in a gymnastic display.

An electoret microphone (ECM) works on a similar principle but is constructed with materials that will retain an electrical charge. However, electrical power is needed to run the pre-amplifier, which is usually contained in the microphone casing. This power is often supplied by a 1.5v dry-cell battery contained in the microphone casing or supplied from the recording machine. This type of microphone is very useful. However, make sure you buy a good one.

We use a Sony ECM 907 with our mini-disc recorders and with the Edirol R-1.

### Contact microphones
Essentially these microphones were developed for recording certain instruments. They are devices that pick up vibrations from a solid object. The whole device vibrates with the surface of the object and the inertia of the inner part creates the electrical impulse. In other words, the mass reacts against  cmaybe a piezo-electric device which produces the signal. Although this is a little removed from the sound as we hear, this type of microphone can be very useful in certain circumstances.

### Pressure Zone Microphone
These microphones are designed to work on a flat surface. They do seem to pick up higher frequencies very well so that they can be place don a table where a discussion is taking place. The mic works on the basis that the sound pressure level close to a surface is greater than elsewhere. It can be placed on the wall or ceiling which will have the same effect. Stage performances can be recorded using this mic without stands and suspension systems.

### 2. By direction

The acceptance of sound by a microphone is never equal from all directions by virtue of its normal construction. In fact microphones that accept sound equally from all directions are specially designed for this purpose. But then do we need this? In recording sound there is as much art in excluding sound as including it.

Let us take an example. We are to record a person giving a lecture to a large and inevitably noisy audience. We need only sound from the speaker and not from the audience. How, then, do we select the correct microphone for the job?

We need to know what the directionality of the microphone is. The answer is to put together a 'polar diagram' of the acceptance of the microphone. Since the microphone can be pointed at the source the axis of the 'plan' is usually along the axis of the microphone or, more specifically, the capsule. The obvious characteristics of the directionality can be loosely classified under various heads and this helps select the right microphone or to compare microphones. If we place the shape of the polar diagram on top of a plan of the situation in front of us we can see which sort of microphone to use.

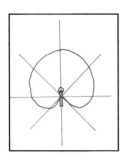

Typically a polar diagram looks like this. In this case the microphone is directional and this is known as a 'cardioid' microphone on account of its heart shaped polar diagram. The ribbon microphone mentioned above has a 'figure of eight' polar diagram. Clearly, the ribbon microphone is not the one to chose to record our lecturer, otherwise we would receive as much sound from the audience as from the lecturer. Again an omni-directional microphone would not be satisfactory. If we list the classification and describe the polar diagrams it will help understand how microphones are chosen.

In more extreme and complex polar diagrams, often the diagram is not correct at certain frequencies. Listening carefully to test runs is perhaps the best strategy. The following is a simple list of the directional classifications:

**Omni-directional** - same sensitivity all round

**Cardioid** - directional, acceptance is heart shaped

**Hyper-cardioid** – more directional than cardioid

**Figure of eight** - polar diagram is like an eight on its side

**Parabolic reflector microphones** - distant wildlife recording

**Gun microphones** - reject close sounds from the sides

Special mics might be:

**Boundary microphones** – these sit on a stage or table for conference recording; another version is the opera mouse is where a microphone is placed in a plastic housing with a slot and a space for the capsule and the whole is placed on the stage to record an 'opera' from the stage without being too obvious. We use an Audio-Technica AT 849 which is a boundary mic.

**Personal microphones** – small mics and for television; these are typically put on lapel or on a tie. These are sometimes incorrectly called *Lavaliere* mics – after Mme Lavaliere who used to wear impressive jewellery around her neck, the allusion being the mic is worn in the same way. However, they can be placed almost anywhere to pick up the voice. Usually these microphones are very small with a very light wire connecting them to the amplifier so that they are less obvious than other types of microphone.

**Radio microphones** – the cable from the microphone to the equipment is a problem from several points of view. In recording for film the cable can be seen. When a performer is moving around then a cable would be a hazard. In both cases it is worth considering an expensive radio link rather than the cable.

**Underwater microphones** – a special microphone that works well under water. These microphones are very expensive because they have to provide extra design facets for the work. A moment's thought and you will see why these are special. The environment is water under pressure and sound behaves differently under water. We are constructing an aural version of the pond-dipping that most children find interesting. Blind children get very little from collecting virtually non-tactile insects, but these same insects talk to each other under water and can be heard. This project is still in the research stage but people from many disciplines are interested.

**Dynamic range** – The range of sound that occurs normally is not a problem. An orchestra and machinery are two problem areas. This may be as much as 130 dB as a sound pressure level, which is a relationship of one to several million. However, care must be taken because although the sound may be converted to an electrical signal at the diaphragm, the first amplifier in the chain may become overloaded and distortion may occur. This may not show in the meters further down the line. In order to avoid this situation 'pads' giving various amounts of attenuation, or reduction in volume, can be placed adjacent to the capsule in various ways. Distortion caused by overload cannot be corrected.

### 3. Extra Equipment for microphones.

Before considering the use of microphones we need to look at some of the ancillary equipment that goes with the microphone.

### Shock and vibration mounts

As mentioned elsewhere sound can reach the microphone via its support. For this reason microphones should be placed in elastic supports to protect them. The lack of such a support can be the source of strange rumbling noises. Often stages and platforms and even lecterns pick up foot movement and the sound of a hand turning a page. There are situations where the microphone is hand-held and this takes some skill. Often sounds come from the movement of the connecting cable; this should be held in a loop to produce isolation from the length of cable which in turn picks up odd vibrations.

### Wind and breath

As one would expect, the diaphragm is very sensitive to the slightest wind movement and certainly breath. For this reason the microphone has to be protected. Often the microphone has a 'muff' made of foam plastic which will serve to protect it from slight movement of air. However, it does need greater protection than this in many situations. When used outside cages covered with longhaired cloth are often used. When a microphone is being used close to a person who is reading or singing, certain syllables produce a powerful projection of breath. Typically 'p' comes over as a 'pop' in the recording. This is usually dealt with by using what is known as a 'pop screen', which is a wire circle with a light cloth cover held on an adjustable support.

### Stands
These should be well-designed and give adequate support. They should not have parts that will reflect sound near to the microphone diaphragm because these will distort the designed function of the microphone. For the same reasons as the directional microphone, it is often necessary to suspend or place the microphone over the head of an instrumental player or a person speaking while in the centre of a crowd of people. For this purpose and obviously others a boom is used to carry the microphone. Another technique for the same purpose is a light hand-held boom which is known as a 'fishpole'.

### Cables
They should be of a suitable type and should be taped to the stand so that the cable cannot be tripped over or pulled. Place a loop at the back of the microphone so that any sound moving up the cable will not reach the body of the microphone. You should note that cables are a frequent source of accidents. In the audio business there is a tape called 'Gaffer Tape' that can be used for fixing down cable. In fact this tape, which sticks to almost everything except some stone, can be used for many temporary repair jobs. While care must be taken, a good insurance policy is essential and in certain cases is a legal requirement.

### Pre-amplifiers
These are particularly useful in natural history recording. The Shure FP23 gives us up to 66dB gain. The amplitude of the sound of speech and the normal sound of the environment is at a level that is easily heard and microphones are designed for this range of volume. There are sound environments that have a lower amplitude than this.

### 4. Mono use of microphone

Mono means one and in this context it means one track. Stereo has come to mean two tracks, but this is an oversimplification. Generally, it is the recording industry that has 'set in stone' this form of stereo. The first stereo demonstration was in 1881 at the Paris Exhibition by Clement Adler. It was not until 1931 that Alan Blumlein patented a system of stereo sound and it was some considerable time after, in June 1958, that a so-called stereo recording on a disc was marketed by Pye. The patent that Blumlein put together is the foundation of modern thinking about stereo audio. Patent number 394,325 was entitled 'Improvements in and relating to sound-transmission, sound recording and sound reproducing systems'.

He frequently used the expression 'binaural', but not quite in the same way as is used in modern stereo systems; what he was referring to was the use of two ears.

The use of a mono track can, nevertheless, give a sense of perspective. If we stand close to a person and they talk, there is less interference from other noises around than if we stand a distance away. Also more of the sound is direct, rather than reflected sound, so the closer that a person seems to be.

In certain instances two microphones can be used and mixed onto one channel. This might be considered where two people have to be recorded and rather than sharing one microphone where one person would have to stand in front of another, two microphones are used and the signal from both are mixed together.

Using a special line and a CODEC (code.decode) it is possible to connect with a studio direct rather than going there in person. Many of us have travelled hundreds of miles to record a few minutes of sound and many actors, musicians and narrators have done the same. You would require a good microphone and a certain amount of equipment to your studio to do this work, but it will become more usual in the future.

### 5. Stereo Sound

By now those who are interested in hi-fidelity sound reproduction will be wondering why we are still talking about one channel. After all we have two ears and most commercial playback systems have two channels! Stereo sound is about sound giving information about space and that is what the word means. Since sound occurs in space (even if it is underwater space) and the reflections of sound are important we need to think about them. In simple terms, when we stand on the pavement and wait to cross a road, we hear a car coming from the left and then one from the right and this way we know which way to check by looking and then we cross. Long ago it was not a motor car, but perhaps a bear or a bison. The human body is wonderfully designed and provides us with a warning system which is also a mechanism that has become part of a complex communication system. Put one hand over one ear and close your eyes. Suddenly what we hear is flat and gives us no clues as to space, except in amplitude reduction and certain types of signals. Remove your hand and space has returned. Perhaps this why we have two ears.

As we consider the sources of sound and the way that sound reverberates in spaces, we realise that it is very complex. Not only this, but there are other messages coming in. Thus, while we need to have some understanding of this complex situation the whole is resolved by listening. With two ears and our pinnae – that is the flappy things on the side of our heads - we can judge distances, interpret sounds, place objects and hear our enemies. Furthermore the brain can decode what amounts to a simple wave form and tell us much about the individual sounds that make up the complex wave form. Most of this we can only do with two ears, not one.

Given two ears then we need two audio channels. Certainly, as we have suggested, other signals and their relationship will give us some indication of space, but the basic need is a channel for each ear. However, when the sound is presented to us via a headset this is true but where it is via several loudspeakers that is another matter. For this we need at least two microphones, or if we are to be very realistic several microphones. However, two channels delivered through two speakers or a headset is amazingly effective and has become standard in most commercial equipment!

Here we are entering a world that is very exciting and has been, and continues to be, carefully considered and written about. Even so not all the answers are available. Right here we will suggest some books that you could well find very interesting.

Jens Blauert, <u>Spatial Hearing, the Psychophysics of Human Sound Localization</u>.[2] This is a classic but very detailed.
Francis Rumsey, <u>Spatial Audio</u>.[3] Here is very clear description of the techniques used.
Durand R Begault, <u>3D Sound for Virtual Reality and Multimedia</u>[4] This book is particularly interesting in respect to virtual reality.

The above books will set you on the right track, but remember that you are dealing with the psychophysics of hearing and that you should also check back to our references given earlier in the book.

We will also point you in the direction of another book that will take you deeper into the history of stereo: <u>The inventor of Stereo, The Life and Works of Alan Dower Blumlein</u> by Robert Charles Alexander.[5] This is the story of a very interesting person who thought up the theory of stereo. If you find this subject interesting and want to know more of the history of the theory of stereo then get hold of a copy of this book. I had a friend who designed microphones and he could quote complete sections from the patent!

So what do we do? For a start we take two microphones and connect them to a recording machine and, surprise, we find it has two tracks. It has two tracks so that it can record in stereo. If we think in terms of a 'sound stage' in front of us which we need to record, then the pattern becomes a little clearer. We can substitute two loudspeakers for the stage and if we feed our recording into this then when side A, on 'stage' left, is louder than side B, on 'stage' right, the sound seems to come from the left. And so on across the 'sound stage'.

# *Microphones*

But what of the microphones that will produce these two channels? We need two cardioid mics pointing out at say 90 degrees to each other towards the 'sound stage'. The little Sony ECM mic that we mention has two mics inside and does this for you and the angle is marked on the controls. Take a look at the picture below which is of two condenser cardioids set up for stereo.

This is whole exciting area; it is also specialised world and so we asked Damian Murphy, who works with us, to say more about this. He is a Research Fellow in the Media Engineering Research Group at the University of York, specialising in Music Technology, Physical Modelling Synthesis and Recording Studio Techniques. In the next section he outlines this huge and relevant subject.

[1] The property that allows a system to store an electric charge.

[2] Jens Blauert, Spatial Hearing, The Psychophysics of Human Sound Localization, USA 1997, ISBN0-262-02413-6.

[3] Francis Rumsey, Spatial Audio, UK 2001, ISBN 0-240-51623-0.

[4] Durand R Begault, 3D Sound for Virtual Reality and Multi Media , USA 1994, ISBN 0-12-084735-3.

[5] Robert Charles Alexander, The Inventor of Stereo, The Life and Works of Alan Dower Blumlein, UK 1999, ISBN 0-240-51577-3

# *Creating Virtual Acoustics Environments by Damian Murphy*

### Introduction

The word 'stereophonic' is derived from Greek, and means 'solid sound', referring to the construction of believable, solid, stable sound images, regardless of how many loudspeakers are used. It can be applied to surround-sound systems as well as to simple two-channel techniques - the original cinema based Dolby Surround system was also known as Dolby Stereo, even though it used a four separate audio channels. However, stereo is most commonly considered a two-channel system, making use of two loudspeakers for playback, and two channel recording media (such as the compact disk) for storage and delivery.

Before considering how to can create a 'good' stereo image it is important to remember what it is that defines an audio event as being stereo. When stereo was first introduced in popular recording during the 60's, no-one really knew what to do with the extra speaker, resulting in some strange pseudo-stereo effects, usually involving half the band being heard from one speaker with the lead vocal and guitar coming from the other. Stereo mixing in modern times (and now surround mixing) is all about placing sounds 'around' the listener.

Under normal listening conditions our two ears, which are separated by our head, are used to locate a sound from somewhere around us. The five main auditory cues are:

- Interaural Time Difference
- Interaural Intensity Difference
- Pinnae differences
- Head movements
- Sight

### Interaural Time Difference (ITD)

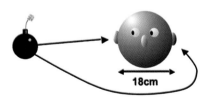

Your ears are separated by a distance of about 18cm. If a sound is placed somewhere around the head, unless it is either directly to the front or the back, there will be a slight difference in the length of the path the sound travels to each ear. This will result in a very slight time delay between the sound at each ear. Note that there will be no delay for a sound placed directly in front or behind us so we must use some other mechanism to help us with these situations.

### Interaural Intensity Difference (IID)

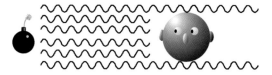

The other main cue that is used to detect the direction of the sound is the differing levels of intensity that result at each ear due to the shading effect of the head. Again this will be equal directly in front or behind the listener. As the source moves away from the centre line, the level at one ear will increase and decrease at the other, furthest away from the source. The intensity ratio between the two ears varies from about 0dB to 20dB, depending on frequency. However, there is a lower frequency limit below which IID is not so useful, due to the large low frequency waves diffracting around the head, minimising the IID. It is not so useful below about 700Hz.

Therefore, in general, ITD is used for localizing low frequencies, and IID is used at high frequencies. However, the crossover is quite blurred, and there are some arguments that state that a form of ITD is still used at higher frequencies. Note also that both of these techniques are (strictly) related to lateral localisation only – they give us no information about height or the difference between front and back.

### Pinna Differences and Head Movements

It still remains to consider the difference between sounds from the front and rear or those that are elevated. The first effect is due to that shape of the outer ear or pinnae. Sounds striking the pinnae are reflected into the ear canal by the complex series of ridges, resulting in very small but very significant delays, giving comb filter interference effects on the sound. These delays are a function of direction of arrival from all three dimensions and they help to resolve differences that cannot be accounted for by ITD or IID. The delays are very small so occur only at high frequencies, typically above 5kHz. The effect is also person specific as everyone has a different head and shaped ears. The asymmetric front/ back profile of the pinna help to differentiate between sounds in front and behind us. This can be demonstrated by cupping your hands behind your ears to give extra-large pinnae to accentuate the effect.

We also attempt to resolve directional ambiguities by moving our heads. Usually when we hear a sound we are interested in we move our head towards it, and may even attempt to place it directly in front of us so as to cancel out any time or intensity differences altogether. Moving our head will also change the relative direction of the sound, and this is position dependent. Therefore a sound from the rear will move in a different direction to a sound above or in front of us. This is one of the reasons we hear headphone sound 'in our head'. The sound is constant no matter how we move our head, so cannot be outside our head so must be inside.

When considering sound localisation we cannot rule out the use of our sight – we will look for the source of sound as well as listen for it and this is often the dominant sense.

### Stereo Recording and Listening
Using the directional properties of the ear it is possible to fool the ear into perceiving a directional effect through just a pair of speakers or headphones. There are three main ways of creating stereo sound images over a pair of loudspeakers:

> The first technique is the use of two or more identical but spaced microphones. These microphones capture sounds at differing times because of their physical separation, and so record time-of-arrival information in the two channels.

> The second is an entirely artificial technique based on Alan Blumlein's work, and uses pan pots to position the sound images from individual microphones by sending different proportions of each microphone to the two channels and so is based on the idea of level differences.

> The third system is that of coincident microphones, using a pair of identical directional microphones, each feeding one channel. The microphones capture sound sources in differing levels between the two channels, much like the pan-pot system, but this time the signal amplitudes vary in direct relation to the physical angle between mics and sound sources.

### Pan Pots and Coincident Techniques – Some more detail
Blumlein developed coincident techniques to overcome the inherent deficiencies (as he saw them) of the spaced microphone systems being developed. Since our hearing mechanism relies heavily on timing information it was thought reasonable to use microphones to capture similar timing differences.

However, when sound is replayed over loudspeakers, both ears hear both speakers, so we actually receive a very complex pattern of timing differences, involving the real timing differences from each speaker to both ears, plus the recorded timing differences from the microphones. This arrangement tends to produce rather vague positional information.

# *Creating Virtual Acoustic Environments*

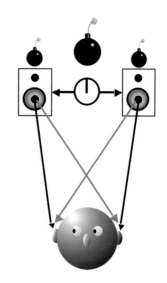

Blumlein demonstrated that by using only the amplitude differences between the two loudspeakers, it was possible to fool the human hearing system into translating these into perceived timing differences, and hence stable and accurate image positions. This is taken entirely for granted now, and a listener is generally happy with the notion that moving a pan-pot to alter the relative amplitudes of a signal in the two channels will alter its position in the stereo image. A 12 to 16dB difference between channels will produce a full left or right image, with about 6dB producing a half-left or right image, although the exact figures vary.

To create stereo images directly from real life, a microphone technique was required that captured level differences between the two channels, but no timing differences. To avoid timing differences, the two microphones must be placed as close together as is physically possible. Hence the term 'Coincident Stereo'. The normal technique is to place the capsule of one microphone immediately above the other, so that they are coincident in the horizontal plane, which is the dimension from which we are trying to recreate image positions. Amplitude differences between the two channels are created through the microphone's own polar patterns, making them more or less sensitive to sounds from various directions. This technique is sometimes called, XY, AB (In the UK), Crossed Pair, or Normal Stereo. 90 degrees is the most commonly used angle of separation. It is possible to change the angle over a small range, to adjust the precise relationship between the physical sound source positions in front of the microphones and their perceived positions in the stereo image. This usable working area in front of the microphone is defined by the polar patterns of the microphones, and is called the 'Acceptance Angle'. Greater than $130^0$ will leave a hole in the middle of the stereo field with central sources falling outside the pick-up angle of each microphone. Smaller than $80^0$ and the acceptance angle is greater than $180^0$. The small focused overlap of the mics however mean that lateral sound sources are attenuated and in general, the aim is to place sound sources around stereo microphones such that they occupy the complete stereo image.

### Spaced Microphone Techniques
The main disadvantage of spaced microphone techniques compared with coincident systems is that if the outputs from all of the microphones in an array are mixed together (to produce a single mono signal), the sound will potentially become coloured because the timing differences between the left and right stereo signals, when added together, act to cancel out or reinforce sounds at particular frequencies across the spectrum. Also all coincident systems have to use directional microphones in order to create the necessary level differences between the two channels of the stereo system and directional microphones aren't so reliable at low

frequencies. By way of comparison, omnidirectional microphones have very smooth and extended low-frequency regions, although do not work well as coincident pairs because they do not produce level differences proportional to the angle of incident sound. Omnidirectional microphones can only be used to record in stereo if they are spaced them apart to deliberately introduce timing differences.

Replaying a stereo recording with timing differences between the two channels leads to a confusing set of time-of-arrival differences for our ears, but the sound is normally still perceived as having width and a certain amount of imaging information, and it usually sounds a lot more spacious than a coincident recording. However the imaging is not very precise and in really bad cases, the recording may even appear to have a 'hole in the middle'. The simplest spaced-microphone technique is to place an identical pair of omnidirectional mics a distance apart in front of the sound source; most engineers would generally choose a spacing of between a half and a third of the width of the actual sound stage. This could be improved through the use of additional directional microphones to alleviate any potential hole in the middle effects.

Other spaced techniques that use directional microphones are often called 'near coincident' techniques because they combine the level difference recording characteristics of directional coincident microphones, with spaced arrays. For instance the ORTF method uses a pair of cardioid microphones with a mutual angle of 110°, spaced about 17cm apart.

### Binaural Recording
Binaural recording is a basic two-microphone spaced-pair technique, but it is rather specialised in that it only works effectively when listened to through headphones. The principle is to replicate the way our ears capture sounds, and replay those sounds directly into the corresponding ear canal. The easiest technique is to simply clip a couple of small omnidirectional microphones to the ears of a willing victim without moving their head, and excellent results can be obtained if the microphones are recorded on a cassette or DAT Walkman as you go about your daily life. A rather more practical method is to use a Jecklin Disc, which mimics the fundamental acoustic aspects of the average head. The disc can be made from Perspex or plywood, typically about 25-30cm in diameter, with a mounting point for the microphone stand on one edge, and fixings for a pair of microphones arranged through its centre. The concept is that the microphone-spacing matches that of our ears, and the disc provides the sound-shadowing effects of the head.

When replayed over headphones, the signals from the disc mics are fed directly into our ear canals, bypassing the effects of our own head- and ear-spacing, effectively transporting our ears directly to the recording venue. The state of the art method of binaural recording would be to use a dummy head such as HATS or KEMAR. Binaural recordings replayed over loudspeakers manage to convey a sense of stereo width and movement without having any accurate imaging qualities. This facet of the technique is often used to advantage in the production of sound effects for radio and television. In general, sound effects -- especially atmospheric effects -- should convey the environment, but must not distract from the foreground dialogue or action, hence the usefulness of not having accurate imaging information in a binaural recording when played over speakers. Binaural playback can be enhanced for speaker reproduction if required using Transaural techniques.

### Increasing Levels of Accuracy – Surround Sound and Virtual Acoustics

Since stereophonic sound reproduction was introduced in the 1960s it has remained the standard playback mechanism for essentially all types of recorded audio. However, well before this, with the cinematic release of Disneys Fantasia in 1939 composers and sound engineers began to develop techniques for a more immersive listening experience, electronically creating a virtual acoustic world using multiple speakers positioned around the audience. Multi-speaker techniques are now commonplace in cinema sound systems and are becoming more readily available in the home with the advent of home cinema systems and DVD. PC soundcards with surround-sound enhancements for games and other entertainment software are also commonly available. Surround-sound audio can also be produced using only standard headphones or stereo speakers together with precise measurements obtained from the detailed physical characteristics of our head and ears.

The ultimate challenge for the sound designer or audio engineer is goal is therefore to electronically manufacture a complex three-dimensional acoustic world that is indistinguishable from what we normally hear around us. The potential result has applications in music composition and playback, art, architectural design, cinema, television and gaming entertainment, telecommunications and user interface design.

### The Impulse Response of a Room

The size, shape and dimensions of a room, together with the actual materials used in its construction, all have a critical part to play in the quality of any sound heard within it, and hence in our perception of that sound event, and the information we receive about the environment in which we are placed. Imagine a gun being fired inside a large room or hall. This short, sharp and very loud event causes a variation in localised air pressure that is transmitted through the air itself and spreads out through the room in every direction - a sound wave. This sound wave will travel unhindered until it reaches an object where it will be partially absorbed and partially reflected. There may also be diffraction effects, where the sound bends round an object or passes through a gap (such as an open door into another room), resulting in further spreading of the original sound wave. Very quickly (within 100ms) the sound from the gunshot has spread throughout the room, and been reflected, absorbed and diffracted according to the room's physical properties. The resulting superposition of the these complex wavefronts can cause acoustic pressure peaks and nulls at various points around the room, in what is known as constructive and destructive interference, respectively. Some of the wavefronts will travel repeated, regular reflection paths due to the geometry of the room resulting in the dominance of particular interference patterns and the enhancement of particular frequencies at specific positions around the room these frequencies are called the room modes.

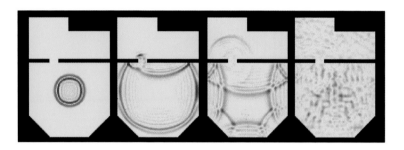

The characteristic build-up of sound in a room as simulated using a digital waveguide mesh model. (left to right) (1) A short, sharp, impulsive sound fired into the larger of two rooms causes a circular wavefront to spread out from the sound source. (2) The sound wave is reflected from the walls and part of it passes through a gap into the smaller room. (3) In the larger room, interference effects are clearly visible; in the smaller room, the soundwave has spread out into an arc, demonstrating the effects of diffraction. (4) A short while after the initial event, the sound energy has spread out in a much more random and complex fashion.

This complex acoustic behaviour can be uniquely captured at a point within the room by using a single measurement called the Impulse Response. The gunshot sound input to the room ideally contains equal amounts of every audio frequency we are interested in, and by measuring (or listening) to this sound at another point in the room it is possible to examine how each frequency has been changed by its interactions with the room. The impulse response itself is not very interesting to listen to lasting anywhere between 0.1 to 10 seconds depending on the size of the room and how reflective the surfaces are and sounds like a click with a prolonged and decaying tail. This decaying part of the impulse response is due to the reverberation present in the room and is typically the characteristic 'hanging on' quality of a sound that can be heard once the sound source itself has become silent. For instance, reverberation can be heard quite clearly in an empty church. However it is possible to take this very boring sound and apply it to any other sound using digital signal processing. The result is that we can make any sound appear to be coming from inside any particular space as long as we know its impulse response.

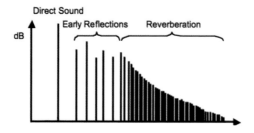

*A profile of the typical characteristic build up of sound in a room consisting of direct sound, early reflections and reverberation.*

The impulse response of a room can be measured directly although for most applications it is usually more practical to calculate an approximation using an acoustic model.

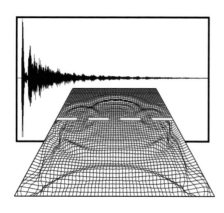

Modelling the acoustics of a room, using a Digital Waveguide Mesh computer simulation. Notice the reflections at the boundaries and the diffraction and interference effects in the partitioned area, caused by gaps in the dividing wall. In the background, a room impulse response obtained from such a model.

### The Impulse Response of the Ear

The wave propagation phenomena present in a room, as discussed above, are equally applicable on a smaller scale when considering the effect of the human head on sound perception. Differences in the arrival time and amplitude of a sound at each ear together with the diffraction of sound waves around the head, when combined with the minute reflections that occur due to the pinnae (the fleshy part of the outer ears), produce particular constructive and destructive interference patterns. These patterns alter the frequency content of the sound that reaches the ear-drums and this direction dependent information allows us to determine the direction of the original sound.

The acoustic behaviour of the head is unique for each person and can be described by a set of Head-Related Impulse Responses, with a left/right ear pair for each sound source direction. Head-Related Impulse Responses last for approximately only 5ms, around 1000 times shorter than that of a typical concert hall, and again sound like a short, sharp click. As with the room based impulse response, digital signal processing allows the characteristics of the Head-Related Impulse Responses to be applied to any audio source. It is then possible to place a sound at any position in a 3-D virtual space around the listeners head, and reproduce it using only headphones (or stereo speakers). Further, if the room impulse response is measured at the entrance to the listeners ears, rather than at a single point, then these two sets of frequency characteristics combine to impart both the environmental and directional acoustic properties of the space being measured. In this way it is possible to generate binaural audio without having to rely on recordings made using microphones attached to a real or dummy head.

Aspects of 3-D sound: (Foreground) KEMAR mannequin head and torso, together with a speaker, used in the measurement of the head-related impulse response. (Mid) Three-dimensional frequency plot of measured head-related impulse responses varying with the direction of the sound in relation to the head. (Background) Three-dimensional model of the outer ear.

## Surround Sound

As discussed previously, when a single sound is played at equal levels from two stereo loudspeakers (or headphones), we perceive the sound as coming from the mid-point between them. This is because there is no difference in the time taken for a sound from each speaker to reach each our ears. Making the sound from one of the speakers louder shifts the sound image towards the louder side, and we perceive the sound as moving either to the left or the right depending on which speaker is now the loudest. This technique is termed panning.

At a basic level a similar technique can be applied to presenting sound images over an array of speakers distributed around the listener. For most cinema or domestic surround-sound systems there are different speakers for different roles in the control and reproduction of the acoustic environment. The front left and right speakers are used for the accompanying music and surround effects. Two speakers are located at the centre of the screen, one of which is used for dialogue, the other being only used for low frequency sounds. There are also two speakers to the rear of the listeners that are used exclusively for surround-sound effects. Sounds can be panned around these speakers to produce various effects. However to produce a convincing effect often other factors have to be considered related to the psychology of how we hear. For instance a Doppler Shift effect can be used to accentuate the movement of a sound as it is panned between the speakers and hence moved around the listener. Doppler Shift is the change of pitch that we hear as a fast moving object moves towards and then away from us this is typically only found in the real world with very fast moving objects over large distances, such as the sound of a siren on a police car, or the horn on a locomotive. However we associate this characteristic effect with sound movement so it will often be used subtly on other sounds to impart the required dramatic result. Another common effect used in cinema surround-sound is to make an aircraft fly over the heads of the audience yet the speakers used to do this are at positions not much higher than our ears when we are seated - they are not placed above the audience in the ceiling of the cinema itself. The sound of the aircraft is actually panned around the speakers from front to back yet we associate the real world sound of an aircraft flying as coming from way above us and so that is what we perceive.

### Generating Virtual Acoustic Environments

ODEON is an example of room acoustics prediction software used for designing, modelling and testing the acoustic characteristics of enclosed spaces, based on geometrical acoustic techniques. It provides a range of capabilities from acoustic parameter prediction at different source locations, reverberation time predication and full RIR/HRTF based auralization. It uses a combination of techniques to calculate the responses making use of image-source and ray-tracing algorithms, together with diffusion reflection modelling at room boundaries. A free demo, publications relating to its use, the manual and audio examples are available from:

> http://www.dat.dtu.dk/~odeon/index.html

A very similar application with a demo available is CATT-Acoustic, available at:
> http://www.catt.se/
Wave Based Acoustic Models

Geometric acoustic models methods are valid for high frequencies only and less appropriate for low frequencies where the wave based properties of sound propagation and the presence of sparsely distributed modal frequencies tend to dominate. They are further limited in their ability to successfully model diffraction effects and hence by extension, sound occlusion due to objects being present in the propagation path, resulting in potential spatialization errors. Diffraction is a wave phenomenon where objects the same order of magnitude in size as the wavelength being considered result in the scattering of the incident wave. This fundamental property is critical when considering building interiors or city plans when the direct line of sight between sound source and listener is often blocked. Diffraction allows the listener to hear someone coming towards them from a space coupled to the one they occupy via an open door. It provides the acoustic cues that enable the pedestrian to work out that an ambulance with its siren on is about to turn a corner into the street they are just about to cross on foot. The Digital Waveguide Mesh is an alternative acoustic model based on wave scattering methods that produces accurate results together with intuitive visuals. RoomWeaver is an application developed at the University of York to facilitate virtual acoustic modelling in this way. The images below show the RoomWeaver GUI and some of the wave propagation effects that can be demonstrated as a consequence of the underlying core Digital Waveguide Mesh based modelling engine. Both ODEON and RoomWeaver were used to generate results for the Coventry Cathedral Acoustic Model referred to earlier.

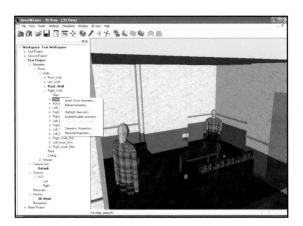

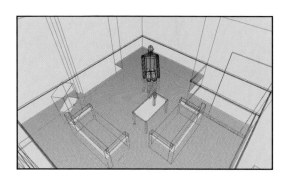

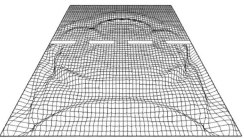

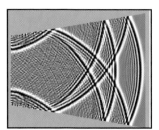

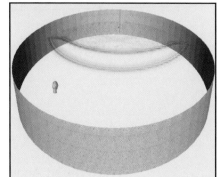

More information about RoomWeaver can be found in the following paper presented at DAFx-04 in Naples, October 2004:

http://dafx04.na.infn.it/WebProc/Proc/P_268.pdf

More information about Digital Waveguide Mesh modelling for room acoustics can be found in a paper presented at DAFx-02:

http://www.unibw-hamburg.de/EWEB/ANT/dafx2002/papers/DAFX02_Murphy_Mullen_waveguide_mesh_modeling.pdf

For more further information on Digital Waveguides and physical modelling refer to Julius Smith's webpage, who was originator of this technique:

http://ccrma.stanford.edu/~jos/

You can experiment with your own impulse response based reverberation/ room modelling using the freeware SIR convolution reverb VST plug-in and Audacity freeware audio editing software:

http://www.knufinke.de/sir/index_en.html
http://audacity.sourceforge.net/

A range of real and simulated room impulse responses are available at:

http://www.noisevault.com/

A basic geometric acoustic modeller suitable for generating your own RIRs is Impulse Modeller.  A demo is available at:

http://www.voxengo.com/imodeler/

**Links**

| | |
|---|---|
| Audio and 3-D sound links: | http://www.wareing.dircon.co.uk/3daudio.htm |
| 3-D Sound Information and Resources: | http://www.3dsound.com/ |
| Dolby Surround-sound developers: | http://www.dolby.com/ |
| Ambisonic Surround Sound: | http://www.york.ac.uk/inst/mustech/3d_audio/ambison.htm |
| Digital Signal Processing: A Tutorial | http://www.dsptutor.freeuk.com/index.htm |

# Mixers and Monitors

The mixing desk appears in almost every publicity shot or advertisement in the audio business. Hundreds of faders in exaggerated perspective disappear into the distance to show the considerable 'macho' control the person in the photograph has over the situation. It is possible to record without a mixer but it is more convenient with one. However, in the area we are talking about it is rare to need more than a few microphones so that a very small mixer is usually sufficient. You may not even need a mixer!

In a complex situation such as a symphony orchestra, which we have done on several occasions, a stereo 'array', or pair, should be sufficient. However, generally a single array is not sufficient because the balance is not quite correct and then the art of the game is to create the correct balance by pulling up, or pushing back, various instruments or sections of the orchestra by using the mixer. Besides this many pieces have soloists who need to be brought forward in the mix and this is done by putting in solo stands and mics to be mixed in. This all take practice but it is so obvious when it is right that it is not a worry. If you are to be governed by egocentric musicians and jumpy producers then you might have real problems so we suggest that you give that situation a miss. For recorded drama you may also be forced into 'mixerdom'. To record the courtroom scene at Brecknock Museum we used a 'dummy head' and two pairs of cardioids small diaphragm condenser mics and mixed these down on the spot through a mixer. This was more complex than most sessions. Listen to a track of this recording on the examples CD.

An alternative to using a mixer is to use a multi-track recording machine. These machines are very expensive at the present time. However, the mixing down of the recording is simply put off until a later stage. There are advantages in this in that another mixdown can be made from the same material. We suggest that you do not need to do this and anyway if you can afford this sort of equipment let us know where you got the money from!

Considering what the mixer can do gives us the real clue as to its form. It takes in the lines from the microphones or other sources and mixes the signals and provides an output, or even several outputs, via 'buses' (the main output), to the output plugs that will be connected to the recording equipment and also to the monitoring equipment. In our case the recording equipment can be a computer and the signal has to be digitised from the analogue signal to something that can be used by the computer.

In physical terms, the input processing is lined up vertically, or back to front, so that there will be as many possible inputs as there are vertical ranks of processing equipment. The input is generally at the head of the mixer where each rank or line has a series of input plugs to match possible lines in. In order down the rank you will generally find:

1. The input sockets of various sorts
2. An attenuation pad
3. An amplifier
4. An EQ system
5. A fader
6. A pan to right or left

The line is then connected to a 'bus' that connects to the output section which, again, is vertical or front to back except on this occasion the signals go from front to back to output connections. This is where the output meters are generally situated – if it goes over the top then you have ruined the recording.

The output section is generally on the right and connects with various output sockets. This line has the main output faders together with meters. Subsequent to the fader is a meter that indicates the output of the mixer unit. This meter is generally a Peak Programme Meter. There is generally a test tone device that connects a tone to the recording equipment. This has to be balanced so that the maximum reading on the meter does not exceed the maximum capability of the recording equipment. Also in this section there will be connections for monitoring by loudspeaker and headset.

In addition at this stage there may be a 'slate' microphone which will put onto the recording the name of the take and other spoken details. Other equipment could include communication connections that are intended to link with others in the recording team.

The above is about an analogue mixer which for our purposes is fine. Digital mixers and controllers play a different role in the overall system and are presently considerably more expensive. The measure of this is that analogue mixers start at a few hundred pounds and a digital mixer at a few thousand pounds. In the set-up which has an analogue mixer, the monitoring arrangement has to be connected with the mixer because that is where it is controlled. Where there is no mixer the monitoring has to be taken off the recording gear, which may be the computer.

## Monitoring

Monitoring goes with mixing and in fact it is difficult to mix without listening to what you are mixing. Monitoring has several functions. The first is to hear what is being recorded or will be recorded and make adjustments on the mixer or make adjustments of the position of the microphones or performers in order to achieve what is required. Also monitoring is essential for editing and mixing. In the case of using one microphone and no mixer the monitoring can be taken off the recording equipment and adjustments to the microphone position can be made on this basis.

Monitoring is a way to spot anything that is or will go wrong. For example the occasional tapping of a foot can be heard. Other faults such intermittent connections may also show up. Some things happen only occasionally and so it is important to keep listening. This is the moment to get it right; it is too late when the recording gear is 'rolling'. Some problems will not show up until the editing stage. For example sub-audible vibration will only show up when the recording is in the computer. Monitoring can be on a headset, near-field monitors or large monitors which all have their own characteristics.

## Headsets

A high quality open headset is usually satisfactory for monitoring but in noisy or sensitive environments a 'closed' headset is necessary; this is one that excludes all external sound. Certainly it is agreed that the best monitoring is from loudspeakers since headsets tend not to give a good two-channel stereo picture. A closed headset can give -27dB noise reduction between the ear and the outside environment – do not talk to someone with a headset on!

We have found that in a noisy environment such as a street carnival, or at the other end of the scale where there is little sound such as recording birds, we need a closed headset. Care must be taken in the volume of sound that is delivered through the headset because too great a volume can damage the hearing. Another advantage of the headset is that generally the acoustics of the surrounding space will not affect the sound that you hear. However, since what you are putting together may be played back using a speaker in a space that has ambience remember that your headset has no ambience. It might be worth adding reverb similar to the ambience of the place that you have in mind to a copy of your master file to check what it sounds like on site.

## Near-field monitors

It is generally accepted that near-field monitors are better for monitoring than a headset. However, there are many situations where headsets have to be used, for example out in the countryside. The loudspeakers are called 'near-field' monitors because they are designed to be close to the person who is either recording or editing. Most of these monitors are quite expensive but very accurate. Digital self-powered are an improvement on analogue self-powered speakers but are presently more expensive. The digital file needs to be translated through the pre-amp to drive the analogue monitors. Even with a near-field monitor the acoustics of the surrounding space will affect what you hear. In practice if your head is very close, this is not too critical although in certain circumstances it could be. All spaces have acoustic character so beware.

### Large monitors

This is a luxury product but it must be realised that the lower frequencies are heard better on a big monitor. However, it is possible to rig another speaker into the near-field situation that will read the lower frequencies. Such speakers are available for 5:1 cinema arrangements. In practice we have never found this necessary. Where large monitors are used the acoustics of the space is critical and there are many articles on this in the professional magazines.

### Low quality playback systems

Much of what we produce will be played on low quality equipment. Poor equipment has its own characteristics and for this reason it is possible to buy monitors that have a performance that is similar to, for example, the tiny speaker in a TV set. However, it is important to understand what the characteristics of the playback equipment are and to take this into account in the design of the audio piece. For example, if the playback equipment has a limited range of frequencies, then there is no point in including and relying on the top and bottom frequencies to give a quality since these will not be heard. Therefore, it is worth checking whether what has been edited using a high quality system, will work on a limited one. Another way is to check what has been recorded is on cheap equipment and there is plenty of that around.

### Ultimate quality

When we consider the ultimate quality of the playback obviously the master must be equal to or slightly better than the playback equipment. It is good practice to reach a sensible level of quality because the master might be used on better equipment than that originally designated for the work. But there is no point spending money in making a super-quality master with extended frequencies when a very simple amplifier and speaker will be used to play the piece.

### Safety

We, as indeed others have, the drop-off in sensitivity of the ear after a long day of editing. The temptation is to turn up the volume to compensate for this loss. In Acoustics and Psychoacoustics,[1] David Howard and James Angus include a section on 'Noise Induced Hearing Loss'. The book contains a section dealing with Loudness Perception, which is not the same at all frequencies. It also contains the inevitable but important list of sound levels in the environment which produce one or two unusual readings. One of these is the sound of an empty concert hall which is 20dB and normal speech at 60dB – not much headroom! In the room we are at present with the radio playing music in the background, the reading on our metre is 60dB and outside in the garden the reading is around 50dB. Although these readings are typical, it does demonstrate that quiet places are not always quiet. Some environments have high levels of sound that will damage your hearing, and playback equipment certainly can. The maximum level before damage is probably 80dB. A dance floor is rated at 110dB.

Some headsets have a mechanism for automatic switch-off at the level at which damage is done and in certain types of entertainment premises there is a cut-off for the speakers if they are too loud. The Noise at Work Regulations 1989, are intended to reduce hearing damage. Within these regulations there are three action levels and employers need to take the first level of action if the sound reaches 85dB with further action at higher levels. If you work for yourself, your ears are no less valuable, so take care.

[1] David M Howard and James Angus, Acoustics and Psychoacoustics, Oxford, 1996, ISBN 0-240-51428-9.

*Peter's old mixer from the 1950s. The same principle applies: several lines in and one out. These days we use two channels and tomorrow we will be using probably eight channels.*

# *Signal Processing*

When a track is recorded digitally, the sound becomes a file usually within the computer. Recording machines with solid state memories process the sound before it is fed into the computer. However, within the computer the file may take one of many forms and you will notice that as you work on a file it could be stored also in other file format and this is shown by the suffix to the file. The most straightforward file form will be WAV which is the standard for PCs as it was developed by Microsoft.

Before digital recording the form of the sound was usually analogue magnetic and these recordings were processed in analogue equipment. Often this was very good, but not always. The processing equipment was usually what is termed 'outboard'; that is a box that is added to other equipment and is not part of a recording machine. Now most signal processing is done within the computer or specialised computing device.

The file in the computer can be manipulated in many ways. It is likely that you will not need many of these processing facilities. Nevertheless, have a go at everything as it is only by trying that you will get to know what the programmes can do for you. Some processes are about making the file suitable for various reasons. Others are very useful for the sort of work that we do such as reverberation – known as reverb – equalisation – known as EQ – and so on. There are also those processes that are used for pop music which are often fun but not that useful to us. Sometimes the processes are not as good as they can be. To get the very best then it is very expensive and outside our range of finance.

We are using *Cool Edit Pro* as our editing programme. It has now become Adobe Audition, but to prevent confusion we will continue to use the former name. The list of processes that *Cool Edit Pro* (as it was ) can do is below. It is pretty impressive and is grouped under the head of 'effects' and some other processes are hidden elsewhere. The processes are grouped under their main functions. You should have the manual and hopefully other books that will go into details. We will outline what we use and how, but remember that programmes change and updates may change the way of doing certain things. There are two books in particular that are important. The first is by Richard Riley and is entitled <u>Audio Editing with Cool Edit</u>.[1] The second is by Roger Derry and is entitled <u>PC Audio Editing</u>.[2]

**Effects**
Amplitude
Amplify – boost or cut volume
Channel Mixer
Dynamics Processing – compression and expansion
Envelope – apply fade in and fade out
Hard Limiting
Normalise – set maximum amplitude of waveform
Pan expand – stereo only
Stereo Field Rotate – stereo only

Delay Effects
Chorus
Delay
Dynamic delay
Echo
Echo Chamber
Flanger
Full reverb
Multitap delay
Quickreverb
Reverb
Sweeping phaser

DirectX – see note
Filters
Dynamic EQ
FFT filter
Graphic phase shifter
Notch filter
Parametric equalizer
Quick filter
Scientific filter

Noise reduction
Click/pop eliminator
Clip Restoration
Hiss reduction
Noise reduction

Brainwave synchronizer
Distortion
Music

Time/pitch
Doppler shifter
Pitch bender
Stretch

Of the above list there are some items of processing that we use all the time and we will describe these. However, for fine detail look at your programme manual and also check for updates.

The DirectX menu item generally refers to connections with other programmes. You may wish to explore this on your machines to see what can be used. Some will certainly crash your machine but it is worth a try. The following are comments on particular processors that are useful to us.

### Amplify
Amplify-boost or cut volume
This is an obvious tool. It can be applied to either track. This can be used to adjust the tracks and this can adjust stereo positions or an inadequate level from a microphone.

### Channel mixer
In this process you can restructure the right and left channels.

### Dynamic range processing
There is a graph that you will be faced with which plots input against output. While the line runs at 45 degrees then input equals output, in other words no change. The line can be moved and typically where the peaks are too high the top right of the graph can be bent down and this will take the top off the peaks. Try the presets to get the idea of how it works. Take a piece of speech and piece of music and work these through the presets.

### Envelope
As a tool this can shape the amplitude of a sound file in the wave section of the programme. This is useful to prefabricate inserts with, typically, a sharp but exact fade in and a sharp fade out. Other shapes become clear when the presets are used. The same tests can be applied to this as the process above.

### Hard limiting
This can be used to bring the body of the file towards the peaks, but this can also be done quite easily in the Dynamic Processing by compressing and expanding the signal.

### Normalize
This is the process we use most. In recording one is anxious not to run the recording level over what the recording device can handle. If

you do then it all has to be recorded again. For this reason you will find that your recordings may be quite low. To normalize, the computer finds the highest peaks and on this basis calculates how much the volume can be increased without running over the top and getting distortion. It is good practice that every file should be normalised before it is put into storage. The volume can be easily reduced to fit the mix that you are working on if necessary. Sometimes a peak will be so extreme, such as where the speaker dropped his script next to the mic, that these should first be reduced or cut out. They can be cut out in the usual edit manner, but if it happens in the middle of what you need to keep the best route is to highlight the peak and reduce it in Amplify by -2dB increments and continues until it is right.

### DelayEffects
Full reverb

This has all the adjustments set out and is therefore a little confusing unless you have some knowledge of acoustics. It is best to try some of the presets to see their results and then try the preview. The best way to check is to process the whole file and then if it is not what you want, go to edit and undo the process.

### Quickverb

This is a simpler version of Full reverb so try the presets again in the same way.

### Reverb

Again this is a simpler version of full reverb. Try as above. Check all the presets in these reverb processors because one may fit what you are doing.

### Filters
Dynamic EQ

This might be useful in special circumstances as it enables the gradual cut or boost of any frequency range over time.

### FFT Filter (fast fourier transform)

You can design your own filter using this process. However, it will take you a considerable time unless you know exactly what you are doing.

### Graphic equaliser

This has a variable number of sliders that increase or decrease the volume at any frequency. Clearly, the more sliders there are, the more accurate the shaping of the sound. Again try everything that you can and see what happens.

### Quick filter

A simpler version of the above.

### Scientific filter

This presents subtleties that you might not have thought of.

### Noise Reduction

We have found that the processes under this head seem to have a limited use in our work. In certain cases we have used the light hiss reduction and this has worked well.

### Time/Pitch

Pitch bender

This can change pitch over time and a graph can be drawn on the computer. But remember that pitch and speed vary as each other. This might be useful in certain situations.

### Stretch

As above there is graph that can be adjusted. However, there are certain effects that have a positive pitch and it is difficult to match sequences and this might help.

---

[1] Richard Riley, <u>Audio Editing with Cool Edit</u> Britain 2002,
   ISBN 1-870775-74-0
[2] Roger Derry, <u>PC Audio Editing</u>, Oxford 2000,
   ISBN 0-240-51697-4.

# *Editing Sound*

The script has been discussed elsewhere and as we have seen it is the equivalent of the drawing on the drawing board. The drawing board is now a little out of date but there does not seem to be a new equivalent of the script as there is in the case of the visual design, or even for the sound itself, as we will show. Everyone has experience with words and putting these together in one way or another. When an actor looks at a script he will immediately tell you what is right and what is wrong from the point of view of reading the script. Read it aloud to yourself to try it out. You will find this quite amazing and very revealing.

The script should contain instructions as to the montage or 'cutting' of the sound and this has been discussed elsewhere. In a word it is the contrast between sections but there is more to it than that.

Before we look at the way pieces of sound should be put together, we need to look at the way that editing is done. Traditionally sound editing was done by cutting tape. Quite simply, the tape passes the playback head in sequence so that if the pieces of tape are spliced in the correct order then they will play after each other. There are other subtleties like the slope of the cut and remembering which piece of black tape is which when it is cut. There was a more complex situation where several tracks were recorded onto one tape. Most tapes were a quarter of an inch wide and carried two tracks, but some were wider tapes and carried more tracks all recorded at the same time. Mostly this had to be dubbed off onto other tapes with a loss in quality. Everyone who is interested in sound editing should have a go at this way of doing things. However, with a little imagination you will see the problems.

With hard disc editing you need to start with the audio files on the hard disc. We have described how to get them there elsewhere in the book. There are now quite a few different editing systems but mostly they are similar in their mechanisms. In Cool Edit Pro the 'wave form' shows a picture of the amplitude in the form of a set of waves. Simply where there are no waves shown there is no sound and you can play the file and the sound is marked on the 'wave form' by the curser. These waves can be cut and placed together in various ways. Unlike the magnetic tape nothing is destroyed by cutting but pieces are called off the audio files as instructed. The wave form shows the edited form and will play it back if asked to do so.

Various effects can be applied to the new file and in this way a piece of sound can be put together.

Having got the pieces of sound as files these files can then be used in the multi-track form of the programme. They are placed in tracks one over another but still playing from right to left. The top line could contain the narrative and the next line down sound effects and the next a line of music. The tracks can be moved with a right press on the mouse and slid from one place to another. There can be 128 tracks expressed in this way but it is difficult to imagine that many jobs would need this number of tracks. So, quite simply, a final set of tracks can be placed and checked. It is wise then to make a 'mixdown' track with all the tracks resolved into two, that is stereo, tracks. And that is about it.

### Designing in Sound

You are the person who holds the brief for sound. You should be the leader of this way of thinking. We have been brought up reading architects' drawings, but most people have not and they mean very little even with intense explanation. The same is true with a script and a computer display. Not only are there words to be understood as a spoken flow of sound, there are also other sounds and the amplitude waves on the computer. We have talked about the principles behind this elsewhere and here we are talking about the presentation of these ideas. In the same way that designs were originally developed bit by bit, the cost of putting together sound is considerable. This is true even if you are doing it all yourself, so the more that can be agreed on the basis of the script the more efficient the whole operation will be.

In <u>PC Audio Editing</u>, Roger Derry refers to 'chequer boarding'. This a technique where the sounds are set up in the manner of a chequer board on the computer monitor and can be sketched out on a piece of paper in the same manner. In the past cutting tape was the only option and this combined with dubbing from one reel of tape to another made up the technology of sound editing. Remember that every analogue dub meant loss of quality!

New computer programmes do things differently. The first programme of this new form that we used was Sadie which is still very good but very expensive.[1] We have underwritten what used to be a programme called Cool Edit Pro and, as we have said, is now Adobe Audition and there are many others in the same bracket but often developed for other purposes such as music composition.

This book does not aim to teach you all about computer editing in Cool Edit or any other programme specifically, so refer to the books we have mentioned above and to your manual for the programme. There is a saying in the audio world, 'If everything else fails refer to the manual!'

Dealing specifically with Cool Edit, the primary edit of the tracks takes place on a section of the wave form part of the programme and the multi-track editing or combining of tracks in another. While this imposes a discipline on the editing, it also helps in focusing on the way of doing it. If at this point the junctions between sounds are worked out then this need not be changed at the multi-track stage. Indeed if you are editing a live recording of speech or music, then there is no need to move into the multi-track mode. However, if what you are editing is to move forward then think carefully about the way you store and name files. In the past, we have spent hours trying to find a small piece of audio tape that has fallen onto the floor but, more recently we have also spent hours trying to find a file that has been lost in the computer or on a huge hard drive. We have a system which seems to work, but it is specific to Cool Edit although the principle could be used elsewhere. Like so many things always try new ideas on a small job to start with.

In the illustration below you can see what you will see in your computer monitor. There is a timeline from left to right which has pairs of tracks since this job is being recorded and edited in stereo with pairs of tracks. This is essentially a multi-track approach which in Cool Edit is contained in a separate part of the computer programme to the detailed editing of the separate tracks. You will note that the patches have in them wave forms that show the variation in amplitude of the recording. The height of the wave will also give you a clue as to the amplitude or volume of the sound. As we have said, it is as well to 'normalise' the tracks so that they do not go over the top or disappear into the background. This process will take the peaks within the percentage of the acceptable volume and bring all of the file amplitude with it. After a short while you will begin to recognise your pieces of sound by their shape as well as their sound.

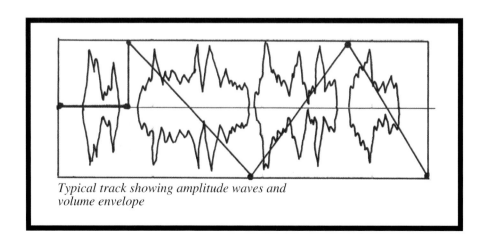

*Typical track showing amplitude waves and volume envelope*

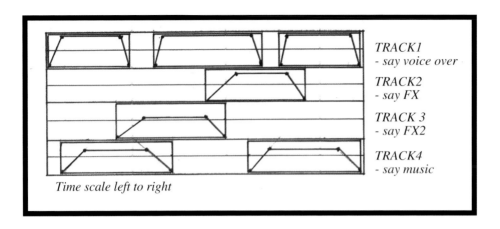

TRACK1
- *say voice over*

TRACK2
- *say FX*

TRACK 3
- *say FX2*

TRACK4
- *say music*

*Time scale left to right*

In the sketch you will see a simplification of the screen shot above. Try to think this way. Cool Edit can raise 126 tracks in its multi-track version. In order to make up a particular sound it is possible that several tracks will be needed but there will probably be only three main tracks. In fact it is generally accepted that except for compound tracks, that is tracks made up with various sounds to make a final sound, two or three tracks are as much as the mind can take in. An example might be that in order to put together the sound of an army marching one file of one set of footsteps can be repeated many many times to sound like thousands. In fact Walter Murch in an article on sound for film says that two and a half tracks is as much as one can take in. Apart from compound tracks we agree with him.

You will note that we have written the file numbers on the chequerboard inserts AND the file number of the main multi-track file. In practice we spend more time chasing files than we wish. At least if the files are listed and the folders from which they come noted, there is a chance that they can be found again even if the computer decides to lose them.

In order to obtain a correct balance for the effect it may be necessary to process the effect to make best use of it. For example if our effect is of the ambience of an environment with birds plus motor cars, which is typical situation, the lower frequencies might need to be reduced.

## Joining

We have discussed the sections and their juxtaposition but an important aspect of the joining is the form of the join. These sound blocks join together and to butt joint them, that is to place one next to another, can be an auditory shock and so the fade was invented. The basic parts that we are going to put together might be:

Music

Dialogue
Sound effects
Silence

These need to fit together or overlap in various ways. In the end you will have to develop your own vocabulary.

We can list the types of join and their use will depend on what is being joined to what. Or what follows what.:

A simple butt joint - brutal
A fade out followed by a fade in - gentler
A fade out followed by silence followed in turn by a fade in – one effect after another
A fade out followed by a butt joint – a dramatic insert
A fade in followed by a steady section followed by a fade out – used where a sound effect is inserted.
Overlapping fades – more complex events.

And, of course, variations on this idea which can perhaps be best illustrated as diagrams that can be applied to our 'chequerboard'. Using the programmes that we have suggested it is possible to shape a sound within a sound envelope in effects and then apply this to the multi track section of the programme.

### Labelling and Storage
The audio files need to be carefully labelled and stored. We transfer to and store all our audio work on a Maxtor Hard Disc with USB connection (around £150). This has a capacity of 160 gigabytes. However, it is wise to keep the original discs or tapes as well. This hard disc has thousands of files on it so the designation of files needs to be carefully thought through otherwise the files will never be found again. We work at standard CD specification so that audio material can be stored on CD, via the programme CD Architect 5.0. It is worth remembering that one minute of CD quality, that is 44.1 kHz sampling rate, takes ten megabytes of storage.

CD Architect 5.0 is then opened up and cleared (file > new). The files are then called up from 'media pool' and placed on the time-line making sure that the first file is set at two seconds into the CD otherwise the CD will not be to 'red book' standard.

When all the files are in order the master can be burned on the computer or on a separate CD burner using CD Architect.

The master can be duplicated on a CD duplicator using white faced thermal printing blanks and then labelled in a TDK thermal printer LPCW

100 (about £100). There are other types of blanks if alternative printing processes are used, such as an inkjet printer like Epson Photo R300. The duplicator is an M Tech 5 disc machine (about £600). The master is placed in the top slot and it prints and checks the five CD blanks in about two minutes. There are now small machines that will duplicate and print the labels of CDs at 50 at a time at very reasonable prices. Since there is a growing market for small productions then this is very important.

The duplicated CDs can be used in portable CD players, or sold, or sent out for outreach work. Putting on one side the processing cost, the blanks cost in the region of 45p each when bought as a 'cake' of 50 but the cost is less for a greater bulk. Obviously there are other costs but if many CDs are made from one master then the unit processing cost is reduced. Where more copies are needed, for outreach for example, there are contractors who will supply copies at a much lower cost. These copies are generally burned onto CD-R stock. Usually the smallest order for these contractors to accept is 25. For large commercial production a glass master is made and the CDs are pressed but this is not economic until the numbers are around 1000 copies although packages for 500 seem to be possible but not very economic.

[1] Studio Audio Digital Editing system.

# *Sound Use and Presentation*

### Introduction

It is stating the obvious to say that audio needs playback systems. These come in a confusing range of types, sizes and models. Under the Innovative Actions programme, funded through Advantage West Midlands, the Trust has been looking at this bewildering array and trying to make sense of them. These playback systems are an essential part of a visit for visually impaired visitors as audio is sometimes the only way they can receive information about a site or venue.

If we consider the design of a core system that will deal with interactive and navigational needs we need to consider its use by a group of people who do not and indeed should not need to understand the electronics. The operational parameters of the equipment need to be very clear. Thus for this reason we need to have simple feed in and out system such as a CD in and audio out. Using WAV or MP3 could also be organised but not much more at this stage.

We have had some bitter experiences with organisations making their own equipment that does not agree with other equipment. It is unrealistic to expect a blind person to have, say, six different systems in a suitcase ready for use. It would be much better if we have to have different systems they should operate with a set of a given national, or even international, performance specifications.

There is already a history of the use of sound in exhibitions. In the pre-technical past there were sounds at fairs and circuses. There were barkers trying to attract attention and circus bands. Even shops and market stalls had the sound of the barrow boy calling out his wares and this goes back to the beginning of selling. We have evidence of the cries built into pieces of music.

At the point where technology comes forward sound is used in a different and more sophisticated way. In 1889 Thomas Alva Edison had a stand at the Paris Exposition where visitors could listen to his recordings. By 1915, the Panama Pacific Exposition in San Francisco had a twelve hundred seat amphitheatre revolving around a huge scale model of the canal as the audience listened to a recorded commentary delivered directly to them via telephone receivers.

# Sound Use and Presentation

The market has expanded greatly over the years since the Sony Walkman was produced in 1979.[1] From this exciting, revolutionary beginning, personal audio technology has moved from tape to CD to solid state and MP3. Having discussed the production of sound, the question remains as to how this will and can be used. Over the last few years there have been several developments in this area and there is a growing awareness that sound can and should be used.

### Research into Playback Systems

The Trust has been able to buy a range of different types of systems, from *Talking Tin Lids* to a personal CD player for under £10 to the latest *Pickup* from Dataton which costs many hundreds of pounds. We needed to test these for ease of loading the material if they were to be useful to people who wanted to produce their own audio. We also tested them out with visually impaired users to see how they managed with the controls and to see if the controls were set out in a logical way. There will be on-going testing which will be put on the Dog Rose Trust website.

While technology has made many things easier for people with visual impairments, it has also enabled manufacturers to make their machines smaller which in turn makes it harder to manipulate the controls if you have poor vision or mobility difficulties. Most personal machines also have a range of options for recording and playback. This especially applies to mini-disc recorders; if you cannot see the screen which tells you which option you have selected, perhaps inadvertently, then your recording could be spoiled. Personal CD players have many different modes for programming the CD, most of which are unnecessary to play a straightforward audio CD. Look at Peter Bosher's guidelines on playback machines in the next chapter.

We have not tested out cassette machines, which still have their place, but their days are probably numbered. It is now more expensive to duplicate and do on-body printing on to a cassette than it is on a CD.

Generally speaking the sound quality from these machines is good. However, the more you try to get on them with compressed sound, the lower the quality will be. We have only included one multi-level 'wand-type' machine, which has options for listening to further tracks. This is because of the practices of the industry where most machines, and some of them are good, are tied to a company which will also want to produce and update the audio for you at prices you cannot afford. Sometimes there is a high cost for the annual licence for the programme. While these machines do provide scope for a large amount of information, the recharge systems for most of these machines adds considerably to the cost. These units usually come in multiples of ten which may be more than you need.

Black Box do supply a wand-type machine, *Tourmate*, with no strings attached which is a good one, except that the layout of the numbers is two parallel lines on the keypad, not the telephone form which visually impaired people are used to. If you feel that this is not a problem, then ask Blackbox about it; their details are below.

Mobile phone tours are now being used for trails in towns and countryside. The site sets up a phone line through a third-party service provider. The user dials a given number which will take then into the options for the tour. The obvious advantage of this system is that it is relatively cheap to set up with little or no running costs. It is also very useful for open-access sites with no visitor centre or reception to hand out machines. Some of the revenue generated from the calls comes back to the site and the average cost to the mobile phone user is considered to be about £3. As teenagers, a notoriously hard market to reach, are regular mobile phone users this is a good way to engage them. Further developments are taking place where mobile phones can receive information directly off the web.

The disadvantages for visually impaired users are the accessibility problems connected with a mobile phone, although the 'talking' mobile phones are a great step forward but still expensive. The system also excludes people who do not use mobile phones for a variety of reasons, and these are often people with disabilities, so a positive outreach policy needs to be in place to make sure they can obtain the information about the site.

An audio tour relayed in this way should give general information about the site in order for a visually impaired visitor to have some idea of the layout and what is accessible to them. The inclusion of mobility details would help people who use wheelchairs.

The concept of space in our curious world is governed by the attenuation of sound. We have to be close to each other to hear. It is a normal part of an audible conversation to say 'I am sorry I did not hear you'. Essentially, it is the inverse square law that the further from the source, the less is the acoustical energy. It is fascinating to be among deaf friends conversing in sign language in a large room because this law that sound reduces communication according to distance does not apply. With sign language it is possible to converse at much larger distances, possibly 30 metres. Space in this case is different. Sadly, we do not speak British Sign Language but we wish we had time to learn it.

It seems that there is some similarity between this and an interesting experiment carried out in Japan and Canada. The use of low-powered radio transmitters has been developed, not as originally for the control of toy cars but as a simple communication system between people. Although the inverse square law will apply, the distance will be larger and visual barriers will have less effect. You will remember that Isaac Newton noticed that the further you are away from the source of energy the less energy will reach you and did some sums. A wooden partition is unlikely to stop radio waves for example. In the book <u>Radio Rethink – art, sound and transmission</u>,[2] there are many exciting essays that describe the use of 'mini FM transmitters' for communication between people and local bases, which could be called radio stations although the interesting concepts of these centres is explored. One particular essay by Tetso Kaqawa deserves attention as indeed do others in this book. The application to our work is obvious.

### Hyper Sonic Sound

Described as being able to 'focus sound where you want it and no place else'.[3] The basis of this technique is to carry audio frequency 'sound' on ultrasonic frequencies which 'decodes' when it hits a person. Although it has not been tried, it could be very useful in terms of navigation and wayfinding. There seem to be two firms in the US that manufacture these speakers. Finding the way in an environment is a problem for blind and partially sighted persons as well as for sighted people and this technique might be a help. Sadly this technique will probably be used for advertising which could confuse everyone and take away from its usefulness. It might, for example, be useful in a free flow situation such a railway station concourse where paths cannot be otherwise defined.

Other factors need to considered in the presentation of sound.

### Power

The cost of getting power to places on site in the countryside is high; this is usually possible in buildings, but not on open or isolated sites. There are some solar powered audio machines but security of the panel and batteries could be a problem. This is a field that needs developing and we hope to follow it up. Checking, charging and changing batteries in any machines on a regular basis could also be difficult with venues with a small staff.

### Portable or Static

According to your needs you have to decide whether you want a 'carry around' machine or a static system which has sensors that trip the sound and can match the exhibit or place. The Pickup is a combination of both but we have not included more information about sensors as their availability is limited at present and they are expensive. Some of the wand-type machines have the ability to trip sound and video as you enter the space.

### Public or Private Sound?

### Public Sound

Loudspeakers are bulky and often not very good to look at so it is best to think of where they need to go early on in the design. Recent designs of flat speakers are very useful and some speakers are designed to be placed outside and are disguised as rocks. What is important is to make sure that the speakers do justice to the sound you have so carefully created. Cheap tinny speakers will produce cheap tinny sound. Sound overlaps and obscures other sounds so this must be carefully thought through. It is worth thinking in terms of absorbent surfaces and shadowing.

An overall background sound suitably filtered can cover traces of other sounds and can give an overall feeling to the exhibition or environment. An example might be the recording of birds in a subject that is rural. Different recordings that have been processed in the same way can be used adjacent to each other if necessary.

The main focused 'frames' of sound can be designed to be intermittent and not conflict. They can be timed, started by pressing buttons, by PIRs or other devices. Modern controls are a great help with this. The use of 5:1 stereo for the frames could be very useful as it gives more tracks that can be played. Specially written music for the situation can be of great advantage. In restaurants this is done with music but this can in itself be intrusive. As in every sound situation everything needs careful soundscaping.

An alternative is the parabolic reflector which can be placed above an exhibit and as the visitor steps under it, it isolates the sound to within a small area under the parabola.[4]

### Private Sound

Sound spill can be a problem. With a headset, there is virtually no spill. By this we can define situations where a personal headset is used and the sound is private to that particular person. Most of the above points apply. However, it is possible to control sound so that it becomes more private. Sound absorbent screens can be designed into situations and absorbent surfaces can be added so that there is less sound spill and in some situations the sound can become virtually private. Another system that makes sound virtually secret is the use of overhead parabolic reflectors. There are several of these on the market and they vary in effectiveness but they can be very useful. For example where there are a row of exhibits and no way to provide sound these devices can be used overhead quite effectively. This is the reverse of the parabolic reflector used with microphones for picking up distant natural sounds such as bird calls.

With sound whose volume is carefully balanced against other sound there are problems when the noise level from visitors rises. Clearly, there is a gamut of situations where at the one end there is little background sound with very few people to one where, perhaps on a bank holiday, the museum or gallery is crowded and the sound level is very high. Given this situation there has to be a sound level monitor that can vary the output of various devices to balance the sound.

Some people comment that they do not like headsets as they cut them off from their surroundings. However, this only really happens with professional enclosed headsets. The headsets should be stereo as these give better spacial information to blind people.

### Infra-red transmission

The Trust used an infra-red transmitter and headsets on its first Dorcas Project, the interactive plan of York. This system was also used for the Glasgow Cathedral Precinct Model. This is a useful system when a listener needs to move around a model or plan, but you have to remember that the sun also emits infra-red and so this produces difficulties if it is placed near a window.

The results of the Trust's research on playback systems are given below. We hope that this will help you to decide which system is best for your venue.

### Research on Playback Systems

These are in no particular order but were probably written up as they were bought.

**Chatterbox by Spotlight Display**, 208 Winsford Avenue, Coventry, CV5 9NB. Telephone: 024 7667 7667.

Spotlight Display makes two kinds of Chatterbox: the new style for indoor use and one for outdoor use. The indoor model is powered by 4 AA 1.5v batteries and outdoor by a 'lantern' battery. There is no mains option. The loading procedures are either directly into the microphone of the machine or via line input socket which is an optional extra; the latter gives better quality. The length of playback time is 1 minute. Speakers are the only listening option.

**Uturn Wind-up audio unit by BlackBox Av**, 25 Aberafan Road, Baglan Industrial Estate, Port Talbot, SA12 7DJ. Telephone: 01639 767007.

This is a very useful audio unit which is powered by turning the handle; no battery and no mains and sound from speakers. The Size is 270mm x 380mm x 105mm deep. The loading is from MP3 computer files via a programme supplied by BlackBox and a Sandisk card reader on to a memory card (as in a digital camera). The length of the playback time is 2 minutes each way you turn the handle but can be longer if sound is put on at a different compression. However, in practice 1.40 minutes is long enough to turn. If you let it stop, then it goes back to the start. There also variations with selections being able to be made which is very useful for additional languages.

We have discussed writing for these wind-up audio units in Scripting but this does need further information. Avoid music or distinctive sound effects at the beginning; if the person winding stops then each time they start again, this same tune or noise will be heard again

An illustration of the machine and instructions as to what to do can help. We have produced metal-etched plates with letters, Braille and a diagram to go alongside the unit. The interpretation boards at the Avalon Marshes incorporate the audio units and the panel alongside them gives instructions and contents.

A sloping position makes it easier to turn, at a level which can be reached by a range of abilities. We have illustrated one we supplied to the RSPB at Ham Wall in Section 5.03.

Fitting needs to be firm and secure. It is important that the back of the machine is protected so that the sound card cannot be removed by unauthorised people. As they cost about £14 each, plus reloading with sound, this is an important consideration.

BlackBox also make the Envoy SB2 Solid State Sound store for exhibitions and displays. It is powered by electricity and loaded from computer files via a computer programme supplied and card reader. Listening via speakers or headsets or PIR. (Passive Infra-red) We are using two in Coalport China Museum for an interactive display so we will report back on them via the Dog Rose Trust website.

**Speaking Sign from RNIB**, Model No. DH124; RNIB, www.rnib.org.uk. See Shopping Section. Powered by 4 AA batteries with a mains option. Loading procedure is  directly into microphone; machine must be kept still while recording. Length of playback time is 20 seconds. The volume control is a milled wheel on the side. Speaker only, activated by PIR or can be a repeated message. Can be wall mounted, optional swivel bracket. An inexpensive way of providing short messages. The RNIB also make another **Speaking Sign**, DH154. This is mains powered and is loaded directly on to the chip or via microphone input. Playback time is 4 minutes and the listening options are speaker only. Activated by push button. Wall mounted.

*Talking Tin Lids* also from the RNIB. Model number DK90. This is designed to do what it says: fit on the lid of tins. It is powered by a small round battery. To load speak directly into the microphone. It plays back for about 8-10 seconds but at £3 is the cheapest thing around for a very short message.

### Nomad Internet Audio Player Muvo MP3 player from Creative Labs.

This very small player can be found at big electrical stores and is powered by AAA batteries. It is loaded with MP3 files off computer via a programme supplied on CD. It stored 64mb of sound, that is up to 20 songs equal to 80 minutes. Listening is via a headset. A neckstrap is supplied. The controls are small and fiddly.

### Nakamichi 3 disc CD Sampling changer, model: MB-K300s from Micro Video Systems, 24 Cobham Road, Ferndown Industrial Estate, Wimbourne, BH21 7NP. Telephone: 01202 861696.

This is a no-nonsense machine that takes 3 CDs which can be accessed in any order. Listening is by headset only on armoured cable. Two can be fitted. This machine is used in record stores so is very robust. It is ideal for stores of audio information such as oral history.

### Personal CD players

The Trust has been trying out personal CD players as they are cheap and simple to operate. The main problem with them is the small size of the control buttons and how they can be mixed up with function buttons which do not need to be touched for a simple audio play back. The CD players the Trust has looked at have been cheap, available at nationwide electrical stores and have buttons which are reasonably easy to access and are in a logical sequence. However, models change quickly and there seems to be a desire to get controls as small as possible. The only really reliable method of finding the right machine is to keep looking and try out possible suitable models with people who are visually impaired. As with all playback systems, staff awareness of the function of the machines is a key to a visually impaired visitor being able to successfully access the sound.

Look for machines that follow Peter Bosher's guidelines: clear separated controls, easy to find buttons, uncomplicated layout. The Expanium CD/MP3 player by Philips came out well with its function buttons along the top of the machine. Although the machine has many functions only three of the buttons along the top are necessary for its operation. A large button for start and pause, a smaller one for stop and twin ones for changing tracks. Visual display for tracks and other information. This machine will also play MP3 put on to CD if you have the facilities to do this which gives longer playback time. The machine 'beeps' when buttons are pressed which is useful, the only one we have found in the lower price range that does this. They are all powered by AA batteries.

**Pickup Audio Guide by Dataton, from Orbital**, 57 Acre Lane, Brixton, London SW2 5TN. Telephone: 0207 501 6868.

Recently we came across a Swedish system with the name of Pickup that seems to be very suitable for self operation and for blind visitors. It is not our job to advertise products, but we are so pleased to come across this particular product we will describe it in more detail. It is good to find a self-operated system where the sound can be designed and altered easily using a sensor. The hand set is very light and weighs only 65 grams and contains rechargeable batteries and a Smart media card. There are two sockets for headsets which is good for two people walking round an exhibition together. Besides the handset there are other accessories such as a charging fitting, a card-loading unit that is connected to one's computer by USB connection. The handset is triggered by a small infra-red 'hotspot' transponder which can be placed adjacent to the object under discussion.

The player has to be pointed at the transponder which then starts to play. However, it is possible to miss and for a blind person this is a definite possibility. The Swedes have used a system of placing the transponder on the ceiling above the object. It might be a useful idea to place a tactile mat next to the object so that the blind person knows when to point the player upwards. Clearly, with a sensor system there are many possibilities.

The hotspot handbook quite rightly divides the preparation of the audio guide into two distinct parts. First, to script, record and edit the sound in the computer. Second, to transfer the files thus prepared to MP3 coding and these are then placed on the 'smartmedia' card.

**Guide Man Wand type audio guide from Ophrys Systems, France supplied by Advanced Thinking Systems** (ATS), 1 South Lane, Clanfield, Waterlooville, Hampshire, PO8 0RB. Telephone: 023 9259 5000.

This is a solid state machine with a keypad and a slight bump on the 5. It has rechargeable batteries from mains and an individual charger can be supplied. Loading is from computer files via a programme which is supplied. Listening is from its own speaker or from a headset. It has a neckstrap. There is no pressure from ATS to do the scripting and recording. Like all machines of this type, it will store many hours of sound.

[1] www.sony.net, Sony History.
[2] Edited by Daina Augaitis and Dan Lander, Radio Rethink – art, sound and transmission, Canada 1994, ISBN 0-920159-66-4.
[3] From the website of the American Technology Corporation; www.atcsd.com
[4] See www.sounddirections.co.uk.

# Guidelines for Designing Accessible Audio Guides
## by Peter Bosher

### Introduction

The aim of these guidelines is to define criteria for the design of audio-guides which will ensure that they are optimally usable and accessible for blind and partially-sighted people.

As part of the Talking Images project, RNIB, in collaboration with Resource (now MLA) and Vocaleyes, carried out an extensive accessibility audit of a wide range of venues where audio guides are in use. One of the key findings was the high degree of inconsistency and difficulty that visually impaired people found in using the equipment, even when the guides were supposedly designed specifically with them in mind.

The recommendations that follow have been based on the experiences of the people who carried out the audit, draw on existing good practice guidelines and are intended to give practical guidance for designing or adapting such equipment in future.

The vast majority of guides in current use are of the 'wand' type, and to avoid becoming too general and abstract, this article assumes that the guide will be in the form of a wand, with a numeric keypad giving random access to items that are stored in solid-state memory. Most of the principles should apply to other carriers such as CD, PDA's (Personal Digital Assistant) or adapted MP3 players, but the wand is the working model.

### General principles

### Layout

Controls should be grouped separately and made distinctive from each other. For example, the number-pad should be clearly separated from other controls, and should be at the top of the panel; the volume up/down buttons should be together, and separate from other groupings.

The number-pad should respect the convention of the telephone key-pad (1-2-3 on the top-row) since this is in far more common use than the computer/calculator layout.

### Visual Indications

• When symbols are used to represent functions or controls, then widely recognisable ones should be chosen.

• An easy-to-read font should be used for all display indications.

• Colour combinations must have a contrast (brightness) of 4.0 or greater. (See Appendix )

• There should be a clear colour and tone contrast between the buttons and the surrounding panel, and/or coloured 'circling' of buttons.

### Audible Indication

Feedback should be given to confirm that a button press has been accepted, or warn if it has not. If the unit is speech-enabled, then this feedback will be in the form of spoken prompts and confirmations of the button pressed. If not, then a simple system of tones or beeps, such as used in mobile phones, will be quite adequate. For example, a short discrete beep means that the press was accepted, and a longer harsher beep means that some sort of error occurred.

### Tactile Indication

• Buttons should be clearly distinguishable from the surrounding panel and from each other, so they should project, be hard plastic rather than rubber, and should give a firm positive click when pressed.

• Shaped buttons can help to confirm functions, such as arrows pointing right and left for moving forward and back, or up and down for volume.

• On the numeric keypad, the widely accepted convention of putting a dot on the number 5 should be respected.

### Functions and Controls

In order to navigate effectively within and between a large number of recorded items of variable length, the following controls are essential, and must have dedicated buttons (not dual function). No existing guide has yet met these requirements.

• Play: starts an item from the beginning when it is selected.

• Stop: stops the item, ready for either re-play from the beginning, or entry of new item.

• Pause: pauses the item mid-way, and resumes when pressed again.

• Scroll forward/back: a group of two controls allowing forward or backward scrolling with audible movement (sometimes called cue and revue).

• Clear/Cancel: returns to default state if you make a mistake.

All the guides reviewed had some combination of these controls, but often had dual-function buttons, or missed some of the essential functionality.

## Other Considerations

### Listening Modes

There should be two ways of listening to the audio: through the wand itself, in the style of a telephone handset, but also through stereo headphones for extended listening or when the audio and production quality are more critical, so a headphone socket is essential.

The type of headphones or earphones should be considered carefully. For example, in most visiting situations, it is important to be able to hear sounds in the environment clearly alongside the audio-guide, but there may be settings where it is important to reduce outside noise with closed or 'in-ear' designs.

### Carrying

Guides should be fitted with a cord or strap, to allow them to be carried round the neck so that hands are free when needed.

### Triggering of items

A number of systems, based on infra-red or radio control 'tags', or GPS location, make it possible for appropriate items to play automatically when the visitor passes the right point, or simply to indicate which item is nearby, so that it may be selected when desired. One of these systems should be used whenever possible, in view of the difficulty of knowing when you are near a numbered item.

### Multimedia Guides

New guiding techniques are constantly being developed, some current examples being multimedia workstations placed around venues, and portable multimedia devices (similar to PDA's) containing all the information content in memory. The principles in these guidelines should be applied to new carriers, in such a way that the information content, whether text, audio, or, where applicable, graphical, be made accessible to blind and partially sighted visitors.

**Appendix**

Display colours

The following are examples of colour combinations which will enhance (or detract from) visual clarity, for the majority of visually impaired people

Examples which enhance clarity:

First colour – Black; Second colour - Any light colour, especially
white     white or yellow.
First colour – White; Second colour – black, or Any dark colour
First colour - Light blue-green; Second colour - Dark purple
First colour - Light blue-green; Second colour - Dark red
First colour - Light green; Second colour - Dark purple
First colour - Light green; Second colour - Dark red
First colour - Light green; Second colour - Dark violet
First colour - Light yellow; Second colour - Dark purple
First colour - Light yellow; Second colour - Dark blue
First colour - Light yellow; Second colour - Dark violet
First colour - Light orange; Second colour - Dark blue
First colour - Light orange; Second colour - Dark violet

Poor examples which may reduce clarity

First colour - Light red (pink); Second colour - Dark green
First colour – Red; Second colour - Purple
First colour – Yellow, Second colour - White/light grey
First colour - Lavender (light purple - pastel colour)
Second colour - Pink (light red - pastel colour)

Peter Bosher is an adaptive technology consultant and trainer specialising in Internet access, and Chairman of BCAB, the British Computer Association of the Blind. He worked as Project Manager with RNIB promoting the benefits of access to electronic information, and has continued this work within the Web Accessibility Initiative, part of the World Wide Web Consortium.

## *Oral History*

### Introduction

*These stories, memories, and traditions are powerful expressions of community life and values. They anchor us in the larger whole, connecting us to the past, grounding us firmly in the present, giving us a sense of identity and roots, and belonging and purpose.*

From The Smithsonian Folklife and Oral History Interviewing Guide.[1]

Oral history is a section of a total spectrum of sound recording and this is just a brief overview. Oral history is recording the memories of people, generally older people but there is no reason why they should not be younger people. However, it is information about the past that is being recorded, not thoughts about present day events.

Remember that the stories and memories you collect are valuable not necessarily because they represent historical facts, but because they embody human truths - a particular way of looking at the world.[2]

This is the Trust's experience of recording oral history and what we have learnt. We are fairly new to it but hope to do further recordings and become more experienced.

### Use of the recordings

Before starting an oral history project, you should have some idea of how you want to use the recordings that are collected. You need to consider if you want to use them in a historical exhibition or display. Do you want to make a CD about your area which includes some oral history? Short extracts can be used effectively on playback systems such as the Uturn wind-up audio units.

When Priory Gardens in Coventry were redeveloped and landscaped, a Visitor Centre was built by the site of the former cloister. A path and trees were laid on the site in front of the building with a sound installation. This sound installation, in the form of tall poles with speakers, plays tracks with people from Coventry telling the story of their lives. The sound is not much louder than a whisper; you can just hear it if you stand under the poles. But as you walk around the area, you catch snatches of sentences and words, just as you would if you were walking around the city.

If the recordings are going to be made public, as these are, make sure everyone knows that before they start and make it clear what you might want to use the recordings for; they may want to say some things differently! You will need their permission with a signed consent form but this can be done at the end of the interview. For the actual interview prepare a list of subjects, but also be prepared to go off in different directions if they sound interesting. Respect the confidential things that people might tell you.

Discuss the subjects that you want to cover with possible interviewees and choose topics that will narrow the field, otherwise the interview could be too diffuse or take too long. The Trust went to the Day Centres in Ellesmere and talked to the people there and asked who had memories about the subjects we needed information on. In this case, we principally wanted childhood memories of playing in and by water of the Mere but one thing led to another and with little prompting we were able to record, at a later date, much useful information that we have been able to use in the audio guide. We then asked the organiser of the Ellesmere and District Age Concern Day Centre to find out who really wanted to be interviewed and she came back with six names, all of whom proved to be 'stars' and thoroughly enjoyed themselves.

Keep people in touch. Send them copies of the interviews. CDs were sent to the Age Concern Day Centre in Ellesmere and they played these at one of their meetings. This provoked much comment and discussion among members.

In the long term, whatever the shorter term use of the recordings is, the master copies should be deposited with the local archives for future generations to enjoy and refer to. The storage of the masters is an important consideration. The medium used should be as up-to-date as possible, then it is the least likely to be obsolete quickly and will not, we hope, deteriorate. The Trust has a range of recording and playback equipment that is very out of date but has to be kept so that older recordings can be taken off; some of these only go back about twenty five years but have been superseded several times over. So check out the technology for storage and then decide on the method of recording.

### Recording equipment, transcripts and other requirements

The section on recording deals with equipment in more detail, but for straightforward recording the mini-disc is suitable at the moment, but there are not many models that have a microphone socket. Many can download sound from a computer or on the internet, but have no facilities for recording directly through a microphone. So make sure you get the right machine. One of the problems of a mini-disc recorder is the small size of the controls and the number of recording modes available. Using the wrong mode can reduce the technical quality to an unacceptable level. Check the controls and see what the screen is reading before starting. Place the machine where you can see the controls and know when you are coming to the end of the disc, tape or battery. Keep the machine running all the time; as soon as you turn it off, the interviewee will say something really important and may not want to repeat it.

Mini-discs are being superseded by solid state machines which are getting smaller and cheaper so it is necessary to be aware of the rapid changes taking place in this field. Richer Sounds[3] is a good source and also Hagger Electronics.[4] Recording devices are dealt with in more detail in other sections of this book.

Whatever method you decide, you will probably have to make a typed transcript of the material which is not an easy job and allowance has to be made for the cost of this. Without a typed transcript, it is difficult to edit the recordings and select out the pieces that are needed for an exhibition or to put the recordings together as a publication. If the material is audio only, then people who are deaf or hearing impaired are excluded so a printed transcript is necessary for them to read.

It may mean that your digital recording will have to be transferred to a Philips Cassette so that it can be put into a transcription machine. However, developments are taking place to make this job easier but at present a digital transcription machine is only made for the Olympus Voice Recorders. This may change.

It is important that the transcript reflects the structure of the dialect and the accents, although these are hard to type out but are so important as they are disappearing so fast. The transcripts must be true to the words as they are spoken. Listen to the recording and follow the transcript to get the full flavour of the person's voice and accent; this is especially important when you are editing or trying to find a particular piece of information. Recently we were trying to find information about a Coalport painter called Chivers. We saw a Mr Trip in the transcript and did not realise it was the same person until we listened to the recording.

The Smithsonian Guide gives a list of other items you should take along such as spare batteries – easy to forget – a notebook, pens or pencil, camera and film.

### Microphones and Recording
The Smithsonian Guide suggests practising on your family and friends before recording people you do not know well. Ask questions that will produce more complete answers rather than 'yes' and 'no' replies.

Take care with the microphone, which is best on a stand, when recording and make sure it does not get knocked or banged by gesturing hands. This is even more important when recording with people who might be nervous. If they are reading from notes or text make sure that they keep it away from the microphone so that it does not pick up rustling noises. Watch out for sounds that can irritate, such as keys or coins jingling in pockets, but if you stop people to point this out it can make them nervous. It is better to sort this out before you begin. Sit where the person being interviewed can see you but can still talk into the microphone. They will naturally want to answer your questions directly and will therefore look at you; if you are in a position which makes them turn away from the microphone then the recording will be unbalanced. If the microphone is hand-held, then keep it still. Outdoor recordings can pick up wind noise and rustle the diaphragm inside the capsule of the microphone, so watch out for this.

It is preferable to record people on their own, or with only one other person present who can be relied on to keep quiet. This is especially important if the recordings are to be used on audio guides, in exhibitions or other presentations. If there is a group, people will try to cap either other's stories or correct each other on facts and dates. The absolute accuracy of what you are recording is not the biggest issue; you are talking to people who remember it as they saw or experienced it. You can always check hard facts later.

Make sure you put people at their ease. Once happy with this and started, most people will talk easily and forget about the microphone. When you begin, say the date, who you are interviewing and who else is in the room and where you are – that will explain any additional sounds that may be in the background of the recording. Try and find a quiet room where you will not be disturbed or away from heavy traffic. Ticking clocks and crackling fires are homely regular sounds, but sounds such as door bells and barking dogs are intrusive.

When you have started the recording, remember not to intervene unless another question or change of subject is required. We have had to work with other people's recordings where the interviewer's interjections are intrusive and cannot be edited out as they are too close to the other voice. Try nods of encouragement instead.

It is very useful if the interviewee gets out photographs and talks about them and identifies the people in them, but this does not make for good audio as the listener does not know what is being discussed. Record a description of the photo. If any good stories or anecdotes connected with it are told, then ask if they can be repeated but with the inclusion of names, objects and places, rather than 'and this is my brother' or 'you see that house there'.

## Managing the Recordings

Accurate record keeping is vital to people who might want to use the recordings in the future. Label all the recordings with name of person interviewed, interviewer, date and place. As with other recordings logging the recording afterwards is very important. This procedure has been described in more detail elsewhere. Listen to the recordings, make a note of the time indicator of each subject talked about. Even if you transfer the recording to another medium where the numbering system may be different, then at least you have the relevant position of items you may want to use. You may think you will remember all the details, but believe us, a year ahead you will not!

If and when you transfer your recording to CD, do make sure that you put the PQs points in, that is labelling the tracks, and keep a note of what you have on each track. Otherwise you will get a 70 minute recording with no way of finding the exact bits you want. Also if you need to transfer the recording back into the computer to find a small section, all the recording will have to be fed on in order to do this. So small sections are easier to handle.

Be wary of promising to include other people's recordings; they may not be of the same quality as yours and it could take much time to improve them and find the pieces you want, especially if there is no transcript.

Finally, enjoy oral history recording. It is living history and you are a part of it.

## Further reference

Ken Howarth's Oral History, published by Sutton Publishing, 1998, is a comprehensive guide to the subject. The Smithsonian Guide covers the subject well in a short space and The Oral History Society has much useful information on its website www.oralhistory.org.uk and there are many other sites that are also helpful.

---

[1] Marjorie Hunt, The Smithsonian Folklife and Oral History Interviewing Guide, Smithsonian Institute, 2003. www.folklife.si.edu.

[2] The Smithsonian Folklife and Oral History Interviewing Guide, page 2.

[3] Richer Sounds is a wonderful chain of no-nonsense audio equipment, usually tucked away in unfashionable parts of the town. www.richersounds.com Julian Richer, who started the chain, set up the Persula Foundation which gives starter grants to small charities. This Foundation gave the Dog Rose Trust one of its first donations 10 years ago and so we have a soft spot for this firm who have a reputation for exemplary management.

[4] www.hagger.co.uk

The Trust does not necessarily endorse these two firms but they have proved very useful and helpful to us

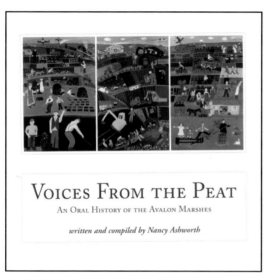

*Oral history is the basis of a true history*

*Visual Ears, Aural Eyes*
*A Cross Sensory Approach to*
*Design Education*
*by Eric Somers*

### Educating the Visual and Aural Designer

Educators in the visual and aural arts often misunderstand the education required for applied designers in contrast to that for fine artists. While fine artists often base their work on self expression, playful novelty, or conscious copying from an established tradition, the applied artist is usually in the position of designing a structure which communicates information to meet the needs of an external client. Thus training for the designer, whether a designer of sound or image, must include learning to think of visual and aural structures as solutions to design problems. Recently I have come to realize that an effective way to teach this kind of thinking is to ask students of sound design to analyze works of visual art then translate those structures and symbols into aural equivalents and, conversely, to ask visual design students to analyze sound compositions and use those structures as organizing principles for visual designs. Mladen Milicevic [15] has called this process "semiotic transformation."

### The Function of the Designer

There is a great tendency to confuse the role of the designer with that of either the fine artist or the stylist. The term "designer" is often applied to the stylist. Most properly thought of, the information designer is a problem solver or information "architect" who takes ideas or information developed by a client and puts it into a form which will communicate effectively. A graphic designer takes text and images which communicate information about a business, for example, and creates a publication which presents the information clearly and interestingly to the reader. The stylist, though often confused with the designer, usually takes a design already produced by an original designer and re-shapes or decorates it to make it more novel or individualistic. Thus a creator of "designer" jeans does not really design a piece of clothing which functions more effectively than the original Levi Strauss product of a century ago, but creates a more novel variation of the original design. Such a "designer" is most properly called a "stylist." The fine artist may develop his or her work in a variety of ways. Some artists consciously copy the tradition of a certain genre of art. Others treat art as a form of free self-expression and create works meaningful to themselves, but which sometimes are not meaningful to others without explanation. Others may try to challenge the viewers' or listeners' expectations or perceptions with art forms that are perplexing or shocking.

# *Visual Eyes, Aural Eyes*

### Visual and Aural Imagination

Clearly the designer of a visual or aural structure must understand the information to be communicated then develop a concept for an effective presentation of that information. Ideally this should be done by understanding the nature of perception in the viewer/listener and developing an idea about how the information to be communicated could be designed for successful perception.

Often art education and design practice fail in meeting this ideal. Too often design is copying of a look, a sound, indeed a "style," and applying it to a problem which may or may not be suited to the solution. One only has to look at the many copy-cat confusing web sites to see this phenomenon, or listen to much popular music. Yet real design progress requires original conception, not ornamentation or augmentation.

### The Integration of the Senses

There is an inherent integration of the human senses as noted by Sergei Eisenstein [6], Erich M. von Hornbostel [20], Oliver Sacks [18] and others. The experience of one sense can, at a minimum, remind one of a sensation of another sense. For example, when most people hear someone talking on the radio, they develop a mental picture of the appearance of that person. William Gaver [7] has noted that in everyday perception of sound in the environment people tend to visualize a sound by associating it with the source they believe produced it. In the most extreme form of sense integration, synesthesia, a person exposed to stimulation of one sense actually experiences the physical sensations of another. Richard Cytowic [4] has documented cases in which people actually see colours when hearing music and feel shapes when tasting food. But true synesthesia is a neurological condition. My pedagogy is an attempt to make use of the inherent "everyday" integration of the senses (in Gaver's sense) in order to allow sense experience of one form to promote creative thinking in another.

### Thinking Visually and Aurally

The idea of an artist studying more than one art form in order to derive first principles is not new. The painter Wassily Kandinsky wrote "One art must learn how another uses its method, so that its own means may than be used according to the same fundamental principles, but in its own medium." He added that "The natural result of this work is a comparison of the elements of one art with those of another. Music is found to be the best teacher." [10] Though perception and creative thinking are certainly related, there is a vast difference between the value placed on visual experience and on aural perception.

Scholars studying the anthropology of communication, especially Edmund Carpenter [3], Marshall McLuhan [14], Walter Ong [16] and David Berlo [2] have noted that literate cultures tend to emphasize sight over the other senses. Western societies, especially, have tended to privilege the sense of sight since the widespread adoption of literacy made possible by the printing press. In such cultures people equate seeing with thinking and use visual terms as a kind of code to describe understanding of thought: "I see your point," "Can you make yourself more clear?" "Your logic is fuzzy," "I get the picture," "Seeing is believing, etc. Cultures which do not equate seeing with thinking would have difficulty decoding such statements in a meaningful way since they do not share the same code.

Cultures which do not have a strong tradition of literacy develop an aural culture with its own particular characteristics and code. In these cultures terms related to thinking often get expressed in aural terms. For example, "I hear you" is often used to mean "I understand you." Though people from most literate cultures would rather go deaf than blind, people from oral cultures feel deafness to be a greater hardship than blindness. Non-literate cultures tend to believe something heard over something seen. Even Plato expressed skepticism and distrust of the then-new medium of writing, believing it to be inferior to word-of-mouth communication. [17] Speech in non-literate cultures tends to make use of several aural and visual elements of expression: the meaning of the words chosen ("diction"), the vocal inflections of the person saying the words, and the body movements, facial positions and gestures of the speaker. Speakers in non-literate cultures, including children in all cultures who have not yet learned to read, tend to use many inflections and gestures. But as people become educated in literate cultures they are often taught to "modulate" their vocal inflections, stand still as they talk, and not use gestures. Thus speech becomes reduced to the single element which can be coded by writing or printing: the meaning of the words themselves. [3, 14,16]

David Berlo [2] and Tony Schwartz [19] remind us that meanings do not reside in words, images, or sounds, but in the cultural experience of each reader-viewer-listener. Thus perceptions bring to mind meanings which may not be the same for each recipient of the same act of communication. The complexity of meaning is apt to be greater than the symbol used for communication. Schwartz writes "A listener or viewer brings far more information to the communication event than a communicator can put into his program, commercial or message." [19] Maribeth Back [1] has taken a similar approach to sound design, letting a well chosen sound evoke a deeper cultural meaning. Miroslav Malik, [12] a Czech-Canadian designer of multimedia exhibits for worlds fairs and other multicultural festivals, often used a "mosaic" design approach in which many different images are presented at once drawn from the cultural backgrounds of different cultures. Viewers from each culture are then able to decode at least part of the message. The ability for a sound, word or image to evoke a complex thought allows for very powerful communication with a minimum of means or a narrow channel. But such associations can also lead to "stereotyping" in which a symbol always brings to mind a single instance of what could otherwise be a multidimensional thought. These symbols become icons that are not analyzed for the information they contain but which simply redirect the perceiver to his/her own stored meaning. Indeed, some people try to find symbolic associations in certain kinds of messages where none are intended. A common example is the preoccupation naive art viewers often have trying to figure out what a non-representational work of art is "supposed to be."

## Context and Imagination

Designer Steve McCallion relates an assignment a professor of his gave in architecture school: "to create an innovative office tower. He insisted that we not reference outside resources — no books, no photographs. . . The result? A depressingly familiar display of foam core and hot glue." [13] Given a lack of context, designers often resort to the stereotypical thinking mentioned above. They tend to recall a stored impression and make it an "original" design by changing small details. They become stylists. By greatly changing the context of a design problem it is much more likely that original designs, not "styles," will result. Thus if one asks a class simply to design a "car" most will create a stylistic variation of the typical car. If however, one stipulates that the car has to be able to cross water and also drive up sand dunes, then the discontinuity of the new context will more likely produce innovative thinking. The architect John M. Johansen has produced some highly original experimental designs — the kind McCallion may have been seeking from his students — by setting for himself some imaginative recontextualizing problems: a structure which hangs between twin skyscraper towers and is supported by them; a theatre which uses magnetic levitation to move people and objects; buildings which "adapt" themselves to changing environmental conditions similar to adaptation in biological forms, etc. [9]

## Discontinuity as an Agent of Contextual Change

Eric Hoffer [8], Peter Drucker [5] and others have discussed how discontinuity leads to innovation. Immigrants to the U.S. have a better-than-average record of success as inventors, business entrepreneurs, and artists. The change of social context leads these immigrants to creative thinking more easily than someone brought up within the culture. Dealing with the discontinuity of change seems to produce creative thinking. Discontinuities can be caused by various forces. Many young people in the 1960s became disillusioned with certain social structures and political policies in the U.S. and sought innovative changes. Writers and painters often travel to consciously experience discontinuities which might awaken them to new ideas and images. In my teaching of visual and aural design I have produced discontinuity as a stimulant to creative thinking by asking students to "re-frame" their visual perceptions in aural terms and to re-frame their aural perceptions in visual terms. This process of semiotic transformation involves the conversion of the symbols and structure of one sensory medium to those of another. It is an attempt to re-integrate the senses so that auditory experience will play a role in visualization and visual experience will play a role in aural thinking.

## Semiotic Transformation as a Stimulant to Design Thinking

There is a tradition of using art of one form as "inspiration" for another. Some teachers of fine art play music in the classroom and ask students to "paint what they feel." A similar approach is used by some writing teachers. In music there is the tradition of "program music" which is intended to bring to mind a specific experience. Thus in Beethoven's Sixth Symphony we hear passages intended to remind us of a storm, of villagers playing, etc. Lest we miss the intent Beethoven thoughtfully annotated the score. The pedagogy being presented here is not related to any of those strategies. Its purpose is not to evoke shared cultural memory of certain images or experiences, nor is it intended to focus the student on his or her own "feelings." It is analytical and structural in nature. The student is not asked to "interpret" a sound or image, but to understand the nature of its elements and how they are related, then create an artwork in another medium which uses elements perceived to be of a similar nature arranged in a similar structure. What sounds are similar to certain pictorial elements, and what pictorial representations would be good "translations" of sound elements, are decisions the student designer must make. The result then is not self expression (the domain of the fine artist) but analytical problem solving (the domain of the true designer).

Sound Composition Based on Sonification of Visual Experience
In teaching a course in sound composition and musique concrète a few years ago I faced a problem similar to that of Steve McCallion's professor (see above). When I asked students to make sound compositions from "found sounds" recorded by them using a portable DAT recorder, I tended to either get compositions that were more or less random collections of sounds or else imitations of non-concrète music. Without a structural framework the students floundered. Since most of these students were media studies majors with no background in music composition, they could not rely on their understanding of the design of music to design these sound compositions. But each student had taken a foundations course in two dimensional visual design. As an experiment I took a abstract painting from the wall in my office and asked the sound design students each to create a sound composition equivalent to the visual work of art. I explained that the students were to study the visual art, break it down into separate visual elements, then find sounds equivalent to each element. Finally, they were to study the arrangement, or composition, of the elements on the canvas and arrange their sound elements so they seemed equivalent in time and sonic space to the arrangement in visual space of the visual elements.

This process of semiotic transformation greatly improved the structures of the student sound compositions. In the following semesters we repeated the assignment successfully using visual works by a number of artists including Ann Wilson, Elsworth Kelly, Mark Rothko, Cy Twombley, and Jackson Pollack. Most recently I expanded the technique by showing two works of visual art and asking students to create a composition which begins with the form of the first visual design and gradually develops into a piece having the form of the second visual composition. In all cases the visual designs presented are non-representational in order to keep the assignment focused on form rather than on outside references. The results can be summarized as follows:

1. By limiting the composition to elements re-mapped from the visual model, students used fewer different sounds and made better use of repetition and variation.

2. Greater structural unity resulted from their "seeing" in the visual model how to think of the sound composition as a structure having multiple overlapping elements, not just a string of linear events.

3. In having to do the semiotic transformations, the students improved their analytical skills by learning how to break down visual and aural structures into individual elements.

4. By re-framing their visual experience aurally, the process of composition became focused in the brain, with the tools of the sound studio more a means of execution and less the means of composition itself.

### Visual Design Based on Visualization of Sound Experience

With the success of the sound composition project, I tested the possibility of reversing the process described above: to use sound composition as a pedagogical aid in teaching visual design. When presenting a student with a visual design problem one often finds that student solutions tend to copy other designs the student has seen. Indeed, some teachers actually show worked-out solutions as models. But this tends, in my view, to promote an emphasis on styling rather than design. I once joked that it would be better to teach visual design by radio (so students would have nothing visual to copy), but then realized that using sound might provide a way to train students to come up with original visualizations. Basing visual art on sound is not entirely a new concept in teaching art and design. In addition to the "listen and paint what you feel" exercises noted above, some major artists have experimented with the visualization of music. Paul Klee, in his Notebooks [11], describes exercises in basing visual art on musical rhythm and structure. He includes an analysis of a three part passage by Bach, but most of his analysis seems to have been made from the musical score rather than from the sound itself. For my teaching experiment, I designed electro acoustic sound clips produced by computer sound synthesis. As with the visual art using in my sound composition exercises, the sounds were non-representational. Again, too, the task was analytical: to find elements in sound that can be represented by equivalent visual structures. Students were trained to make the transformations a step at a time. Small, short sounds were produced and students asked to produce visualizations of them. Then longer sound passages were presented and students were given time to create drawing which represented both individual sound elements and the relationship of these elements to each other. In the most advanced stage four minute compositions were played and students were asked to create color paper cut-out collages representing the sound piece.

Several results were noted:

1. There was sufficient formal consistency between both the elements and overall compositions to indicate that the semiotic transformation from the sound events was genuine. An example can be seen in the three drawings below, each a different student representation of two plucked string notes, one louder than the other:

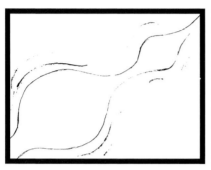  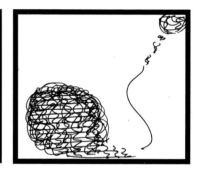

Figure 1: Student sketches by Bill Miller, Frank Corridori and Sophie Phan

2. Though nothing was ever said to the students about how the sounds were produced, many of the visual images showed a striking understanding from the aural perception alone. The examples below are based on a sound produced by modulation. The visual reproductions are clear representations of structures where one element controls (or modulates) another:

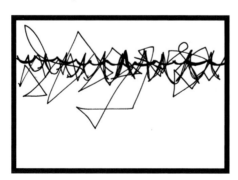 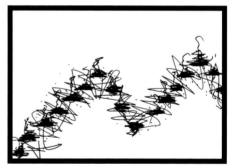

Figure 2: Student sketches by Jay Diesing, Ashley Benner and Frank Corridori

3. The students developed a remarkable ability to articulate their reasons for making visual choices based on their sound perceptions, thus supporting the analytical purpose of this pedagogy.

4. Many of the student visual compositions were interesting and original visual designs completely pleasing on a purely visual level.

5. Many of the students felt the experience helped them to understand the design process better.

**Conclusion**

With the specialization inherent in much of modern society, it is often easy to forget a past where an educated person made simultaneous contributions to several fields including visual art, theatre, music, the natural sciences and philosophy. In such a context the idea of using one's ears to aid visual thinking, or the reverse, would probably not have seemed unusual. Today, when someone asks "what do you do?" they sometimes seem unsatisfied by any answer that can't "peg" you to a certain narrow area of specialty.

Sometimes specialization is necessary. One probably cannot be a noted concert violinist and a accomplished oil painter simultaneously because of the amount of time it takes to study and practice the technique of each art. But with the aid of modern technology, especially the computer, one can design sonic information structures and visual ones and can perform tasks that are both technical and artistic. With the visual-aural demands of a multimedia culture, it is not unreasonable for a young person to want to understand the underlying principles of both aural and visual design.

The experiments I have done and described above show that semiotic transformation can be a useful tool of design education. Thus the multi-sensory pedagogy described in this paper seems to be an appropriate direction for design educators to consider in the 21st century.

NOTE: This article first appeared, in slightly different form, in the proceedings of the 1998 International Conference on Auditory Display (ICAD '98) under the title of "A Pedagogy of Creative Thinking based on Sonification of Visual Structures and Visualization of Aural Structures."

References
1. Back M. "Micro-Narratives in Sound Design: Context, Character, and Caricature in Waveform Manipulation." In: Proceedings of the International Conference on Auditory Display, 1996.
2. Berlo D. The Process of Communication: An Introduction to Theory and Practice. Holt, Rinehart, Winston, New York 1960.
3. Carpenter E. Oh, What a Blow That Phantom Gave Me!. Holt, Rinehart and Winston, New York, 1972.
4. Cytowic R. The Man Who Tasted Shapes. Tracher/Putnam, New York, 1993.
5. Drucker P. The Age of Discontinuity: Guidelines to Our Changing Society. Harper and Row, New York, 1969.
6. Eisenstein S. Leyda J (ed and trans) Film Sense. Harcourt Brace Jovanovich, 1942.
7. Gaver W. "Using and Creating Auditory Icons." In: Kramer G. (ed) Auditory Display: Sonification, Audification, and Auditory Interfaces. Addison Wesley, Reading MA, 1994.
8. Hoffer E. The Ordeal of Change. Harper and Row, New York, 1963.

9.     Johansen J.  A Life in the Continuum of Modern Architecture. L'Arca Edizioni, Milan, 1995.

10.     Kandinsky W.  Concerning the Spiritual in Art.  George Wittenborn, New York, 1947.

11.     Klee P., Spiller J. (ed), Maheim R. (trans)  Paul Klee Notebooks Volume 1: The Thinking Eye.  The Overlook Press, Woodstock New York, 1992.

12.     Malik, M.  Private conversation with the author (though some references to his work can be found in various reviews of the Czech pavilion at Expo '67 held in Montreal).

13.     McCallion S, Muoio A (ed.) from a profile in "They Have a Better Idea . . . Do You?" Fast Company, August-September 1997.

14.     McLuhan M.  The Gutenberg Galaxy. University of Toronto Press, Toronto, 1963.

15.     Milicevic M.  Private conversation with the author after hearing a presentation of preliminary findings from experiments with the pedagogy presented.

16.     Ong W.  Orality and Literacy.  Methuan, London and New York, 1982.

17.     Plato, Phaedrus.  also discussed by Ong (see above).

18.     Sacks O.  Seeing Voices: A Journey Into the World of the Deaf.  HarperCollins, New York 1990.

19.     Schwartz T.  The Responsive Chord.  Anchor Press/ Doubleday, Garden City (NJ) and New York, 1973.

20.     Von Hornbostel E.  "The Unity of the Senses." In Psyche Vol. VII No. 4, April 1927.

Eric Somers is Professor of Design and Communication at Dutchess Community College of the State University of New York, where he served as Chair of the Department of Visual and Performing Arts for 15 years.  He began his career as a fine arts television producer which triggered a life long interest in the relationship of sound to image.  He currently maintains a production service, The Sandbook Studio, which specializes in visual and aural documentation of the fine arts and in presenting workshops related to high end sound and image capture and reproduction. Professor Somers has served as Chair of the New York section of the Audio Engineering Society (AES), President of the International Community for Auditory Display (ICAD), and President of the Museum for Preservation of Illustrative Art.

## *Touch Literacy*
## *By Rachel Sullivan*

The exploration of methods by which visually impaired people can participate in art as both producers and consumers has led me to believe that alternative ways of learning are not only possible, but are absolutely essential.

The enhancement of experience for all disabled people, through the multi-sensory approach and through touch exhibitions, has become the norm throughout the country. Galleries and Museums have been involving visually impaired people to a much greater degree, and yet the feeling persists that still we have barely touched the tip of the iceberg. I believe this to be true. This is both exciting and challenging.

We need to know so much more about the senses and how they interrelate - their cause and effect. I want to concentrate on one of the senses - touch - and show how it can stimulate, activate and unify the senses as well as being a powerful aid to comprehension. The use of very simple aids will demonstrate how the basic vocabulary of art can be learned and understood through touch. This in turn helps to develop the ability to concentrate and to focus, which then greatly enhances the experience of touch.

Does the historical and cultural aspect play an important role in the use of the hands as tools for investigation, communication and evaluation? If touch literacy is a means and an end in itself, could it not be the key to many rooms as yet unexplored?

The assumption that blind and visually impaired people have the innate ability to understand through touch must be challenged. If it is true that such tools of comprehension are largely learned, as work done at the Centre would seem to indicate, then surely it is unreasonable to expect anyone to understand, without first learning how to understand.

If we briefly consider the cultural and historical backgrounds of touch, we begin to have a better idea of why it is that people are not generally at one with the world through the medium of touch. In other cultures, the reverse can be true.

For each generation of people, education has a duty to pass on aspects of the culture deemed important or worthwhile. By perpetuating the myth that sight and sound are superior, touch is devalued. We have only to consider the world of advertising and pop music to understand these facts. In this world of instant requirement who has the time or inclination to stop, touch, respond and interpret?

'Do not touch' is perhaps one of the first sentences we learn from our parents. We are prohibited from touching from the moment we leave our mother's breast and arms. The suckling action of the tongue on the nipple is replaced by the speech action of the tongue formulating words. Are touch and language very closely linked?

Touch differs from the other senses in that it always requires the presence, at once and separately, of the body or object we touch and our body with which we touch. We feel something inside ourselves when we touch. Does the way in which we touch affect this feeling inside ourselves? I believe that it does. It would seem from my work in teaching art to blind, visually impaired people, and people in general, that the mode of address of the hands to an object and the requirement to focus upon this act, are fundamentally important to touch as a perceptual process.

The course in touch literacy has evolved from this work. The methods devised are a direct result of the needs of the people involved and my own limitations as a teacher. I had, and still have, twin obsessions - art and natural form. From childhood I had built up a modest collection of plant, animal, mineral and fossil remains. These, together with play-bricks and toys left over from my own children, became the source for exploration, study and research.

We began with a ruler and a wooden ball. In two dimensions these became a straight line and a circle. These are universal symbols. They can connect us to language, culture, history, religion, the universe, mathematics, myth, legend and mystery.

Each thematic scheme of objects aroused responses which connected us to the other senses and to other systems. Touch both unified and elucidated; demonstrated absolute simplicity and utter complexity; gave both pleasure and horror.

Gradually the basic vocabulary of sculpture, the edges, flat planes and curves, became familiar, could be understood and applied to both the making and the enjoyment of art. Visits to museums, galleries and exhibitions enhanced this understanding and enjoyment. The close scrutiny of objects and ideas was invariably followed by the drawing of the outline on paper with a pen or wax crayon according to taste. The concentration necessary to find and fix the drawn image required absolute focus. The shape of the object, the making of the image, was far more relevant than the drawing itself. The process was all. In this way a large repertoire of images could be built up in the mind. Sounds, scents and colour play vital roles in the perceptual process.

Rhythm, pulse and body language are all part of the artistic process. Each time we make a mark on paper these forces come into play. Why is it that the making of marks appears to be an essential need in the human animal; look at cave painting and modern graffiti? Visually impaired people must be given every opportunity to explore their potential as makers of marks in both painting and drawing. These made marks, for each individual, are singular – like a thumb print.

Conceptual exercises have woven their way through the theme of work. The vital importance of giving structure to joys, fears, ideas, thoughts, poetry and prose cannot be overemphasised.

What advantages are there in touch literacy for blind, visually impaired people and people in general?
- Greatly improved finger sensitivity and hand dexterity.
- Enables periods of concentration and focus.
- Better control of the hands for skill acquisition.
- Establishes an independent spirit through discovery, discernment and decision taking.
- The possibility for concept building and the ability to make cross references.
- The enlargement of experience.
- Special literacy.
- The basic vocabulary of art. This leads to a better understanding of the language of art and the arts in general.
- Clues to the structure of the universe: how the harmony between natural form and mathematics can relate to nature and manmade objects, landscape and cityscape.
- The ability to make connections in the arts and in life situations.
- It is great fun!

Who would benefit most from touch training? There are infinite advantages for children. They are quick to learn, eager to explore; they naturally like making and breaking. They can be curious , inquisitive, bold and courageous They can equally be timid, shy, retiring, completely lacking in self confidence. For blind and visually impaired children it would seem to be an enormous advantage to be touch literate from a very early age.

The sharing of skill learning in an integrated situation mean less time for blind and visually impaired people and children for concentrated study in order to establish their own basic needs in the learning situation. To be touch literate would seem to be a great advantage. The resources needed to set up a touch literacy workshop are very small indeed. The thematic and systematic arrangements of objects gradually build up an awareness of the vocabulary of art and the connections necessary for cross reference and concept building.

It can be used in schools, hospitals, day centres, and workshops, or in any context; for example museum handling sessions; museum workshops relating to current exhibitions, using selected source material in order to create connections with the main exhibition; art, sculpture and pottery workshops; institutions for the elderly and infirm. Allied with clay workshops, a whole stream of experience is possible using the simplest of source material.

The vital ingredient of any touch workshop is the enthusiasm of the enabler. The objects and ideas used can be illuminated by this enthusiasm. My own enthusiasm happened to be natural form and art. Yours might be insects or collectible toys – it just does not matter. It is the projection that is all.

Rachel Sullivan is a Sculptor and was an Associate Director of the Richard Attenborough for Centre for Disability and the Arts in Leicester.

# *Touch*

### The psychology of touching

The academic psychologist is concerned with touch in different ways to general psychologists. The touching of human beings each other is of great importance in life and therefore is important in the consideration of design. A corridor that is too narrow and causes people to brush past each other is a classic example. However, people do touch each other in the way of living a full life, and environments need to take this into account; a dance floor is a good example. More intimate forms of design and communication will also need to be considered. Books such as Touching by Ashley Montagu add to our deeper understanding of touching.[1]

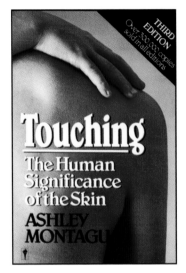

In a more formal sense, The Psychology of Touch, edited by Morton A. Heller and William Schiff, contains a series of interesting essays on a wide range of subjects within the subject of touching. Morton Heller engages our interest as designers in the first page of his introduction.

> The hand is a remarkable instrument, but it is not the exclusive organ of the sense of touch. If sensations were the source of perceiving, as many have explicitly and implicitly argued, then we can experience tactile sensations with our entire skin surface.

The book does not contain a set of rules that the designer can pick up and use, but it does contain much of interest, especially the section on tactile perception for the visually impaired person. In this book, Morton Heller himself has written a paper on haptic perception.[2] John M Kennedy, with Paul Gabias and Andrea Nicholls write on Tactile Pictures[3] and Susanna Miller on the production of tactile drawings.[4]

The division between disciplines is always arbitrary, except where legal responsibility is a matter of importance. For this reason researchers seem to be very individualistic in their ultimate approach even when part of a 'school' at some academic institution. The divisions are often slight and so the next section is close to the work set out in the book we have just discussed.

### Psychophysics

To start with the overall concept of touch in terms of psychophysics is more complex than simply what we touch with our fingers and how it works. I sit on a chair in front of the computer. I feel the base of the chair with my feet, through thick winter shoes. I feel the stem of the chair support with the back of my leg. My bottom feels the seat of the chair. My back rests against the back support. I scratch my head and then go back to typing and so my hand has given me two sets of information within moments. I get up and walk to the door and feel the different pieces of carpet on the way. My foot tells me that I have I have reached the door sill. As I sit at the computer which faces the large window onto the garden I feel the radiant loss of heat from my body and the radiant gain to my back from the room heater.

As I move my body the nerves within each part tell me where the parts of my body are in relation to each other. This is called Kinaesthesia and it is very relevant to how we move and how the body operates. Nevertheless it is not simply an internal mechanism, it is something that we use in relation to all sorts of actions.

In psychophysics there are some very sensible divisions. Michael Levine gives them as follows:

Proprioception – the sense of position of your body and limbs in space.

Tactile sensation – the sense elicited  by non- painful stimuli placed against your body surface.

Nociception (pain) – the sense elicited by noxious stimuli applied to your body.

Temperature – the sense elicited by stimuli that are either warmer or colder than your body surface.

There are many types of receptors that provide input into the sensory system and we should be aware of their construction and their function so that we can design for them. At this level we are looking at the psychophysics of the situation and at the next we must be considering the cognitive action that follows. The study of cognition is facilitated by researchers from various disciplines.[5] Sadly there are no designers amongst these researchers.

Many of the subjects that are part of the study of cognitive science appear to be relevant to designers. In Cognition, by Daniel Reisberg there are several subjects listed that are indeed important to designers such as 'visual knowledge', 'judgement', and the 'acquisition of memories'. [6] If we regress slightly then we can see that these could apply to designing for various senses.

All of this should be considered in the design of an environment, but it is not thought of as part of decision-making in design. If we are aware of what our body is saying, then great pleasure and functional opportunity is in front of us. So often we do not think about our movement or the broader meaning of touch but only a superficial set of sensations through our hands. We seem to have lost our way.

We have talked about wayfinding and the broader definition of touch applies. It is possible to change the texture of the floor for various routes and texture of handrails to help direct people. Similarly one could use the feeling of heat to provide radiant heat beacons which, with sophisticated control, could maintain a sensible temperature and could easily be altered to change routes. The aesthetics of this belong to our broader definition of touch. Much of this is exciting and frequently considered but usually not installed in architecture.

Our particular experience relates to the more restricted definition of touch in two and a half dimension and three dimensional tactile forms. The way that a piece of communication with a texture operates is different to the three-dimensional version of touching. In terms of the technology of manufacturing, the texture is frequently seen as 'two and a half-dimensional (2 ½ D)'. This is where the depth of the 'texture' is given as a unit throughout the machining; in other words where there are two levels in the finished piece. Three-dimensional work has, as one would expect, three dimensions (3D). An example of work 2 ½ D might be the making of tactile diagrams and Braille texts. 3D work could be models of architecture. We have worked on both of these categories of manufacture, a term which implies mass production, but repetition is not usually something that we are involved in although some techniques that we have used have been quite sophisticated, for example laser cutting and machine milling.

The way in which 2 ½ D pieces are read with the fingers is different to the way that 3D objects are read. The actual techniques that people use are complex. The techniques are discussed.

We have discovered that different ways of manufacturing Braille brought up special problems. In order to deal with this we developed our own Braille type faces to match the method of manufacture. The original form of Braille was pressed through thick paper and therefore had a characteristic profile. Where the Braille is etched in either a metal or polymer sheet the sides of the 'raised' profile are straight. This is a by-product of plate etching for the printing industry. The result is that if the etching is done on the basis of 'visible' Braille which is usual with such processes, then the dot is too large. In our font for this purpose the position of the dot is kept but the dot size is reduced. Other processes require different dot sizes and we have a range of dot sizes for this purpose.

### Technical comment on processes

Various techniques are used by the Trust and information is available on these. The following are abstracts of the information on some of the techniques:

### Two and a Half Tactile Forms

1. Tactile silk-screen Printing – The Dorcas panels

(as you will read elsewhere Dorcas, with her owner Eric Sayce, was the first Guide Dog to be part of the team.)

### a. Analysis

The evolution of the resins that can be cured by ultra-violet light has taken time. Part of the reason for its evolution was that solvents used in the past are very harmful. As part of this development a resin with bulk was discovered. It has taken the Trust some years to follow this research and promote the application of the bulk resins to forms suitable for tactile reading. The initial research was done in conjunction with Bill Appleton at GLOSCAT (Gloucester College of Art and Technology). Subsequently this was picked up by the silk-screen firm Gardners in Cardiff who continued the development. The basic problem was that of all visual and tactile signs which is to give the maximum facility to provide visual images and also superimposed tactile forms that relate to it.

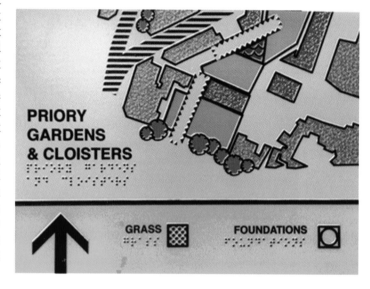

*Detail of the tactile silk-screen printed plan of Coventry*

### b. Synthesis

In the present system the bulking resin is silk-screened on top of images digitally printed onto powder coated steel sheet. This is then covered by a transparent membrane to protect the image. There are possible variations to this technique but so far the technique has resisted vandalism.

### c. Production

The design and manufacture of the panels has become relatively streamlined. The design is developed in a layered graphics programme in the normal manner but with an additional layer to represent the raised layer. The raised layer is normally around .6 mm. The approved files are sent to the manufacturer, who then checks the art work, confirms the form and sends this back as a fax. The form is confirmed and the signs are then manufactured.

Fixing is either by adhesive and/or lips around the edge of the panel. Because repeating the form of the panel is relatively easy several are made at the same time to provide spares in case the panel is damaged.

### 2. Acid-Etched, Two and a Half Dimension Pieces
( co-polymer can be etched in a similar manner)

#### a. Analysis
The craft of etching has been used for years particularly in the printing industry. Given a deep etch, the reversed images are tactile provided the form is correctly designed. Often the medium that is etched is a metal such as zinc. Another more recent method is the use of co-polymer plastic; this is the product of work in the area of package printing. It has the advantage that the co-polymer can be transparent and therefore the reverse can be printed with an image and text. In the case of the opaque, metal colour can be placed in the etched parts and the whole run through a milling machine to clean the surface.

As it is lightweight, it is suitable for interpretation and labelling; many visually impaired people can read images when they are placed close to the eyes, in a position suitable for the particular characteristics of the eye. The position of the sign should be carefully designed and placed so that it is free for a person to move it or themselves in relation to their eyes.

Braille has a different characteristic when etched rather than the traditional punching through thick somewhat crude paper. It is therefore important that the correct dot size is used in the art work that produces the manufactured Braille.

#### b. Synthesis
All the above need to be synthesised to produce a final design. The Trust has established a basis for the various aspects of standard design but many projects need individual designs.

#### c. Production
The etching is produced in a traditional manner. A photo-sensitive resist layer is placed on the material to be etched; this protects the appropriate part of the surface from the action of the etching media. A similar technique can be used on stone except that the resist film has a mechanical strength to stop the shot-blasted sand from injuring the surfaces that need to be protested. In this type of work everything is raised and there are no visual forms under the raised parts.

### Techniques that can Provide 3D and 2.5D Forms
Casting Tactile Objects

#### a. Analysis
It has to be assumed that the main design work has been done already in the making of the master, but there are some other parameters that are of importance. An example of this might be the size of a cast glass form that needs to be drilled and fixed. Another example is a model that has to be anchored. It is worth remembering that a large bronze casting is very heavy and needs to be handled without damage. Self damage, that is from its own weight or form, must also be taken into account. A problem that faces all castings is the possible vandalism. Materials like glass are surprisingly strong.

The method of casting is important to consider. Most metals and glass can be cast in two ways: first, simply in sand with open tops and second, with lost wax which is expensive but gives very fine detail. The amount of detail required needs to be analysed. Colour and finish are either part of the raw material or applied afterwards. Decisions need to be made on this before casting takes place.

#### b. Synthesis
The casting has to be part of a final design and must be designed as such. Although the focus of the tactile form is to assist blind people, others enjoy touching and looking at models and facsimiles, so lighting needs to be considered whether natural or artificial.

#### c. Production
The production is usually via a specialist nominated sub-contractor. Care has to be taken to select a suitable firm. Where a large model is being made, it is as well to check if the sub-contractor can carry and fix the casting. We have found that there are misconceptions and views about certain materials: for example, glass is a very sturdy material if correctly designed and bronze, which is expensive, seems to be a favourite amongst councillors - perhaps it goes with the 'gold chain' syndrome! Stainless steel is a fine material but is not generally liked despite its obvious advantages.

### 2. Making tactile objects using Computer Aided Design (CAD) and Computer Numerical Control (CNC)

#### a. Analysis
The evolution of CAD systems has been fast and effective. The Trust has been precluded from development in this area by the cost of programmes and suitable computers. However, the Trust has carried out

one piece of research for the Nuffield Foundation on the development of tactile plans from architects' drawings that had been generated in CAD.

A by-product of CAD working was the development, by the Trust, of laser-cut veneers to form the elevation of buildings in a tactile manner. This method, though, belongs in the two and a half-dimension category.

It is possible to feed regulations into a CAD system that will define the parameters of the design. Our own experience, plus the research work by the French Ministry of Education, could make up a useful package of controls in respect to touch. For example the anthropometrics of a pilot can be checked against the CAD design of controls in an aircraft, so a tactile design could be controlled so that it has an optimum form.

Three-dimensional copies via probe or laser measuring devices can make digital files of the spatial form of an existing object which can be manipulated and reproduced. Museums and galleries need to understand that most people enjoy being able to touch objects. This is particularly important for blind people who cannot see the content of glass cases.

### b. Synthesis
All the above need to be synthesised to produce a final design. In certain cases the Braille has to be inset in the form of a cast or etched plate otherwise the substrate has to be fine enough for the machine to describe the Braille.

### c. Production
The production can be via almost any machining device. Often this is a milling machine. Although further copies can be made from a computer file, the machine is expensive to run. However, it does make replacement simple. Wood is a useful tactile material and can be machined in this way. In some situations a specially devised material developed for prototyping can be used and this can then be used as the master for casting.

---

[1] Ashley Montagu, <u>Touching</u>, USA, 1986, ISBN 0-06-015535-3.
[2] See also: Morton A Heller, <u>Touch, Representation and Blindness</u>, Oxford, 2000, ISBN 0-19-850388-1.
[3] See also: John M Kennedy, <u>Drawing and the Blind, Pictures to Touch</u>, Yale 1993 ISBN 0-300-05490-4.
[4] See also: Susanna Millar, <u>Understanding and Representing Space, Theory and Evidence from Studies with Blind and Sighted Children</u>, Oxford, 1994, ISBN 0-19-852142-1.
[5] Ed. Neil A Stillings, et al., <u>Cognitive Science an Introduction</u>, USA, 1995, ISBN 0-262-19353-1. This book contains essays that relate various disciplines to cognitive science.
[6] Daniel Reisberg, <u>Cognition Exploring the Science of the Mind</u>, USA, 1997, ISBN 0-393-96925-8.

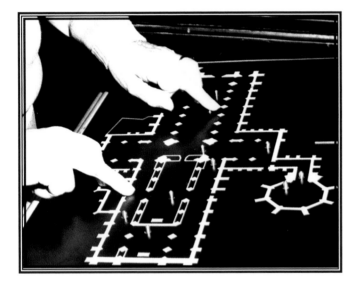

# The Use of Tactile Information

Some years ago The Trust carried out a research project on the production of tactile work with the De Montfort University in Leicester, funded by the Nuffield Foundation. This was to explore tactile manufacturing methods, how effective they were and the interface between CAD programmes and the machinery the manufacturers used. We decided that the sign industry would be a good place to start and sent out a questionnaire to about one hundred firms. We asked what they produced and how and if they include Braille in their work. Many said that following the introduction of the first parts of the DDA, they had begun to offer Braille on their signs. Some of them also said that they had discontinued it because the demand had not been there.

The situation has improved and Braille is used more often on signs and notices, but mainly as information that is repeated – toilets, office, reception and other regularly recurring words. One-off Braille words on signs is still relatively expensive to produce.

As our interest is in combining information for both sighted and blind on one panel or sign, we will set out some examples of how we have carried this out.

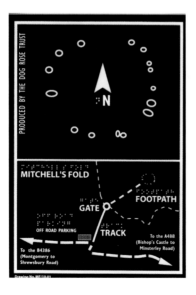

Before creating an information panel you need artwork. For some years we have worked with Matthew Lloyd of *Think Graphic Design* to design panels that satisfy both visual and tactile needs. Before we started work with Matthew we designed our own plans. Much of this early work was the production of maps to accompany our audio guides. We produced A4 black and white tactile plans for the walks around Clun, Craven Arms and Mitchell's Fold. Eric Sayce and Denise Collier checked these for us against the words we had written as well as for ease of reading the information in a tactile form.

# The Use of Tactile Information

This part of the work is essential and the sequence of consultation before final production is:

    1. Initial design thoughts
    2. Discussion with end-users
    3. Draw up more detailed designs
    4. Produce plans as 'swell paper' copies and send out for consultation
    5. Test the final design with the access groups

The National Centre for Tactile Diagrams at the University of Hertfordshire specialise in this work and can give advise on design.[1] 'Swell paper' has been mentioned in several places so we need to explain it. This is a magic paper that is used extensively for raised diagrams and pictures.

*Tactile silk-screen printing at Gardners*

Put simply, the paper consists of millions of micro-capsules (containing alcohol) in an emulsion paint-like formula which is spread on to a backing paper. Once an image or diagram is produced on the ZY®-TEX2 Swell Paper, this is pushed through the ZY®-FUSE Heater machine. The black areas on the paper then expand in the heater whilst all other areas stay flat, hence creating a raised image that can be read by tactile contact.[2]

The 'swell paper' images are not very durable and to make then last longer they can be backed and sprayed as we did for Gloucester Cathedral and as Street Thoma describes in his paper.

The black and white silk-screen printed plans have proved successful and durable as they are suitable for outdoor use. Like all screen-printing, the set-up costs are high but the running costs comparatively low.

When we had mastered the silk-screen techniques with Gardners we went on to more ambitious work with the larger full colour panels. The first of these were

*Some of the Shysters
feel the tactile
plan of Coventry*

installed at Ham Wall in Somerset and in the city centre of Coventry. They have now been there for long enough to be sure that the colours are durable and the materials stable. We currently have one in the deep freeze being tested out for northern winters. It periodically comes out, thaws out and returns.

Others have been hanging out in the garden for a long time as our initial contact with Gardners goes back to the original Dorcas project many years ago, so York Minster has been out there for that length of time and is still tactile. Richard Gardner and Andrew Collins have put hours of time into the development of this work and the Trust is very grateful for this.

Vandalism is always a problem and one of the first things that a client asks about. We do not have, like everyone else, the definitive and positive answer to this, but we can say that the Coventry plan has been there since 2002 and is still intact. The vandals have had a go at most other things in the area but have left this alone – so far. We printed several extra copies, just in case, and we always advise clients to have a spare set run off at the same time.

This plan was an offshoot of the Disabled People's Development Advisory Group, which has been written about elsewhere, and the idea was that other similar ones would be put around the city. However, this has not materialised yet.

Bi-lingual tactile panels were created for Clynfyw in mid-Wales. These showed maps of the walks around the woodlands as well as some of the birds and trees that are found in the area.

### The Avalon Marshes

Somerset County Council received funding to produce interpretation for the villages around the Somerset Levels and we worked with Richard Brunning, the Moors and Levels Archaeologist, on interpretation panels with the history of the area on them. They were to be both visually attractive and tactile as they combined photographs, drawings, maps and timelines. These were designed with Matthew Lloyd and produced by Gardners. The series of 39 panels, 3 panels to each wooden stand, is the largest that we have ever been involved with.

Complementary to the panels is The Avalon Marshes – a History in Sound and four U-turn Wind-up audio units. Some of the wonderful oral history that was recorded in the area in 2001 is included, capturing the accents of the people who have lived and worked on the peat moors all their lives. Photographs of some of them are also shown on the panels.

Choosing which items to make tactile from the material provided is not always easy; the photographs are usually not suitable so parts of them and the drawings had to be abstracted and shown in a larger, more readable form. We asked for more graphic material so that it would lend itself to being interpreted in a two-dimensional form but this was not always possible.

It was a pleasure to work in this historic area with someone as knowledgeable as Richard and to find out about the ancient trackways as we knew little previously. The most famous is the Sweet Track and we discovered that it was called after the peat digger who found it – Ray Sweet. It was exciting to meet him at the launch of the oral history book, Voices from the Peat, and even more exciting to be able to record some extra pieces from him. Living history indeed!

We hope that now the technique for these tactile panels is established that their use will become more widespread and people will think in terms of making their information truly inclusive. There is more nformation about the Dorcas Panels in Chapter 4.11 by Matthew Lloyd.

### Acid-Etched Signs

Acid-etched signs were made for the Bridges Community Centre in Monmouth. Some of the building is late 19th century and has fine wooden doors for which name plates were required. The Trust designed these in a suitable typeface with Braille and a dark green background, as requested. Photocast produced the names for all the rooms as well as the toilets and kitchen.

This technique has been used for other work where there is need for a simple robust plan or map; everything in the design comes out raised, so great care has to be taken in creating the art work. It is essential to test out the designs with visually impaired people.

The map of Ludlow has been in the entrance to the Tourist Information Centre for many years to help blind and partially sighted visitors learn about the town. This is not the place to discuss how much it can serve as a map for finding your way around as this is a very complex subject, but at least it does give some orientation of the town and its significant places such as the Castle and the Church. Like everyone else, some blind people find tactile maps very hard to read, but others manage well; map-reading on journeys can be a great cause of strife between couples!

The plan of the Abbey Gardens at Bury St Edmunds was more colourful. This was to show the location of the Sensory Garden. As you would expect, each colour expressed a type of surface – brown for the gravel and green for the grass.

We have produced many toilet signs with this acid-etching method and they are solid and durable; however they are also apparently desirable as two were stolen off the doors at the Midlands Arts Centre. We have slightly altered the standard toilet symbols to make them more readable. The man has his legs further apart and the woman has a longer dress. Words and Braille are also included.

We have also produced plans of the layout of accessible toilets. We were requested to do this for the new toilets at Coventry Library; so far they have not been stolen.

Acid-etching is a versatile and useful form of raising diagrammatic information. You can do lettering in a limited quantity as it has to be quite large to be easily read. Braille comes out well and is read with no problems, but the dot size has been carefully considered to suit the production method.

As these are 'one-offs' each one costs about the same; if you have more than one produced at the same time it is marginally cheaper, but this does not often happen except for repetitive signs such as toilets. There is a wide range of colours that can be used for the images as well as the backgrounds. Smaller signs can be fixed on with double-sided tape but larger ones need counter-sunk screws to fix them.

**Other Methods**

Co-Polymer Etching can also be used for making raised information. This is another method where everything on the surface is raised. However, reverse printing can be done on a transparent base before etching out the raised information on the front. This leaves the printed design showing through the clear material.

We have only tried this method once and technically it worked, but blind people who tested it found the Braille rather sharp and spiky. The production companies need to understand the technique for producing Braille and tactile information.

We have to mention our late lamented lightbox plans. We loved this method and were just getting it to a state with which we were satisfied when the firm closed down, literally overnight, and we have not been able to find another company to do this. Essentially these were plastic panels with the raised information, including Braille, put on in resin coloured with florescene with a 'plotter'. Areas of the plan or item were computer-cut in vinyl, which was then fixed to the panel. The panels were fitted into a lightbox with a florescent lamp making the florescene in the resin glow. At first we raised the writing but when we found that the vinyl on the surface could be damaged, we put it on the back of the clear panel with the lettering printed on it. Braille readers found the texture of the dots easy and comfortable to read.

This colourful method was developed by the Luminart system by a firm in Northampton and we worked there with Andrew Gorman, another person who put a great deal of time into meeting our demands. We met the firm first at *Sign UK*, a show where we have gathered much useful information over the years.

We produced two for Coventry Transport Museum, three for Brecknock Museum with both English and Welsh lettering and Braille as well as symbols, one for Llanelli Town Centre,[3] two for the Belgrade Theatre Coventry and for our finale, one for MAC, the Midlands Arts Centre[4].

There are other etching, routing and cutting methods which we have not fully explored but hope to in the future. The production of the carp, which is fully described in the Appendix, goes some way towards this.

*Lightbox plan of Midlands Arts Centre*

[1] http://www.nctd.org.uk/

[2] From the website of Zychem, one of the biggest suppliers of machines and paper in the UK. www.zychem-ltd.co.uk.

[3] This was for the Carmarthenshire Blind Society where we worked with amazingly energetic Ray Clarke who is an inspiration to us all with his dynamic fund-raising.

[4] MAC also had silk-screen printed tactile plans of their auditoria.

# Introduction to Braille
## by Sue Nicholls

There does not appear to be a precise figure for the number of Braille readers in the UK, but the RNIB estimate that 20,000 people are currently making use of this system of communication. The National Library for the Blind have about 6,000 members, of which 300 are children; and support a further 100 youngsters via education establishments.

It is not easy to learn Braille which consists of many signs and numerous rules for their use, and requires a good memory and an enhanced sense of touch, plus a high degree of motivation. It is, therefore, more easily mastered by young people who are eager to learn to read for the first time, or those who, due to severely restricted vision, can only see large clear print in tiny sections, sometimes as little as one letter at a time, making it frustrating and almost incomprehensible. The code can only be acquired by a systematic approach and regular reading and writing practice. Self-learning can be very difficult, and occasional lessons frustrating, there being no substitute for regular support and encouragement from a competent enthusiastic Braille user. People who are used to reading print fluently get something of a culture shock as their eyes are used to seeing a considerable amount of material at once and scanning easily through a document, whereas one can only read the Braille sign which is under one's fingertips, thus necessitating endless patience and practice to develop sufficient speed to facilitate comprehension and enjoyment.

Braille is normally read with the upper half of the padded part of the forefingers, with fingers slightly bent and relaxed. The other fingers are used to track the line across the page. Both hands work together so that as the right hand moves towards the end of the line, the left hand moves down to the beginning of the next line, thus ensuring a steady flow.

The need for, and use of Braille varies tremendously from those people who use this system daily, for reading and writing, in employment, education, leisure, general information, marking and labelling, etc. to those who use Braille to label food packets and tins, CD's, cassettes, etc, to record addresses and phone numbers and to mark household equipment. The former tend to be proficient, often long-term users, who depend on Braille as much as most people rely on the printed word; whereas the latter group are 'survival' users who don't necessarily need to know the whole of the Braille code or to read at speed.

# *Introduction to Braille*

Whilst computers have, in some instances, reduced people's dependence on Braille, many have electronic Braille notetakers and/or Braille displays attached to their computers; and many more would do so if they were less expensive. Braille and/or other tactile signs in public places can be useful for confirmation that one has located the correct door or reached a particular spot on a journey. However, their usefulness is limited because, unlike visual signs which can be seen at some considerable distance, a blind person will not know that there is a sign until he/she touches it and, as safe mobility requires a good deal of skill and concentration, feeling walls, doors etc in the vague hope of finding a sign could actually impede one's progress quite drastically. If tactile signs were to be a regular feature in any particular area, they would need to be well and frequently publicised and strategically placed to maximise their usefulness. The most appropriate position would be approximately nose/forehead height, i.e. five feet to five feet eight inches. Audible signs can, in many cases, be more suitable as their information can be gathered as one approaches.

Whilst audio books have become increasingly popular over recent years, particularly amongst older people and those with touch difficulties, proficient Braillists would say that there is no substitute for independent reading which requires no equipment or light, and allows the reader to interpret the material in their own way.

In addition to the standard Braille code, there is a Braille shorthand system which enables a shorthand typist to reach speeds of up to 120 words per minute. This was a popular occupation amongst blind people for many years but, sadly, is a skill which has largely been superseded by technology. Another code is Braille music. Its main drawback is that one cannot play directly from music notation as the hands are needed for both skills, but blind musicians can use it in order to learn pieces of music.

In the past, the production of Braille involved skilful Braillists punching out dots by hand, a long laborious process, followed by careful proofreading, and resulting in very few books and little information being available in this format. However, with the increasing use of computers, the vast majority of Braille material is now produced electronically, quickly and economically, allowing for the speedy transcription of individual documents or multiple copies of books. Hence, the number of books and amount of general and personal information available to the Braille reader has increased and should continue to do so with technological developments, implementation of the Disability Discrimination Act and the Freedom of Information Act. Its main drawback is its bulk and weight. However, to those who find Braille an essential part of their daily lives, this is a small price to pay.

Sue Nicholls is a Braille Tutor for the RNIB

# *The Use of Braille*

> *Braille holds a special place of honour in the lives of those who use it, not only as a tool for true literacy but also as a tool for personal dignity, privacy and independence.*

Judith Dixon, National Library Service for the Blind, Washington DC.[1]

**Introduction**

Braille is a tactile method of reading where the letters are made up of raised dots. There had been many developments to produce raised type for many years; the earliest recorded is a blind Arab professor who used a raised method to make notes and identify his books. Until Braille was developed there was a system of raised letters in many different systems, but these were difficult to read and could only be produced on a printing machine.

The system we know today was named after Louis Braille, a Frenchman who developed the system in 1829. As a child Louis Braille became blind in both eyes following an accident and an infection. At his blind school in Paris he had to use raised letters which he found hard to read. His breakthrough came when he met a soldier called Charles Barbier who had developed a system of raised dots for reading messages in the dark. Louis recognised that this could be used for blind people and the rest is history, as they say.

The Braille system is used around the world and allows blind people to read material on the same level as sighted people. It is based on a system of six dots, arranged like the six on a domino. There are 63 symbols made up of all the variations of these dots: 26 are for the letters of the alphabet and 10 for punctuation.

There are two grades of Braille: Grade 1, which is letter-for-letter and Grade 2 which is contracted like a shorthand. As Braille takes up a lot of space, Grade 2 is used for books and lengthy documents to make them less bulky and easier to read. The use of these grades is discussed below.

To read Braille, the fingers should be able to glide gently over paper that has been embossed with the Braille. Braille is read by the tip of the index finger and this determines the size of the dot which must remain constant however large the print around it is. Think about it in these terms: 'Ordinary writing is the art of speaking to the eyes, that discovered by M. Barbier is the art of speaking to the fingers'. From a report written in 1823 by l'Académie Royale des Sciences in Paris.

For note-taking, a pointed instrument is used to punch out the dots on paper held in a metal slate. The readable raised dots appear on the other side of the paper.

### The use of Braille

Braille and raised images are challenging but there is no reason not to use them both. Writing about the use of raised maps, Charles W Holmes of the Canadian Institute for the Blind wrote: 'The eye cannot help seeing much that it is not looking for, but the finger reads only what it can actually touch.' The French philosopher, Denis Diderot, considered that of all the senses, 'touch was the most profound...'

So don't be put off from using Braille by being told that no one reads it. There are a considerable number of people for whom Braille is their reading language. There are also people who have become blind later in life and have managed to learn the Braille alphabet. They can manage to read Grade 1 Braille. It should be considered that not everyone can manage even Grade 1, so large print and clear, well-lit lettering is also important, together with audio for those who cannot read either.

Consider being confronted by an interactive piece of equipment with no instructions; you are not sure whether to push, pull or turn. A single word in Braille could be the key to getting it to work. The Trust has put simple Braille printed on clear Perspex next to push buttons for starting a sound track.

Even more importantly, finding out which toilet is which is very basic, but the wrong choice could spoil someone's day. Large straightforward standard raised symbols should be produced with Braille under them. These could prevent misunderstanding. Braille Guides are useful and should be produced in Grade 2, but their size should be limited owing the problems of carrying them around on site. Longer Braille guides are best reserved for sending out and reading at home before a visit.

Positioning of the Braille is also important. Obviously it needs to be within reach and in a position where it can be comfortably read without obstructing other people. The angle it is placed at varies, but generally speaking it either needs to be flat or at a suitable angle of about 45°.

### Examples of the Use of Braille

Way-finding is another place where Braille is useful. It can be put under handrails to give direction, in the entrance to Galleries to confirm you have reached the right place and on the showcases to link up with audio, large print or Braille guide. There is more about the use of Braille for wayfinding and displays in the Soldiers of Gloucestershire Museum Case Study.

For an award-winning wayfinding scheme, the Trust used Braille in both English and Welsh on signs, alongside letters and tactile symbols. The symbols are important so that the words and the Braille can be left off as the person follows them and so the signs can be made smaller. This project is given in more detail in the Case Study on Brecknock Museum.

We believe that it is important to use Braille for those people who need it and that it should be integrated into the main displays. For Somerset County Council full colour panels were produced with tactile silk-screen overlay; the Braille will go over the images that are not being raised. However, this does raise issues about the length of the text. As we wanted as many people as possible to be able to read it, it was produced in Grade 1, which is about two and a half times as long as the equivalent print. Louis Braille himself recognised the problem: 'Since the methods of writing and printing take up a lot of space on paper, we must compress the thought with the fewest possible words'. We try to encourage short and concise text, as recommended by Louis Braille, but this is not easy as curators and site managers want to cover as much as possible.

If you are trying to combine text, images and Braille on the same panel and if the written text is long then there is no option but to shorten the Braille text. In his V&A Guidelines, Barry Ginley advises against this, but with skilful précising there is no reason why the information should not be the same but said in a more concise way. In fact, writing for Braille text teaches us to be more concise and produces tighter and, perhaps in the end, more satisfactory information; no more than 100 words should be used for information in Grade 1 Braille. If the Braille is being produced separately from the lettered text, then there is no need to shorten it, especially if Grade 2 Braille is being used.

Which Grade to use is controversial and advice conflicting. The RNIB website says that Grade 1 'is seldom used, as it takes up a lot of space and is comparatively slow to read.' Eric Sayce would disagree: as a late Braille learner, he can manage Grade 1, albeit slowly, but if Grade 2 is used it excludes him completely. An RNIB Braille teacher asked us if we used Grade 1 or 2. We firmly said 'no' and she said 'good' to our great relief.

Cambray Jones and Emile Fane, who are expert Braille readers and have proof-read our Braille for many years, have not commented on our use of Grade 1. We have only met one person, who is a Grade 2 reader, who said they could not read the Grade 1.

The best advice we can give is that it depends on how you are using Braille as to which Grade to use and consult with end-users in your area. However, some access groups, even with visually impaired people as their members, advise that 'no one reads Braille so it is not necessary to include it.' Yes, people do read Braille and for those who need it, it is very necessary. It gives them an independent literacy that no other method can match.

### Braille Production

Braille was traditionally produced by paper being punched up from below to produce a round dot with a flattish top. Until the widespread use of computers the Perkins and other Braillers were the most common methods of production. Now there are many computer driven machines such as Index and Tiger that produce Braille fast in large quantities.

The method of production of Braille for exhibition and signage purposes is probably the key thing as there are several ways of producing it and your choice depends on how you want to use it to fit in with the rest of the display. Some of the most common methods are:

- Raised silk-screen printing
- Chemical etching on metal
- Casting
- Etched or milled plastic

This group is more suited to panels, signs and information boards and can be produced in low quantities or as 'one-offs'. No method is cheap and all these have comparable prices.

There are also less frequently used methods:
- Flocking
- Electro Static
- Pressed paper

These methods are more suited to big runs such as greetings cards. The set-up costs can be very high but the unit cost cheap when printing large quantities.

Some of these methods are discussed in more detail in the production of tactile materials in the touch section.

There are some simple solutions for producing Braille in the short term. An adapted Dymo embosser, which has a Braille font, can be bought from the RNIB.[2] Perkins Braillers are typewriters with Braille dots instead of letters. They can be used to produce short texts and labels, but now Braille books and longer texts are set on a computer programme and produced on big and fast machines; the local Resource Centre for the Blind will be able to do this for you.

### Producing the Braille art work

The text for the Braille for production or manufacturing needs to be done in what is sometimes called 'Visible Braille' – that is, just the dots are printed out but not raised. The Trust sets its own Braille but there are companies who can do it; ask at your local Resource Centre for the Blind as they may set Braille. We do it ourselves as it often has to fit into a defined space and therefore needs to be set on a graphics programme.

A Braille font can be downloaded from the University of Birmingham's website.[3] Care must be taken when using it; if you want to try and set it yourself, do simple words and sentences at first as some of the rules for such things as websites and punctuation are complex. Numbers are the first ten letters of the alphabet, not the numbers on the keyboard and need a numerals symbol before them; this looks like a back-to-front L (#). The RNIB, who do not have a downloadable font now, have some manuals on Braille and these should be referred to before starting to attempt anything.

The Trust has developed its own font using the programme Fontographer and the dot size had been scaled to suit different manufacturing methods. At present this is not available commercially and is only for use by the Trust. Duxbury Systems market Duxbury Braille Board for Windows which can be used with graphics programmes. It has been developed specifically for sign making and is scaleable.[4]

Always get the Braille proof read by a fluent Braille reader as there are lots of pitfalls. This is easier said than done when the timetable is tight so leave plenty of time. It is hard to read it visually and be sure that the spacing and layout is correct. Barry Ginley includes layout in his guidelines, which are at the end of this section.

### Moon

Braille is not the only raised system for blind people; the other is known as Moon as it was developed by Dr William Moon in 1845. He became blind as a child and could not get on with the existing systems of embossed writing so developed his own.

The Moon Alphabet consisted of raised simplified forms of Roman letters suitable for reading with the fingers. His students quickly got to grips with the new system but his school committee would not financially support its development. His first benefactor came forward in 1847. Moon founded the first of a dizzying number of societies and institutions to further his educational and social aims. The adaptation of recognizable traditional letter forms remains a strength of Moon's system.[5]

Once widely used, its use declined but recently it has had a revival as a reading system for people who cannot access Braille or print.

The main message, though, has to be that you should think about universal communication and offer a range of options to users.

[1] From <u>Braille into the next Millennium</u> published by the NLS - National Library Service for the Blind, Washington DC, 2000. All quotations are from this source and we are grateful to the NLS for sending us this book.

[2] http://onlineshop.rnib.org.uk/

[3] www.education.bham.ac.uk/onlinelearning/braille/intro/equipment. htm#virtual.

[4] For further information see www.duxburysystems.com

[5] From http://www.scip.org.uk/moon/mooncode.htm

## *Braille Guidelines*
## *by Barry Ginley*

### Introduction

Reviewing the Braille labels produced for the British Galleries, the following guidelines have been produced for Handling Collections and Touch objects:

### Label layout

All pull-out Braille labels need a blank boarder of 15mm around text. Ensure that there is a 15mm space at the top of the label once the label is pulled out.

The title and date should be on the first line. It should start with an indentation of one Braille space, if the title goes into a second line then that line should be indented too.

The start of the main body of the text should not be indented.

The words 'museum number' needs to be indented by one Braille space. If there is not enough space for the number itself, then it should start on the line below, with Braille space indentation.

If space allows, all Braille labels should have a blank line between the title and main body of the text, and a blank line from the main body of the text and the museum number.

All pull-out Braille labels need to state 'Pull out' at the bottom of the label. In accordance with the *Sign Design Guidelines* this should be in grade 1 Braille. However if the rest of the text is in grade 2 this could be confusing and therefore we suggest that 'Pull out' should be in grade 2 for consistency with the text.

Where objects can be touched and have accompanying Braille text, there should be a small hand symbol to identify what can be touched. Ideally the hand symbol and Braille panel should be in the same colour – any colour could be used – but a bright colour helps identification, especially helpful for accompanying guides to quickly locate objects with Braille for the visually impaired or people with a learning disability. The colour of the hand symbol should contrast strongly against the background colour.

### Line Drawing Plates

Line drawing plates should be as simple as possible. Only details, which are mentioned in the Braille, should be in the plate.

The more relief in the plate the easier it is to read – wherever possible a model should be used.

### Braille Text

All Braille text should be produced in Grade Two Braille.

As a general principle the Braille panel should contain the same text as the print label. Occasionally there may be a need for slightly different information in the Braille panel but this should be the exception.

The Braille should conform to British Braille guidelines and only use Braille symbols such as: punctuation; number signs, or letter signs. The use of American Braille with capitalisation must not be used.

### Positioning

Braille panels should be located either: flat on a surface with the handling object; or as a pull out panel. The Braille panels should never be located flat on walls.

The specified height from floor level of the panel should be no less than 700 mm and no higher than 760 mm. This allows children and wheelchair users who are Braille readers to have access to the information.

### Management Procedures

All Braille panels must be checked by a Braille reader before any manufacturing takes place.

On receipt of the Braille panels, proof reading by a Braille reader must be carried out before installation.

During installation a Braille reader must be on hand to check that the panels are being installed at the correct object.

Barry Ginley is Access Officer for the Victoria and Albert Museum in London. These guideline have been drawn up him for use in the V&A and we would like to thank him for allowing us to include them. Copyright: Victoria & Albert Museum

# Tactile Models

**Introduction**

**Historical Architectural models**

Architectural models have been made from antiquity to the present day for a variety of purposes which include presentation of ideas to the client and fund raising. More models were made than have survived; this is known from accounts that were paid for the model to be made. The work was usually carried out by a skilled craftsman and many are works of art in their own right. Probably the most famous model in this country is Sir Christopher Wren's Great Model of St. Paul's Cathedral, constructed in 1673. This impressive model was 6.3 metres long and big enough to allow a detailed exploration of the interior of the building. Wren's friend, Robert Hooke, 'walked through the Great Model' in February 1674. It cost £600, a huge sum at that time.

Other models were more modest, both in size and cost, but the 17th century architect, Sir Roger Pratt considered that they saved money. He wrote:

> ... the Italians will hardly ever undertake to build anything considerable, or of expense, without [a model] and do count it money saved, though otherwise the charge be great which is expended on it. The model ... will not only prevent future alterations in the building, a thing of most vast expense, but will likewise avoid all complaints of the master and abuse of the contriver ...[1]

Models were built to demonstrate how the roof would be supported and in the case of Shrewsbury, Shropshire, to elicit funds for the building of a new bridge. The model, commissioned by the Shrewsbury architect John Gwynn, was sent down from London and displayed in an enclosure with a man to guard it. The people of Shrewsbury could come and view the model and of course subscribe to the scheme.

**The use of architectural models today**

Architectural models are still made today to show how a building or layout will look, but they are being replaced by virtual reality computer imaging. Technology though moves on quickly and rapid prototyping, in use for sometime in industry, can produce elaborate models, from a range of materials 'at the touch of a button'.[2]

In some cases the architectural profession is going back to the finely crafted model to show work that has been done on prestige buildings, bridges and townscapes – the 'wow' factor much loved by the Deputy Prime Minster, John Prescott. Each year the Royal Academy in London has a show of models which are very popular and there is little doubt that models of buildings or towns appeal to most people. In an interview, the curator of the RIBA Drawings Collection, now at the V&A, was asked what was the big attraction of the new exhibition. 'Models', he replied without hesitation.

### The Value of Models in Interpretation

Although the introduction and most of this section is about architectural models where we have had the most experience, much of what we have learnt can also be applied to other three-dimensional models. Further information on tactile replicas or representations can be found in the section on the research for this subject and the production of the carp.

Perhaps we need to define the word model. Dictionary definitions include: 'representation in three dimensions of projected or existing structure or material object',[3] or 'an imitation of something on a smaller scale'.[4] These definitions set out how we should think about tactile models and differentiate them from tactile images which are produced in what is known as two and half dimensions.

Tactile scale models should be for everyone to touch and look at and where applicable listen to. They should be designed and produced on Universal Design principles which are discussed throughout this book. They also be included in overall interpretation and wayfinding schemes and should be part of the message that you want to convey about your site. Unfortunately funding does not always allows for this luxury so we have to make the best of what we can get.

However one organisation that has the funding to create a dedicated museum, The Museo Tiflologico, is ONCE (Spanish National Organisation of the Blind) in Madrid, thereby demonstrating the importance of this form of interpretation to people with visual impairments.

It is specially designed for the visually impaired with contrasted colours, lighting and tactile flooring, which all contribute to smooth orientation within the exhibiting halls. Sound has been installed at all entrances so that visitors know at any moment where they are in the museum. Walking and exhibition areas are clearly differentiated thanks to a combination of different flooring textures.

Of particular interest is the exhibition of models of architectural monuments worldwide. It is almost impossible for a blind person to have a full perception of a real life architectural monument, but models are the ideal compensatory tool: they allow for a comprehensive representation; they also make it possible for a blind person to 'see' the different components of a monument and measure them one against the other.

For each model, information organised in two levels is provided through a complex audio recording system: 'basic-level' information to help the tactile exploration of the model, and documented information on the history and other facts relating to the model.

The models are of excellent quality. As an example, the model featuring the Taj Mahal is made of the same marble stone as the original: the material was specially brought from the Agra region in India to make the model. [5]

There are other issues that need deciding before starting on a tactile model as Rebecca Fuller, a model-maker from the USA, outlines:

When setting out to create 'tactile exhibits' there are a number of questions to ask yourself: Questions such as, 'What do you want to accomplish with a tactile exhibit, what type of information are you trying to convey - and what level of information are you trying to get across?' [6]

The Orientation and Mobility mailing list carried correspondence on the internet which covered tactile models and their use with blind children. Richard Larson wrote:

It appears that little attention has been given to this topic, which is surprising. In reviewing the literature for my dissertation on tactile maps, I came across practically nothing on tactile models, while I found a good deal on tactile graphics and tactual perception. Tactile models can certainly be helpful in teaching blind children, but one must remember that they do not convey information as readily to blind children as they do to sighted children. It is always best to use the real object when one is teaching blind children, if possible, but when this cannot be done, models should be considered. Those models which are the closest in size to the real object are the best. For example, a model which is half the size of the real object is better than one that is one-fourth or one-eight the size. When a sighted child is given a model, he is usually able to understand what the real object looks like with little or no instruction - the sense of sight allows us to see the whole object at the same time, and therefore we are able to see the various features and proportions of the model almost immediately, and our visual imagery allows us to recognize the same type of object if it is much larger or if it is made of different materials. This is not the case with the sense of touch. Information obtained by touch is sequential and has to be integrated by the mind. - this information does not give us a 'gestalt' as visual information does. Consequently, if a blind child is given a model and then is allowed to examine the real object with the real object being several times larger than the model, it is very likely that he will not recognize the real object. One blind boy had a toy cow, which he became very familiar with, and then one day he went to a farm and was shown a real cow. When he was told the animal was a cow, he replied, 'This isn't a cow!' He thought of his toy as a cow, and to him there was no resemblance between his toy and the real cow. When we use models with blind children, we need to provide verbal information to help the child to understand the information he is getting from his fingers. Many things will not be as obvious to him as they would be to a sighted child. We need to explain that the animal has long legs or short legs, that it has a slender or broad body, and if there is something unusual about it, such as the neck in the case of a giraffe, this should be pointed out. If there is a difference between the size of the model and the real object, this should be carefully explained. For example, if a model of a dinosaur (a favourite subject of children!) is being studied, the size of the real object should be compared to something the child is familiar with, such as a school bus. When a child is given a toy which is really a model, he should never be told, 'This is a car', or 'This is a tiger'. He should be told, 'This is a model of a tiger - a real tiger is much, much larger'. Even if a model is about the same size as the real object, it will probably be made of different material, and this difference between the model and the real object should be carefully explained. Stuffed animals are excellent for providing information to blind children about animals, but even these are not quite the same as live animals, since they do not have the same consistency - they are hard rather than soft - and they are not warm. These limitations are minor, but they need to be explained to blind children. [7]

Although Richard Larson is writing about children, his observations could be applied to all blind people, in particular those who have never had sight. His ideas are endorsed by Eric Sayce:

Tactile models are an essential component of any interpretation system providing the information with the fingers which the eyes cannot see. They must be accompanied with information in an accessible format written specifically to guide the fingers with an explanation of what is being felt.

It is hard for the sighted world to appreciate what is missed by those with no sight. In a conversation about audio description of ballet with Emilie Fane, we mentioned that the different types of leaps in the air were described by making the words long or short. Emilie, although a medal-winning ballroom dancer herself, had not realised that ballet dancers left the ground as no one had thought to tell her; it did explain to her why they injured themselves. In a similar way, a tactile model can put other things into context.

This is particularly true of the model of the centre of the City of York, which the Trust has been involved with. On the scale model the Minster dominates its surroundings in a way that cannot really be appreciated because of the enclosed nature of the site. When you are close to the Minster, the adjacent buildings seem larger than they really are. Although the Minster does appear to be a very large building, it does not seem to tower over its neighbours as it does on the model. The model therefore serves one of its purposes - that of demonstrating the scale of the Minster compared with its surroundings and gives this information to everyone. For some people this information comes through sight and for others through touch.

The model of the Palace of Westminster also demonstrates that the Clock Tower, better known as Big Ben throughout the world for its chimes, is not as high as the much lesser known Victoria Tower. These two towers stand at either end of this remarkable building.

### Work on tactile models by the Trust
The Trust has been involved in the creation and production of tactile scale models over many years. The aim of these models is to help everyone understand and appreciate the building or environment. It is therefore important the model expresses the form and character of the location involved. The work began as part of the Cathedrals Through Touch and Hearing project, when models of English Cathedrals were made. During the life of the project, technology was moving fast and the interactive commentaries moved from transcriptions machines with mini-cassettes to adapted players with standard cassettes. The Trust was convinced that this could be moved on further to take advantage of up-to-date systems.

The sound systems were developed for the Trust by Dilwyn Morgan of Eos Electronics in Barry, South Wales. The Trust had been looking for an affordable interactive electronic playback system for sometime and Dilwyn was the only person who was prepared to try and do this. The first demonstration wooden model was made in his workshops in 1994 and the sound installed there. The basic idea was to modify a

CD player so that it would pick up tracks from the remote buttons on the model via a multi-cable. Sound could be accessed through speakers or headsets. If the number of tracks was under twelve then a computer was not required. More than that number and a computer needed to be installed to speed up the selection process, otherwise the pick-up time was too slow.

As the Trust had been working at York Minster on an audio guide and had drawings of the layout of the building in hand, they were used to create wooden ground plan. At the same time, the Trust was also researching and trying to develop tactile silk screen printing and were pointed by Jonathan Ionides, a cousin in the print trade, in the direction of Gardners in Cardiff. So began a long and productive relationship with two firms, who happened by chance to be within a few miles of each other. Both firms put a tremendous amount of time and money into the development of the Trust's ideas and without them these ideas would not have come to fruition. Dilwyn has now retired but work with Gardners continues today, as well as the research into new technology for producing sound on models at an affordable price.

Advanced Thinking Systems are developing a system called Tap-Tap. When an area is tapped on a tactile picture, model or plan it activates the sound. As this is a sensitive system it will only set off the sound when the hand is tapping the area near the object. There is a limitation on the type and thickness of material that will work but it is an advance in this type of technology and one of the few interesting and imaginative schemes around.

*Cambray Jones with the original Dorcas Project model*

The only other person we have met who has produced a similar interactive tactile plan is artist Street Thoma, then living in Baltimore, Maryland. We were able to meet him when we were in the US on a Churchill Travelling Fellowship in 1997. The ideas of Street and the Trust coincided in a very exciting way and the friendship and exchange of ideas continues today and we are delighted that he is a contributor to this book.

The prototype plan of York Minster with its interactive buttons and infra-red headset showed that this system worked well. In typical optimistic frame of mind, the Trust expected the interpretation world to welcome it with open arms. Many years later the waiting still goes on. The Dorcas Project, we have said, was called after the beloved first Guide Dog of Eric Sayce, was much enjoyed by people with visual impairments and it still seems astonishing that the idea was not taken up by designers. The technique was the obvious way to present a building, environment or whatever to everyone, especially those who could not see it. Perhaps though there is some distinction in uniqueness: there are, at present, only five Dorcas Project sound systems in the world.[8]

### The design of tactile models

The parameters for designing and making the models of buildings and their plans were based on what had been learnt and observed during the years with the Cathedrals Through Touch and Hearing Project and also from our work in architecture and architectural history, but much of this applies to all models. Accuracy is important in most aspects; for instance, if the building has flying buttresses they needed to be shown as they are very hard features to describe and imagine. However, the components of the building, such as piers or columns in a Cathedral plan, often have to be slightly pulled further apart than they actually are so that the fingers can explore them and read them as separate items rather than as a mass.

The materials used for models should be sympathetic to the touch and also compatible with their surroundings. Wood, usually lime wood which is very good for modelling and carving, was used for the Cathedrals with a darker wood for the ground plans so that the outlines contrasted with the board.

Sharp points, jagged edges and rough surfaces have to be avoided and fingers should be able to move easily over the surfaces as the item is explored. The tall pointed spires of Cathedral can be a problem and their designs need to be considered carefully. Clear varnish or lacquer helps to give a smooth finish as well as with keeping the model clean but does not obscure the detail. The amount of detail to include is a decision that has to be made. Too much and the model becomes fussy and hard to read. Too little and it does not do justice to the building. Reducing a building the size of York Minster to a model of a scale of 1:625 means that such details as the carving on the West Front would be so small as to be unreadable. That is where the commentary comes in to fill that gap; it will be covered with at the end of this section.

The overall size of the model is important, especially when the subject is a townscape or landscape. The size of the footprint of the model is usually determined by the reach of someone in a wheelchair. From that position they should be able to feel the middle of the model without straining. Similarly, the width of the overall model is dictated by the span of the arms; one hand should be able to remain on a reference point while the other explores other parts of the model. The user then can return to this reference point for orientation or location purposes. The size of a model of a single building or object should be comfortable for the hands to explore.

Remember that Richard Larson has commented on the linear nature of tactile exploration.

The height of the model is somewhat determined by ergonomics and a person's reach. Therefore a very tall building in a townscape might determine the scale of whole model to make sure that it is all within reach.

**Commentary for the models**.
Richard Larson has also already stressed the need for verbal help to assist the blind person 'to understand the information he is getting from his fingers'. So tactile models need an audio commentary in some form to accompany them.

The content of the script for the commentary will depend to some degree on the way in which it is going to be played. The length of the tracks or information could be restricted by technical limitations or by the time that people need to stand and listen. Attention spans are getting shorter so the more concise the information can be, without loosing clarity and conveying the character of the place, the better. The ideal situation is being able to sit at a desk and take time to listen and explore as at Chester Cathedral

The same questions asked about the model itself, can be asked about the commentary so it is worth repeating them in this context: "What do you want to accomplish with a tactile exhibit, what type of information are you trying to convey - and what level of information are you trying to get across?

If it is a single building, then what do you want to communicate? For a Cathedral, perhaps it is the function of the different places such as the Nave and Choir and what takes place there. This might be important to the understanding of the building for someone who does not go to church or comes from a different religion. If the building is particularly notable for its architecture of a certain period then this should be emphasised. If the commentary can be multi-layered then the overall picture of each area can be given with more details on the following track.

Is the tactile model an aid to way-finding and understanding the layout of the urban area or park? The commentary then needs to take this into consideration and should be written in conjunction with visually impaired users as their requirements, as we discovered at York, might differ from those of sighted users. Consultation with end users applies to all commentaries. Read out what you have written while someone who is visually impaired tries to follow on the model. They will point out the tactile directions that are confusing  or where the information does not make sense.

A commentary about outdoor areas should reflect the characteristic sounds of the place, 'sound icons', which can be recognised when they are encountered, but make sure they are sounds that will be regular and long-term. Big Ben chiming on the Palace of Westminster is certainly there to stay! If you can be sure about recurring smells then mention them too; some of our advisers in York used the smell of baked bread and pies coming from Thomas the Baker to tell them that they were near the Post Office.

An interactive sound system allows for random access to the commentary on a model. Press the button wherever your hand is and your can hear about that space. A commentary played on a tape is linear and there should be a way to stop the machine and rewind to listen again. A CD player gives more flexibility as the tracks can be short and then repeated, but it should easy to stop after each track to allow the listener to manually explore that area and move on to the next place, having been given the instruction on the previous track.

An outreach package with CD or tape and tactile plan allows the user to listen in their own time and also to bring a familiar machine with them when they visit. However, the publicity for the outreach has to be very thorough and maintained over a long period in order to reach the people who might like to hear about it.

### Glasgow Cathedral Precinct

The first models that the Trust produced using an interactive sound system were Glasgow Cathedral with its Precinct and The Palace of Westminster.

The Trust worked with Strathclyde Regional Council, as it then was, and Jim Agnew and Cath Simpson of the Resource Centre for the Blind in Glasgow on a project entitled Communities in Touch. The idea was to link the religious organisations in the city by creating tactile models of their key buildings for everyone to enjoy. The buildings included Glasgow Cathedral, the Catholic Cathedral, the Mosque on the River Clyde, the Episcopalian Cathedral and the Synagogue. Funding was a problem but was temporarily solved when the Provost of Glasgow Cathedral donated a wooden scale model of the Cathedral and its precinct. This had been made for the redevelopment of the area and had been put away in the lower church once this was completed. This demonstrates that there are probably models out there, stored away, that could be used for this purpose. It was fortunate that this model had been made of strong materials, which is not always the case. Architects and developers need to consider if their models could be put to further use once they are no longer needed for consultation purposes.

# Tactile Models

The model was returned to the model makers in Glasgow as it needed some minor modification, such as the replacement of the trees which were made of a material that was not durable enough. John Knox was restored to the top of his column. Some of the nearby Necropolis burial ground had to be sawn off with a band-saw as the whole model was too wide for someone in a wheel-chair to reach. One or two of the buildings had changed and therefore some alterations were needed. A sound system was installed with brass buttons which, when pressed, activated the commentary. This was listened to through infra-red cordless headsets via a transmitter mast on the stand. This enabled the listener to walk around the model and not be concerned with the leads of captive headsets and is the only time the Trust has been commissioned to use this method. Strathclyde funded the alterations and the sound system and Heritage Scotland paid for the stand which housed the electronic sound system. The sound came off the CD player system that had been developed.

Unfortunately Communities in Touch went no further. Shortly after the first model was officially opened by the Convenor, Strathclyde Regional Council was split up into smaller authorities who had more on their minds than providing models for blind people. Now the mantle is being taken up again by sculptor Alec Keeper, who is working with Jim Agnew, at the renamed Centre for Sensory Impaired People in Partick, Glasgow. They are working on a project called Tactile Govan, with Alec building on the experience he gained in The Lace Market Unveiled in Nottingham. He has written about these projects in this book.

### The Palace of Westminster

The Trust has always been rather inclined to take on challenges and making a tactile model of the Palace of Westminster, better known as the Houses of Parliament, presented quite a challenge: it has twelve hundred rooms, 100 staircases and 3 kilometres of passages. Until we worked there we had not realised that behind the façade that the public see from Westminster Square is a series of open courtyards that vehicles can be driven through from one end to the other.

After much deliberation and many stops and starts, it was decided that the model should show the overall form of the whole building and a ground plan of the so-called 'Line of Route' all at a scale of 1:400. This is the route that the Queen takes when she opens Parliament but she only goes, according to the custom of many centuries, as far as the House of Lords. Visitors to the Palace go on the same route but continue on to the House of Commons and Westminster Hall, the great ceremonial hall which has been in continuous use for over nine hundred years. It was the one part of the Palace that did not get destroyed in the fire of 1834 and the bombing of 1941.

Such a large building required a large model and the Trust worked with the same Glasgow model makers; they have since closed and we now work with a member of the model-making team. The model needed to keep within the parameters set out above and yet retain the details of the architecture which are such an important part of its appearance and character. As this detail is repetitive on the front façade with its rhythm of buttresses and windows, it was cut out by laser and several layers were glued together and fixed on to the base block model. The accuracy of the laser produced these details very well and was the first time this method had been used on a tactile model. In retrospect they should have had more strength in them, but overall they have survived well during the years the model has been installed.

As the aforementioned courtyards have had extra, but ostensibly temporary, one-storey buildings installed over the years, decisions had to be made about what to include. Eventually those that appeared to be the most permanent were put in. The ground plan needed to show only the principle rooms on the Line of Route, otherwise it would have been much too complex. The plan and model were mounted on boards on a 'desk' that housed the sound systems. They are at an angle of 20 degrees. The desk now would be smaller now as technology has moved on very fast but at that time there was little available that would be suitable or fit in with the budget.

*The launch of the Palace of Westminster model with the then-Speaker*

Lettering and Braille were added to both the three-dimensional model and the plan. The lettering was also cut out by laser but has not worn so well and needs to be replaced after six years. The Braille was produced by drilling holes in the base on which the model and plan stood and inserting small brass pins. We were puzzled when some of them disappeared; this was only solved after we found a tiny thread caught in one and realised that as people reached over the plan or model their sleeve caught a pin and pulled it out. The pins thereafter were glued down.

The model was to be put into the Queen's Robing Room, where she puts on her crown and state robes before opening Parliament. The stand for it, therefore, had to fit in the surroundings and also with other furniture in the Palace designed in the 1830s by the architect, A. W. Pugin. We were able to find drawings for a Pugin table and use it to design the stand, which was very ably made by Ludlow craftsman, Roger Dolphin.

The description of the Palace on the commentary had to cover a very wide range of subjects for each area, such as function, architecture, furniture, decoration of the space and so on. Each track had to be concise and pack this information into a maximum of two minutes for each interactive button. The important areas have two buttons: one round topped which describes the area in more general terms and a square topped one which gave further details of function and decoration.

The narrator was Edward Kelsey, well known for his portrayal of a grumpy old farmer in the radio serial *The Archers*, but in real life a superb reader who has worked with the Trust on many occasions. We spent an extraordinary Saturday in the Palace working our way around from area to area. Sound effects such as Big Ben striking and the Jubilee fountain playing are included on the sound track. As the Palace is such a timeless building where little changes, the text for the commentary has not become dated, unlike other places the Trust has worked on.

The sound is relayed through captive headsets on armoured cables for strength; these are housed in the front of the cabinet behind sliding doors. Infra-red transmitters and headsets were proposed but rejected for logistical reasons. Two separate sound systems, one for the plan and one for the model, were installed in the case, with backups. They can easily be switched over in case of failure.

Although intended for people with visual impairments, the model has turned out to be an exercise in Universal Design. The guides who take groups along the Line of Route, now use the model to point out the way they will be going. Groups with special needs also enjoy learning about the building from the model and its commentary.

The Trust naively thought that a model for such a high profile building would publicise the benefits it would bring for visually impaired visitors and that other venues would follow suit. How wrong we were: it was to be sometime before the model of Chester Cathedral was commissioned.

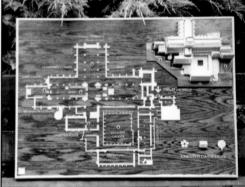

*Chester model and plan*

### Model of Chester Cathedral

The model of Chester Cathedral was designed to be part of a new interpretation display in the undercroft. Although not one of the 'top ten' English Cathedrals, Chester is nevertheless very interesting and receives a huge number of visitors who are attracted to the City, its historic centre and its shops. As funding was limited, it was decided to make a small scale three dimensional model of the Cathedral and a larger ground plan, with an interactive sound system.

The Cathedral decided that the route on the ground plan should follow the route that visitors take when they follow the trail on the leaflet

of the building. This was marked out on the plan by brass pins, this time firmly glued in. The stand for the model was made by the Cathedral's own works department.

The commentary was limited to 12 buttons so that a computer would not be necessary. As users followed the route they came to buttons which then activated the sound track about that area. Nicholas Fry, the Visitors Officer, is also an actor and so recorded the commentary in the Cathedral. Particularly effective is the section about the shrine of St.

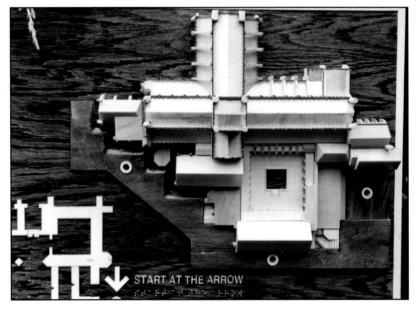

START AT THE ARROW

Werburgh. The pilgrim puts his head into a niche of the shrine and says a private prayer. The sound reverberates around him. Since then David Lubman, an American Acoustician, visited Chester Cathedral with us and recorded a prayer first outside the shrine and then with his head in the niche. The results have been written about and played at the Acoustical Society of America.[9]

# Tactile Models

### Model of the Parthenon for the British Museum

The British Museum had already established a good reputation for access for people with visual impairments with the Parthenon Galleries. One of these room has been specially designed with tactile exhibits and accompanying audio commentary. There was also a complementary silk screen printed tactile book with audio. The different parts, including tactile casts of the amazing carving on the Parthenon Frieze, explanatory tactile panels and display of actual stones made up an excellent whole which is greatly to the credit of Ian Jenkins, the Assistant Keeper of Antiquities, who masterminded the project. After the Gallery has been completed an evaluation process took place, carried out by access consultant Rebecca McGinnis. Many useful observations were made by the visually impaired people taking part and the main thing they felt was missing was a tactile three- dimensional model of the Parthenon that would show the overall shape of the building, put the other objects in context and demonstrate the position of the carved frieze on the building.

*Mock-up for the model of the Parthenon*

Sometimes the details of the buildings themselves dictate the design: for the model of the Parthenon a card mock-up was built of a section of the colonnade surrounding the inner temple. One of the main purposes of the model was to demonstrate to visually impaired users where the frieze was situated. As it is high on the outside of the inner temple and inside the colonnade, this meant that the fingers had to go between the columns and up to the top of the inner temple to find the row of studs representing the frieze. The mock-up was to make sure that people could get their hands between the columns and after a try-out with a visually impaired group, it was clear that the columns needed to be set a little further apart. A scale of 1:50 was decided on.

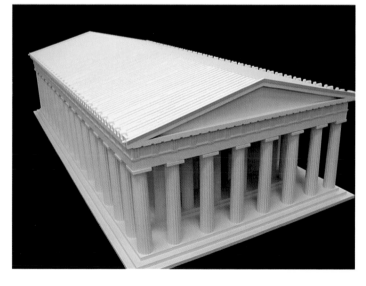

The model shows the Parthenon when it still had its roof on. It needed to convey the character and beauty of the building but at that scale it would not be possible to show much of the wonderful detail. The overall size of the building meant that the model had to be of a length that it might not be possible to span with the arms and it was hoped that this would not cause a problem. The building is the same on both long sides with the shorter ends only slightly different, so apart from locating the frieze inside the colonnade, it is not a

difficult building to 'read' with the hands.

The model was made in wood and painted white to resemble the Pentelic marble of the actual building. At the time we were working on the model, we went to Athens to visit a cousin who lives at Pendeli (or Penteli) near where the mountain where the marble came from. We went up the mountain to see where the marble had been taken out and saw the tracks, also made of marble, on which the huge blocks were lowered down the mountain to the city. It was very moving to see the deep grooves made by the ropes on the even larger blocks of stone as they restrained them on their journey.

The model had to be made with great strength so that it could be available for everyone to touch, including the hoards of school children who invade the British Museum at all times of the year. The Louvre in Paris has a model of the Parthenon with a lifting roof so that interior can be seen and felt. However, this was kept for educational purposes only and this option would not have been possible with the model on open access to all. The figure of a man, shown just inside the colonnade at the front of the Parthenon for scale comparison purposes, disappeared rapidly and a replacement needed to be bolted on.

*Hal Studdert testing the revised audio guide*

*Discussing the Parthenon model with Isabel Murdoch*

The model was made in Scotland by Robert Munn of Omega Models and the stand was made in-house at the British Museum. After its installation the audio guide needed to be updated to include the model. Much of the previous script, written by Ian Jenkins was retained; this covered the tactile panels and casts, admirably. The Trust wrote new sections for the model and for other modifications that had taken place following the evaluation. The rewritten script was recorded in draft and tested out by Judy Smith and Hal Studdert who were members of the consultation group. The final recording took place with Edward Kelsey and actress Janet Wantling. Music, based on ancient Greek instruments, was composed by Adrian Williams.

The Parthenon gallery is the most complete scheme that the Trust has come across in its years of working in this field and we were pleased to have been a part of it.

### Model of the Centre of the City of York

The model of the centre of the City of York was commissioned by three of the York Rotary Clubs acting on behalf of the York Conservation Trust. As York is a big city a decision was made on what area to cover so that the model would be of a size able to be encompassed by the hands. The extent of the footprint of the part for the city for the model was determined to some extent by having the key shape of the Minster almost at the centre of it with the River Ouse on one side. Apart from the Minster, this area is very densely packed with historic buildings and because of scale only the twelve most important were modelled in more detail. These scale of these was slightly distorted so that they could be felt with the fingers. The other buildings would show variations of their age by their rooflines. Again the Trust worked on this model with Robert Munn and he went up the tower of the Minster to take photographs of the roofscapes so that these could be reflected on the model.

Robert made the original model in lime wood at a scale of 1:625; this would be used for casting in bronze using the lost-wax method which, although a longer and perhaps slightly more expensive process, takes the detail very well. As the Minster was so large it was cast separately and welded on to the base. This work was carried out by Brian Caster at Powderhall Bronze in Edinburgh.

*The wax casting of York Minster*

It was important that the model should give as much information as possible to blind and partially sighted people and therefore the design had to be carefully thought through and consultation with end-users was a key part of this. When Robert had completed most of the components of the model but not stuck them to the base board, he brought them to York for a meeting with members of the York Blind and Partially Sighted Society. The Trust had already contacted members by telephone to ask them about the routes they used into the city and the characteristics of them. From their replies it was realised that some of the roads that were used most would have to

be wider so that fingers could go along them. At the meeting comments were made about the width on the model of the roads and the position of some of the buildings which could all be altered at that stage.

The completed wooden model, with lettering and Braille for the street names, was then checked by the clients before being sent to Powderhall Bronze. The important historical buildings had numbers in circles next to them and the key to their names was put around the sloping base of the model.

The stone plinth for the model was designed by Stephen Calvert of Pearce Bottomley Architects. The bronze model was brought down from Edinburgh and installed, near the West End of the Minster, by Brian Caster and the contractor who built the plinth. The model has proved popular with all visitors, but what did the Trust learn from it?

We learnt that it is a large undertaking that took more time that expected to complete. Consultation is a lengthy process and if there are several people involved in making a decision then it will be even longer. A deadline needs to be set for responses and if necessary a 'if you do not reply by ...then we will assume that you have no comments' type of letter.

There should have been more contrast between the lettering and the base of the model so that it stood out for people with partial sight. The Braille was made by a firm we had worked with on many occasions; they printed dots on Perspex using a liquid resin but these could have been raised more. The dedication plaque was made by Photocast Products of Liverpool, who we also work with, and this came out better in the casting process and we would use their metal etching method again; they already work with Brian Caster on projects. It is only after the casting has taken place that these observations emerged and then it is too late to change them, but they are lessons learnt for another time.

Over the years the bronze of the model will weather and change colour, but it should be almost resistant to vandalism, 'almost' because if someone took a sledge hammer to it, it would probably crack. Brian

# Tactile Models

is sure that it could be repaired, whereas a resin model would probably have to be cast again. As the model is in an unprotected site in the city centre, bronze was probably the only feasible material for longevity.

*The wooden model after the casting*

We need to emphasise again the need for verbal explanations for all tactile objects, from models to diagrams. It was not possible to install an interactive electronic or even solar-powered sound system in the model which is in the York Conservation Area and its heritage protected. Now we could have run it off mobile phones; that technology was not advanced at that time, but it does need to be considered for the future.[10] The only option was to supply, through the York Blind and Partially Sighted Society, a separate audio guide and a tactile plan. Funding for this came from the Lottery Awards for All.

The Trust spent several days recording the characteristic sounds of the city, such as the bells of the Minster, the Morris dancers in a square, the buskers in St. Helen's Square, the crowds strolling around the Shambles and the boats on the river with the trains running alongside. This would help to build up a sound picture of the city for the listener. A script was written which reflected these sounds and 'walked' the fingers around the model as well as walking the listener around the streets. This was recorded in draft and sent to several members of the Society for comments. We met with the group and went through their comments which were incorporated into the rewrite. The recording was done at the Music Technology Department of York University with Jacqui and Peter Taylor whose voices were well known from the audio description they do at the Theatre Royal in York. The end result was produced on both cassette and CD.

Inevitably there was a problem getting sufficient information about the area of the city covered by the model on to an A4 tactile plan. A larger size such as A3 causes logistical problems such as posting, storage and carrying around. The simplified plan was put on one sheet and a key to the streets and buildings on another. It was not totally satisfactory, but it was the best that could be achieved within the budget as at least 50 of copies of each had to be produced. They were printed by Tactile Vision of Canada.[11] The idea was that visitors could obtain copies of the audio guide and the tactile plan before coming to the city, so a supply was sent to the Society in York. Copies were also given to the Minster so that they could loan them out on request and some were kept by the Trust. Publicity was circulated so that people would know where to get them from. Take-up from the Trust has been limited and highlights again the difficulty of getting information to those who might want to know about a project.

# Tactile Models

### Other Models

Over the years as we have travelled we look out for interesting work for people with visual impairments and this includes models. Edinburgh has a topographical model by the mound outside the National Gallery and Glasgow has several. There is one at the entrance to the pedestrianised Buchanan Street showing the layout of the city and other at the West end of the city. There are two on the Cathedral Precinct. English Heritage has installed a resin model with Braille of Helmsley Castle in Yorkshire which Eric Sayce found very helpful on the day we visited with him.

*Model of Helmsley Castle, Yorkshire*

However, as it was raining hard he was conscious of the water collecting in the moat – as it should – and other places which made it unpleasant to touch. We asked about drainage holes, which would have been easy to drill holes in the resin but were told that it was not thought necessary. Perhaps this has now been put right.

Of course we have seen many indoor models under glass, but that is another story.

We have looked at a number of outdoor bronze models in other counties, including Milan in Italy, Valencia in Spain and Parnu in Estonia. There are a series of indoor models at Oviedo showing the ninth century churches; these are intended for touch.

*Model of Valencia Cathedral*

Some are more satisfactory than others. Those that are handmade with clay as the base model are artistic but not able to not produce enough detail.

Maintenance and refurbishment are other issues to consider. The tower of Valencia Cathedral has had a knock and leans like the Pisa Tower and the ceramic tiles are cracked around the base of the Buchanan Street model in Glasgow. The York model so far has sustained little damage apart from cigarette burns and felt tip pens. The plinth is covered with footprints of children climbing up but these are minor problems.

So ask yourself Rebecca Fuller's questions about what you want to achieve before setting out on any definite path.

[1] From a paper given by Anthony Cleminson at a conference on The Early Eighteenth Century Great House at the Department of Continuing Studies, Oxford, January 1996.

[2] An article in <u>Building Design</u>, January 28, 2005, by Amanda Birch, covered the advances in this technology for the production of models; pages 18-21. BD as it is known, is an outspoken weekly paper for architects.

[3] Oxford Illustrated Dictionary, 1970 edition.

[4] Chambers Concise Dictionary, 1992 edition.

[5] From <u>A Survey on Museum Accessibility for Blind and Partially Sighted People in Europe</u>, 2001.

[6] From a paper given by Rebecca Fuller at The International Conference on Tactile Diagrams, Maps and Pictures, 2002 at the University of Hertfordshire.

[7] Letters from Richard Larson, Oklahoma School for the Blind. 29 February, 2004, on the <u>OandM@list.Msu.Edu</u> on the internet, click on Tactile models in the alphabetic list. Item no. 44. We have tried to contact Richard Larson by email but received no reply. We apologise for using his very perceptive letter without his permission and hope to hear from him one day.

[8] Glasgow Cathedral, The Palace of Westminster, The Wall Street Journal at Wolverhampton Art Gallery, The University of Birmingham Campus, done with the Cathedrals Through Touch and Hearing Project, and Chester Cathedral all have interactive sound systems.

[9] For further information on this paper, see <u>http://www.aip.org/148th/lubman.html</u>

[10] Information about this is included in the section on Playback systems.

[11] http://www.tactilevisioninc.com/

# The Production of Tactile Models for Exhibitions - A Research Project

*I feel strongly that the strength of this medium is the removal of the divisions between display material targeted at the sighted and unsighted.*

Tim Chalk of Chalkworks, who took part in the research project.

The Trust selected a small group of artists and craftsmen to produce tactile exhibition panels for use in museums and heritage sector. We knew that those we selected had the ability to produce pieces which would have good tactile qualities l that could withstand being touched by everyone as well as visual appeal. Another important issue was the ability to produce Braille. With this in mind the Trust commissioned a panel which contained the image of the fish and the words Common Carp in both lettering and Braille. Some of the craftsmen and producers were already known to the Trust and some were recommended.

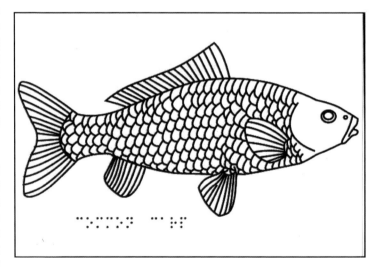

The Trust believed that if this was achieved then the door is open for other more interesting work to replicate images for museums and galleries. There could be no excuses about not being able to find the right craftsman or producer to make the object in the right material at the right price.

The materials used ranged from copper and glass to wood and resins. All the producers were given freedom to interpret the fish as they thought best, but the size must be A4 in either landscape or portrait format.

The other key requirements were:

- Durability
- Tactile properties
- Use in various situations, including outdoors
- Consideration of method of fixing
- Safe to use and touch with no sharp corners

The carp was chosen as the shape is a recognisable one and the fins and scales make good tactile features as well as being a typical museum or exhibition subject. It was interesting to see the different interpretations that came from the same image. We asked all those participating to write about their work.

The image of the common carp was produced by the following:

**1. David Green, High Weald Furniture Ltd.,**
**45 Summerheath Road, Hailsham, East Sussex, BN27 3DR**
**Telephone: 01435 810402**
**Email dave@highwealdfurniture.com**
**Website www.highwealdfurniture.com**

High Weald Furniture work with local authorities and charities around the UK designing and making a range of quality furniture from home-grown hardwoods. Their name was given to the Trust by Allan Linfield, an Access Consultant in East Sussex, who has done interesting and innovative work on outdoor sites in the area.

The material used is Seasoned English Oak. The firm has made similar tactile work which has been tested by visually impaired user-groups with positive results. The Braille was produced, with no problems, by placing brass pins in pre-set holes. The user group found this easy to read. The feel of the wood proved popular because it has its own texture and also a warmth.

David Green said he can make any size or shape of panel, with any required tactile images, raised lettering or Braille and that he can respond to any comments and suggestions and produce pieces which are tailored to the particular needs.

**2. Ian Hughes, Ian Hughes-Lifeforms,
Garth, Llanarth, Ceredigion, Wales, SA47 0NQ
Telephone: 01545 580778
Email  ianhughes@lifeforms.freeserve.co.uk**

Ian Hughes is an experienced modeller and has worked for many museums and zoos including the National Museum of Wales, the British Museum of Natural History, London Zoo, Edinburgh Zoo, Paignton Zoo and Chester Zoo. At least four of his exhibits (all of which involved other people too) have won Museum of the Year or Interpret Britain awards.

The material used was epoxy sculpting putty on a plaster core and plywood backing panel. This was Ian's first experience of Braille and he commented that he 'finally got round to producing it'; he solved the production of the Braille in an interesting way, as you will find out below.

He also said that he had cast 'many fish but never a carp so that was a fun experience although the cast itself wasn't much use in the end. Modelling fish scales is a laborious process. I probably should have gone over the model once more for accuracy but a family discussion decided that rougher scales would be easier to feel'.

Ian adds: 'Given time (or money) a real carp could be acquired and cast to a high degree of accuracy. This could be reproduced in rubber.' He thought that 'coating with olive oil or hand cream if used for handling sessions would give a realistic if rather messy feel.'

Casting the fish is a more economical way of doing it rather than modelling, so that is a point to bear in mind when selecting an object to be replicated. Additional copies can normally be made at around half the original cost depending on texture and colour detail.

Ian does community workshops and makes all kinds of natural history models and displays of geological, botanical and zoological subjects. They have ranged from an elephant calf to crocodiles, bears, deer, dinosaurs, enlarged fleas, spiders and worms, leaves, flowers and mixed dioramas. He also makes reliefs where the texture of an image is slightly raised and has been developing a tactile prehistoric timeline among other things. At Dudley Zoo in the 1990s he started an initiative called *See by Touch* where a variety of casts and models were available for visually impaired people.

Feedback from similar projects has called for backings or matrix to be as smooth as possible in contrast to the model. In the case of leaves, the underside is better because the veins are raised rather than sunk.

Technical Details

Materials
- Rough cast crystacal plaster core
- Overmodelled with epoxy resin
- Cast resin head with steel barbel
- Model screwed to marine plywood backing panel
- Coloured with acrylic paints and coated in acrylic (floor grade) varnish
- Backing panel painted with cellulose paints

**Method**

The body cast from the live fish provided an armature which was smoothed down and overmodelled with Epoxy sculpting putty. The head was produced by casting the head of a live fish using dental alginate. The alginate mould was used to produce a plaster cast which was then moulded in latex. From the latex mould an epoxy copy was made which forms the head of the final model attached to the sculpted body. All fins are hand sculpted. One pelvic fin is splayed open whilst the other is held against the body. The model is produced to look like a cast 'taxidermy' style specimen with thick backings to the splayed fins. This gives the fins strength and gets rid of any sharp edges. It is best described as a medium detail model.

Ian wrote:

What you have is the original model made of epoxy resin. I have made a mould from which casts could be produced in resin, plaster or rubber etc. The eyes can be replaced with glass eyes which not only give a very lifelike look but also feel perfectly smooth against other textures. The model has a 'blind side' which is quite normal for fish casts and sculptures, but can be rectified by a little extra modelling or casting. The scales can also be brought to a higher level of detail and accuracy with more fiddling. The board (from a sustainable source) can be drilled, screwed, nailed or bolted into place and is biodegradable.

And finally, Ian's irresistible account of trying to cast the fish had to be included.

When I received the specifications I decided it would be better to cast the fish as this would give a highly accurate replica with no artistic licence. I asked fisherman friends and they said carp are hard to come by these days. I stopped off at fisheries that I came across and indeed they were all working with trout.

I searched the internet and found a website, among many with titles like carpisking.com, that led me through various links to an address in my own village. I rang this one and other fisheries that mentioned carp. I left messages on a BT answer phone system. The only reply I got was from the Llanarth fishery, my local. A gentleman called Nigel left me a message saying we should get together to 'try and take this forward.'

Meanwhile I had been searching for a way to produce Braille. I have the Braille alphabet on card but to cast from it would have lost detail either through the casting medium soaking into the porous card or through putting a protective layer on the card. I thought that perhaps I might be able to write Braille using pins or small nails and set about looking for some of the correct size. I could of course, sculpt the Braille but this would take so much concentration that I could see myself having to run around for half an hour after every letter to release the build up of tension. So, in the meantime I looked for some sort of Braille producing machine on the internet.

The fabulous internet, that I curse so much led me, of course to the RNIB site and their shop. There you may buy, for the price of a car or even a holiday home with a sea view, a machine that presses dots into pieces of paper for you. I panned down the list; it seemed hopeless. I only needed to type two words but they did have to be on a material I could cast. But very low down on the list and with less text than all the rest was a contraption for £35, a thing that we used to call a taka tape thingy, those hand-held devices everybody used in the 1970s to label everything with embossed plastic strips. It not only produced strips of Braille but translated normal letters to Braille letters. A week later, there it was in the post box, just what I'd hoped. Needless to say the whole family instantly went Brailling mad and I quickly had to impose a Brailling embargo lest they use up all the taka tape stuff. I had my source of Braille.

So I drove down the track to see Nigel the carp man. Nigel didn't walk too well and got about his land in a golf cart. We introduced ourselves outside his house overlooking the valley, and I explained what I wanted which was an eleven inch common carp that I could cast. He explained to me that carp, to him and his kind are, well, sacred really and he wouldn't like to one of his fish, which incidentally are worth £60 for the smallest, to come to any harm. I explained I have cast live amphibians before and thought I might be able to get a good enough cast from a live one if he was willing to let me have a go. I offered him money for the service but he was intrigued and said he wanted nothing. Nigel is a straight talking chap and very friendly. We'd been leaning on his fence while he explained to me how he used to be able to stand in just this spot and look across the Euphrates River and watch ostriches grazing in the valley. Fortunately I knew that the village river, the Llethi, flows into the Euphrates and that there used to be an ostrich farm round here, otherwise I would of been searching for excuses to leave.

'Jump in the cart and I'll take you down to the pools', he said. 'H'm!', I was thinking, 'this site doesn't look flat enough for a little golf cart like this. After all it said on the web site that the place was fully accessible for disabled anglers. There must be a flatter route down into the valley than that steep stony track we are facing.'

We proceeded at no small speed to what I can only describe as a precipice and then began a roller coaster ride down into the valley through stone and mud and sharp bends while Nigel made small talk and I replied politely whilst thinking 'Watch out for that drop - that rock, that log - aaaaaaahhh!' As we descended I saw glimpses of water through the trees where there were about a dozen fishermen each surrounded by a 'campsite' of hi-tech tackle and bait. 'Sometimes you can't see the banks for the fishermen,' Nigel told me.

We went round the pool and spoke to each of the fishermen amongst whose fishing tackle they all had 4x4 all-terrain gas-guzzling vehicles. They were all from the West Midlands. In fact they were all from Dudley and Tipton, an area I knew well from working at Dudley Zoo for several years. Two of the fishermen lifted their keep nets out onto the bank for us. They were wriggling with masses of common and mirror carp panicking and slapping about. Amongst them were several that looked exactly eleven inches long. We agreed to do the casting in about a weeks time.

A week later I returned with materials and buckets. My 11 year-old son Jake was with me to assist and take photos. We drove/slid down into the valley in my little old Nissan Micra and Nigel came along behind in his golf cart. He instructed a fisherman to empty his net and from it I removed an 11-inch specimen and placed it in a bucket of pond water. I had with me a rectangular bucket in which I mixed up enough dental alginate to cast the fish in. Dental alginate is the material dentists use to cast the inside of your mouth. It comes in pink and green, has a nice minty smell, sets from liquid into a rubbery material in around two minutes and is completely harmless, unless you drown in it and this was the risk for the carp. I know carp can survive out of water for over an hour but I was a little concerned about getting alginate stuck in its throat. Fortunately the technique for stopping a carp wriggling also stops it from swallowing casting material; you put your finger into its mouth, as far as it will comfortably go.

I mixed up the alginate, grabbed the fish, stuck my 'pinky' in his chops and dunked him gently into the alginate. The carp performed wonderfully, at first. It lay absolutely still as we waited for the alginate to set. The low temperatures extended the setting time of the material and we waited more like four minutes. Nigel watching me closely and professing his love of the fish talked continuously and gave Jake jobs to do which prohibited him from taking photos. I could feel the alginate setting around my fingers; I was seconds away from my goal. Unfortunately the fish felt the change in consistency too and gave a sudden struggle.

'Slappity flip flap slap' went its tail spraying alginate over my hands, forearms, coat and face. Alas the wriggle had occurred just as the alginate was gelling and whilst some detail was good I was not happy with it and asked Nigel if he minded me having another go. Looking up at him I saw that he, his glasses and his golf cart were covered in alginate. I had a second go and the fish did the same thing again. So I did a third mould just of the head and this turned out to be the only cast part of the model. The specimen I cast from had lost its barbels to a fisherman's hook so these are modelled in.

There is no doubt I could get a good cast but it would mean buying a fish, acquiring a dead specimen or at least bringing one back to my studio to work in a more comfortable atmosphere with everything I might need to hand. Jake had taken pictures of the process but with my underwater camera which has a viewfinder rather than SLR and when we got in the car we discovered a big splodge of alginate on the lens too!

**3. Tim Chalk, Chalkworks**
**183A Dalry Road, Edinburgh, EH1 2EB**
**Telephone: 0131 623 2363**
**Email: info@chalkworks.com**
**website: www.chalkworks.com**

Tim Chalk wrote:
I have a wide experience in conducting all kinds of community workshops. Many of my works result from a consultative and participative process. I have worked in this way with schools, community groups and many other situations. My work ranges from autonomous commissioned artworks to interactive models for a wide range of museums and visitor centres.

I have always thought relief sculpture particularly suited to work for partially and unsighted people, but this was my first opportunity to produce a piece with this as a prime aim, and I found it very interesting to concentrate on this aspect of the work.

Although used to the process of interpreting form in three dimensions, I have never produced a work which had to rely solely on its tactile qualities. I found it unexpectedly challenging to detach myself from the visual aspects of the sculpting process and concentrate solely on the tactile. I kept checking myself as I was seduced by visual considerations, and found it very interesting to have my tactile senses heightened in the process. From a technical point of view I used tried and tested modelling and casting techniques, so this was a straightforward matter.

This small-scale tester convinced me of what I had already thought; relief sculpture has huge potential as a medium for interpretive display, providing a language that speaks to the sighted and the unsighted on an equal footing. The tester panel shows only one depth of relief, but there is considerable potential for larger scale panels using a range between very shallow relief and deep relief. My introduction to Braille has impressed me with how sensitive the ability to pick up subtle information by touch is. I often use letter cut text in my relief sculpture, and I think this, combined with Braille, lends itself well to this type of interpretive display. My panel combined the use of acrylic casting compound (Jesmonite) and bronze. The combination of different materials (carved wood could also be incorporated into a similar work) and textures could be used to great tactile and visual effect to produce narrative work of equal appeal to everyone.

## General

The panel is a cast from an original modelled in wax. I made two casts from the same mould, showing the carp in a different colour/tone from the background. One is Jesmonite pigmented in two different colours (black/terra-cotta), and the other is Jesmonite and Resin Bronze (black/green). I have done two to illustrate, using the same mould, that there are a huge variety of colours and finishes possible; for instance, if more visible text were required this also could be picked out in a contrasting tone. The Braille was achieved with pin heads incorporated into the original wax which was effective.

## Durability

Jesmonite is a very durable material. It is plaster and acrylic based, and in this case, reinforced with chopped glass strands. It will withstand all non-malicious attention, but has its limits if dropped or struck hard; this applies to everything. It is ideally suited to indoor situations, but can be used outside if in a form where puddles will not gather, and if treated with a proprietory sealer. However, if an outdoor situation is planned from the outset there is a concrete based version of Jesmonite available, which is fully weatherproof. The base colour of this material is pale grey, but like this version, it can be coloured with pigments. There is a very slight cost implication here, but this is governed mostly by the large quantity required for a minimum order of this material; the larger the overall size of the job the less of an issue this would be.

### Hanging and Fixing

Jesmonite panels up to a certain size and weight can be stuck to backing panels using a strong epoxy adhesive. Panels of this size and weight and over, if in a situation where they receive a lot of wear and tear, would probably benefit from the incorporation of fixings at the time of casting, such as projecting threaded rods, for bolting through a backing panel, or recessed hanging fixings. A great variety of fixings are possible and can be specified to suit any particular context. For example, I have produced large scale relief panels which have been recessed and incorporated seamlessly into curved walls.

And finally, the only amusing snippet to report is the rather predictable but potentially disastrous muddling up of the 'A' and the 'R' in 'CARP', spotted in time by my son.

### 4. Ralph Jandrell, Ralph Jandrell Pottery
### Coalport China Museum, Coalport, Shropshire, TF8 7HT
### Telephone: 01952 586579

**Email: pottery@ralphjandrell.co.uk**
**website: www.ralphjandrell.co.uk**

I was approached by the Dog Rose Trust and asked to produce an image of a fish following their example and specification. They wanted something that would be interesting to blind and partially sighted people as well as the fully sighted.

There seemed to be two main ways of approaching the subject in ceramic terms.

1. As a freely modelled one-off piece which would allow for varying degrees of texture and detail. This could be made in a variety of different clays depending on what finished colours and textures were required.

2. As a moulded piece allowing for repetition of the image. This limits the degree of 'three-dimensionality' achievable because undercuts must be avoided so that the mould will release properly, but allows certain

other clays to be used such as Bone China which is a very white strong clay and a good background for colour work.

I decided to explore the second method as this seemed the more interesting one as far as the Dog Rose Trust might be concerned.

### Making the Fish Plaque

I was supplied with an A4 image of the fish in question. I had decided to use Bone China slip to make the final plaque. After experimenting with this I found it would shrink by about 10% so my first job was to enlarge the original fish image by 10%. I did this on a photocopier.

The next step was to model the fish shape in relief so that I could make a mould of it. I used the enlarged image of the fish as a guide and, on a rolled out slab of clay, used a pin to prick through the paper on to the clay leaving the basic shape and features of the fish. After several attempts and experiments with different textures and approaches, I produced a relief image of the fish which would be suitable for taking a mould from, i.e. no undercuts, and would be texturally interesting to a blind person. The Braille lettering was an additional challenge. I tried various experiments to find the best way of producing Braille in ceramic form: slip-trailing, using a point pressed in clay to make a negative mould etc, but finally settled on making a plaster negative of the Braille into which I pressed clay which, when applied to the slab of clay, formed the clay Braille positive. The clay original was then surrounded by wood cottling (walls to contain the plaster) and then plaster of paris was poured over it. This was then dried thoroughly.

Into this negative plaster mould I poured my Bone China slip, left for 40 minutes, then poured out. After a period of drying the cast was removed from the mould. This was then dried completely, fired in the kiln to 1200c, cooled, dipped in a clear glaze and then fired in the kiln to 1120c. Although the technique was very successful there are further possibilities: the plaque could be painted, a coloured or textured glaze could be used and the degree of relief and texture could be increased if required.

Ralph Jandrell has his own pottery workshop at the Coalport China Museum at Ironbridge.

**5. Richard Taylor, Coppersmith Sculptor.**
**Box Cottage, Rock Road, Crossgates, Llandrindod Wells, Powys., LD1 6RR**
**Telephone: 01597 851 930**
**email: gardensculpture@richardktaylor.co.uk**
**Website**: www.richardktaylor.co.uk

Richard wrote: The material used for sample was copper.

### The positive results of the work

The project set an interesting challenge to find a means by which a potential series of one-off hand-beaten copper tactile pieces (usually

a relatively high time consuming operation) could be effectively and economically produced to a high standard. It required an innovative approach to find a method that maximised the capacity of copper to be readily formed into a high profile tactile product but that controlled its tendency to distort and stretch during the making process.

Copper proved itself to be very amenable to creating the Braille and after a little experimentation with a few test pieces, the right weight of hammer blow onto a sharp punch applied to the reverse of the copper produced a satisfactory result. Accuracy was the major consideration but the problem was solved by scanning and reversing the supplied Braille configuration which was then taped to the reverse side of the copper to provide an accurate template.

With a dummy run or two it was possible to control beaten copper's tendency to stretch and distort and actually use it to advantage. The punching of the scale texture caused a considerable amount of stretching; in fact it produced a concave version of the fish, which with a little judicious persuasion with a soft-faced mallet was able to be reversed so that the stretched copper was taken up in the convex body of the finished fish.

### The Concept

The key lay in developing a process that permitted sufficient controlled distortion/stretch of the flat copper plate to be taken up the convex body shape. It would be all right to cause less stretch because the 'doming' could always be increased (judicious application of the soft faced mallet again). Too much stretch would cause the flat plate from which the fish emerges to 'cockle,' which would have difficult to remedy.

### Further Development

It would be interesting to explore possibilities of mounting beaten copper profiles (outlines) onto other material. It could offer tactile, and even thermal variation  Copper is an excellent conductor and rapidly 'warms' to the touch. It would be possible to detect a difference between copper and marble for instance.

Copper profiles would reduce the problem of distortion in beating a form out of a flat plate. However, since copper so readily accepts Braille, the flat plate background might be desirable.

### Community workshops and other work

I do schools and community based workshops and residencies, usually on large scale pieces with many component parts made by individuals and stamped with their name.

Major projects for Arcady in Central Powys which include lots of one-off or short run sessions with social support and development groups, such as MIND, Gingerbread, Women's Aid,  Informal Education Groups and Youth Clubs.

### Work with visually impaired people

I have done nothing specific, but one of the contributors to the Arcady Fabulous Water Beast project has a fairly severe visual impairment but was able, with a little assistance, to hand-beat a component piece for the sculpture to a very high standard. She commented specifically on how warm copper felt to the touch. I would be interested to explore the possibility further and, with advice, develop sculpture-building projects specifically designed to engage and enable  people with a visual impairment take an active creative role.

**6. Frank Triggs, Wood Forms
The Poplars, Gwern-y-Brenin, Oswestry, Shropshire SY10 8AR
Telephone: 01691 680196
Email:** frank@woodforms. co.uk
**website:** www.woodforms. co.uk

Common Carp

The carp was produced by CAD and CNC using a maple wood.

Frank wrote:
Thinking about the work with the Carp I thought it might be useful to record some of my deliberations. Mostly they pose more questions than they answer. However, this work gave

me the chance to extend previous design work for special needs clients including taking part in a 'sculpture for the blind' exhibition at Walsall Art Gallery.

Supposing you have never seen a fish. How do you know that this peculiar wooden half-model is supposed to be an entity called a fish without the normal cross sensory affirmation?

We are using an essentially drawn representation of the scale pattern which is in itself a visual shorthand rather than a tactile one. Is this technique more appropriate to strengthening indistinct visual information than providing a 'fishy' tactile experience?

A carver approaching representation of form in relief thinks about light and shade. Only in producing some aspects of false perspective do they deal with planar edges. The edges of planes, steps, strata, and curves where surfaces intersect might be more easily read as relating more to the tactile world.

Areas of texture are another place where I am guessing. How does aggressive/ sharp/hard/abrasive surface feel? Is it actually distracting like discordant, highly saturated colour? Is the domed profile of Braille more finger friendly? Creating the Braille was not easy. The finest tooling my equipment will take is 1mm in diameter; this means I cannot make the Braille dots with a definition (the clear space between) that would be ideal. The smaller type faces are also at the absolute limit of what is possible on my machinery at the moment.

Can surface quality embody emotional information? Does information interfere? If a textured surface crosses another one what happens? Can the scale pattern and the fish shape be perceived separately? How many layers of overlaid tactile information can be achieved before confusion sets in? I had no real problems creating the fish; as a sculptor it's what I do every day. However being able to discuss finer points of design with the Dog Rose Trust made things easy. The decision to emboss or engrave form is an aesthetic decision for a sculptor, but is very significant to someone experiencing the work only with tactile sense.

Overlaying different materials to give visual/tonal contrast could give problems in timber; different timbers have different rates of movement. Timber choice is critical as woods are needed that will hold the detail without damage from use and can be machined easily.

The carvings were planned specifically to give an image that would be clearly readable by touch. They could be developed to give differing tactile qualities between surfaces; textured background with a smooth embossed image or variations within the image for instance. Later pieces have used a locating notch to help with finding the start of the Braille inscription.

I think we have to be very careful not to be directed too strongly by the high contrast easy-to-read graphic, ideal for the visually impaired, to the detriment of those more reliant on mainly tactile information. I need to be more clear on just how forms are read by those without visual back up.

There is nothing like starting to ask questions to make me realise my ignorance. A sculptor, and I just don't know the answers to how tactile forms are understood using tactile sense! I can not even begin to describe how I FEEL form without using words like 'picture' and 'visualise' .

These problems are probably more difficult to address with representations of the natural rather than the manufactured world, where selection, simplification and abstraction are matters of degree rather than quality.

Frank Triggs  has worked as the Coalbrookdale Museum of Iron and has created interactives based on the work of Modigliani for Birmingham and Walsall Museum and Art Galleries. He had produced highly tactile computer carved plywood panels and complex surface carving including a recent work using 3D Islamic text as well as carved digital terrain maps of mountain areas and 3D urban landscapes, used usually in architectural models.

### 7. Peter and Russell Blood, The Osprey Company
**Guards Road, Coldstream, TD12 4E**
**Telephone:01890883127**
**email:ospreyco@ednet.co.uk**
**website<u>www.signsbynature.co.uk</u>**

The Osprey Company specialises in the design and production of outdoor interpretation and signage for nature reserves and heritage sites. It has a reputation for being innovative in introducing new techniques and approaches.

The fish was produced in timber on a CNC routing machine using special 3D software. The software allows you to design items from scratch, allocating profiles to the main shapes of the fish such as body and fins. Then by blending these shapes together, designing and adding textures for the scales etc. and employing various finishing techniques, it is possible to create very realistic effects.

We have deliberately exaggerated some of the textures on the fish in order to make it quite tactile rather than purely visual. The design process is quite involved but once a design is completed it can be kept on file and reproduced at any time in the future. We hope to build up a library of designs in the same way as we have for our wildlife images. The physical process of cutting the design from wood is done with various sizes of routing tools, reducing in size as the job progresses in order to achieve more detail. It is a lengthy process; the fish took about 4 hours to rout but the process is totally automated and can be left to cut unsupervised.

As for the lettering and Braille, this could also be done as part of the routing process. However, because it would add quite considerably to the time taken to produce the job, it may be more cost effective to produce this by some other means and then attach it to the 3D plaque.

**8. Jaqueline Cooley, Glass Artist**
**Unit 3, Sutton Hall Farm, Sutton Maddock, Shropshire**
**TF11 9NQ.**
**Telephone: 01746 781280**
**email: jaqueline@ jaquelinecooley.com**
**Website: www.jaquelinecooley.com**

The fish was made using the lost wax method of casting.

1. First of all, I modelled the fish in clay and took a rubber mould from the clay model, so that I could make a plaster fish, which would be easier to carve and achieve sharper detail.

2. When I was happy with my plaster fish, I stuck it in the centre of my bought frame. I made the text bar in clay, featuring the raised Braille lettering and raised text and stuck this in place too. This is a 'positive' model.

3. Using a type of rubber which can be chopped up and melted like jelly in a microwave oven, I poured the liquid rubber over the whole surface of the fish and frame and waited for it to cool. The rubber mould is a 'negative' mould.

4. When the rubber has cooled and set, I peeled it away from the model. I melted wax and poured it into the detail of the rubber mould, filling the

mould completely. I left it to cool and then worked on the surface of the wax with metal tools to re-carve any detail and fill any air bubbles. The wax model is a 'positive'.

5. Mixing potters plaster with other ingredients which help to hold the mould together during the firing, I pour the plaster mix over the wax model to make another 'negative' mould.

6. The wax is steamed out of the mould, leaving negative detail which I fill with coloured glass powders and large clear glass chunks.

7. The mould is placed into the kiln and put on a long firing programme which takes about 4 days. Slow cooling is crucial to prevent stress in the glass which could cause cracking.

8. When the kiln is cold, the plaster mould is broken away from the glass panel. Cold working usually takes place to grind and polish any rough surface or edges.

Jaqueline Cooley is an experienced award-winning glass artist who has carried out many commissions around the West Midlands.

## The Tactile Cups of Coalport

As well as having its own song, *Here's to Coalport China*, the China Museum at Coalport also has tactile cup shapes, funded by the Heritage Lottery Fund. The curator decided that visually impaired visitors would find it interesting to be able to explore the evolving shape of Coalport teacups over 150 years. She chose six distinctive shapes.

For obvious reasons the cups in the collection could not be handled except under strict supervision and we all wanted the display to be available to everyone. Different ways of producing these were discussed. It was eventually decided that the display would show half-cups with an emphasis on the shape of the handles and that they should be slip-cast by potter, Ralph Jandrell.

It would have been very time-consuming and therefore expensive for Ralph to have created these from scratch. The originals could not be used, so imperfect ones were found locally at an affordable price. Each cup was put onto an A4 panel with lettering and Braille created by Frank Triggs of *Woodforms*.

1. To produce each panel for the cup project the following process was followed:

2. Each cup was set into a rectangular slab of clay leaving half exposed and with no undercuts. A Braille panel was then also set into this slab.

3. The slab was surrounded by walls known as cottling, and then plaster of paris was poured over the form and left to go off. The original form was removed from the plaster, with greater or lesser success as three cups did not survive.

4. Bone china slip was then poured into this plaster mould, poured out after 40 minutes and the resulting cast removed from the mould and left to dry. This cast was then biscuit fired to 1200c. The cast was dipped in a clear glaze and fired again to 1120c.

5. Finally the lettering on the fired panel was painted with enamel and fired to 780c.

6. This process was repeated for all six cup panels. They were then fired and the finished results put into a frame.

The result is six cup panels which link directly, in ceramic, the individual cup shapes to their Braille description. A sound system was added so that each cup had its own audio description.

The three cups that survived the casting process have now gone into Coalport Museum's handling collection.

# Tactile Exhibits: A Model Maker's Perspective
## by Rebecca Fuller

The goal of Universal Design is to make information and experiences accessible to as wide an audience as possible. This audience will include people with varied intellectual and physical abilities, people of different sizes and ages, as well as people with different backgrounds and interests.

Tactile exhibits fill an important role in providing a multi-sensory experience for all museum visitors by providing a 'hands-on' experience for everyone. Additionally, the tactile exhibit may be the primary tool that provides access to the information being presented to the audience with visual impairments.

When setting out to create 'tactile exhibits' there are a number of questions to ask yourself: Questions such as, 'What do you want to accomplish with a tactile exhibit, what type of information are you trying to convey - and what level of information are you trying to get across?'

Tactile exhibits vary widely but some broad categories of their function are Orientation, Interpretation and Comparison.

**Orientation**

One possible goal for a tactile model is orienting people to the physical layout of your site. The Brazo's Bend State Park model is an example of a 'Tactile Orientation Map'.

By providing a tactile, or raised graphic map, you give the visitor a method, through touch, of understanding the relationships of the site's different elements. The Brazo's Bend map conveys information such as, 'if I leave the Visitor's Center and travel west on the Loop Road, when I reach the point where I can turn left on the trail, I will be half way to the fishing pier.'

It is important that an orientation map keep the information clear and concise. There is no need to know that you pass 32 trees between the Visitor's Center and the fishing pier.

Another possible goal of an orientation map is to locate the Park within a larger geographic area. A model such as Pecos National Historical Park tells the visitor that the park is located below the bluffs and that both the Interstate and the Santa Fe Trail pass through the park. All visitors get a 'bird's eye view' that would only be possible if they were in an airplane.

Other tactile models are designed to give a greater understanding of a site to the entire audience. A highly realistic 'tactile' model of a tunnel passing through a mountain - such as the model of Natural Tunnel State Park - allows children to reach into the tunnel on one side of the model and touch the fingers of someone reaching from the other side.

Along with interpretation provided by the naturalists, it enables people to feel and understand how a tiny stream found it's way through a crack in the mountain and eventually eroded away so much of the mountain that a train can now travel through the passageway.

*Model of
Pecos National Park*

*Natural Tunnel State
Park model*

Some sites, such as the prehistoric cliff dwellings at Mesa Verde, take a great deal of physical effort to reach. In this type of situation a large portion of the audience may not have the ability to make the climb, or may not have the desire to go to the height necessary to reach the caves. A tactile model of the cliff dwellings will provide an understanding of the site to all visitors.

Tactile models can be used to facilitate making comparisons between different things. One example is an exhibit that discussed how the physical structure of a jawbone allows one to draw conclusions about the diet of an animal. This was illustrated by: increasing the size of a mouse skull, decreasing the size of a moose skull and recreating a wolf skull at its actual size; thus making it possible to compare the shape and locations of the teeth and jaw, and to see that each animal was 'built' to handle a completely different diet.

Tactile models can be used to facilitate making comparisons between different things. One example is an exhibit that discussed how the physical structure of a jawbone allows one to draw conclusions about the diet of an animal.

This was illustrated by: increasing the size of a mouse skull, decreasing the size of a moose skull and recreating a wolf skull at its

*Moose, wolf and mouse jawbone model*

actual size; thus making it possible to compare the shape and locations of the teeth and jaw, and to see that each animal was 'built' to handle a completely different diet.

Another important example of using tactile models to make comparisons was an exhibit of Bath House Row at Hot Springs National Park. Here the designer worked with the Park to use four different scales to increase the visitor's understanding. A 'bird's eye view' model used texture to distinguish and locate the area of the Park within the surrounding landscape. In this model the buildings in Bath House Row were approximately the size of sugar cubes, and the entire row of buildings is perhaps 6 inches long.

In the next larger model, Bath House Row is 6 feet long with individual buildings ranging from 4 to 9 inches wide. At this scale the texture of the roofs and the indentation of the windows and other architectural details are distinguishable both by sight and touch. The third enlargement shows the facades of two of the Bath Houses at a scale large enough (one façade is 14 inches wide, the other is 24 inches wide) to include a high level of textural detail. It is possible to distinguish the carving of the Indian head above the door of one of the buildings. An

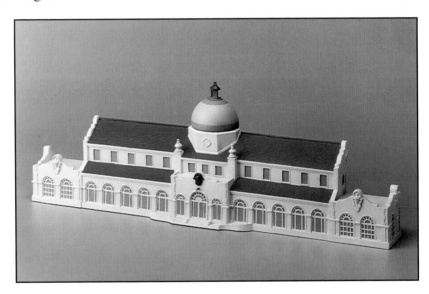

*Model of Bath House at Hot Springs National Park*

exact, full-scale replica of the Indian head architectural detail which was made by creating a mould of the actual architectural detail, casting it and putting it inside on the wall where all visitors can explore the intricacies of the carving.

The exhibit at Hot Springs National Park is an excellent example of using the comparison of different scales to give all visitors a clearer understanding of the rich architectural detail of the Bath Houses. It is

# *Tactile Exhibits*

also a perfect example of Universal Design deepening and enriching the learning and experience of every visitor.

The possible applications of tactile models are limited only by the imaginations of exhibit designers, model fabricators and site interpreters. The wide range of durable materials now available; from bronze, which has been used for thousands of years, to plastics and space-age polymers, allows for an endless variety of tactile models.

This article was first published in Access Today – Fall 2001. Credit: National Center on Accessibility, Bloomington, Indiana. www.ncaonline.org/rec-leisure.shtml. email: nca@indiana.edu.

Rebecca Fuller as been involved in creating museum exhibits for the past 24 years. For the past 17 years a growing portion of my focus has been on designing and fabricating exhibits that are tactile, and therefore work for the blind and low vision audience. The use of multi-sensory techniques, such as tactile elements for presentation of information, is also very beneficial to people who have different learning styles. She has an MFA in Sculpture and an extensive knowledge of materials and fabrication techniques. She emphasizes durability when deciding which materials to use because of the demands placed on tactile exhibits by an enthusiastic public.

# *Looking at Paintings*
# *by Street Thoma*

When we look at a painting hanging on the wall of an art museum, we see the picture (the simple subject matter), and we are moved by it. We feel excitement, anger, wonder, repulsion, whatever. And sometimes, we have an 'Oh Wow!' This is the simplest version of the 'art experience'.

Next, we have a dialog in our heads, with ourselves: What's this picture showing? Why do I think its interesting? What's the painter trying to say? Why is it important to other people? Look at that color! It's so tiny and delicate, how did the artist make it? What's the big deal about this? Why do they even show it? They want how much money ... for this!!??

Then we listen to someone else's comments - the friend who is with us, another visitor, a museum guide. Perhaps we read the wall label, the exhibition catalog, or a book about the artist. As we gather more information about the painting and more responses to it, in other words as we see it from more and more perspectives, our understanding grows ever more complex. The painting speaks to us on many levels. This is also a part of the ' art experience'.

This process of building complexity is similar to learning a language or going to school. As babies we start with the first sounds we can make (ga ga, goo goo), and revel in them. Then we build upon them (ga goo spliftzzzz). We learn words (da da), nuances of emotion and meaning (DA-dee, pa-LEZE), and we string them together into sentences and stories. We move from infancy through kindergarten, to first grade, elementary school, high school, and on to our post-graduate studies.

Let's go back to our first look at the painting. We are moved by it. We want to know more, and we start asking many questions. In our excitement, these questions quickly become complex. We want to look at everything, see everything, all at once - NOW! We want to write our doctoral dissertation before finishing elementary school. Have you ever listened to a child having the most wonderful, excited conversations with herself when she first learns to make sounds? How we, too, can hear all of the 'sentences' she is saying, when it is actually just gibberish. We find the child's efforts sweet and enchanting, we imagine her growing up to be a doctor, or the president. So can she. Fortunately, however, we realize that this growing process will take time. If we allow only our excitement and desire to lead us, the child will go too fast, she will not be able to process all of the information coming at her, she will feel frustrated by her lack of comprehension and will very soon lose interest. It is the same with the language of art. If we move too fast, this wonderful world will close to us. Therefore, we must force ourselves to proceed one step at a time. The more time we take to look at a painting, the more we will see, and the more we will be able to see.

Educators and tour guides in art museums interpret and contextualize works of art to help us understand those works on multiple levels. I make Touchable Interpretations of paintings to help museums give blind and visually impaired visitors access to the works of art in their collections. I think of these interpretations as 'looking from a different perspective'. They help those who cannot see to see, and they help everyone to see what they are looking at.

I am an artist, a sculptor. I am fascinated by how people, especially myself, perceive the world around them. In 1983 I met Kurt Milam, who is blind. Sharing similar outlooks and interests, we became (and still are) the best of friends. It was for him that I created my second[1] Touchable Interpretation of a painting, a Piet Mondrian Christmas card in 1984. Over the years, incorporating his continuing input together with the work and ideas of many other people, professional and lay, I have been improving and refining the initial concept.

When preparing an interpretation of a painting, I start by asking the commissioning museum a series of questions. What paintings do you want to show? What do you want to say about them? Do you want to be able to compare several works by one artist, by similar artists, by very different artists? Who will make the presentation of the painting (an education teacher; a museum guide; texts provided in print, Braille, and recorded audio)? Will each visitor come only once, or will there be a program of multiple visits?

My Touchable Interpretations, as I make them today, consist of three basic parts: a verbal description, a series of diagrams, and a construction. The verbal description is the most important of the three parts because it uses the most familiar language - words. Each verbal description is carefully structured and crafted.[2] It follows one basic principle: if it isn't absolutely necessary to the objective understanding of the picture, leave it out. I start with first grade material, even if the visitor is impatient (and he usually is). By the time I work him through to the construction, however, he recognizes (and usually comments on) the benefits of starting with basics. Only in this way, by beginning with the most basic picture, can an interpretation lead to an understanding of what a painting, a great painting, is all about - that it is much, much more than a picture.

For describing Touchable Interpretations, I will use as an example an interpretation of *Saint Francis Receiving the Stigmata*, attributed to Jan van Eyck, and dateable to A.D. 1430, which I completed for the Philadelphia Museum of Art in November 2004.

I start with two sentences about the room where the painting hangs, and tell the visitor where he stands in it and in relation to the painting. I tell the size of the work (Its the same size as a CD jewel case). Next comes a short series of sentences to provide an overview of the subject. (It shows two men up close to us, almost filling the whole painting. The man on your left is kneeling, facing your right, and holding his hands up in front of himself as if to say 'the fish was … oh…about this big (a loaf of bread, maybe). The other man is sitting on the ground just in front of the first man, on your right side, and he is also facing right. The second man rests his chin in the palms of his hands. His eyes are closed.) These basic descriptions of size and subject approximate to the very first glimpse a sighted person gets of a painting.

As I say these descriptions, I simultaneously direct the visitor's hand to a color Xerox that is an actual sized copy of the painting, glued onto a ¼" board on the wall. I tell the visitor 'If you were to touch the original painting, which you can't because it is much too fragile, it would be this big and feel smooth, like this Xerox copy'.

We then move on to a series of black and white, raised-line, textured diagrams to build up the composition and help understand some of the details. In the case of the Saint Francis, which is a very small painting, I made the diagrams two times larger than the original. I made five diagrams in all for this picture (the number of diagrams required depends on the composition of each painting).

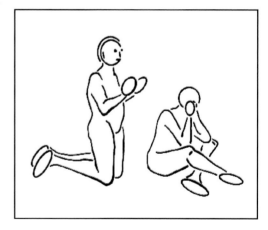

*Diagram 1.*

The first diagram shows the outline of only the two men, with their drapery removed. They are the most prominent features of the composition. The verbal description continues by providing the visitor with the title and date of the painting, and telling the basic story that the painting illustrates. I then tell the visitor 'In the top center of the diagram you will find the circle of the kneeling man's head, with the dots of his two eyes and the lines of his nose and hair.' While I am saying this, the blind visitor is feeling the diagram. I watch his hands as I speak. When he finds the head, I interrupt with a 'yes' and keep describing. If he has trouble finding the head, I give him a minute to let him catch up. I may touch the tip of his finger when it passes over the circle of the head and press lightly to stop it, saying 'there', or I may gently take his hand or fingers and lead them to the circle. I choose which method according to each person's comfort level and success. I continue with this process through the rest of the first diagram, spending perhaps two to three minutes on it. I give only objective information here. No story. No subjectivity.

We continue with a second diagram. This diagram adds the two men's robes as they are represented in this painting. I continuously watch the visitor's hands as I speak, and interrupt my description with interjections such as ' yep, right there'. I try to touch as little as possible, or to just give a tap on the visitor's fingertip as confirmation ('here').

These first two diagrams are critical because it is through them that the visitor first encounters, and learns, the new language that he will use throughout the rest of the interpretation. A clear foundation now allows him to comprehend the complexity later. And, indeed, even if the visitor stops at this point and does not look at the rest of the interpretation, he will go away with some understanding of the painting.

In the second diagram I have begun to bring in some of the details that make up the visual narration of the story. ('Their robes have been painted brown to help identify both men as Franciscan friars.') In the third, fourth, and fifth diagrams, I continue this process, weaving in more and more pieces of the story as I proceed ('Jan van Eyck was one of the first artists to exploit fully the technique of painting with oil based pigments.')

*Diagram 3.*

Finally, I arrive at the construction. The diagrams, although tactilely legible, are two-dimensional, like the original painting. They illustrate the technique of making a painting, of building up and arranging symbols on a flat surface. The construction, on the other hand, is a fully three-dimensional rendition of the painting, itself, complete with fore-, middle and background, smooth water, bumpy rocks, and prickly trees.

The construction of *Saint Francis Receiving the Stigmata* emphasizes detail because van Eyke's original painting is incredibly detailed, and is very much ABOUT detail. Other constructions might emphasize other features. One of a self-portrait by van Gogh focuses on brush strokes, while one of a grid-like Piet Mondrian abstract concentrates on components and colors. The interpretations as a whole must also work on a visual as well as a tactile and aural level because most people who are legally blind have some vision, and more people are visually impaired than are blind. And indeed, access (inclusion) works both ways. We (sighted art educators) help a blind person look at a painting. Through his seeing, we too learn to see on levels not otherwise accessible. Art is many things for many people.

So, how do I make the touchable parts of these interpretations?

### Diagrams

I first create a drawing in pen and ink on mylar (yes, I am an artist with many years experience at this, but I found the work of others helpful.[3]) I then xerox this drawing onto swell paper[4] and pass the swell paper through a heat machine.[5] The black areas of the diagram (its lines and textures) absorb more heat than the clear areas, and they swell up. Voila! You can feel the lines and bumps. I mount the swell paper diagram onto ¼" Gatorboard (it's like foamcore but has a much harder surface). I use a cold mount, sticky paper to do this (peel off the backing from one side, apply to diagram, burnish, peel off the backing from the other side, apply to Gatorboard, burnish, sand edges to make it comfortable to touch). Finally, I spray the diagram with clear polyurathane from a can.[6] I apply several light coats and I do so improperly so that the coating does not quite come together into one smooth layer but leaves a slightly textured surface that is MUCH more finger-friendly.

No matter how large the original painting, the maximum size of a diagram is 17" square. This is the average distance that a person's two hands can spread apart with the thumbs still touching tip to tip while the fingers are open wide like a fan. It's important that the thumbs are kept touching because only then is it possible to judge the distances between the other fingers and thus between objects at the extreme edges of the diagram. Similarly, it is easier to explore a diagram by finding one readily recognizable feature (for example, the circle of Saint Francis's head), keeping one finger on it, and feeling around to other objects using the original feature as a constant reference point by which to understand the relative locations of all objects. I also describe to the visitor different ways to feel, using different parts of the hand.

### Constructions

In the case of Saint Francis, the construction is made of a multitude of materials including wood, metal screen, screws, angle brackets, gypsum cement (a super strong plaster), several different textures of cloth, paints, steel wires, two (albeit rebuilt) WWF wrestling dolls, and epoxy. In addition to being an accurate representation of the original painting, the construction is made to be touched. I protect the fabrics with scotch guard, use durable paints and finish coats, and build the compositions with an enormous amount of structural support and bracing.

*Beginning the construction*

Just about now you might be saying that making a Touchable Interpretation like this is an awful lot of work! Sure, it all LOOKS beautiful, but why go to so much trouble when the same access might be given with much less effort? My answer is that Touchable Interpretations are, themselves, works of art, from the words, to the diagrams, to the constructions, to the equally important presentation. And that is WHY they are so effective at interpreting works of art. They demonstrate what they are interpreting.

*Middle stage*

Now you've got the idea and process of Touchable Interpretations, how can you use them? First and foremost is having access to the original work of art. At the very least, the experience of being in a museum, in the gallery with all of the other visitors, is paramount and not to be underestimated. After all, inclusion is what this is all about. Equal access. Conversing with other visitors. Also, keep in mind that a Touchable Interpretation is first and foremost about providing an objective foundation on which the blind visitor can build his or her own, subjective impressions and understanding of the work of art.

Ideally an experienced guide takes the visitor through an interpretation, spending about twenty-five minutes on the process, either in an office, or a studio, or a conference room, or (ideally) the gallery where the original painting hangs. Like any tour, the guide tailors the interaction to the

*Completed construction*

needs of each visitor and adapts as they get to know one another.

At the Philadelphia Museum of Art, we also occasionally install interpretations on a shelf in a stand-alone public display. In these instances, we place the printed text on the wall, the Braille text on the shelf, and, most importantly, the verbal text on CD so that a visitor can use headphones[7] to hear the narration, leaving his hands free for the tactile experience.

It is at these public displays that sighted visitors often stop and say 'Whoa. What have we here?' Indeed, such displays provide fully sighted visitors with an opportunity to look at art from a different perspective, too. After all, isn't that what an artist him or herself does, make us look from different perspectives? Van Eyck, for example, shows us his subject's perspective (Saint Francis seeing the source of his stigmata), his own perspective, and the perspectives of his culture, religion, and patron; it's this very multiplicity of perspectives - these feelings, responses, conversations - that constitute the LIFE of the painting, it's history, its art history - even its artistry, its very essence. And so, when a visitor asks 'Why is this painting great?' might they not equally ask, 'What makes a human life great?' And, voila! It becomes easier to answer because a work of art, like a human life, is not just a picture or even just a painting, but a web of object and context. When you have access to explore this web, then you are having a full-blown 'art experience'. You are speaking the language of art. You are participating in a history of art!

OK, OK I got a bit carried away at the end, there, but you get the idea. A blind person can look at a painting. We can create for them the opportunity to see some of what is in a work of art, and thus provide them the ability to create their own 'art experience'. And, sometimes, they will have their own 'Oh Wow!!'

---

[1] My first touchable interpretations were the sculptures I made (for myself) of my own paintings.

[2] I have learned from many sources over many years, especially from practice. I give in these notes just a few of the resources and materials I have found particularly helpful. For verbal description see <u>Art Beyond Sight: A Resource Guide to Art Creativity and Visual Impairment</u> (published by Art Education for the Blind, distributed by American foundation for the Blind Press), pp. 229 - 237.

[3] Eriksson, Yvonne and Monica Strucel. <u>A Guide to The Production of Tactile</u>

Graphics on Swell Paper.  Enskede, Sweden: TPB, The Swedish Library of Talking Books and Braille, 1995.

[4] Capsule Paper, made by J. P. Trading Co.

[5] For heat-activated imaging machines, I prefer the Stereo Copying System for the Blind made by JP Trading. Repro Tronics and Zychem of Cheshire also make a similar machine.

[6] I use Varathane Diamond Wood Finish (crystal clear waterborne, semi-gloss, interior) from a spray can.  This product is by Flecto, an RPM company. It really does not yellow.

[7] Sony Walkman model # D-E220 allows the user to play, pause, stop, replay, forward, and adjust the volume at will, and it automatically returns to start when finished. It also shuts itself off at the end when left alone. I attached a neck strap for hands free use.

Street Thoma is a sculptor, a painter, co-creator with Kurt Milam of the *You Are Here Directory Map* (for blind visitors), creator of Touchable Interpretations (in use in the Getty Museum of Art and the Philadelphia Museum of Art, among others), and, currently, Manager of the Office of Accessible Programs at the Philadelphia Museum of Art. He  graduated from the Maryland Institute, College of Art in 1969 with a Bachelor of Fine Art degree in sculpture. After two years in the US Army, he worked for the architectural and engineering firm of RTKL Assoc. Inc. establishing their scale model building shop. In 1979, he left there to pursue self employment as an artist and scale model builder. In 1983 he met Kurt Milam, a rehabilitation specialist for blind people who is himself blind. Between '85 and '88 they co-created the You Are Here Directory Map (for blind visitors). Street improved and marketed it through 1999. During these same years, "84 to the present, Street was creating and marketing his Touchable Interpretations of paintings (described above) and building his career as an accessibility consultant and educator as a part of this process. The National Library Service for the Blind and Physically Handicapped, the Library of Congress, the Washington National Cathedral, the Maryland School for the Blind, the Getty Museum, and the Mid Atlantic Association of Museums are but a few of his many clients. In 1999, the Philadelphia Museum of Art hired him as their part time ADA Coordinator and in 2002 appointed him Manager of their Office of Accessible Programs.

Photographs of Diagrams 1 and 3 and the final construction are by Graydon Ward courtesy of Philadelphia Museum of Art. The two other construction photographs are by Street Thoma.

## Beyond the Screen and Please Touch
## at the Museum of Fine Arts, Boston, USA.
## by Elly Rubin and Hannah Gordon

> *When a man constructs a house, embellishes
> it with fine furnishings and dwells there in, he finds it
> difficult to avoid an attitude of proud satisfaction. Since
> each of these things is the finest of its kind, how can I
> not feel outwardly at ease and inwardly in harmony, my
> body at peace and my mind joyful?*

This is a quote from the wall text in the *Beyond the Screen*
exhibition and is included in the Braille and large type text which augments
the exhibition at Boston. It exemplifies the ideas of universal design where
visitors can use all their senses to enjoy the ambience of the gallery and to
learn about Chinese furniture of the 16th and 17th century.

One approach to the exhibition galleries brings a visitor to a
courtyard. The visitor immediately encounters sculptural stone stools
which function both as interesting objects and as seating in the gallery.
A visitor feels free to rest and to explore the images carved in relief on
the stool's side surfaces. The tranquility of the courtyard is a feature of
the exhibition design and is palpable. If one wanders from the courtyard
to the scholar's study, music played on a traditional stringed instrument
is heard. The recorded sounds are triggered by the visitors' presence. In
the carpentry area, examples of joinery are at hand for tactile exploration
by all.

### Setting up the Project and Consultation Process

With the support of VSA Arts (formerly Very Special Arts of
Massachusetts) in 1999 the Museum of Fine Arts (MFA), Boston, was
able to develop materials to augment the barrier-free design of this
exhibition. Additional materials were developed to assist visitors who are
blind or visually impaired in visiting this exhibition without making prior
arrangements. The coordinators of Access in the Museum's Education
Department created satchels of tactile materials designed to assist individuals with visual impairments in exploring this collection. These satchels
are available at the Museum's Information Centre.

The project was divided into four phases. In the first phase, a
survey was created and distributed. The results were used to educate our
staff about tactile tours at a variety of museums. The accumulation of
information from this survey informed our project plan. The decision

was made to create a satchel of objects for use in a specific area of the Museum as a pilot project to increase access for people who are blind. The Beyond the Screen exhibition was chosen because it already contained many accessible features.

In the second phase, an advisory group was formed to work on the project. The group included people who are visually impaired or blind, and people who teach mobility skills to individuals who are losing their vision. Staff of Massachusetts Association for the Blind and the Carroll Centre for the Blind assisted this project.

During the third phase, Museum of Fine Arts, Boston staff visited two sites to learn first hand about the needs of their students or clientele. They visited Perkins School for the Blind to meet with staff there. Museum staff observed classes in progress and explored ways in which the Museum could create opportunities for Perkins students. At National Braille Press, they met with the director and several other staff members who are blind. While there, they made arrangements for Brailling the tour text. The text in both Braille and large type was to be placed in the satchels along with objects of tactile interest.

Finally, tactile materials were researched, tested, and purchased. The materials include small reproductions of furniture such as one sees in the exhibition's reception area and items such as inkstone and brushes. The inkstone, brushes and a fish-shaped water dropper, represented the display of objects in the scholar's area of the exhibition. Pieces of textured fabric like those in the 18th century bedroom were placed in satchels. Also included is fragrance in a small cloth pillow which evokes the incense that would have been burned in the reception hall. These items were chosen after being tested by adults with congenital blindness and adventitious blindness. Text in Braille and in large type was tested as well.

### The Audience
The primary audience for this project is individual visitors who are visually impaired or blind and who wish to visit the collection on their own. This primary audience might include families with children who are blind or a blind parent with a sighted child or many other constellations of family, friends, college students, or visitors from out of town who include a person who is blind.

By involving people who are blind in the project's development, we cultivated interest in the resulting materials. Now a varied group of people from many institutions serving the needs of people who are blind is invested in the success of the project.

Through this pilot effort we will continue to learn more about which items actually serve people's needs well and we will make replacements and substitutions as the needs dictate. Though these materials were developed for the *Beyond the Screen* exhibition, they will serve to increase access to the permanent collection of Asian art as well.

Upon entering the exhibition, a visitor literally passed 'beyond the screen' The Braille and large type tour texts told the visitor. The screen was one of the earliest forms of furniture, a portable piece of architecture used to create privacy, to deflect drafts or to ward off evil spirits. As one prepares to leave the exhibition, an inscription carved over the doorway (and described in the tour text) reads: 'Prolonging longevity with beautiful thoughts'. The Museum of Fine Arts, Boston hopes that all who entered this exhibition left with 'beautiful thoughts' of the objects encountered.

### Please Touch

The new self-guided tour, almost completed, focuses on five of the Museum of Fine Arts in Boston's *Please Be Seated* collection of unique handmade chairs and benches; these are located throughout the galleries and may be sat in, touched and explored. This is structured similarly to *Beyond the Screen*, and although it is suitable for all ages, it is designed with young people in mind.

The variety within this collection is wonderful, ranging from simple elegant pieces to sculptural benches. Four of the benches on this tour are made of wood, and one is cast glass.

The text in the *Please Be Seated* tour includes descriptions of each piece, a little about the artist, suggestions for exploring it, questions to ponder, and directions for the tactile objects. We would like the text available in both large print and Braille, as well as tape.

A woodworker, Dan Paret, helped choose the pieces to be included; he has given gallery talks to the general public and tactile tours for people who are blind or visually impaired of the Please Be Seated collection and helped choose the pieces to be included. He also created sample joints to go with one of the pieces and wrote notes on the characteristics of the benches and intent of the artist. In addition to the joints that Dan created, there are raised line drawings of each piece, different grades of sand paper, dowels, and a slice of a tree with bark still attached. The development of the text and objects has included Museum staff, two interns, an art teacher from Perkins School for the Blind, and consultant consumers. It is our hope that if this tour is successful, we will be able to build on it, adding more pieces as we go, or perhaps making a second tour.

The benches that were chosen for this self-guided tour are fairly stable in their locations (one of the criteria for choosing them) but they do occasionally move short distances, say from one side of the gallery to another, obviously a problem for a self-guided tour. And then there is the same difficulty to getting around that we have with *Beyond the Screen* - the occasional closing of galleries and corridors.

To solve the problem of navigating through the MFA in changing circumstances, we have decided to train all of the Visitor Services staff, volunteers with the Visitor Services staff, and Protective Services in being sighted guides, making sure they have information about our two self-guided tours. While this seems a fairly simple solution, and would certainly provide assistance to other areas of the museum, the number of people involved, and the variety of schedules that people work, make it a complicated project. Our thought is that eventually it should become part of basic training and orientation to have visual guides at the information desk and with training materials so that people can review it periodically, and to train all trainers. We offer sighted guide training as one of our monthly access seminars that are available to all staff and volunteers, and perhaps we could offer more. With two part-time staff responsible for access, it still seems a big job to make it work right, and we welcome all suggestions!

These articles were first published in <u>Barrierfree</u>, the Journal of the Museums and Galleries Disability Association. For more information on both projects, look at the website of Museum of Fine Art and their accessibility programme on http://www.mfa. org

Eleanor Rubin was the Coordinator of Access for Visitors with disabilities the Boston Fine Arts Museum for many years. She was instrumental in making more exhibitions accessible to people with disabilities. She has now left to pursue her own career as an artist. Hannah Goodwin took over from Eleanor Rubin and is continuing the excellent work done at the Museum. She has a new, shorter title, Manager of Accessibility, and can be reached at hgoodwin@mfa.org

# From Objects to Drawings: Introducing Tactile Graphics to Congenitally Blind Children
## by Boguslaw Marek

The paper shows how a wide range of concepts which are acquired by sighted people with the help of vision can be "translated" into other manifestations of these concepts, and how they can be accessed through touch. It also shows how careful and well planned introduction of tactile graphics can assist visually impaired children in acquiring and reinforcing the understanding of concepts based on visual experience and spatial relations. Fundamental to the effectiveness of any tactile graphics is the understanding of the relation between three-dimensional objects and two-dimensional drawings. The article shows how this notoriously difficult problem can be solved with the help of a simple educational set and a series of structures exercises.

What would a totally blind child, confronted with a tactile version of the picture below, make of the drawing?

Fig. 1

Probably not much. A chaos of meaningless straight lines stretching in all directions, curves, loops and dots would be the closest and the most accurate description if one's eyes could not be fooled by the various conventions used in drawings. Various deformations which are to show different angles of viewing, make two dimensional representations of even familiar everyday objects very difficult to recognize through touch. Add to this the conventions used for creating an impression of distance, and spatial relations such as between, in front, behind, above and under, and it must become clear that understanding tactile graphics is not as straightforward as it might seem and that it involves a lot more than sensitive fingertips.

To fully appreciate the scale of the difficulty which a child born blind faces while trying to interpret a tactile illustrations, one only needs to look at the drawing of a bus made by a five-year-old totally blind girl. The three lines – one for the step, one for the pole she holds on to while boarding, and one for the seat, making a complete picture of a bus, with all the essential components accessible to the child.

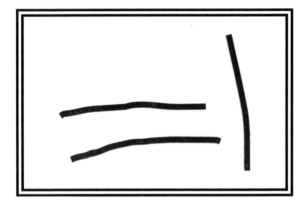

Fig. 2.

The important lesson one can learn from the above drawing is that for children with a severe visual impairment direct experience is the key to the understanding of concepts involving spatial relations. The tactile representation of a bus differs considerably from one which might come from a sighted child. The blind girl had no interest in, and probably little awareness of the existence of such visually prominent features as windows and wheel, which are always shown in 'sighted' drawings of vehicles. But the direct experience reflected in the picture is revealed in the dynamic, temporal organization of the lines which represent each of the stages of 'exploring' the bus.

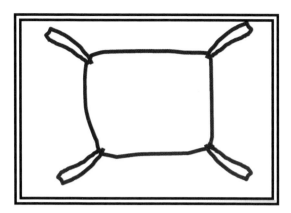

Fig. 3

The same temporal organization and sequencing can be found in another drawing frequently made by a congenitally blind children – a drawing of a table.

The drawing reflects the way in which an experienced blind child would explore an object the size of a table – first going over the table top with sweeping movements of both hands, and then passing on to each of the legs. It is therefore not surprising that the simple drawing below, showing a side view of a table, was greeted by a congenitally blind child with an enthusiastic expression of success when he exclaimed "I know what it is! These are three lines!"

Fig. 4

Indeed, how could a totally blind child possibly recognize a table, a chair, or a bed shown as two dimensional representations drawn with just three lines? And how useful would it be to learn these conventions without understanding the concept of a vertical projection? How could a congenitally blind child be expected to make sense of the complex spatial relations found in the drawing shown in Fig. 1? These are not just rhetorical questions. They must be addressed by designers and producers of tactile graphics if drawings are to become important tools for helping totally blind learners understand concepts based on visual experience and spatial relations, and if visually impaired learners are to enjoy rather than be frustrated by tactile adaptations of illustrations in story books, maps and diagrams.

The obvious suggestion which comes to one's mind when planning a meaningful tactile adaptation of Fig. 1, is to eliminate all unnecessary details. The decision as to what is and what is not essential depends on the purpose which a particular drawing is to serve. In the case of Fig. 1, the drawing illustrates an English as a foreign language task – identifying the location of the three books and comparing the sizes of the three balls and of the three animals. This means that a lot of detail can be disposed of.

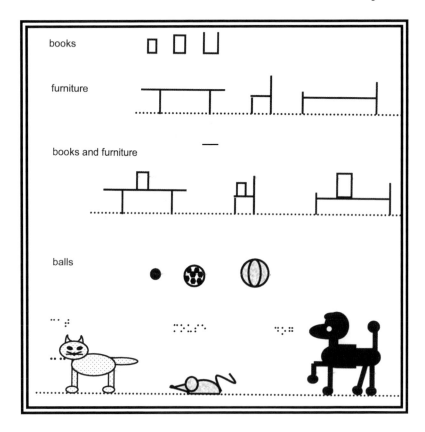

Fig. 5.

The problems which do remain are the distortions and conventions used in two-dimensional representations of objects and the drawings of the animals, illegible due to the angle from which they are shown.

Some answers of how to explain the relation between three-dimensional objects and their two-dimensional representations are prompted by blind children's drawings shown in figures 2 and 3. The sequencing suggests that the drawing should be divided into three separate sections, each limited to the task involved – the furniture and the books, the three balls and the animals, with the books and the furniture first shown separately, and only then presented in configurations present in Fig. 1.

While recognizing books shown as rectangles may not pose a problem, the highly schematic representations of the table, chair and bed may require more careful explanation. Following the observation that direct experience is the best path to understanding, a simple tool called a 'Transfograph' can be used to help even a totally blind child understand why a straight horizontal line is sufficient to represent a tabletop, and why there is no need to draw all four legs of a table. The same tool explains the 'mystery' behind a simplified side view of a chair and a bed.

The name 'Transfograph' was chosen to stress the capability of the tool to transform objects into simple graphics. This educational tool for explaining the relation between 3-dimensional models and 2-dimensional drawings easily changes models of different objects into tactile outlines, helping a blind learner understand what happens when a 3-dimensional object is represented as graphics on a flat sheet of paper. Models of objects such as table, chair, bed, desk, refrigerator and a chest of draws slide into matching slots in exchangeable lids of a box, revealing an easily felt "relief" of the frontal or side view of each of these items. A comparison of the model with a real table allows the child to establish the relation between corresponding parts and get an idea of the whole shape of typical tables, which are usually too large and can only be explored one part at a time. All one needs to do is to explain that that the horizontal

Fig. 6. Transfograph

Fig. 7. Drawing a table with transfograph

edge of the tabletop and the two front legs which stand out above the level of the box and which the child can feel under the fingertips is exactly what a sighted person can see when standing directly in front of a table. Understanding that there is no need to draw the legs in the back because their view is obstructed by the front legs usually helps resolve the mystery of "the three lines" and of the relation between objects and drawings.

With this introduction, a book with tactile illustrations of different pieces of furniture will certainly make more sense not just to a blind child but to any first-time user of tactile graphics, regardless of age.

Drawings of animals and people pose a different set of problems solving which can be achieved by following the same principles of sequencing and direct experience. Another educational set containing a teddy bear, a wooden teddy bear puzzle and a book with tactile illustrations has turned out to be an effective tool for explaining body parts – a useful introduction to understanding the human body and the different 'shapes' which the human body can assume in different situations – sitting, lying or kneeling down etc.. The effectiveness of the set can be confirmed by the reaction of totally blind children with little experience in tactile graphics, who fail in recognizing a drawing of a 'complete' teddy bear shown in Fig. 8, but have no problems with identifying it after a session with the

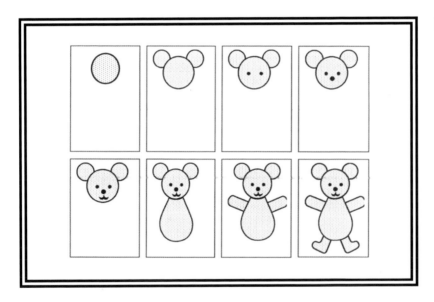

Fig. 8.

tactile story book, in which the teddy bear is introduced gradually, one part at a time. The wooden magnetic teddy bear puzzle which comes with the set is used as an intermediate shape to help relate the real teddy bear with its two-dimensional tactile representation.

Figs. 9 & 10
Tactile Teddy
Bear book

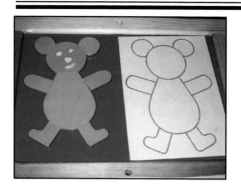 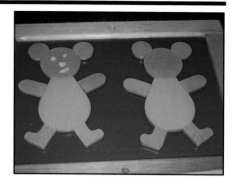

The magnetic puzzle and a tactile overlay can be used to reinforce the understanding of the relations obtaining between different body parts by engaging the child in an activity which can be a non-sighted version of a colouring book.

The importance of engaging young totally blind learners in activities involving tactile graphics can be confirmed by the problems encountered by a ten-year-old totally blind girl who had problems with deciding which of the two teddies shown in Fig. 10 was 'coming' towards her, and which one was 'walking away'. The face was no indication for her of the direction in which teddies, or people, are moving. Thus, tactile graphics can be an important tool for filling various gaps in the

"Now I know
what
a man on a ski"

knowledge of the world of children deprived of visual experience. But with time and carefully structured exercises even children born blind can become competent and confident users of complex tactile graphics, understanding images as abstract as this ski jumping must appear to someone who cannot see.

But the greatest benefits of engaging young totally blind learners in drawing and in reading tactile graphics is the confidence they gain that even with poor vision or without sight they can be in command of the space around them, that they can understand and enjoy maps, drawings and diagrams similar to those used by their sighted peers and that questions like "How can you see a big mountain through a small window" will no longer be a mystery.

Boguslaw Marek, better known as 'Bob', is a professor of English at the Catholic University of Lublin, Poland.

Bob's interest in tactile graphics stems from his involvement in teaching English as a foreign language to visually impaired children. The need to produce adaptations of the highly visual content of foreign language course books has forced him to design educational tools which would prepare congenitally blind children for their first contact with tactile drawings, maps and diagrams. Bob has run workshops on tactile graphics and seminars for teachers working with young learners with a visual impairment in Poland, Lithuania, Estonia, Finland, UK, Belgium, The Netherlands, Hungary, Slovakia and Dubai.

The English for the Blind programme which Bob started in 1999 relies entirely on volunteer involvement. Six totally blind university students studying English and twelve totally blind children aged 6 –14 benefit currently from the programme, for which, in 2002, Bob received the Order of the British Empire.

Hungry Fingers is a one-man company specializing in designing and producing educational tools for young learners with a visual impairment. The tools are designed to help totally blind children understand difficult concepts based on visual experience, and on spatial relations needed for reading tactile graphics. The relation between objects and drawings, symmetry, rotation and perspective are just some of the problems which can be addressed with the help of the tools. Listen and Touch books, produced in co-operation with the Dog Rose Trust (UK) and Tactile Vision (Canada) explain, in an entertaining way, concepts related to body parts and drawings of animals.

The mission envisaged by Hungry Fingers is to give visually impaired children the confidence that with poor vision, or even without sight, they can be in command of the space around them if they can understand it, that space can be divided and altered in many different ways, and that they are the ones who decide how they want to change it.
www.hungryfingers.com

# *Access for All to Exhibitions?*

*'Good design enables, bad design disables'*.

The motto of the European Design for All declaration adopted on 9 May, 2004 in Stockholm.

## Introduction

This section includes brief information that will help to make exhibitions more accessible to everyone, including people who are blind and visually impaired. Access for all to exhibitions and galleries is a huge subject and entire book on its own, and indeed many have been written as you will see below; we have directed you to publications which we have found useful and informative over the years.

Regrettably, though, universal inclusion and multi-sensory design for exhibitions and displays is not understood or taken into account by most exhibitions designers. People with sensory disabilities are not included in the main design and facilities for them are usually added-on afterwards, when there is little money left.

The multi-sensory exhibitions that are put on are often low budget in small museums and have usually been organised in-house by a committed member of staff. Barrierfree has many examples of these excellent events, which usually depend on one person to drive them through.[1]

The best work is often found in the smaller museums which have little funding and have to rely on their own resources, imagination and skills to create accessible displays. Surrey Museums are a good example of this. They have been in partnership on a European project with Fetsund Lenser, the logging museum near Oslo, which is another place doing innovative work on a small budget.[2]

Until Universal Design is taught as main component of architecture, exhibition design and museum courses, the principles and advantages of inclusion will not be understood by architects and designers. We realise that there is much to cover in these courses but inclusion should be written into the curriculum, not viewed as an add-on or optional subject.

# Access for All to Exhibitions?

The Trust was invited to the end of year exhibition of one of the architecture schools, which also included a course on exhibition design mainly, but not exclusively for commercial purposes, not museums. The designs were good and inventive but none of them had considered people with sensory impairments and in some cases mobility had not been thought through. We asked about this aspect of their work and found that access for people with disabilities, let alone Universal Design, was not included in the course.

We asked a design company, who were supposed to be working with us on a job, to come around one of their exhibitions with ourselves and our blind colleague, Eric Sayce, to see how just a little extra thought could make it accessible to him. There were plenty of hands-on exhibits and interactives but there was no way that he could find out how to work them. If they had observed Eric trying to find his way around the exhibits, as John Veverka did with the school children, they might have understood a little more about how to design them so that he could use them. The person in charge of access had conveniently disappeared the day we visited and the receptionist was so embarrassed by Eric that she could only talk to Harry, the Guide Dog. This sort of situation is improving but Eric could write a book about his experiences of this sort.

You will notice that we have not mentioned touch tours or special events put on for people with visual impairments. We are concerned with the person who does not want to book ahead and would just like to drop into a museum, gallery or whatever and is able to find something they can access along with the rest of their family or their friends.

We have also not included much direct information about facilities for people with hearing impairments; we hope that their inclusion is implicit in all we have said on multi-sensory design. There is much good work being done in this field by DeafWorks and Jane Dewey with the Deaf Astronomer's Club and they have far more expertise in this field than we have. We may have said this before, but to repeat, our own expertise is in the field of interpretation for all with an emphasis on those visitors with visual impairments.

Below we have set out some thoughts about some of the aspects of design that could make a difference to a wide range of user groups.

## Labels and information

Written exhibition labels are probably the area that most visitors find the most irritating and unsatisfactory. They find them too high, too low, too long, too short; the print is too small or the print is too large making the label intrusive. Some people think a picture or object should speak for itself and others want more information. It is an almost no-win situation and can become a battle-ground between curators, designers and the people who work on access.

Audio is another contentious issue. Public sound is only usually allowed in the children's sections. Wolverhampton Art Gallery has been adventurous in this direction and we recorded 'cow' sounds for an exhibition called Moo. If there are aesthetic objections to sound in the 'temples of art' then what about a quiet day, like the quiet carriages on the trains? What about a large print label day? Some galleries have days where they raise the lux levels on works that are light sensitive. If we are going to make inclusion, in all senses of the word, meaningful in our cultural institutions we have to break down the barriers and think imaginatively. The quiet of an art gallery can be inspiring to some, but off-putting to others.

Many people cannot read print or Braille and so need audio to describe the works. This then leads into the avenue of what sort of audio, how much will it cost and all the simplicities and complexities that we have outlined elsewhere in this book.

Back to the printed information. Some museums, such as the V&A and Tate Britain, provide large print versions of the labels in booklets in the galleries. These can then be viewed at an angle that suits the visitor. But it does raise the issue that labels in larger print might be better for most people.

The population of Europe is an ageing one and whether we like it or not our eyesight becomes worse as we get older, especially when it comes to reading small print. Many of us were patronisingly amused when our parents and grandparents constantly said, 'Where did I put my glasses?'; now it is our turn to find that we can no longer focus on the print as it is getting smaller and our arms shorter. People who wear glasses for reading are constantly taking them on and off: on to read the labels, off to walk around the gallery and go up and down steps. Large print size would make all this much easier.

It is not only the print size that is important though; lighting, as briefly outlined below, colour contrast and positioning of labels can also make a considerable difference. It has long been advised that black on yellow was the best combination for print, but this is now being reconsidered. What is important is that the contrast between the background and print should be at least 70%. Fancy fonts, especially Gothic typefaces, italics, justification, back-printing of images and photos make the print harder to read.

The position of the labels should ensure that they are comfortable to read, without bending down too low, and they should be near to the objects or paintings they relate to. Inexperienced gallery visitors may be unaware that the label for a sculpture in the centre of the room is actually on the wall by the door. Labels printed on the glass or Perspex of the case are also hard to read because of the low contrast.

Information and design guidelines for exhibitions can be found in many publications. We have put the titles and information out in full here as we highly recommend them.

Two straightforward ones are:

Smithsonian Guidelines for Accessible Exhibition Design can be downloaded off the internet at http://www.si.edu/opa/accessibility/exdesign/start.htm[3]

Designing Exhibitions to Include People with Disabilites, A Practical Guide, by Gail Nolan and published by the National Museums of Scotland in 1997.
ISBN 1-901-663- 00-0.

Other practical publications are:

The Informability Manual, Wendy Gregory, HMSO, London, 1996, ISBN 0-11-702-038-9 which has already been mentioned.

Exhibit Labels, An Interpretive Approach, Beverley Serrell, Altamira Press, 1996, ISBN 0-7619-9106-9

A book with more specific information relating to a particular user group is Access in Mind, Towards the Inclusive Museum, by Ann Rayner.[4] This was a research project by Intact, The Intellectual Access Trust to provide access for people with learning disabilities and has a common-sense approach to providing access for everyone. It is highly recommended.[5]

Two other specialised books are:

Access for deaf people to museums and galleries, A review of good practice in London, Deafworks, London, 2001.

Arts for All? This was another research project, carried out by Mencap, on the 'accessibility of arts and cultural venues for families with children with a learning disability'. Published by Mencap in 2003, it is a salutary read about how these venues fail to make everyone welcome.

A very useful site for all kinds of accessibility information is from Ontario, Canada: http://www.equalopportunity.on.ca

Also from Canada is Design Guidelines for Media Accessibility, 1994, ISBN 0-662-20651-7

### Lighting

It cannot be emphasised too strongly that good lighting can assist many more people with poor eyesight to see properly. 'Adequate and appropriate lighting are important factors for people with visual impairments'. The importance of good lighting and making use of what vision a person has is put into practice much better in the Nordic countries. Recently we were talking to an opthalmist who said he was continually advising residential homes to provide angle-poise type lamps for their elderly clients, but without much success. He stressed that it would make so much difference to their ability to read if they had lighting to suit their individual needs.[6]

This is a big subject and all we can do here is to urge you to take into account the words 'adequate' and 'appropriate' for lighting for displays and exhibitions. This is not always easy as some of the exhibits might be light sensitive; some galleries have a day of the week where the lights are at a higher level. In places where this is not a problem then some lighting that a visually impaired person can adjust themselves for level and angle would be very welcome. The positioning of lighting is important and glare should be avoided.

The RNIB can give further information. Their book, <u>Building Sight</u>, has a section on lighting.[7] The University of Reading have carried out research on lighting with the Group for Inclusive Environments.[8]

### Symbols

We see symbols almost every day, standard ones such as road signs and toilet signs, that we understand without thinking too much about them, except when taking our driving tests or wanting to find the ladies or gents. Generally a universally accepted sign is used for toilets, but some venues decide to express themselves by having cavalier hats and ladies' bonnets or other unintelligible pictures.

You would think that it would be a practical solution to develop a dictionary of other symbols that would help make life easier for a range of people, including those with visual impairments or learning disabilities. This is far from the case. It has been a frustrating problem for those working in this field. Meetings are held but nothing gets decided at a higher level. Designs are drawn up but there is no agreement to use them nationally.

Imagine driving around the UK and finding the road signs were all laid out in different colours in different parts of the country. To some extent that is the situation with footpaths, countryside and town maps and information leaflets.

# Access for All to Exhibitions?

We have tried to use symbols where we can and designed them for the signs at Brecknock Museum, but these applied to only that museum. For keys to maps, such as the consultative maps we produced for Coventry for consultation, we tried to use symbols in current use. This was not easy as there were no standard symbols for some of the things we wanted to include, such as the bus station. We could draw a bus, but it would probably be different from a bus drawn by someone else for another map of Coventry. Consistency for items that reoccur frequently in the same city would be very helpful, let alone around the country.

A useful source for us has been <u>Symbols</u> from the British Tourist Authority, now renamed VisitBritain, and no, that is not a typing error.[9] It comprehensively covered most eventualities, including a section on symbols for disability, but strangely nothing for a bus station. It was also produced in a loose-leaf format so that symbols could be scanned on and used in a document. This has been updated in-house but has not been published again.

Good clear graphic disability symbols under the Disability Access Symbols Project have been produced by the American National Endowment for the Arts in Washington, DC with the Graphic Artists Guild Foundation.[10]

In 2001 the Countryside Agency piloted a range of symbols for paths along the Thames in London which aimed to tell walkers about facilities around the paths and let them decide which one to take, especially if they had mobility difficulties. This work has now been taken further and the symbols researched and developed are used on the Oxfordshire County Council's website, under free and downloadable easy access 'Paths for All'. http://www.oxfordshire.gov.uk. Work has been carried out on these maps by Linda Francis who consulted members of the RNIB in Cardiff to make sure that they could be read by people with visual impairments. They are not, at present, designed to be produced on tactile maps although they are easily downloadable for the website and could be made tactile with the use of 'swell paper'.

Another project is the *Common Visual Language*, which was proposed by Bob Jones, of the Forestry Commission, in a paper given at the 2000 Scottish Natural Heritage Conference.[11] This project has been carried forward by Scottish Natural Heritage and is moving slowly with Dougie Pollock in charge.

The focus of the *Common Visual Language* was on pictograms for behavioural signs such as no fires, no camping and dogs on leads. The aim was to make them as accessible as possible to a wide range of users, such as people with visual impairments and colour blindness, although it was not intended for them to be read easily in a tactile form and this was not a prime consideration. All images were to be easily routed in timber and almost instantly recognisable.

The plan is for the images to be adopted in Scotland as well as England and Wales, through their countryside agencies. Stumbling blocks have been what sort of dog to use: a Scottie for Scotland? A labrador for England? A sheepdog for Wales? Why not just a generic dog with four legs and a tail?

Symbols are used in a coordinated way for communication for people with learning disabilities, such as with Makaton:

Makaton is now in such common widespread use that it is in the Oxford English Dictionary 2005 edition and in the OED online version. The word 'Makaton' is defined in the dictionary as 'a proprietary name for: a language programme integrating speech, manual signs, and graphic symbols, developed to help people for whom communication is very difficult, especially those with learning disabilities'.[12]

Makaton is both a pictorial written language and a signed one, based on British Sign Language. It can be learnt on three levels depending on the user's ability.

Another pictorial-based system is Widget. This was 'designed to develop literacy using pictures, symbols and words, particularly for learners who have a measure of difficulty in developing traditional orthographic skills'.[13] This is a written language and not a signed one. Programmes for the symbols can be bought for computers. The websites for both these systems will give full details about their work and programmes.

There are a number of picture and photo libraries that are worth consulting. People First, 'an organisation of people with learning difficulties speaking up for ourselves', has developed a picture library which is on CD-Rom, Access 2 Pictures. It has over 800 pictures 'which will makes sure people with learning difficulties can understand your information more easily' and is divided up into sixteen subjects and has clear instructions on how to place any pictures within documents.[14]

Valuing People has a clip art library.[15] These are popular with younger people, especially if there is a cartoon element about them. The site, www.easyinfo.org.uk, has more information about these libraries.

Designing for Special Needs was sent to us for review and is full of common sense design ideas for everyone, including a wonderful outdoor sculpture of a dog by Elizabeth Frink that acts, as the book says, as a location marker and as decoration at a residential school. A very upmarket sign post! At this school they use pictures for communication such as PECS – Picture Exchange Communication System – for indentifying rooms, storage and other necessary information. This system is particularly useful for children with autistic spectrum disorders. Have a look at  http://www.specialschool.org/pecs.htm for some video clips of PECS in use.

The 'one symbol fits all' will take a great deal of consultation and design work to achieve. Although this would not be impossible in the limited range of public information signs, from toilets to public parks, as a wider communication system it would be more difficult. Some people with learning disabilities prefer photographs to other forms of pictorial representation. However, unless they are very clear and graphic, photographs would not be so useful for people with visual impairments.

A research project, Improving signs for people with a learning disability, was carried out for the Disability Rights Commission by the Joint Mobility Unit Access Partnership.[16] There are some useful points in it, especially regarding consistency of the image on the sign, its background colour and the use of pictograms.

### Colour
Colour has been mentioned in connection with scripting and now we look at some practical ways in which colour can be conveyed to someone with little or no sight by means other than sound.

The RNIB's on-line catalogue may give you some ideas about innovative and inexpensive items that could be used in an exhibition.  A simple method of identification around the home are Bumpons. These raised bumps are on self-adhesive sheets and come in a range of sizes and colours. They are a simple way to mark items such as on/off positions of electrical appliances. Although we have never tried them there is no reason why they could not be used for identification of objects in museums. Their shapes are familiar to many blind people which is a good start.

Also from the RNIB, and familiar to blind people, are the Indicating Buttons. They 'are designed to help people identify items in everyday life'. There are 16 shapes each representing a different colour. They can be sewn on to clothing  and stand up to washing and ironing.

A system has been developed by Tactile Colour Communications to identify colours by textured vinyl material. This is available in twelve colour/texture combinations: each colour has a different texture and there are different shapes for each texture. They are now based in Canada.[17]

Combining smell, sight and touch are Zychem's *Smelly Vision* papers.[18] There are 11 sheets of different coloured paper which have a scent embedded in them which is released when they are scratched. Smells include strawberry (red paper) and liquorice (black paper). The

RNIB used to sell scented crayons so that the user could tell what areas of the paper they had covered.

Also coloured are *Wikki Stix*; these are colourful yarn and wax sticks that can be bent to any shape and will stick to paper so pictures can be formed with them. They peel off easily so they are reusable. We used them to show the blind members of the Coventry Access Group new features that were being put around the city as part of the Phoenix Initiative.

More sophisticated for those interested in fashion is the c Swatch. This was an entry for the Design Challenge Awards at the Royal College of Art in London. They are organised every year by the Helen Hamlyn Research Centre which promotes inclusive design.[19] The c Swatch won the Inclusive Design prize with its clothing tag system which represented a wide range of colours and sizes through a clever classification of over 60 colours. Unfortunately it has not been possible, so far, to take this idea into production. Patenting is too expensive and a retailer has not taken it up.

But colour need not be confined to identification. The RNIB's Low Tech/No Tech Factsheet includes the information that 'some people find that changing the colour of the background can improve their reading, either by removing the glare from the white paper or because an alternative colour makes the print appear clearer'.[20] Their suggestion is to put the document into a coloured transparent plastic wallet. A range of colours to hand might help someone to read your information more clearly.

### Management and Evaluation
We have mentioned in the Outreach section the need for long-term thinking about exhibitions and now we stress the importance of the management of them. If you are providing facilities for everyone, including those who are visually impaired, then make sure they are kept in good condition and maintained in working order.

All staff should be aware of where Braille guides, audio guides and other items are kept and check that audio machines have batteries. How often we have heard in Cathedrals: 'Do you know where the keys are to the Touch and Hearing Centre?' We went to a much-recommended exhibition in America to listen to the audio description and the machines there would not work because of flat batteries and no one could leave the building to get more as they were short-staffed. We read the text instead; fortunately we were able to do so but others cannot.

It is not easy to make sure everyone knows about everything with so many volunteers working in such a large place as a Cathedral; Winchester, at last count, had around 700 doing different tasks on a rota.

However, the people at the desk, the sharp end, should know.

For information about working with volunteers consult Voluntary Action or the Community Council. Our local South Shropshire Voluntary Action publishes good practice guidelines on Volunteering in Vole, Voluntary Opportunities and Local Energies. Both organisations also run courses on volunteering and many other useful subjects.

Evaluation is something that we all know we should do and leave until the last minute or try and forget about. There is always so much else do that is more interesting. We are as guilty as anyone in this direction. If you can evaluate, then you will learn much about the needs of people with disabilities. In this book, John Veverka has written about the evaluation of interactives and the most positive thing we can do is direct you to a paper called Ask the Audience. This was put together and edited by Emma Hawthorne for the West Midlands Regional Museum Council, as it was then; it is now MLA West Midlands.[21]

And finally, two important websites in the design world.

First, The Design Council in London, organiser of the Millennium Awards. The Dog Rose Trust and several other organisations in the field of disability and medicine gained awards under this scheme. Regrettably, the projects chosen did not get the publicity they should have done as there were some brilliant ideas. The original idea may have been to display all the projects in the Millennium Dome, to celebrate British design and invention, just as the Festival of Britain did in 1951. However, this did not happen and our names were confined to a structure called the Spiral which was outside the Dome by the River Thames. If you wanted your actual object displayed then you had to pay for it and few people did. Now the Design Council site does not carry any information about the Awards and little was found on an internet search. This was a wasted opportunity. However the Design Council does carry useful information about design in general. http://www. design-council.org.uk

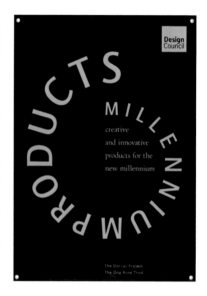

The second site is for the European Institute of Design and Disability http://www.design-for-all.org/. Their motto, 'Good design enables, bad design disables' is quoted at the top of this section. This site is full of information about design across Europe and some inspiring work is being done.

[1] <u>Barrierfree</u> is the journal of MAGDA, the Museums and Galleries Disability Association. <u>www.magda.org.uk</u>.

[2] <u>http://www.surreymuseums.org.uk/</u> and http://www.fetsundlenser.no/

[3] The Smithsonian Guidelines for Accessible Publication Design can be obtained by emailing Beth Ziebarth on <u>ziebarth@op.si.edu</u>. Beth, Director, Smithsonian Institution Accessibility Program, is a great supporter of universal design and accessibility for all.

[4] <u>Access in Mind</u>, Edinburgh, 1998, ISBN 1-901-663-18-3.

[5] A search on the second-hand book site, <u>www.ABE.com</u> came up with two copies – one in Florida and one in New Zealand. However, the books only came up when we put in Access in Mind, not when we refined the search by author and ISBN. ABE is a wonderful site, but think laterally and put in different search words if it cannot find what you want. The book may not be there but it is worth trying other options.

[6] From http://www.norfolk.gov.uk/social/sensory/Rehabilitation.htm

[7] Peter Barker et al, <u>Building Sight</u>, London 1995, ISBN 1-85878-074-8

[8] http://www.rdg.ac.uk/ie/research/fit/fit.htm

[9] Symbols for tourist guides, maps and countryside recreation, published by the British Tourist Authority, London 1993. ISBN 0-7095-5552-0.

[10] This was produced, around 1993, in conjunction with the Graphic Artists Guild Foundation. They can be found on their website: <u>http://www.gag.org/resources/das.php</u>

[11] <u>Natural Codes: Towards a Common Visual Language</u>, Bob Jones, a paper given at the Scottish Natural Heritage Conference – Enjoyment and Understanding of the Natural Heritage, 2000. The papers given at this conference were published by the Stationery Office. ISBN 0-11496-290-7.

[12] From the website of the Makaton Vocabulary Development Project: <u>http://www.makaton.org</u> Programmes for Makaton can be bought on this site.

[13] For more information see <u>http://www.widgit.com</u>.

[14] The CD can be bought off their website: <u>http://www.peoplefirstltd.com/Information.htm</u>

[15] <u>http://www.publications.doh.gov.uk/learningdisabilities/access/</u>. The company that did these, Community Living, have brought out more pictures in a similar style and called it the Valuing People Clip Art collection. <u>http://www.communityliving.org.uk</u>. Information from Zoe Porter of Valuing People Support Team.

[16] <u>www.drc.org.uk/publicationsandreports</u>

[17] http://www.tactile.org

[18] See <u>www.zychem-ltd.co.uk</u> for more details.

[19] For more information see <u>http://www.hhrc.rca.ac.uk/</u> and DBA Challenge 2002.

[20] <u>www.rnib.org.uk</u> and search for Factsheets. There are many useful ones that can be downloaded and printed out.

[21] http://www.mlawestmidlands.org.uk/

MUSEER FÖR ALLA
I NORDEN

Om tillgänglighet för
människor med funktionshinder

Nord Kultur

Underlining the declaration at the beginning of this chapter is *Museer för Alla* in Norden by Elisabet Svensson. The Trust was happy to be able to contribute to this book which was published in 2000.

# *Community Audio*

### Introduction

The Heritage Lottery Fund (HLF) and Advantage West Midlands (AWM), through *Innovative Actions* funded the Dog Rose Trust to run audio courses for people working in the heritage sector and community groups. The project aimed to overcome reservations and nerves about recordings and convince people that they too could do it.

The aim of the HLF *Audio for All* project was to create a 'bank' of audio for venues to draw on, involving the organisation's own staff and volunteers from the local community. Two venues were involved in this aspect: the town of Ellesmere in Shropshire and Coalport China Museum, Coalport, Ironbridge, Shropshire.

Both these projects also involved the production of tactile items so that everyone, including visitors who are visually impaired, could enjoy both venues through sound and touch. The third element of Audio for All was to work with the Shysters, from the Open Theatre Company in Coventry, to produce an audio picture of their city entitled The Shysters Discover Coventry.

An essential component of encouraging people to feel at ease and produce a professional job was to have an experienced voice-over actor running the course. The Trust was fortunate to know the actor, Richard Derrington, who admirably fitted this role. His first task for us was to produce a demonstration CD, based on a brief we had all written, of the techniques that he has used over the years and which have worked for him.

This CD is at the back of this book. We all stress that it is based on Richard's own experience as a voice-over actor and also on his one-man performances with such diverse subjects as Richard III and a poacher. Another actor, Janet Dale. has also been working with the Trust. As a neighbour and friend of Richard Derrington, she sometimes shares his studio and is experienced in radio and voice production.

### Coalport China Museum

The Trust worked closely with the Curator of the Museum and other members of the Ironbridge Gorge Museum Trust to work out strategies for creating sound and touch at the Museum, principally for the benefit of visitors who are visually impaired, but for everyone to enjoy.

The Museum also wanted to have a closer connection with the people of Coalport so Jennifer Thomson, the Curator, organised an open evening with the Friends of the Museum for local residents to come and have a look at the Museum. The Trust put together some tracks from oral history recorded at Coalport China Works more than thirty years ago by Ken Jones. By stepping in when he did, Ken was able to capture the voices of people who had been employed at the Coalport China Works before it closed in 1926 and in doing so created a unique archive. These were played during the evening and comments invited on the content. People were also asked if they would like to put their names forward as narrators or voice-overs for audio to be created for the museum.

*Richard Derrington with Carolinbe Kennedy Morris*

Six people put their names forward and the next move was to meet them all for an informal chat. We met in a local pub, suitably situated by the River Severn which served as the transport system for the Coalport China Works. We then arranged a recording date. The Curator sent an outline of the points she wanted to include on the theme of Transport and Industry at Coalport; we then put this into a draft readable form and then spent time going through the words and dividing the paragraphs between the four readers. We put some of the words into the first person and these were allocated to William Reynolds, a key figure on the development of industry in the area and one reader took on this part.

The readers were coached by Richard, then read their parts into the microphone, listened to the recordings, discussed them and then read each piece twice again. The group showed themselves to be efficient and accurate readers as well as being conscious of the meanings of the words they were saying, so some were changed yet again as we went along. The results were very satisfactory to everyone and the group surprised themselves by how much they had enjoyed doing it and wanted to do more.

The same group came for the second session, which was to read descriptions of six tea cups for the tactile cups display as well as short 'captions' for some tactile images. This time the script, which had been easier to put together, was in better order and had been circulated to the group well beforehand. Preliminary readings showed up words or sentences that needed changing and ironed out phrases and pronunciation that might prove difficult. The 'faintly fluted' description of the shape of a cup could have caused problems without trying it out several times.

The descriptions had been allocated to each reader to suit the character of the cup. The group ably demonstrated that they had learnt much about recording from Richard, who was unable to come. The session went very smoothly, apart from the persistent sound of the small planes going over the Gorge from a nearby airfield and clearly heard in the Museum's conference room where we were recording.

From the editing point of view, and this is described in more detail elsewhere, the more accurate the reader, the easier and faster the job. With computer editing the script does not need to be read in order from beginning to end, as this would entail readers constantly changing places, but good clean 'takes' make the whole job easier.

The recordings will be used in Coalport China Museum. The description of the cups will be accessed by pressing a button beside each cup in a display in the Introductory Gallery. Sound will be accessed via two headsets. The playback system is an Envoy SB from Black BoxAv. The tactile cups were produced by potter Ralph Jandrell who has a workshop at the Coalport China Museum.

The industry and transport recording will be used in the Social History Gallery. This will be accessed by sound from speakers triggered by passive infra-red (PIR) off another Envoy SB.

Sound effects have been collected from the Long Workshop with the demonstrators working the machines, as well as other sounds from the working machinery at the Gladstone Pottery in Longton, Stoke on Trent. These will be used to give character and atmosphere to the narrative.

Additional sound will be provided in the Long Workshop by an MVS Nakamichi 3-disc player. Some of the oral history, relating to Coalport China Works and the social history of the area, have been put on to CDs so that visitors can sit and listen to these during their visit. Other provisions included tactile panels of four key pieces in the Introductory Gallery. There were photographed to be printed in full colour on metal panels with a tactile raised silk screen layer over them.

# Community Audio

Consultation for the project was carried out with blind colleagues Anne Donnelly and Eric Sayce. Anne and her husband John visited the China Museum and gave a report on the spot about the interpretation they would like to see there. We were pleased, and relieved, to hear that these ideas coincided with what we were planning to do.

### Ellesmere

At Ellesmere, Shropshire's Lake District, HLF funded the Trust to work with the community to produce an audio guide as well as a range of sound that could be used in different situations. Here the Trust worked with Shropshire's Countryside Service and Qube, Oswestry Community Action. Again, the aim was to make the area as accessible as possible to people with visual impairments.

As this is an outdoor site, a different approach was required. The story of the town needed to be told by the people of the town and the Trust had met many of them already during *Footprints Round the Mere*, which was organised by Qube and managed by the Trust and funded by Leader +, a European measure. A series of workshops was held to encourage local people to put forward their ideas about interpretation of the Mere. The script for the audio guide was based on these workshops, which included story telling, bird watching, archaeology and trees.

Visually impaired colleagues came to Ellesmere on several occasions to put forward their ideas for the interpretation and one of the workshops was about using all the senses.

The Trust asked local people if they would record sections of the guide. The town's historian described some of the notable buildings, a retired forester talked about the feel, character and shape of the trees, a story teller told the legends of the Mere, a retired blacksmith talked about his work on the canals and the community archaeologist told the story of medieval Ellesmere. We also collected oral history from the members of two day centres.

*Denise Collier and Eric Sayce at Ellesmere*

The oral history and the audio contributions then needed linking together and for that the Trust turned to the Ellesmere Amateur Dramatic Society. Four volunteers came forward, none of whom had any experience of working with a microphone. The script was a straightforward one and the facts had already been checked with local experts and organisations, so little needed to be done to it on the actual recording day. This meant that all efforts could be concentrated on the words and reading them.

*Script discussion at Ellesmere*

Finding a venue was almost the hardest part. Ellesmere has a busy main road running through it so traffic noise is a big problem. This ruled out the Town Hall, where some of the oral history was recorded; at times it sounds almost like a motorway outside. All other suitable venues seemed to be booked so we hired a room at The Red Lion which was away from traffic and proved to be reasonably noise-free. Janet Dale was the coach and the whole day went very efficiently with good results.

During the day we also recorded links for the Uturn Wind-up audio units. These machines are described in more detail in the Playback Section. The extracts from the oral history and other contributions were already in place, only the links needed to be done. It is not easy, either in the writing and editing, to keep the content down to less than two minutes for each side and much will depend on the speed of the speaker. As we tend to talk rather fast, we get a lot of words in during that time, but we are conscious that we cannot rush people who are not experienced.

Twenty people took part in the audio guide, together with all the recordings of events such as the Carnival, the Triathlon and the music composed at the schools; this is written about in the Community Music section. There was a lively local interest in the project which was exactly what we wanted.

With an audio guide, the most important part is the first few sentences – the welcome, setting the scene, creating the atmosphere. For this reason and especially with inexperienced readers, it is often better to start the recording in the middle of the script and do the beginning when everyone is more relaxed and confident. However, do not forget to record it!

Remember to log up everything. There are more details about this in the Scripting for Audio section.

**Summary**

1.      Give yourself plenty of time to arrange dates for meetings with people who already have many commitments.

2.      Leave time for the script to be circulated for comments. It can sit on someone's desk for a long time so put a deadline for reply on it.

3.      Keep all the comments. Someone will come back and say that a fact is wrong, then you can produce the evidence that they did not tell you.

4.      Get your material together in good time and leave time enough for scripting and discussion before the recording session. You can then come prepared to start recording without delay.

5.      Find a quiet venue.

6.      Make sure you get the script to the readers in advance. Preparation makes a big difference to the end-product.

7.      Non-professional readers can do a perfectly satisfactory job given time to prepare and the right production.

8.      Involve as many people as is practical; it spreads the word.

# *Community Music*

### Community Music

The Heritage Lottery Fund (HLF) awarded grants to the Dog Rose Trust to compose music for the *Audio for All* projects. Over the years we have included music with many of our projects as we feel that this gives character and atmosphere to an audio recording and links the sections of it together. Although HLF made no conditions about how the music should be created, it was decided to do this as community projects with the schools in Ellesmere and Much Wenlock, both in Shropshire.

*John Kirkpatrick*

Together with the head of music, we organised a music workshop at Much Wenlock School with 17 pupils from year 10 who played a range of different instruments. The workshop was taken by internationally renowned folk musician, John Kirkpatrick. John demonstrated his skill on the accordion, melodian and squeeze box before asking the children to join him in some traditional Shropshire folk music. Although perhaps not initially their taste, feet were soon tapping and by the end of the day even the electric guitars were joining in the Morris dance rhythms. The object was to produce some music for use at the Coalport China Museum and catchy folk numbers such as *Not for Joe* and *Sheepskins* blend in well with the oral history of the area. As an extra bonus, John wrote a song called *Here's to Coalport China* for the occasion, using the oral history recordings of Coalport as the inspiration for the words. This was recorded during the day with the children as an audience.

Two music workshops were held in Ellesmere. The first was to compose *Music of the Mere*, the large stretch of the water by the town. Fourteen pupils from Lakelands School took part. The workshops were led by Keith Alexander and Lorraine Ross; Keith is disabled himself with only one arm, but plays his guitar expertly with a metal hand. The Trust had sent him recordings of the sounds of the Mere – water, birds, seagulls, ducks – so that the theme of the day could reflect these. The music teacher, Carol King, had worked with the class on these themes and some of the pupils had written poems which were put on a board in the music room.

The words for the vocals came from the poems. The music that was put together by the class expressed the different moods of the Mere as dawn came and the sounds of the day started up. Each group of instruments, after practice, recorded their piece separately and afterwards Keith mixed these together on his 16-track machine.

The second workshop was with twenty eight children at Ellesmere Primary School. Again Keith and Lorraine led the day and this time the theme was castles. Their teacher, Lynn Bartley, had worked with them on this and they had all the right words ready to put together to form the song – dragons, moat, horses, singing. The majority of pupils played the wide range of interesting percussion instruments and there was also a recorder group, a keyboard player and a guitarist.

*Keith Alexander*

The basic tune was worked out and then each group played their part and recorded it ready to be mixed. Then the whole class, plus the Headteacher, got together to record the song. The children enjoyed the day so much they did not want Keith and Lorraine to go or to go home themselves.

The Trust believes that music is important as everyone can join in, from making amazing sounds with something as deceptively simple as a rain stick to complex patterns on a keyboard. The end results can be used in a creative way in audio work and enhance the spoken word.

*Keith Alexander and Lorraine Ross*

# *Audio Case Studies*

### Aston on Clun, Shropshire

The first audio course that we ran, under the Innovative Actions programme, was for the Shropshire Museum Service. Coincidentally, the head of the Museum Service was having a meeting with three members of a committee from the small village of Aston on Clun in Shropshire to discuss their plans for interpretation of the site of the Arbor Tree.

They joined the course and were shown a Uturn, wind-up audio unit, which was just what they needed for playing sound to accompany a display about ceremony of dressing the Arbor Tree, which is an ancient fertility ritual revived in the 18th century. The site has no power to it.

The Dog Rose Trust then showed the group how to load the sound files on to the audio unit. Rosie Evans, a member of the group, was then able to produce some exciting music and words for the interpretation of the tree to complement the written information displayed there.

*The Arbor Tree*
*Aston on Clun*

### Herefordshire Museums

Herefordshire Museums wanted to provide audio information for visually impaired visitors but had no funding to commission the work. With advice and a specification from the Dog Rose Trust, they were able to buy the necessary equipment to carry out their own audio production.

The first audio work was produced as CDs giving information about Herefordshire's five museums, including opening times and contact numbers as well specific information about the collections.

More audio was produced at Hereford Museum and Art Gallery as part of the on-going provision for visually impaired visitors, who can now listen to the CDs which describe items from the collection. This gallery also includes large print versions of the labels, highlighted objects in the showcases and Braille books with tactile pictures and items such as fabrics. There are also many objects to handle. The recordings were made by Lara Latcham, a member of staff, and listeners commented on how much they liked her voice. Herefordshire Museums now have the facilities to produce further CDs and can amend existing ones as the need arises.

### Soldiers of Gloucestershire Museum

A few years ago the Trust was asked to put forward ideas to make the Soldiers of Gloucestershire Museum in Gloucester more accessible to people with visual impairments.

There were two main problems: there was very little money and most of the exhibits were in glass cases because they were fragile, precious or dangerous. We suggested an audio guide that told the story of the regiment and its soldiers through key objects in some of the cases. During the consultation process, colleague Denise Collier and Guide Dog Rebecca came to the museum to give their advice. We found that although the building is on three floors it is a compact space so navigation did not present too many problems.

Clear tactile panels with Braille and lettering, showing images of the key objects, were then put on to the front of relevant show cases. These panels were produced on Perspex with raised 'uv-cured' gel lines plotted on them. They were unobtrusive but were easy read with the fingers. The audio guide gave information about where to locate the panels and as these were put in the same position on each cabinet they were not difficult to find. Each room had a clear Braille Perspex plate with a number and Braille so the audio guide listener could make sure they were in the right place.

We wrote the audio guide in conjunction with the Curator, George Streatfeild. He was the main narrator and was recorded in the rooms of the museum, giving information about the displays and directions to find them. The script, written around the objects in the cases, was in the form of stories, some told in the first person and some in third. The Battle of Corunna was told from the point of view of one of the soldiers who fought there. Appropriate sound effects were added.

George enlisted the help of the Cheltenham Amateur Dramatic Society to record the narrative pieces and they did an excellent job; the Battle of Corunna was particularly effective.

### Brecknock Museum, Brecon, Powys
### 1. Courtroom Dramas

Brecknock Museum is a lively place with a reputation for mounting excellent exhibitions of Welsh arts and crafts. The museum building had been the court and when it became a museum the fittings of the courtroom were retained. Our colleague, electronics engineer Dilwyn Morgan was providing the sound system and asked us to create the sound to accompany the period costumed figures placed in the Courtroom.

Before the figures could be made, the story had to be written using an actual case. We used the local newspapers and directories of the 1890s so that the bilingual Welsh and English story could be based on real people and places. Two different scripts were written and recorded at the same

time. As it was important that the Welsh accents were correct for the area, the museum asked local people to play the parts. All were amateur in the sense of not being paid, apart from Edward Kelsey (Joe Grundy of the Radio 4 programme, *The Archers*) who played the judge and the prosecuting council. His role was also to help with rehearsals and make sure the production went smoothly. In the end, everyone, was so professional that all he had to do was play his own parts. Even the curator and his assistant took part.

The Dog Rose Trust recorded and edited the production which was then put on to a computer and programmed to work with lights to make up a sound and light show of ten minutes. While the hardware for this was expensive, the actual production costs were not. Lunchtime conversation took place in Welsh and English as the six native Welsh speakers debated about the right words to be used.

It was agreed that instead of having two versions of the story, one in Welsh and one in English, that the languages would be interwoven. For example, one of the 'witnesses' did not speak English so the 'local teacher' had to translate for him. The on-lookers in the gallery spoke in both languages, with the other group picking up words so that it was understood by all.

The benefits of making the audio in this way was that local people were involved and felt they were contributing something to their museum and the recording has authentic local Welsh accents. In addition, everyone seemed to enjoy themselves.

### 2. Signage for All

The Trust was asked to design some signage for the museum that would be suitable for a wide range of visitors as well as fitting in with the historic fabric of the building.

The use of two languages meant that extra space was needed so it was decided that symbols would be used where possible for each area of the Museum to replace words. Symbols were designed to reflect the contents of the gallery such as a bird for wildlife and a house for town-life and the colours chosen to tie in with the existing guide book. These were cut from coloured Perspex so that they would be tactile.

The signboards were made of chestnut by a Ludlow craftsman and designed in a modular form so that sections could be replaced or added. Large contrasting lettering in the two languages was put on the main board in the reception area, together with panels containing Braille, symbols and tactile arrows. In some areas the lettering was left off with just the symbols and arrows remaining.

To encourage visitors into the Museum, colourful tactile panels with backlighting were put in the entrance hall. These showed that the Museum covered three floors and the same symbols were used on these as on the signs. The scheme won a top award for Wayfinding from Sign UK in 2003.

### Museum of Transport, Coventry

The Dog Rose Trust worked with the Museum of Transport at Coventry over a period of time to make the displays more accessible to people with visual impairments. As the Museum is in a large rambling building it presented many challenges.

The Trust worked with Steve Bagley, the lively imaginative curator, on a scheme that would fit in with the small budget that the Museum had at that time. Eric Sayce and his Guide Dog Harry were an important part of the discussions to see what could be provided so that someone who is totally blind, like Eric, could navigate their way around the building and enjoy the exhibits. It was decided to concentrate on three key elements:

- tactile tracking for wayfinding
- an audio guide to take visitors around the Museum
- models to understand the shape of the cars

The first job was to find a suitable track that would go around the long distance required to cover several areas of the Museum, as well as go over concrete and carpet. It was not to impede wheelchairs but would stand up to cars being driven over it as they went out to rallies and shows and most importantly would be affordable.

After many telephone calls and enquiries nothing had been found for the right price. In the end we settled for plastic matting that is used to go beside machine tools to stop the operative slipping. A sample of this was tested out by several blind users with long canes and all of them found they could pick it up and follow it. We chose blue and a large roll arrived at Coventry which then had to be cut in half to make it go even further. Black plastic carpet edging was put along the sides to keep it down. At points where there was a choice of route we put tactile rubber squares of a different texture to alert people.

The track not only served its purpose for blind people but proved popular with teachers, who told their class to 'follow the blue track and wait at the end of it'. 'An example of Universal Design', we thought as we watched the children doing this one day.

*Testing out the Blue Track*

The audio guide was to take people around the Museum, through the ten decades of motoring by highlighting representative cars. Models of these were made by Coventry University's Automotive Modelling Department; these aimed to show the overall shape of the vehicle, rather than details which could be felt on the actual cars placed next to the model. The favourite was the Daimler Jaguar because of its sleek elegant lines.

While all this work was going on, Eric and Steve recorded an outreach tape to send to local talking newspapers and other sources which blind people might listen to. Eric appealed for visually impaired people to come and try out the ideas before they were finalised but despite circulating this widely, few people came forward.

The narrator for the recording was Patricia Greene, better known as Jill Archer of *The Archers,* together with Eric Sayce, Harry and members of the Museum's staff. Eric was in charge of the tactile descriptions of the models and actual cars, as well as the directions, which had all been worked out with him beforehand.

To bring the vehicles to life, the sound of their engines was recorded as the staff at the Museum started up all these marvellous cars beginning with the 1898 Daimler. Steve described what it was like riding on a 'bone-shaker', an early type of bicycle, and his colleague Lesley talked her way on and then off a penny-farthing. To add extra character to the guide, music was composed for each of the ten decades, starting with a tune on the theme of *Daisy, Daisy* for the early bicycles.

The track was laid, the models with Braille labels were put on stands near their cars, other Braille labels and wayfinding clues, such as rails and cords, were put into place, the audio guide was ready to be launched. Then the Museum became a designated collection and received money to redo its displays and so a complete redesign was undertaken over the next few years. Unfortunately, this has not included as much access for people with visual impairments as Eric Sayce and his friends would wish, but it is hoped this will happen in the future.

What did become apparent was that the appointed designers of the new galleries had no interest in making the displays accessible to people with visual impairments, despite the brief, written with the Trust, stating that this full accessibility should be included.

The accessible parts of the displays have been produced by Steve Bagley and his team, not the designers. When the Victorian street part of the Museum, *Memory Lane*, was being redesigned the Trust, with Steve Bagley, wrote a report on how to make this more accessible without a separate audio guide or other aid. Audio commentaries at various points explained features to everyone and these were used to direct people to the next place. Audio clues were given such as 'watch out for the barking dog'; as you passed the mock-up pub, you heard the dog bark. Handrails and cords were retained to act as unobtrusive guides and a letterbox on a wall was used as a tactile clue.

# *Coventry Access Group*

### Consultation in Coventry

For the Millennium redevelopment of some parts of the centre of the city of Coventry took place under the multi-million pound project, The Phoenix Initiative. A consultative group was brought together from disability organisations across the city to advise on the work. The group represented a wide range of disabilities, views and interests and satisfying everyone's needs was going to be a difficult task.

The meetings, ably chaired by Chris Beck with Peter Collard, were held monthly while the major work was being carried out. These provided a forum for people to air their views, ask questions, give their opinions and generally contribute to making the wide-ranging changes as accessible as possible.

Site visits were part of the programme, both with work in progress and completed. The landscape architects were invited to come and join the group on a visit to the newly-created Priory Gardens,. It was unfortunate that they did not take up the invitation as they would have learnt that some of their steps did not work for blind people: the handrail on the bridge and steps was too wide for a comfortable grip and the end of the ramp without a handrail was a hazard for many people. We all could have asked who designed the un-ergonomic benches; great for lying on to sleep away the day but no good for sitting.

The group was able to influence the design of bus shelters and where the buses would be stopping. And this is where the Trust came into the work. We were asked to produce tactile plans of the changes to the city so that the blind members of the group could join in the discussions.

We first produced an overall map of the city that had reference features that are familiar to people with visual impairments. These were the Cathedral and Cathedral ruins, Herbert Art Gallery, Museum of British Road Transport, Belgrade Theatre and the Bus Station. Others were to be discussed with the access group. For this preliminary stage, we used plans raised on A3 'swell paper' with a separate key on another sheet. A brief audio commentary was included.

Using these reference points, we then created maps that showed the area that The Phoenix Initiative would cover and then progressed to detailed plans of some of the newly created areas such as Priory Gardens, The Garden of International Friendship and Millennium Place. Some of these formed the basis for the plan that was put out in the City; we have described this in other places.

The new bus hub and stops caused the most discussion at some meetings; this was an important issue for people who rely on public transport. We produced a schematic plan of the proposals so that specific questions could be asked.

The group also visited other cities to see how they had managed their changes and also to look at street furniture and paving. We went with them to Nottingham and Alec Keeper was able to join us and show them the *Lace Market Unveiled* panels.

When the main work of the Phoenix Initiative had been completed, the group continued to meet, sometimes monthly and sometimes every other month. There are still many changes going on in the city and their advice is needed for such major developments as a new football stadium.

The Disabled People's Development Advisory Group is a good example of consultation with end-users over a period of very active development that has been sustained and needs to keep going for the future. For the project managers, it was an opportunity to learn about access requirements and to explain the reasons why something could not be done the way the group wanted it. The group found that their suggestions and complaints were listened to and acted on where possible and understood why it was that their recommendation could not always be carried out.

*Tactile plan showing the toilets at Coventry Library*

# Exhibit Evaluation
## by John A Veverka

**Exhibit evaluation for Children's Exhibits - The Kirby Science Center Experience.**

### Why Ask?

Evaluation has long been a part of any interpretive planning strategy, especially for interpretive center or museum exhibits. When you consider the costs of exhibits to agencies (estimated at $300 per square foot of exhibit floor space) you would think that before the exhibits were delivered the agency would want to make sure they 'worked', i.e. accomplished the objectives they were designed for. Unfortunately this evaluation process rarely happens and many exhibits quietly 'fail' to make any contact with visitors.

I was recently a part of the Derse Exhibits team to plan, design, build and 'evaluate' exhibits for the new Kirby Science Center in Sioux Falls, South Dakota. They had three empty floors and wanted top quality science exhibits to fill the building – a $3,000,000.00 project. Part of the total project the client wanted was a thorough evaluation of exhibits to make sure that each exhibit accomplished its specific interpretive objectives. This short article will summarize what and how the evaluation took place and what I and the team learned from this 'wrenching' experience called evaluation.

### What were the exhibits supposed to do?

Before you can evaluate anything you have to first know what it was supposed to accomplish. Part of the total exhibit plan was an 'Interpretive Exhibit' plan. This consisted of each individual exhibit having – in writing – a specific concept the exhibit was to present, and specific learning, behavioral and emotional objectives each exhibit was held accountable to accomplish. We would later evaluate the mock up exhibits against those stated objectives.

### The evaluation strategy

For this evaluation strategy I developed several different evaluation methods to be used for the total evaluation. The evaluation would take approximately 4 weeks to do. We set up draft or mock-up exhibits in the warehouse of Derse Exhibits, evaluating approximately 15 exhibits each week, representing six different science subject areas. We then arranged with local schools for teachers to bring in their classes to

# *Evaluating Exhibits*

'test the exhibits' for us. We would test each set of 15 exhibits over the course of one week. The evaluation strategies included:

### A written pre-test and post-test

We brought in school busses of children from different schools to be our 'audience' for the evaluation. Before being allowed to use the exhibits each group took a short written multiple choice and true/false pre-test relating to each exhibit's objectives. After the pre-test the children could then go and 'use' the exhibits. After spending about 45 minutes with the exhibits they came back for a written post-test. We wanted to see if there was any change in what they knew about the tested science concepts from before seeing and using the exhibits – and then after they interacted with the exhibits.

### Observational Studies.

This part of the evaluation used a trained observer stationed at each exhibit to simply watch and record what the children did or didn't do. This told us a lot about things like 'instructions', graphic placements, and subjects that children did and didn't have any interest in.

### The quick fix – and fix – and fix again

Essentially our plan was to have two groups of children test the exhibits on Monday of each of the four weeks. We would then analyze the test results and our observational results, make any changes to the exhibits on Tuesday, bring in two new groups of students on Wednesday' make any more corrections on Thursday, do one final test on Friday, make any final adjustments, and then ship out the completed exhibits from that week's testing on to the Science Center over the weekend. We would then repeat the evaluation process the next week for 15 different exhibits.

### What we found out – Oh the pain!

What did we learn from this experience? We learned that if we had not done the testing the great majority of the exhibits we 'adults' planned would have been failures! Virtually EVERY exhibit we tested had to be 'fixed' in some way. Here are a few of the things we observed.

For example, with an exhibit on 'magnetism', shown in the pictures below, you were directed to move the magnet on the chain UNDER the objects; the magnetic items would then move. Not one child followed these directions. They only used the magnet from above! They wanted to see the magnet on the chain interact directly with the item in the exhibit.

We fixed this by changing the directions and raising items in each container so magnetic objects would react with the magnet held from above. We discovered that children found any written directions to be 'invisible'. In 98% of the cases the children did not look at or read any directions unless an adult suggested they do so. If they had to read complex directions to do the activity – they usually left the activity.

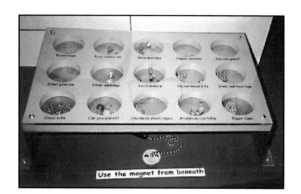

Another interesting example of what and how children think was our 'how bats find food' exhibit. The exhibit has a sensor beam that beeped when a person walked in front of it. As the child would walk closer to the exhibit the beep would beep faster, to illustrate bats eco-location ability. We found that the children made games out of the exhibit beeper trying to run past the beam, crawl under it, etc. They were only interested in the beam and how it worked – they could not care less about bats!

We also were able to test the construction of the exhibits themselves, and some of the exhibit tools. For example, our 'indestructible' microscopes didn't last a week! With constant use, and having the children lean on - push on - tug on the microscopes, they quickly came un-mounted. The exhibit designers had to experiment with a fastening system that was 'difficult' for children to break. Break-proof exhibits for children is 'a dream'! Most of the exhibit design team, used to doing exhibits for adults, found children's exhibits to be an emotional and creative challenge. Children don't think like adults – surprise!

### What we learned
This month-long evaluation process taught us all a lot, the most important of which was that if we hadn't done the evaluation we would have built exhibits using adult ideas of how children learn that children would NOT have learned from.

### Some key points
From the pre-post tests, we found that there were some subjects students already had a good concept level understanding of – pre-tested at an 80% correct response or higher on the written test; and some areas

they had a very poor understanding of – with correct responses on the pre-test of 50% or less. We did find that when comparing the pre-test and post-test results, there were often increases in correct answers on the post-tests, depending of the individual exhibits. So the exhibits were generally working – but the initial post-test improvements were generally very weak, may be only 5-15% improvements on post-tests at the start of the week (Monday testing). But by Friday, after the exhibits had gone through many changes in design, instructions presentation, and concept presentation, we were at an average of 80% comprehension or better on post- testing for most exhibits. By doing this formative evaluation through out the week of testing, we were ending up with 'very good to excellent' exhibits as far as having their educational objectives accomplished at a 70% level or higher (our goal).

We found that EVERY exhibit we evaluated over the 4 week period (about 60 exhibits) had to have some 'improvements'. Some exhibits just needed a little fix – such as the addition of a label that said 'push the button' (otherwise the button to start the activity would not be pushed), to some exhibits needing a major re-design.

We found that children did not even look at, let alone read any 'written' instructions. But we did have success in redesigning instructions in cartoon or 'comic book' formats – more visual presentation instructions. The instructions themselves had to look fun or interesting. For many of these exhibits to be used most efficiently would require a docent, science educator or teacher to help facilitate and direct the learning activity. But the exhibits did work effectively on their own after evaluation-driven re-designs. When our researchers facilitated the learning by explaining directions, etc. the exhibits worked wonderfully.

The design team and the client all learned that the ONLY way you will know for sure if you have a 'successful' exhibit, not just a pretty exhibit, is to evaluate it with your intended target market group. The visitors will tell you if your exhibit is successful in communicating with them or not – if you ask them!

### Summary

This short article only begins to touch on some of the many complex educational issues and design challenges we encountered by doing this evaluation. My goal was to provide an introduction as to why evaluate, and how the process helped us to finally design and build exhibits that were really educationally successful. We believe that based on all that we learned about exhibit users for this museum, that evaluation for any exhibit project is not an option but a requirement for true exhibit success.

**References**

Veverka, John A 1998 <u>Kirby Science Center Exhibit Evaluation Report</u>. Unpublished report for the Kirby Science Center, Sioux Falls, South Dakota.

Veverka, John A. 1994 <u>Interpretive Master Planning</u>. Acorn Naturalists, Tustin, CA.

Veverka, John A. 1999. 'Where is the Interpretation in Interpretive Exhibits'. Unpublished paper available on line at: www.heritageinterp.com (in our LIBRARY).

John Veverka runs John Veverka & Associates, a firm that specialises in Interpretive and Heritage Consultation and Training. John works at heritage sites all over world and is often in the UK giving seminars and workshops.

This article, in a shortened form, was first published in <u>Interpret Scotland,</u> Issue 4, Autumn 2001. This excellent little free publication, which comes out twice a year. To subscribe and to download back numbers, look at their website: http://www.interpretscotland.org.uk/

## Disabled Visitors at the City of Science and Industry, Paris
## by Marie-Laure Las Vergnas

Situated in the Parc de la Villette in the Northwest of Paris, the Cité des sciences et de l'industrie is a huge centre devoted to the popularization of science, technology and industry. It provides a display ('Explora') of permanent and temporary exhibitions, exhibitions specially devised for children (Cité des enfants), a Planetarium, a multimedia library, a congress centre. It covers today's major issues, such as genetics, energy, plate tectonics, astronomy, exploration of space and ocean, environment, health.

From the beginning it was decided to make the Cité accessible to any visitor, including all disabled visitors: wheelchair users, deaf, visually impaired and mentally impaired persons. The aim was to make these visitors as autonomous as possible and to make it possible for everybody, disabled or able-bodied, to visit the same exhibitions at the same time and, by so doing, to help them meet and understand each other.

To perform this task a specialised architect was commissioned to check all the projects from the accessibility point of view, as well as a special team ('service Accessibilité') employing disabled persons was created before the opening, in February 1986.

*Space exhibition being explained in sign language*

In December, 1989 the Cité was awarded an Accessibility prize by the European Community under the Helios Programme and in May 2001 it was the first cultural venue to receive the label ' Tourisme et Handicap ' for the four major impairments. The Cité produces its own guidelines for accessibility.

Today nearly everything is accessible to visitors with mobility problems: circulation between floors is possible by lift or escalator and flat or ramped access is provided everywhere. Only a very few exhibits are inaccessible (such as the real - and narrow- submarine outside the building, near the Géode).

Visits in sign langage with a deaf guide are offered to deaf visitors. The Cité produces films in sign language on scientific matters, which are integrated in the exhibitions and sold to schools, associations and individuals.

For visually handicapped visitors, tactile elements, such as real objects, models and hands-on pictures, are integrated in the exhibitions to reinforce their accessibility. In the multimedia library, the Louis Braille Room provides reading computers. The City publishes books with raised pictures, large print and Braille.

Many exhibitions are interesting for mentally deficient children and grown-ups ; the Accessibility service helps them make their choice and organise their visit.

On the whole every visitor can spend a few hours or a few days in the Cité des sciences et de l'industrie enjoying himself and never getting bored.

### How Do We Proceed To Make Accessible Exhibitions?

We think it is not a good solution to make an exhibition for 'valid' visitors and to conceive a series of add-ons for the others. We always prefer to make exhibitions accessible for every visitor, that is to say exhibitions in which different visitors can use the same exhibits.

*'The Sounds'- a tactile and visual exhibition*

To achieve such a goal we stick to a few rules.

### Rule Number 1.

We organise a lot of (and more) awareness raising: it encompasses not only the agents in contact with the visitors, but also the professionals involved in the process of exhibition making.

### Rule Number 2.

We integrated disabled persons in the team in charge of the project. It makes the designers   understand quicker and the proposals are more adequate and realistic. We have also built partnerships with associations of disabled persons; they help us test the exhibits beforehand and evaluate the exhibitions after their opening.

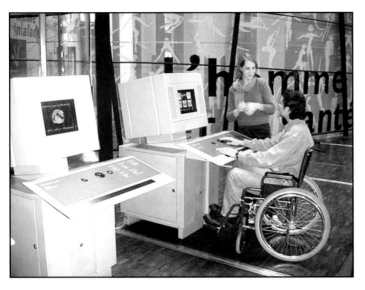

*All the exhibits are accessible to everyone*

### Rule Number 3.

It is essential to remember what we have done and to capitalize the successes and failures. We try to incorporate them in the guidelines of the establishment.

### Rule Number 4.

We always work as early as possible with the teams in charge of the exhibitions and at all the major phases of the exhibition delivery. We try to make them take the point of view of as many users as possible and understand that this can make the exhibition more interesting for everyone.

**A few examples :**

• hands-on models are good for everyone. For instance, in the exhibition Rocks and Volcanoes it was decided to have a tactile volcano usable by every visitor, instead of having a picture for well-sighted visitors and something tactile on the side for the visually impaired. The visitors can also touch lava stones and other tactile models explaining the theory of Plate tectonics. It makes the explanations more understandable by every visitor.

• subtitles for video displays are useful for everyone in a noisy environment.

• directions for use of interactive exhibits : we need to explain to the visitor what he has to do. Using pictures showing what to do, instead of written directions, we help not only deaf visitors, children, mentally impaired visitors, but also foreign visitors, persons with reading difficulties (10 to 15% of the population) and lazy visitors, who are fed up with reading labels.

• non-verbal clues inducing simple and intuitive use (buttons for pushing, levers for pulling, round handles for turning) make it easier for everybody and save energy.

*Smelling the way home, like an ant*

• the presentation of essential information through different modes – pictorial, verbal, tactile – enables every visitor to choose his own best channel for understanding.

For the designers it is a new way of conceiving exhibitions. In the *Cité des sciences et de l'industrie*, we can measure the evolution from the opening. The designers understand more and more that accessibility is not the addition of more and more rigid rules, but that, on the contrary, it enhances their creativity.

Marie-Laure Las Vergnas is in charge of the « mission Accessibilité Générale », which tries to make the Cité des sciences et de l'industrie accessible to every visitor.

# Cultural Heritage Accessible to All
## by Sari Salovaara

The Finnish National Gallery has taken a major role in Finland in the attempt to make cultural facilities accessible and welcoming to everyone. The Gallery consists of three art museums and covers 700 years of Finnish and international art history. The education policy takes into consideration the diversity of different audiences and aims to create inclusive programs. There is a variety of customized services available. Periodically some of the exhibitions and festivals carry themes that involve disability community's views and representation.

Finland is a small country and international relations are extremely important in order to keep up with the developments in different parts of the world and contact with outside organisations is important to us.

Here at the Finnish National Gallery we are very keen to make our exhibitions as accessible as possible to everyone.

**Examples of services available in the Finnish National Gallery**

- Guided tours are offered in sign language and easy-to-follow Finnish. Guided touch tours are also arranged for visually impaired visitors.
- Teleloop amplifies, amplified headsets and an induction loop system are available
- Raised maps/plans of the Ateneum building are mounted on the wall beside the cloakroom and filed in a folder at the information desk.
- Sound pictures of classic works of Finnish art are available at the information desk (twelve in Finnish, one in English).
- Visually impaired visitors are welcome to touch selected works in the collection. Cotton gloves are available for loan at the information desk.
- Magnifying glasses are available for loan at the information desk.
- A website exhibition designed specifically for the visually impaired features a combination of spoken and written text in three languages, images, detailed descriptions and background history: www.fng.fi/hugo.

### Culture for All Service to promote equal access

Culture For All Service is a joint effort funded by the Ministry of Education and coordinated by the Finnish National Gallery's Art Museum Development Department (Kehys). The service promotes equal access to culture and removes barriers to participation. The service works in collaboration with various experts, organizations, cultural institutions and communities.

Access-related guidance and support is offered primarily to providers of cultural services. These include:

- Expert advice and counselling
- Training
- Surveys of facilities and services
- Production and distribution of information material
- A web site www.kulttuuriakaikille.fi

### Networks

The Finnish National Gallery and Culture for All Service collaborate with various cultural institutions. One example of a project promoting accessibility to cultural heritage is entitled ACCU, Access to Cultural Heritage: Policies of Presentation and Use (2004-2007). The project is funded from the Culture 2000 Programme of the European Union. It promotes cooperation between operators in the field of heritage management and offers new tools for professionals to use on accessibility issues. Cultural institutions from six European countries participate in the project led by the Finnish National Board of Antiquities (Helsinki, Finland). The three-year project will include several conferences, the publication of web pages and a DVD with the title OPEN DOORS, Making Cultural Heritage Sites and Exhibitions Accessible, and a travelling exhibition. The DVD and the exhibition are planned for 2007.

Another network is The European Design for All e-Accessibility Network (EDeAN) which was established in 2002, in accordance with one of the specific goals of the eEurope 2002 Action Plan. The Action Plan was agreed on and committed to by the European Commission and all the member states. One of the objectives of the eEurope action plan is the integration of older people and people with disabilities into the information society. This will only come about as a result of designing mainstream products and services to be accessible by as broad a range of users as possible. This approach is termed "Design for All".

Sari Salovaara is the Project Adviser for Culture for All. She has been active in promoting access for all in the Finnish National Gallery. She was one of the leaders of the sessions in Athens in March 2003 at a Cultural Access Institute organised by Very Special Arts in Athens; the Dog Rose Trust was also taking part there.

# The Lace Market Unveiled
## by Alec Keeper

The Lace Market Unveiled was launched in May 2002, in the historic streets of Nottingham's Lace Market. A series of eight sculptural reliefs and accompanying audio guide offer a unique and tactile journey exploring the architecture and heritage of the Lace Market.

*St Mary's Church, The Lace Market, Nottingham*

The audio guide, narrated by Joanna Lumley, was made available from the Lace Market Heritage Point at the Galleries of Justice, a local tourist attraction. The guide is delivered via Walkman-style cassette players and headphones.

### Beginnings

The Lace Market Unveiled, or LMU, had developed from proposals I had exhibited at the Kelvingrove Art Gallery & Museum, Glasgow. The exhibition was the result of a project carried out by Bellarmine Arts Association on behalf of the Centre for Sensory Impaired during Glasgow's reign as European City of Architecture.

# *Lace Market Unveiled*

My proposals considered both route marking and tactile 'images': as a photographer I wanted to produce images that could be understood without sight, and created images of architecture in both glass and granite. I was interested in the combination of these – routes through cities defined by sculpture and street furniture.

### Initial ideas

In Nottingham I discussed these proposals further, and the idea of a heritage trail soon developed. Support was gained from the Nottingham City Council's Access Officer and Team for Visual Impairment, as well as the Nottinghamshire Royal Society for the Blind.

Funding support was required, and Experian, based in Nottingham, was approached. They committed to the idea and Nottingham Trail for Vision Impaired People (NTVIP), a group of volunteers, was established to oversee the project.

Further support was soon gained from Nottingham City Council and the Lace Market Heritage Trust. NTVIP and Experian began work on a bid to Arts and Business, while NTVIP pursued an award from the Local Heritage Initiative to meet the full cost of the project. The project itself began in March 2001.

### Sculptural reliefs

Eight buildings were selected to form a route through the Lace Market, from a 14th century church to a newly opened ice arena. These were photographed and the process of translating these images into 3D reliefs began.

The first stage of this translation was to create the reliefs in clay. Over a four-month period I worked alongside clients in the Nottinghamshire Royal Society for the Blind's (NRSB) art room, who were busy on their own pieces. As the clay models progressed guidance and feedback was sought from various individuals around the centre, with varying levels of vision. The ideas and aims of the project were discussed, both informally and through talks.

*Detail of sited LMU sculpture*

With a clay model arriving at a comprehensible state it was time for the next stage: translating the clay into the final material. For seven of the eight buildings, this material was white Italian Carrara marble. Cooperative Funeral Services in Glasgow provided me with workspace and facilities to carry this out. Using a sandblasting technique I had developed I worked on the stone to match the clay model, employing limited tool finishing as required. Returning to the NRSB, feedback was now sought on the stone version and adjustments made as required.

The eighth building on the trail, the ice arena, was the only modern building. To reflect its building methods in contrast to the others and its function, resin was chosen as the final material. A mould was made from the clay model and an ice-like resin cast produced.

*Testing of the LMU audio guide*

### Audio Guide

The audio guide that was to accompany these sculptural reliefs had two main functions to perform: it had to navigate the viewer's hands around the piece, while conveying stories about the building and area. Initial development took place at the NRSB, creating a framework for the navigation side. This was developed in conjunction with volunteers at the Centre, again with differing sight abilities.

Andy Barrett, a Nottingham based writer, worked on the history aspect of the guide, researching the buildings and their place in the Lace Market story. With the navigation reaching a working level that catered for a broad range of vision, Andy combined these two aspects into one narrative for each building. The guide was now ready to be tested.

Testing of the guide took place over several sessions at the Council House in Nottingham. Around 15 volunteers of different ages and with different levels of vision took part. The sculptures were covered over for sighted volunteers and their response noted: not used to using touch, they were surprised at the small size of the sculptures, thinking they had been considering a much larger area. As throughout the project, feedback was noted and adjustments made until a final version was arrived at.

This final version was recorded with the assistance of 96 Trent FM, a local radio station. The guide itself is delivered via Walkman-style cassette players. These were the most economical choice that would allow free movement of both hands.

### Accessibility

The physical presence of the trail itself demanded certain considerations. The look and feel of the supports for the sculptures had to be practical, accessible and carefully sited. The Lace Market is a conservation area and this too placed demands on the appearance of the trail: quality materials were used throughout. In order to achieve a successful result the project had to engage with several organisations.

I worked closely with Team for Visual Impairment and consulted with Nottingham City Council's Access Officer, Nottinghamshire Blind Alliance,
The Royal National Institute for the Blind and the Joint Mobility Unit to ensure that good practice was adopted throughout.

The development of the route itself, tactile mapping, audio directions and all associated signage and information was carried out in conjunction with Team for Visual Impairment and ensured the full accessibility of the trail.

A flexible approach allowed other ideas to be incorporated as the project progressed. Additions included the use of brass tactile pavement indicators, granite tap rails and the offer of the audio guide in Braille as well as text versions of different sizes. Map carry bags were also made available.

### Presence

The Lace Market Unveiled has been received as a positive enhancement to this historic part of Nottingham, both in its physical appearance within the street fabric and as a valuable asset to promote the heritage of the area.

Its presence helps draw the attention of the general public to the history and beauty of the buildings located in this area. The permanent installation of the trail serves to raise awareness of vision impairment and issues surrounding access, and to keep these firmly in the public domain.

### Awards

The project document of the LMU, a funding requirement, was presented as a website. This website was designed to be fully accessible via browser reading software and was awarded a Commendation at the National Library for the Blind's Visionary Design Awards 2002. It is still online, and can be visited at:

www.lacemarketunveiled.org

The LMU project itself was shortlisted in the Arts & Business Awards 2002.

### Development of the LMU in Glasgow

In the months following the completion of the LMU, I began to consider its development and the possibility of this happening in Glasgow. Touting the idea around different departments of the City Council and other city-based organisations produced a very positive response. Different incarnations of the trail concept around different locations in the city were all discussed. There was definitely an encouraging level of support.

### Tactile Govan

Tactile Govan started in February 2004 as a pilot study to explore the potential for a tactile heritage experience in Glasgow, fully accessible to both sighted and partially sighted audiences. Funding support was provided by Scotland in Europe, Glasgow City Council and Govan High School.

Similarly to the LMU, this experience is to offer citizens and visitors a sensory introduction to the City's architectural heritage, through a series of tactile sculptures with accompanying audio guide.

Tactile Govan offers the opportunity to build on the experience of the LMU project. As time passes, better ways of doing things present themselves: whether in the actual process of creation, or in the delivery to the public of the finished piece.

Observing each aspect of the LMU as a finished product has provided many key points of consideration. In particular the breadth of content of the sculptures themselves, and the effect this has upon their function as both tactile object and visual highlight; the method of delivering the audio guide, and the impact this has upon its range of functions and appeal and the importance of assigned ownership, proper maintenance and promotion to ensure longevity.

*Sculpture and audio detail, Tactile Govan*

### Working Method

One of the main purposes of the pilot was to demonstrate a working method, through the selection of one example building to study. The Pearce Institute (the PI) in Govan was chosen. Together with pupils from Govan High School we considered its architectural form and heritage, with attention to descriptions for those with partial sight.

While in residence at the school I produced an example sculpture, this time selecting only a detail of the building. As before this was produced in clay, although the final material, blonde sandstone, was carved. The Masonry Department of Cooperative Funeralcare again provided me with workspace and advice.

The pupils were guided through a similar process. Each chose a detail from the building and produced tactile panels in clay. Together, their pieces created a sensory description of the building.

A visit to the Sound Sight exhibition in Glasgow provided the pupils with a comprehensive introduction to many issues surrounding vision impairment. This annual exhibition displays a wealth of information and tools to assist those with partial sight.

Sound artist Mil Stricevic was invited to work on the development of the audio element of the study. An example guide was produced to accompany the sandstone sculpture. This time however, the guide was created in two separate sections: one conveyed reminiscences of the buildings life, while the second was a description of the building's appearance. Proposals as to how this guide could be delivered were investigated, aiming at a solution that could make the sculptures 'speak'.

### Tactile Govan Exhibition

The resulting exhibition of the pupils' and artists' work was exhibited in the PI itself, in June 2004. Responses to the Pearce Institute were presented in the form of tactile descriptions, an example sculpture and accompanying audio guides. Outline proposals suggesting different forms of a tactile heritage experience for Govan were displayed.

The Tactile Govan pilot demonstrated an inclusive working process which can be adapted to meet the needs of various educational or community groups. Such a process is ready to be expanded to create permanent works, to be realised in whichever form as appropriate.

The exhibited proposals have engaged the imagination and commitment of several organisations. A management group has since been set up to carry these proposals forward and with the recent receipt of an award from Govan Community Forum we now look forward to the next stage: realisation of these ideas.

Alec Keeper is a professional photographer and artist based in Glasgow. His photographic practice covers both commercial and social assignments. He has been involved in many community arts projects over the last fifteen years, both as a freelance and as an associate of Bellarmine Arts Association. This involvement has seen Alec come full circle, from participant to documenter to coordinator.

The photographs in this article are by Alec Keeper.

## *About Umcebo*
## *by Robin Opperman*

*Beaded
Killerwhale
banner*

**Umcebo is a Zulu word meaning treasure**

The *Umcebo Trust* is a public benefit non-profit organization, which was registered on 22 May 2003. The main aim of the trust is to establish a studio workspace for people with special needs to use and develop their artistic talents as a means of personal and creative development, as well as to generate income.

*Umcebo* is committed to the broader education and the development of skills of people with special needs, but also aims to include those who have various abilities – encouraging contact between all people no matter what their abilities. The idea is for people to develop mutual understanding and awareness of each other in a mutual exchange of ideas and skills. *Umcebo* believes that personal empowerment and improved self-awareness is brought about through artist creation and the learning from and teaching of others. It is this collaboration that works towards inclusion of participants in the fullest sense.

**Where we come from**

*Umcebo Trust* is the brainchild of Robin Opperman, the Head of the Department of Art and Technology at *Ningizimu School for the Severely Mentally Handicapped*. Robin's eleven years of work through the school have provided a working model for *Umcebo*. This work has resulted in a sound working relationship with communities around the school.

*Umcebo* aims to take this work further, and offer it more broadly, through establishing an art workspace where individuals and organisations throughout Durban can get together to develop art and crafts, to learn, and to teach. Through this process learners and members of surrounding communities will be able to educate, empower and inform themselves about the potential and possibilities of art and crafts.

### What we hope to achieve

There are two aspects to the vision of *Umcebo Trust*: firstly, to assist people to generate income, building on the model that has been established through the art programme at *Ningizimu School*; and secondly, to offer training and starter kits for educators who have no resources to help them be more effective at their own work. The training would assist them with the skills to start and grow an art department.

We hope that all involved will dream beyond the confines imposed on them by society, to feel the freedom to come up with workable and realistic ideas that will show their full potential and challenge the stereotypes of what work is fitting and suitable for them. The studio workspace would serve as a hub for people to share their skills and draw skills and inspiration, which they can take back to their communities.

### Our Ethos

*Umcebo's* work is guided by a number of fundamental principles:

- community participation: which is encouraged through members of diverse communities visiting the workshops and becoming involved in the process. Becoming involved includes attending the workshops, sharing skills by training others or being trained, active mentorship, donating waste/ recyclable materials and lending moral support, which builds a real sense of community ownership;
- enhancing individual participants' self-esteem, sense of self-worth and social standing through creative participation, the learning and sharing of new skills and income generating capacity;
- providing a non-threatening and secure environment where a diverse range of people can gather to collaborate on group and individual projects;
- promoting an attitude shift in the broader community's views on marginalised people - where special needs participants and people are valued.

*Umcebo hand-beaded traditional beer mug*

### The work of *Umcebo*

- facilitating the creation of unique art works and functional craft items using a combination of reclaimed waste and other materials;
- facilitating training in, and sharing of, craft production skills;
- generating income for individuals through giving participants the opportunity to create and sell the art works and functional craft items;
- participation in various publicity and

awareness generating events which showcase *Umcebo's* project work;
    • fostering links with organisations that share a similar vision, in order to share expertise and extend the reach and accessibility of the *Umcebo* aims.

### Projects
The projects create the working platform for achieving the aims of *Umcebo*. The projects can be divided into two main areas:

### 1. Creative production-based workshops
The outcomes of these workshops are saleable products, generating income, informal learning and skills transfer. Local communities are encouraged to connect with *Umcebo* by bringing their old newspapers, toilet roll holders and other donated recyclable materials.

Commissioned art pieces: consists of unique and individual banners, 3-dimensional sculptures or specially commissioned projects.

*Aids banner: a celebration of life and colour*

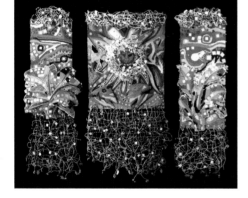

Banners: large and smaller scale cloth wall hangings, jewelled and embellished with wirework, intricately applied beadwork combining found and recycled objects, sewing, embroidery and other painting and cladding techniques. Imagery and patterning is individual to each banner. The final effect is one of a colourful mosaiced, embroidered and sculptural wall hanging.

3-dimensional sculptures: large, freestanding pieces of sculpture involving structural wirework, sewing techniques and other sculptural and painting techniques. The patterned cladding is achieved through using many of the above-mentioned banner techniques. Subject matter, imagery and patterning will also be unique to each sculpture.

Eclectic Collectables: a line of products consisting of functional home-décor items and accessory pieces, which, while functional, still retain a one-of-a-kind, art feel. The line consists of beaded and wirework *objet* pieces and bags, mats, basket and vessels woven and crocheted from reclaimed plastics. This line is constantly developing and will see lots more new additions.

Fire Blocks: non- toxic fuel material is made from pulped paper-waste. These are not only sustainable sources of fuel, but are also cost-effective for low-income households.

### 2. MAPPP-SETA Create South Africa pilot *learnership*

# Umcebo

Umcebo has formed a partnership with Create South Africa, the implementation arm of MAPPP-SETA, to implement and deliver a craft-production *learnership* for special needs learners. The learnership offers a National Qualification Framework (NQF) level two certificate in craft production. The National Skills Fund and MAPPP SETA fund this project jointly.

Umcebo aims, through this project, to formalise and accredit the informal learning and skills transferral that take place through involvement in the creative workshops. Accreditation is given on a learner and/or trainer level. Participation in the *learnership* allows learners and trainers to partake in other more advanced *learnerships*, learning programmes and or pursue formal employment in a post-workshop environment.

Commissioned work as well as the Eclectic Collectables product line continues to enjoy increasing support both nationally and internationally. At present we have sent work to France, Germany, Japan, the Netherlands, the UK and the USA

*Ntokozo Mnyandu making scrap plastic ornamental baskets*

*Detail of bead and crystal work*

In 1993 I joined Ningizimu School for the Severely Mentally Handicapped as a volunteer, and then as the Art Teacher. In 2001 I became Head of Department for Art and Technology. Out of the work that we have done at the school, we now run an incoming-generating art and craft projects which we formalised into a trust called the Umcebo Trust to open the work up to a broader community. Our aim is to get a diverse range of special needs and community members together in an inclusive environment, and to get them to produce high-end fine art and craft pieces, now being exported overseas. We want to ensure that our crafters become trained and experienced in craft production, marketing and sales, thereby ensuring their independence. Robin Opperman.

E-mail: robino@telkomsa.net          Web: http://home.telkomsa.net/tabby

# The Development of the Outdoor Tactile Dorcas Panel
## by Matthew Lloyd

### Introduction

From my personal experience, the graphic design taught at schools and colleges makes one very large assumption: that the intended user has good, clear colour vision.

And why not? The history of art and design is dominated by the visual – we define our experience by what we see. Graphic design students learn how the combination of image and type carry meaning and metaphor to the user, and that the infinite possibilities that result make graphic communication a fascinating, powerful, and engrossing medium.

Yet when presented with the opportunity to create designs intended not to be seen, I felt no compromise. On the contrary, the challenge of communicating through graphics to the unsighted was, and very much still is, a fascinating proposition.

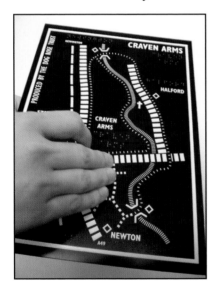

### Early work

I already knew Julia Ionides and Peter Howell as clients of the printers where I was employed as an artworker. I worked then as I do now, with digital designs created on an Apple Mac running applications such as Adobe Illustrator, which has proved to be the most flexible application for the creation of tactile design. Having shown an interest in their work, Julia provided an opportunity to become involved on a project producing tactile material to support a walk around the nearby town of Craven Arms. The material consisted of portable way-finding maps, which were for an audience that was either completely blind or had very poor vision. The considerations then are still valid today. We broke down the requirements something like this:

Completely blind user
Portable and durable format
100% tactile communication
Text in Braille
Graphics and symbols to be specially designed and legible by touch
Annotated with key

Visually impaired user
High contrast design
Large print
Clear graphics with bespoke but easily understood symbols
Annotated with key

Key to our success was to be a solution that was able to combine all of the above into one design.

### The Media

The manufacturing process was new to me - tactile media was virtually unheard of, and I had not seen anything like this before – so I was breaking much new ground right from the start. I was introduced to a process that used screen print to create a raised element, on a pre-printed board. White graphics were printed down first for the visually impaired, and then an overlay of a succession of high-build passes of UV-cured varnish built up the tactile element. The panel itself was made from a light yet stable plastic, approximately 1mm thick. Sized at A4 to make them easy to store and carry as well as cost effective to produce, the panels were a delightfully simple solution developed by Peter, Julia and Gardners of Cardiff, a screen print company.

### The Graphics

The design work was initially a struggle. How do I to read Braille? Indeed, how do the blind 'read'? This was very much an alien world for me. I had much to learn, but with Peter and Julia's guidance and lots of 'feeling', I was able to begin to get to grips with a solution. Strangely, my work on the visually impaired aspect was not as difficult – all I had to do was take my glasses off. Being very short sighted and therefore needing glasses at all times I had forgotten just how bad my eyesight was. By removing my glasses I have a visual range that from the first few inches to infinity is a complete blur. Testing the graphics simply requires me to hold a laser print out at arms' length, and I quickly discover whether my typography is too small or the mapped roads too narrow. For designers with better eyesight, I suggest that they squint and place their print out in shade to test for clarity – this gives an insight into how difficult it can be for the visually impaired.

### What we learned.

For the visually impaired, the base artwork was printed in pure white onto a pure black background giving a contrast of 100%. As I worked, it became apparent that artwork with a lower contrast is also workable, and a limit for monochrome artwork was found at around 70%. This information has proved essential, as today we work with full colour graphics and the contrast between coloured type and its background should not fall below this value. The best way to reveal the contrast is to convert the design into monochrome, greyscale artwork. Once this is done, the image can be viewed with an image editor and greyscale values measured with a sampling tool. However, we have found that our eye is a very good judge of contrast and the sampling tool has only been used in times of doubt.

At this time we developed a number of 'standards' that have been used again on all subsequent projects. Tactile textures were tried and tested, and the most important feature of a texture was revealed to be its 'rhythm'. Variations on line thickness and spacing allow us to differentiate between roads, paths or rivers for example, backed up with an annotated key. Some of our symbols worked better than others, and the factor here is the size of the symbol and its relationship to the size of the finger reading it. Too big or too small and symbols cannot be differentiated from one another. Ensuring that the stroke on a symbol is not too thick also helps to avoid this problem.

Vitally, good user feedback was available, and when combined with our criteria for ease of use and simplicity in production, we were able to develop a new tactile graphic language. Overall, I was amazed at how adept unsighted users can be. Clearly life without clear vision honed other senses, touch being a good example. They were willing to meet us halfway, forgiving some of our early unclear design. But we always knew that the system could be improved and refined, and I took each project as an opportunity to do just that.

### The First Outdoor Panel

It was to be a project for the RSPB at Ham Wall in Somerset that changed everything. I was commissioned to produce a series of panels that were part of a larger outdoor interpretive project in the middle of the Somerset levels. The very same criteria were applicable as with the early designs, but the methods of manufacture had since moved on.

### The Media

This was to be my first experience of working with tactile etched zinc panels. This process, manufactured by Photocast, had been extensively tested by Peter and Julia in the creation of tactile maps and orientation panels, and offered a bold and durable solution for the blind. They also offered the sighted and visually impaired user a workable if unusual system, and this method was selected for the production of the orientation map part of the display. We also had some interpretation to introduce to the display, and Gardners had evolved the tactile screen print process to a point where they were able to apply their high build UV inks to full colour dye-sublimation printed metal panels. We now had a much broader gamut for our base artwork, and took the opportunity to create a design that included the sighted, visually impaired and blind user in one panel.

### The Graphics

The zinc etched panel required artwork that was extremely clear and not fussy. Strong lines, textures and bold symbols were essential, and this played into our hands as the resulting design proved most effective for both the blind and visually impaired. Colour was added by painting, by hand, directly onto the panel. This allowed us to differentiate between dry land, reeds and water. Similar systems for defining paths and furniture as created in the Craven Arms panels were used and this too worked well.

The Gardners-produced panel gave me an opportunity to work much more visually, and sighted text was used as a bold sans serif font with a dark colour fill over a pale background. We also added some illustration to this panel to illustrate some of the bird and plant life to be found nearby, and took the opportunity to 'raise' these illustrations along with the screen-printed Braille. Outlines were drawn around the illustrations in order to provide a simple tactile silhouette for the blind user. Braille was then set over this panel in an area below the sighted text to avoid any clash between the two. It had to be heavily cut in order to make it fit, as being a fixed size Braille takes up some four to five more times the room than sighted text at an accessible 18 point.

### What we learned.

The resulting display was very successful, and as part of an interpretive project that won an AHI Interpret Britain & Ireland Award we did indeed feel very pleased with ourselves. It combined many different manufacturing processes: etched zinc plate, screen-printed colour panels and sandblasted wood (not part of my remit). But one issue stood out very clearly – we had missed an opportunity. The Braille on Gardners' panel worked very well, but leaving the base layer beneath it clear was totally unecassary. Because the overprinted tactile layer was so clear, we could have easily used this space to say more to the sighted or visually impaired user. Also, the combination of the illustrations with the raised outlines had worked very well, and here we also felt that there was a greater opportunity to create a solution where we were able to convey information to sighted, visually impaired and the blind users even more effectively.

### The Ludlow Tactile Panels

By 2004 Think Graphic Design comprised three permanent designers and one freelance. Around mid-2004 we were commissioned to produce panels by a committee consisting of the Ludlow Civic Society and Ludlow Historic Research Group. They arrived at our studio with completed research and a rough layout of the panels. We were required to create artwork following these guidelines and produce tactile panels.

We immediately learned something here – that committees such as this, knowledgeable though they are, do not nessesarily understand what make a good interpretive panel. Although all of the information was well researched and collated, it was apparent that it was not held together by a clear theme or story. An opportunity had been missed and we felt that we should try to help the client remedy the situation. It was not to be. The client group had committed much time and they found it difficult to make concessions. However, we set out to produce panels that were creative, accessible and a showcase for our ability to communicate with tactile systems. The same audience criteria remained as before, the only other demands being that set by the client group as described. Two panels were to be produced, one orientation/interpretive panel, the other purely interpretive.

### The Media

This time we were confident that our panels produced by Gardners would be able to convey all the information; instead of creating etched zinc sections for the orientation maps we would make our tactile map large and lay it over the sighted artwork without any worry that it would cause compromise. In this way they are easier to install, as they comprise of one piece, and every user benefits from finding all information in one panel. This also proved to be an economical solution; one panel – one fixing saves much time and material.

## The Graphics

The sighted information, once much of the copy had been cut, was straightforward and much like any other work we do. The interpretive panel called for illustrations of street elevations, and these were created directly in Adobe Illustrator allowing for clean and editable artwork, with the bonus of saving time when creating the outlines for the raised layer. Here we were able to convey the street's changing rooflines, window arrangements and comparative scale of the buildings to the unsighted – a totally unique piece of design. The Braille was kept as succinct as possible. We find that cutting the copy for the unsighted a very cathartic process – if all we need to say is here, why does the sighted copy have to be so long?

The orientation panel was a bit of a tight squeeze. The client group was asking for a lot here and we wished to leave off the interpretive material. With some compromise we were able to make the map large enough for the visually impaired and still have space for a little interpretation. The tactile map uses exactly the same artwork as that for the sighted, only much larger. Knowing that we were able to lay our tactile information over any sighted artwork, we allowed the raised map to spread as tall and wide as the panel allowed. This was necessary as the map was very dense in parts due to the town's mediaeval street layout, and to annotation was a struggle at any smaller size. Interestingly, the tactile map left no room for the interpretation, making for a neater, more succinct design. The sighted artwork would have benefited from this.

## What we learned.

The early stages of panel design are vital. Exactly what is to be said in a panel must be established before any design work is undertaken. The message must be defined before the means and every user, sighted or not, will benefit. A far more effective panel results when we know what and to whom we are communicating, as this dictates how it is said. Copy must be clear, free of jargon and succinct – doubly so for the unsighted. Images must also be clear, and maps must be pared down to exactly what is necessary and annotated clearly. Question everything and assume nothing, and good design will follow!

Matthew Lloyd is principal of a small lively design consultancy in Ludlow. The name of the organisation is Think Graphics.

Email: mail@thinkgraphicdesign.co.uk

Website: www.thinkgraphicdesign.co.uk

# Interpretation, Multi-Sensory Thinking and Universal Design for Gardens or Outdoor Sites

*Keep out of doors as much as you can, and see all you can of nature: she has the most wonderful exhibition, always open and always free.*

Advice to A.A. Milne from his father.

### Introduction

Multi-sensory thinking should be applied to outdoor sites as well as indoor; it will enhance communication with everyone.

Sensory Mapping has been developed by the Sensory Trust. Lars Stenberg, Communications Officer for the Sensory Trust, has written about this process which encourages people to assess what a park, or other outdoor space, 'has to offer to the five main senses, and also to record other feelings that a particular space evokes'.[1]

So think about your site in wider terms. In the outside world smells are everywhere. Taste is a little more difficult but it has been a key issue in our culture since time immemorial and could become an engineered facility in the future. References to taste could relate to the plants growing; for instance, the sage plant could be linked to sage and onion stuffing.

Interpretation and other features should be designed so that they can be used by a wide range of people of all abilities. People come in all sizes and physical abilities and this must be considered in the provision of both communication and functional forms.

### Tactile Interpretation

#### Tactile maps or plans

Like everyone else, people who are blind and visually impaired like to know where they are going. It is only by having a model of the site, a site plan or a portable tactile plan, that they will be able to find out for themselves the extent of the area concerned and what the options are for walks. This does not mean that they will want to come to the area alone, but it does give them the chance to make independent decisions on where they would like to go. The plan should have lettering and Braille on it.

The cheapest form of raising images and Braille is on 'swell paper'; the result is the same as a photocopy, cheap but not long lasting. Your local Resource Centre for the Blind can advise you; involving them will help with publicity.

Test out tactile plans and drawings with your potential audience and generally seek their advice before doing anything permanent. After all, they are the end users and should therefore be happy with what is being done. Since change is part of the way interpretation develops it is worth maintaining this interface with groups.

However, care must be taken in the interpretation of anything on the basis of one person's evaluation. It is important to get as many views as are possible. A simple raised image is produced using 'swell paper' which is then circulated to a group of blind people. Drawings are then modified in the light of their comments.

To read a tactile plan takes time and is not easy; the Trust tries to provide accompanying audio information, but this is not always possible for an unattended outdoor site. Spotlight Display produce an outdoor version of their *Chatterbox* one minute playback system. This is described in more detail in the section on Playback Equipment.

### Tactile Objects

Touching gives most information to people who cannot see and helps them to understand objects through multi-sensory design and interpretation; sighted people also get satisfaction from touching objects. The use of sound alongside would add even more to the experience of people who are visually impaired.

*A group from Forge with the seat they carved*

Try and imagine exploring public parks through touch and that will lead you into exciting directions. Consider tactile versions of some of the birds, butterflies and other features that can be found in the area. There are many ways in which this can be achieved: carved shapes on seats or picnic benches or resin cast sculptures or reliefs of natural objects. Unnatural intrusion on a natural site should be avoided, so careful design is essential.

Members of the Forge Centre visually impaired wood carving group in the Forest of Dean, Gloucestershire, created leaf-shaped seats around a large

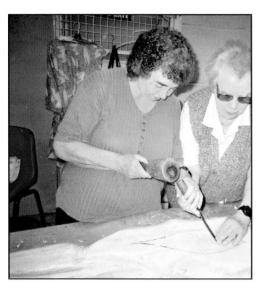

*Two members of the wood carving class*

tree in the Arboretum. They went on to create a tactile sundial which is very impressive. The Forge Centre is an independent local charity which has established a resource centre for blind and visually impaired people in the Forest of Dean.

This lively group had already produced a pre-visit pack for use on the Arboretum trail that had been made accessible. It followed the lines of the excellent pack developed for Wandlebury Country Park in Cambridgeshire, which contained taped information about the site and tactile pictures. Forge decided to adopt this outreach approach as they had the view that 'this makes it unnecessary for the Visually Impaired visitor to use a personal stereo on site and they can therefore hear the natural sound around them and hold a conversation with their companion'.

The shape and feel of leaves vary so much that tactile versions of some of the most common on the site would be appreciated. If you plant trees near to the path then these can be touched without having to go off it into rougher ground. Texture is important; think about the bark of trees and describe it so that the tree can be recognised. Try building up a picture of the whole tree through non-visual means. Where is the tree in the woodland hierarchy? Is it high, medium or low canopy? What birds are usually found in it? What insect life does it support?

Vernon West, a retired forester in North Shropshire, explained how to look at tree on the audio guide of Ellesmere. You can hear this on the audio examples.

A blind friend in the Czech Republic suggested that being able to feel the details of the shape and form of some of the smaller more delicate wild flowers would be very helpful and give her great pleasure. Resin copies of these could be made; possibly some natural history departments or museums might already have some that the mould could be taken off.

*Eric Sayce explores the bark of a tree*

# *Outdoor Interpretation*

There are splendid ones which are used for teaching horticulture to blind students. Tactile models can also be made in ceramics and cast glass, such as the cast glass fossil which are very tactile.

A multi-sensory display at a Visitor Centre could be made with the sound of the trees and the shape of the tree itself and its leaves and the texture of the bark and seed pods/cones as tactile forms, together with mention of any characteristic smells the leaves might have. Try to make the displays as organic as possible using natural materials, even if these have to be renewed. Perhaps the local school could be involved in collecting them.

*Cast glass fossils*

At all times it is important to consult with the end users – people who are visually impaired themselves and those with other disabilities. This is easier said than done as deadlines approach and there are not days enough left to consult properly, so leave plenty of time for the design process.

### Interpretation in Sound
Sound can be used in the following ways:

- for guiding people around the site by use of 'sound icons'

- to bring the site to life for people who cannot see it

- for on-site use during the different seasons

- to identify birds that are more commonly heard

- to bring to people's notice what can be heard rarely around the site, such as the unusual birds

- to differentiate the sound of the trees and reeds; for instance, do the delicate rustling leaves of the silver birch sound different from the more sturdy oak?

- To explain tactile objects

- To evoke a mood or atmosphere. The sound of the site will be very different on damp, foggy days and bright sunny ones.

### On-site Messages and Outreach Information

On-site messages are what they say – for use on the site; to guide people around and tell them about what can be seen. They can either be in the form of an audio guide for the site or they can be so-called 'listening posts' that are accessed when certain points around the site or along the route are reached. If the latter, then there must be a tactile indication underfoot or other indication when one of these is reached.

### Contents and information of audio

Much of this is essential to help the visitor get the most out of the site.

• Directions to get to the site. This could include public transport details as well as the route to reach your venue by car.
• Information about the site. It is important that people are able to have information about such neccessary facilities as toilets, cafes and seating. It is useful to know if there is shelter, where the site can be enjoyed even in wet weather
• What is there. There is little point in someone who is blind or visually impaired visiting the site if there is nothing there to tell them about it. Getting the information beforehand is very useful.
• Directions around the site. Information for all visitors about the site is useful and if it is available beforehand then the visit can be made more pleasurable. Information needs to include the area covered, type of paths, distances to walk, type of terrain (flat or hilly), how much open water there is, as well as other details. If there is a trail, are there steep hills? What is the degree of difficulty? How long is it? Are walking boots needed?
• Are there lakes, ponds or streams? Some guide dogs love to swim and so the owners need to be warned if they do not want a soaking wet dog. When Eric Sayce came over with Harry for the first time we took him to the woods for a run. A drainage ditch ran alongside the path, but Eric assured us that Harry did not like water. The next thing we heard was Harry in the ditch, sploshing around like a little boy in his wellies!
• Information from experts. Those involved with the site should consider taking part in an audio recording as they know it better than anyone else. They can not only talk about the birds that can be heard regularly but also those that might be heard if you are lucky. They can describe the site in all seasons and can get this atmosphere over to others.
• End-users taking part in the recording. Consider involving visitors who are blind or visually impaired in the recording. They can then ask questions about things that they want to know and which are relevant to them. Eric Sayce, who is totally blind, was the interviewer on the Mitchell's Fold Guide.
• Bird Song and Calls. This is an important element of most outdoor sites and it would be very useful to have a recording of the most common birds heard there, including their alarm calls and variations during

the year and send it out to people who are interested.

One person said it would be particularly interesting for her to be able to hear the sound of the birds that are around the site, before a visit. Then she hoped that she would be able to recognise them when she came to the site. Jessica Finch, a friend who is blind, started compiling the sounds that birds make in terms of phrases that can be remembered; the yellowhammer and 'the little bit of bread and no cheese' is an example and the red grouse's 'go-back go back' is another.

• Sound effects. Include any characteristic sounds of the site, such as running water, creaking logs on a bridge, a murmuring group of silver birches. These are the same as photographs in a visual text.

• Archive recordings. If there are archive recordings of the local workers and other people who have been involved with the site in the past; it would be added interest to include them if possible. These would help to explain what the site once was, especially if it has changed as much as the worked-out peat beds in Somerset.

*John Fleming recording birds in Stowe Churchyard with the Telinga field microphone*

### Written Interpretation
Clarity, large print and brevity are helpful on interpretation boards. Get the message across in as few words as possible. Images printed too strongly behind the text often make it hard to read. Clear line drawings can often be easier to make out than paintings or photos. For someone with no sight, additional tactile information needs to be added.

Whatever is decided, make the design consistent, use the same symbols, plans and information all over the sites. This helps everyone, but especially people with visual impairments and learning disabilities. Consider labelling some of the more interesting trees in Braille and large tactile print.

### Outreach Strategy
Your outreach strategy has to be well organised. A pre-visit pack has already been mentioned and could include a tactile plan and images of birds, leaves and trees found on the site and sent out to such places as the Resource Centre for the Blind and libraries. All information should be offered in a range of formats – large print, Braille, audio (cassette and CD) and computer disc. Many people who are blind or visually impaired use computers with voice synthesisers. Make the audio information interesting by including typical sounds around the year.

### Wayfinding and Navigation

Around the site, make sure the paths are well defined with positive edges, so that it is easier for a person who is blind and visually impaired to keep to the path with a long cane. Often the edge could be used as a tap rail. This information should be included on outreach material.

Way-marking needs to be useful to everyone. Tactile way-markers were made for the Forestry Commission; the texture of these matched the textures used for the walks indicated on the map and are fixed to posts along the route. They are also colour-coded to match the map at the beginning of the walks. To emphasise again, all maps and plans should be the same – not one for the leaflet and a different one for the interpretation boards.

Include 'sound icons' and wayfinding clues, such as water and echo or create some if possible. For example, if there is running water anywhere, add some stones so as to create a small waterfall or ripple effect. Other ideas could be:
- Wooden wind chimes

- Japanese-style water running over different materials such as bamboo or hollow wood
- A bowed shape with strings in a position that will play when the wind blows through it
- Anything else that relates to the site organically

The sound of these should also be on any outreach and audio information.

### Interpretation along the route

If you are putting interpretation along the route, you will need to let people know it is there. There are several ways of doing this:
- Change of texture in the path. This can be done with textures that are either harder, such as setts, or a softer material such as matting for playgrounds.[2]
- Tactile strips across the path. These can be made with organic materials such as sleepers or other wooden indicators.
- Humps in the path that are high and wide enough to be felt but not so that they impede wheelchairs. These were used effectively at a site in Brazos Bend, Texas.
- A break in the tap rail or a change of the sound; metallic or hollow wood for example.

*Waymarker for a forest walk*

# Outdoor Interpretation

Are interpretation boards at the height that small children and people in wheelchairs can see them comfortably, but not too low for tall visually impaired people to read without stopping too much? Do the paths enable a blind person, a guide dog and a helper to negotiate them with ease?

Try and use recycled materials for paths, seats and other features. There are several organisations with information about this such as *The Paths for All Partnership*.[3]

*Discussion between Bob Marek and Eric Sayce about a forest walk in Shropshire*

The National Center on Accessibility in Bloomington, Indiana, USA has information about work that is being done in America. Ray Bloomer, who is visually impaired, has been at the forefront of research into accessibility.[4]

For guided walks of outdoor environments TDK's *Outloud* CD wallet would be useful. This handy gadget contains built-in, flat-panel stereo speakers, a pocket for a personal CD or MP3 player and pouches for 24 CDs. You can play as many bird sounds as you want on a walk to a group. It weighs under a kilo so is very portable.

One of the best ideas we have come across recently came from Alan Linfield in Sussex. He put an induction loop into a hide so that people with hearing impairments could hear the birds and other natural sounds. He took along his uncle who has poor hearing and found that it worked so well, he complained about the birds being too loud. Brilliant!

Don't forget the underwater sounds. Our hydrophone has picked up interesting and mysterious noises which will give an intriguing picture of what goes on under the water, yet to be fully interpreted. The nearest identification we have got so far is the screech beetle.

**Accessible Playgrounds**

The leisure industry has been at the forefront in reminding its members about accessibility. This was probably financially driven as it is a highly motivated and well organised sector. Some useful information has come from the leisure magazines and press.[5]

The Trust has been interested in accessible playgrounds since meeting with Susan Goltsman in the USA in 1997. She showed us pictures of the wonderfully imaginative playground her company, Moore, Goltsman and Iacofano had designed in Portland, Oregon. Unfortunately there was no time to go and see it when we were in the area but the memory stayed and we became convinced that more exciting but accessible playgrounds could be created. A good example can be found on the EIDD site: A new accessible playground in Copenhagen.[6]

This interest has led to a collection of articles and catalogues about accessible equipment but no opportunity has arisen to put ideas into practice. These ideas for making the playground and its equipment more accessible for children with visual impairments include:

• A tactile track leading to the most accessible pieces of equipment

• A tactile plan showing where these accessible pieces are

• Small scale models of the equipment which would help the child to know what the size of the equipment is and how it functions

• Sounds to warn the child that a piece of equipment is moving; a bell could be put on a swing that would ring with the movement and the child would be warned to keep out of its way or a sound on a roundabout would help with location as well as warning that it is moving.

### Further References

A useful site for accessibility guidelines and standards comes from the U.S. Architectural and Transportation Barriers Compliance Board. These are updated from time to time and comply with the ADA (Americans with Disabilities Act).[7]

The Association of Play Industries has a directory of its members which is also published by Stable Publishing for the Association. www. playindustries.org.

The Alliance for Technology Access has information for 'children with communication, sensory, developmental or physical challenges.' See www.ataccess.org and search for Playgrounds for Everyone on the site. More information can be found at www.playworldsystems.co.uk.

Comprehensive catalogues of play equipment accessible and otherwise are produced by:
Wicksteed Leisure Ltd., www.wicksteed.co.uk
Hags of Sweden: www.hags.com
G. L. Jones Playgrounds Ltd., telephone: +44 (0)1248 600372
Sutcliffe Play, www.sutcliffeplay.co.uk

---

[1] Sensory Mapping, Sensory Trust Newsletter 5 on www.sensorytrust.org. uk/newsletters. There are back numers on this site with interesting articles.

[2] Wicksteed make a matting; see contact details above.

[3] www.pathsforall.org.uk has useful information about surfaces and paths in Scotland which can apply to any site. Also see www.colas.co.uk/. This company has worked with Alan Linfield, access consultant in Sussex to develop surfaces that are acceptable in a conservation area.

[4] See http://www.ncaonline.org/about

[5] The DDA Leisure Directory, from Stable Publishing. ((0)208 288 1080) This is a lively look at the implications of the DDA for the leisure industry.

[6] See the site of the European Institute for Design and Disability: http://www. design-for-all.org/ The item about the playground is in the Tourism for All section.

[7] The site address is http://www.access-board.gov/play/guide/intro.htm

## *The Accessible Marches and Interpretation Day at Mitchell's Fold Stone Circle*

The Accessible Marches was a European-funded project carried out by the Dog Rose Trust to make the area more accessible to people with visual impairments through universal communication, a multi-sensory design approach and joined-up tourism. Over the years The Trust has worked on several projects in the countryside of the Marches, a beautiful region on the borders of England and Wales, with high rugged hills and low-lying valleys with rivers and streams, iron age hill forts, castles. There are the small historic towns that grew up in the area as well as old railway lines and lead mines, and trees and birds, butterflies and flowers, cream teas and real ale and lots more.

The project aimed to make this idyllic holiday destination, the real England, accessible to people with sight problems and blindness through a series of initiatives which we hoped would benefit everyone.

On this project we worked with Eric Sayce and Denise Collier and their Guide Dogs Harry and Rebecca. They, and other colleagues, provided valuable guidance and advice as well as acting as interviewers for the audio recorded about the country and urban walks and visitor attractions.

We have often been asked why blind people want to visit the countryside if they cannot see it. Well, the answer is that all areas, whether rural or urban, have their own characteristic sounds, smells, feel and in some cases taste; local foods for instance or Shropshire locally brewed ales.

For the project, the Trust organised a two-day break for a group of visually impaired and sighted friends plus two guide dogs to test out some of our ideas for the Accessible Marches. Over the two days they cycled on tandems, walked along muddy trails and over stiles and streams and visited museums. At one of the pubs a brew called Christmas Cracker went down a treat and will long be remembered by everyone. Multi-sensory interpretation was admirably demonstrated by Tom Wall of English Nature when he told Eric Sayce about what can be found on the Stiperstones, the rugged hill country of Shropshire.

There are flowers to smell, birds to hear and so on. Tom handed Eric thistledown to feel and a reed to explore and a blueberry to taste. This kind of multi-sensory interpretation is of benefit to everyone. Listen to the Stiperstones track on the CD.

In this project the Trust combined Universal Design and communication and sustainable tourism. The facilities that the client group were being told about existed already; nothing new was created to use up scarce resources or create extra traffic. It was also linking up existing tourist venues with events in the area. For instance, along the riverside walk on the Onny Trail, there is a reference to the alder trees and then to the project which is producing charcoal from the alders that are being thinned out to allow more light into the river; this in its turn will encourage more fish and plant life and the otters are returning. The project encouraged people to buy more of the local charcoal from sustainable sources and visitors may want to come to the area with the chance of seeing an otter. Mention the blueberries, or whinberries as they are called in Shropshire, and that links with the special whinberry basket that can be found in the Museum in the town of Clun.

An excellent example of joined-up thinking and sustainability was the Parish Welcome Scheme run in South Shropshire. All the parishes were brought together to discuss the dates of their events so that they did not clash; they attended workshops for producing posters and have talks from organisations on how to deal with the safety and comfort of those attending.

The events that the parishes are putting on are a good example of sustainability as they are taking place anyway to raise money for the church, village hall or some local cause; they are small scale and do not create large traffic problems; they may appeal to some people with disabilities who cannot cope with large noisy crowds and the extra income generated by additional visitors could make all the difference to the village itself.

The work focussed on several areas. One is the Onny Trail which is all relatively flat and so easy going for anyone who is reasonably mobile. Stiles were improved and had tactile waymarkers on them; there were dog gates for the Guide Dogs, and the aim was to produce a tactile plan of the walk, and information in audio, large print and Braille. Unfortunately due to funding problems and then foot and mouth this never happened and the moment passed and has not been revived. This is unfortunate as this walk is particularly interesting as it combines natural history with industrial archaeology. A wide range of birds can be heard along the river bank and in the trees.

The trail follows the path of the Bishop's Castle Railway which opened in 1865 and closed, after being bankrupt for most of its life, in 1935. You can also hear the modern trains passing close by at one stage and the main road running parallel, but as you move into the old railway cutting this sound gets blotted out and nature begins to take over. A willow burnt by lightning makes an interesting experience of both touch and smell.

Similar work was carried out for hill walks which include the iron age fort known as the Bury Ditches.

Another project was improvements for the path to Mitchells Fold, a prehistoric standing stone circle high on a hill with far-reaching views of the Welsh Mountains. The singing of the skylarks is breathtaking on a spring day and this can be combined with the mystery of the standing stones and the many stories and legends that have been woven around them.

After the path had improved the Trust put on an interpretation day at Mitchells Fold.

### First steps

A meeting was held to discuss the best way to interpret Stapeley Hill in Shropshire in general and Mitchell's Fold Stone Circle in particular to people who are blind and visually impaired leading up to an 'open day' in the spring. The meeting included local experts, countryside managers and consultants with visually impairments, plus their Guide Dogs.

*Paul Saunders and Eric Sayce at the Stone Circle*

The question was asked: 'what does Mitchell's Fold mean to you and how would you convey it to others, especially those who cannot see?' It was agreed that the important feature of the area was its atmosphere and the reasons for this needed to be explored. It was considered a magical place, a place where something is about to happen and the sense of history and long-time span was stressed. For some, the starting points were the myths and legends about the area, in particular the one of the cow and the witch as this can be followed up by a visit to Middleton-in-Chirbury church. Others thought that the visitors should be left alone at first to feel the atmosphere and initially make up their own minds.

The literary connections and industrial history, such as the lead-mines, all need to be included. The initial discussion resulted in a decision that the actual facts and information about Mitchell's Fold and the surrounding area need to be kept separate from the 'atmosphere' which is a variable issue according to personal responses.

The organising group walked to Mitchell's Fold and several of them wore simulation spectacles so that they could experience for themselves what it was like not to see what was around them. Their guide described the surroundings and scenery.

At the stones the shape of the Circle, which is actually egg-shaped, was discussed with the archaeologist who described the information that had been gathered about the area. The local vicar talked about the Circle as a place of worship and its importance to local people and the service he holds each year to reconcile the links between the church and the Circle. A geologist spoke about the geology of the area and the fact that the carriage route went over the hill because of the marshy nature of the valleys below.

On return to the hall, the question was asked again:
'How can we convey our knowledge of the area to those we are presenting it to - in this context those who are blind and visually impaired? What points need to be emphasised? What had the day achieved?'
1. The peace and quiet
2. The track across the hill and its undulations created over many centuries
3. People took more notice of their surroundings
4. Raised an awareness of needs and made people realise that what is
   being done already, can be improved on
5. The need to learn special interpretation skills
6. The consideration of a large number of issues and practical arrangements for an interpretation day
7. The interpreters should react to the experience of others
8. More fun and enjoyment of the event on the actual day
9. It helped to make members of the group realise how the picture could be
   painted for a visually impaired person
10. The importance of the input of local people was considered important
11. The realisation of the isolation of blindness and the development of
    other senses to compensate

The Trust then carried all these ideas forward to organise an interpretation day six months later.

**Publicity and marketing**
It was decided the venue would be Chirbury Village Hall and a British Sign Language interpreter was booked for the day. Although

publicity was circulated to people with hearing impairments in the end no one came.

Publicity material was sent out to relevant organisations and publications, including the following:

The publications Disability Now, RNIB's New Beacon, Viewpoint, the magazine of the National Federation of the Blind, On Track, the newsletter of the Confederation of Transcription Services. Soundings, a tape magazine for people with visual impairments.

Radio 4 programmes *In Touch* and *Open Country*, local radio and journalists who have shown interest in the Trust's work. To local and regional talking newspapers. One of the participants heard about the event on his talking newspaper in Hertfordshire. Playback in Glasgow is a popular talking magazine widely listened to across the UK.

It was also on the Coventry Talking Newspaper. In addition about 100 letters were sent out to visually impaired people and organisations who are on the Dog Rose database. The information will be added to the database following the event.

An article was written for Explore the Marches, a tourist magazine which comes out every Spring. An advertisement was booked and over 150,000 copies were distributed across the country, and in particular in the Marches area.

An article was written for Barrierfree 10, the magazine of the Museums and Galleries Disability Association (MAGDA) about the day and a photograph of Eric Sayce and his guide dog Harry accompanied it.

### Summary of Publicity Requirements

Widespread publicity is necessary to get the information around to those interested in attending. Although this takes time, it is usually all free. The only publicity paid for was Explore the Marches.

Participants were asked how they heard about the event and Soundings was the one most of them listened to. One person had heard about it from Playback and its offshoot Grapevine from Falkirk. Another received the information from Insight issued by the RNIB.

Suggested sources of publicity were the Tourist Associations and Cheshire seems to have a well developed and useful one for visually impaired events.

### Participants

• People attended from a wide geographical area.

• A group of 11, 5 visually impaired, came in a minibus from the Milton Keynes Walking Group for the Visually Impaired. They brought two rangers from Milton Keynes Parks Trust with them who could observe and pick up ideas. They also brought guides to go with them on the walk.

• A group of 7 came in a minibus from a visually impaired club in Aberystwyth – 4 visually impaired people with guides and 3 Guide Dogs.

• Other people came from Hertfordshire (2), Cheshire (3), Herefordshire (2 plus a Guide Dog) and Shropshire (7) plus one Guide Dog.

All participants were active and able to walk at least up to the Stone Circle. Large print name labels were supplied, for the benefit of the sighted helpers so that we knew who we were talking to.

### Information in Sound and Touch

Participants were given an audio guide to Mitchells Fold on CD to take home. Two additional sections had been recorded for the final version of the audio guide. Stephen Harding, a voluntary warden on Stapeley Hill, described further historical aspects of the area and Gill Mayhew, also a warden and local resident, described what she sees on the hill when she walks her dogs every day around the year.

Participants were also given a tactile silk-screen printed plan of the Stone Circle. The plans were distributed during the morning talks so that people could understand the route they would be following and the form of the Circle. One hundred copies of the plan were printed and 50 copies of the CD made.

It had been decided not to send out the CD to participants before the event as it was to be given out more in the form of a souvenir to take home. It would have been preferable to make a short version to send out before so that people would have more information about the place they were visiting. This could be an informal package of essential details about where, how, when and why. For those with email (the leaders of the two groups and one other participant communicated that way) the script could be written and then be sent out by email.

The script of the audio guide has also been typed out so that people who have hearing impairments can read it. This is a job which takes a long time as much of the audio guide was unscripted and spoken conversation is hard to type out convincingly.

### Information to be sent out

For a day and walk of this type, detailed information should be sent out beforehand. This should include:
• Type of terrain that will be encountered
• Obstacles that might be encountered – stiles, narrow bridges, no dog-gates
• Length of the walks and if there are options as to the length
• Positive aspects of the walk
• Footwear and outerwear requirements
• If snacks and drinks are needed on the walk
• Refreshments that are being provided
• Provision or not of toilets on the walk and before and afterwards. This is a basic but very important issue to many people.
• Make sure that participants know that both guides and transport can be supplied if necessary. Both should be made available, perhaps

through the local walking club and Dial-A-Ride service.
 • Mobile telephone contact number for emergencies on the day

### Practical Considerations

Allow plenty of time. It takes a long time to get people on and off transport, get boots on, queuing for toilets and other activities. The timetable, as set out, was ambitious and hard to keep to as both mini-buses arrived late.

In addition the number of people attending was larger than expected. We did not want to discourage people from coming as we were keen to get as wide a geographical spread of people as possible in order to demonstrate that there is a demand for this kind of activity and to tell people about Mitchell's Fold and what a magical place it is. We also wanted to include as much information as possible to make people feel it had been worthwhile coming a long distance. However, it may be preferable to limit the numbers of blind and visually impaired people to 12. Again, availability of guides and transport can be factors when deciding on numbers.

### Form of the day

The form of the day comprised talks about Stapeley Hill and Mitchell's Fold:

Stephen Harding talked about his role as voluntary warden and what the area means to him, as well as some tales about it. He has a very distinctive voice and has taken part in the audio guide and would also be the leader of the longer walk over the hill in the afternoon.

Andrew Jenkinson talked about the geology of the area and how Stapeley Hill was formed millions of years ago. He brought geological samples with him that people could touch and explore. These had Braille and large print labels attached to

*Setting off for the Stone Circle*

them.

Emma-Kate Burns explained about the archaeological finds in the area that had been left by people living there in the Bronze Age. She brought original artefacts and replicas with her for handling; these also had Braille and large print labels attached to them. As she and Stephen Harding have pleasantly differing views on some of the finds on Stapeley Hill, they made a good double act which kept everyone entertained.

*Paul Saunders plays the medieval pipes on Stapeley Hill*

### Handling objects

Working out how to organise the handling of objects in the time available for such a large group was a difficult problem that we still need to resolve. We had planned to put the items on tables around the rooms with someone nearby who could explain about them. This was the only solution for some of the geological specimens which were heavy to pass around. However, during the talks, especially the archaeological one, people asked if the items could be passed around. We did this but the problem which arises from this approach is that, as it is passed around, people are examining an object sometime after it has been discussed and are having it explained to them while the speaker is talking about the next item. In the case of archaeology, real artefacts are scarce and precious, although Emma-Kate did bring several, and replicas are expensive so it is not possible to obtain many.

Tom Wall of English Nature talked about the birds that can be heard in the area. These were played from a CD which had been specially put together for the event to illustrate the wide range of bird life in the area. The audience was well informed and knowledgeable about them. Tom also distributed combs and greaseproof paper and got everyone to 'cuckoo' with them. Paul Saunders then tried out bird calls on some wooden pipes but the audience, although amused, was not convinced of their accuracy. He then called everyone to lunch with his medieval bagpipes.

Also attending the day were:
Two guides and a volunteer from the Bishop's Castle Walking Festival. They hoped that they might be able to include a walk for blind and visually impaired walkers in future programmes.
Two members of the Shropshire County Council Countryside Unit who wanted to learn more about the area and how to organise a similar day and a member of the Shropshire Hills Countryside Unit who is responsible for access in its broadest sense.

After lunch everyone went by mini-bus or car to Stapeley Hill where they walked up the track to the Mitchell's Fold Stone Circle, led by Paul Saunders and his medieval bagpipes. The track and approach, of nearly one mile, is fairly smooth walking and everyone made good progress in the rather windy but dry conditions.

Along the way, Emma-Kate talked more about the people who had inhabited the area and Andrew explained more about the geology and what was underfoot.

Everyone listened delightedly to the skylarks who performed perfectly. Some people heard a curlew and the ravens were croaking. Tom suggested some people might like to walk through the dried bracken to enjoy the crunching sound underfoot.

At the stone circle, Paul got out his medieval harp. The strong wind plucked the strings in Aeolian fashion, which added to the mystery and atmosphere of the area. Paul then told the story of Mitchell's Fold and the magic cow and the witch.

People walked around the Circle, explored the stones and then those that wanted to walked a further 3 miles, led by Stephen and Emma-Kate. The mini-buses then took the others back to the hall for tea before going back up the hill to meet the walking group.

Those in the hall were asked for their reactions to the day and all had enjoyed the day and learnt a lot about the area. The group enjoyed the longer walk and the mini-buses picked them up to take them back to Chirbury for tea. They walked faster than the mini-bus drivers had expected and were waiting for us to collect them. This emphasised the use of mobile phones for this type of communication, providing there is a signal in the area.

The day finished later than we had intended owing to the late start and the time it had taken to get people around. Unfortunately there was not time to visit Middleton in Chirbury Church, but perhaps next time. There is a description of it in the CD.

The lesson we learnt from this is that it would be preferable to have a base where we could walk from and not to have to transport people to where they are to start the walk. However, this is not always possible: either there is no suitable hall or meeting place, which was thought necessary in case the weather is poor and so that information can be given about the places being visited. Many halls are in small villages, and lanes around, which are often narrow, must be taken into account when walking with a group of blind and visually impaired people. Traffic can be another problem, both from the point of view of the danger of moving vehicles and also obscuring the sound of the country environment.

As far as the interpretation was concerned, it is assumed that visitors would know little about the area and therefore the main story of the place to be visited should be the focus and the other talks hinged around that. We did this to an extent but could have made it even more pointed in that direction.

**Conclusions**

The Interpretation Day showed that there is a demand for this type of activity. There are a number of visually impaired walking groups around the country.

Publicity has to be widespread and sent out well in advance with reminders at a later date. Information has to be produced, or available on request, in a range of formats – large print, audio and Braille. Speakers and guides need to have training on interpreting and guiding visually impaired people. It is particularly important to stress the use of appropriate language and not use information such as 'over there' and 'up here'.

People are willing to pay a reasonable amount towards the cost of the day but it would still need to be subsidised or sponsored if speakers and others taking part are paid, as is reasonable. Participants seemed to appreciate the range of subjects that were covered and all said they had learnt something.

We asked people if they would like to know about future events, either put on by the Dog Rose Trust or other organisations. They all said they would and had no objection to their names being passed on to organisers of similar events within the parameters of the Data Protection Act.

You can hear tracks from the Accessible Marches and Mitchells Fold on the CD.

The Interpretation Day was funded by the Shell Better Britain Campaign and the South Shropshire Countryside Unit.

## Access for All at Ham Wall, near Glastonbury, Somerset
### by Sally Mills RSPB

*Recycled plastic boardwalk , with tactile handrail and modular sign*

The new RSPB visitor facilities at Ham Wall, Somerset, are in the Walton Heath area of the reseve and are aimed to benefit user groups that may be unable to access easily other nature reserves and the countryside in general. The target audience are sensory impaired and infirm or visitors who use wheelchairs.

Prior to the visitor facility project completed in October 2002, the reserve offered very limited opportunities for visitors. However, now the installation of the first phase of works has been done, the intention is to learn from feedback received from users and to develop the facilities further in following years.

### Access
Access to Walton Heath is off Ashcott Road (which runs north to south between the villages of Ashcott and Meare), at Ashcott Corner, along the disused Glastonbury to Highbridge railway line. This railway line dissects Ham Wall in two and provides excellent views over the habitats that have been created. Although uneven in places, it provides good access for wheelchair users and the less able. Approximately 500m along the railway line is the entrance to Walton Heath, where there is a gated parking area for two cars for Radar key holders only.

*below:*
*Viewing platform with six foot cedar sign*

### Viewing Platform
Opposite is the new 5m x 15m elevated viewing platform, which looks over the main reserve. This is a simple area made from clay and topsoil, built up in layers and surfaced with crushed stone. A low handrail to enable good visibility for all users surrounds the area and there are four basic perches in each comer, which take up limited space, leaving plenty of room for groups and wheelchair users. On the eastern end of the platform is a large, 6ft tall cedar sign, with sand-blasted images of the local area,

which is visually attractive and useable by people who are visually impaired and children.

### Interpretation
Opposite the viewing platform, there is information about the site on a modular sign. This modular sign is an adaptation of the sign that is currently widely use by the RSPB on most of its visited sites.

The following adaptations have been made:
The sign is at a suitable height so that wheel chair users and children are able to read and reach all the information All the information is repeated in Braille and different media have been tried out to see which is most successful.

The whole sign is angled so that Braille readers are in a more comfortable position.

*Tactile modular sign*

We have experimented with contrasting colours to cater for the partially sighted.

The handrail at the front provides support for people who are not able to stand for long periods.

Information has been provided, both with the written word, pictorially and through the use

of symbols and Braille, again to cater for a wide range of audiences.

From the modular sign, a recycled plastic boardwalk leads out to the main viewing areas. A tactile wooden handrail accompanies this section of boardwalk. The handrail is sand blasted half round soft wood timber. The sand-blasted imagery includes raised text, (taken from poems written by local school children) accompanied by raised images of reserve wildlife and Braille plaques. The handrail is 26m long and leads to the first viewing screen, which looks east across the reed-beds and open water, with the backdrop of Glastonbury Tor.

*Below: Recycled plastic boardwalk and viewing screen*

### Viewing Screens
The screens are of a simple construction, with open backs, made from half round timbers, with viewing slots. Their floors are a recycled plastic as a continuation of the boardwalk. The first screen has been specifically made to accommodate motorised wheelchairs, offering more turning space. Each screen has been designed for wheelchair access and use with full-length knee projections and low level

viewing slots. The boardwalk continues to a further two screens, looking southeast and west, offering different views across the Walton Heath area.

### The Plastic

The recycled plastic used is normally available in black or brown but a range of other colours are available to order. It is manufactured from recycled High Density Polyethylene (HDPE) from plastic bottles and other plastics from wastewater and gas piping. This is then washed and granulated before being mixed with a colorant. The colorant is ultra-violet-stabilised so does not fade in sunlight. This mix is then melted and either pushed into moulds or an extruder that gives a continuous profile that can be cut to prescribed lengths. The plastic can be treated like timber, for cutting and fixing and is very easy to work with. The walkway is 1.2m clear width with an upstand/tap rail of 9cm high, which is a guide for long cane users and prevents wheelchairs from falling off the path. The plastic forms a very giving and flexible surface, but strong structure with a rough texture, providing a good non-slip surface. The handrails are made with a smooth finish, so not to graze or cut and course there is no worry of splinters!

A passing point has been installed 3m x 1.2m with a low rail, 50m down the boardwalk from the parking area. In between the passing point and the raised walkway, a tactile seat with designs by Meare School children, sand-blasted into the backs, enables people to rest and look out over the pool.

### Using Recycled Plastic
### Advantages:

The plastic is very flexible and so moulds to variations in the substrate, providing a 'cushioned' surface for wheelchairs and pushchairs.

It is very tough and does not chip, split or snap even under great deals of stress.

Although it will melt under continuous or extreme heat, but it does not burn.

It requires no treating and so is essentially maintenance free.

It does not degrade or leach any chemicals.

It does not weaken with time.

*Boardwalk leading to tactile seat*

The decking is non-slip as it has 'grain' included in the mould.

Handrails however can be moulded very smooth so as to not chaff or graze.

The material can be drilled, sawn, screwed, chiselled etc. without specialist tools (however due to its nature it should be noted that wear is increased on saws, drill bits etc.).

It is water resistant and handrails or benches can be wiped down and not remain damp like wood. Graffiti can be cleaned off much easier than wood.

It is easy to 'add on to', if work is to be undertaken in phases.

**Disadvantages**:

The initial cost is greater compared to wooden decking, rolled stone or tarmac.

It is very heavy and therefore difficult to move about safely. (Each 3m section requires 4 or more people to move into place.)

There are only a limited number of suppliers of this material so may be difficult to source locally.

Ham Wall reserve provided the RSPB the excellent opportunity to create a nature reserve from scratch. This was not only in terms of habitat development but also in providing facilities for visitors. The RSPB managed the site for 7 years before installing any infrastructure and comprehensive information. This was a conscious decision, to allow time for the site to establish itself and mature a little. After this time with a blank sheet of paper, I was able to consider and propose what the ideal visitor facilities could be for the reserve. During the development of Ham Wall, I was able to gather a lot of the information needed to provide suitable facilities for the audiences we could get using the reserve. The visitor whole project took 2 years to plan, from designing the proposal, gaining planning permission, securing funds, consulting the different potential user groups to working with contractors. With a blank sheet, my aim was to benefit a wide spectrum of visitors and not just the stereotyped user. To be able to achieve this I needed to undertake a long consultation process, getting many groups out on site – being open to suggestions and then finding practical ways of achieving our intentions on the ground.

Sourcing proper and informed guidance on what to provide for different audiences was the most difficult obstacle to overcome. Installing ramps, boardwalks and basic infrastructure was straight forward, but knowing how to cater for the visually impaired and children out on site, was entirely different from anything myself or the RSPB had really done to any extent before. I have been very pleased with what we have achieved and visitors have been very complimentary. However, making the project a success whilst continuing to run and manage a nature reserve was very difficult and demanding on time. I do feel that in order for more site managers

*A sound box in use*

to undertake such works on nature reserves, the process needs to be made easier. Sourcing information and getting support for new ideas, together with how practically to achieve certain results needs to be more accessible if providing 'Access for All' facilities in the countryside is to become more widespread.

Sally Mills is the RSPB site manager for Ham Wall, an area of reedbeds reclaimed from worked-out peat beds. On the other side of the road from Ham Wall is Shapwick Heath, managed by English Nature. The site warden, Melvyn Yeandle, is also committed to make this site as accessible as possible to everyone.

All the photographs are by Sally Mills.

## The Stiperstones, Shropshire, 'All-ability Trail' by Tom Wall, Site Manager, English Nature

*Dorethy Jeffery trying out the all-ability trail*

The Stiperstones is a National Nature Reserve owned and managed by English Nature; it is of international importance for its upland heathland and geology. The Stiperstones, Mary Webb's 'Diafol Mountain', which 'towers in gigantic aloofness, a mass of quartzite, blackened and hardened by countless ages', is one of the toughest, roughest, hardest, most angular of Midland landscapes. Over the years many have clambered up it fit and game, only to toil back down with twisted ankle or torn tendon. It can be a grim place, but also an exciting, awe-inspiring and invigorating one; a place for wildlife, a place to enjoy, a place to share. But how, given its physical difficulties, to share it with anyone other than the physically privileged?

I was driven to ask myself that question a few years ago, less, I confess, as a response to the Disability Discrimination Act, or a burning desire to spread accessibility, than from a need to provide a significant, grant-justifying, accessibility quota to a habitat re-creation project. Back to purple: conserving and restoring The Stiperstones, a project run jointly by English Nature, the Forestry Commission and Shropshire Wildlife Trust, won support from the Heritage Lottery Fund for heathland re-creation and enhancement of other wildlife habitats, linked to community involvement, interpretation and improvements to access. Part of this last element was the creation of a 500 metre 'All-ability Trail'. Additional funding came from English Nature (through the government's Capital Modernisation Fund), Landfill Tax Credits (courtesy of Tarmac) and the European Community.

Because of site constraints it was an expensive project, but in terms just of length, it remains, I must admit, a modest contribution to improving access. You can walk for more than 5km along the ridge of The Stiperstones, albeit at risk to your ankles. What are we offering instead? A mere 500m, non-circular route along the contour. Yet even this short length has caused me some heartache. This is a wild place. Is it right to saddle it with a municipal-style, wheel-chair friendly, bound surface,

# Stiperstones; All Ability Trail

tapping rail, comprehensive drainage, tactile ground cues, benches and sound-boxes? To be honest, I've yet to entirely convince myself that the answer is 'yes'. But we have, undeniably, provided a facility which has been widely appreciated, and which, though short, has much to offer. True, wheel-chair users are infrequent, cane-wielders exceptional, but we welcome many with lesser mobility constraints: push chair pushers, and the arthritic, the self-confessed unsteady, weak-hearted, over-weight, poorly coordinated, halt and lame, all keen that their mobility problems should not deny them the chance to enjoy open country, contact with nature and fresh air. They may not get the complete, rugged, elevated, Stiperstones experience, but this gentle stroll on the flat offers broad, peaceful vistas, the profile of some of The Stiperstones and all of another Shropshire icon and major wildlife site, The Long Mynd, and verdant valley views through to distant Shrewsbury. Along the trail relict white Wood Anemone flowers blush with pink in spring, and Gorse glows gold through into summer, when Heather blooms, Whinberry (Bilberry) fruits and Gatekeeper butterflies patrol. In autumn, Fieldfares and Redwings feast on the haws and forage for worms in the adjacent fields. In winter, indeed at any season, Buzzards 'mew', Ravens 'cronk' and Red Grouse shout 'go-back' from the ridge.

*John Fleming testing the tap rail*

*This is a comfortable seat*

This is a stroll along the edge of The Stiperstones, and 'the edge' provides the interpretive theme. Working with the Dog Rose Trust, personnel from Shropshire County Council and Shropshire Wildlife Trust, and with professional input from Glynis Powell, we've worked up 'the edge' theme into a series of six sound box recordings trialled with mixed-ability audiences and individuals. These recordings describe the geological edge adjacent to the trail, and the environmental edge between wild country and the domesticated agricultural land along which it runs. This environmental edge is an economic divider too: those in the valleys did relatively well, but those who lived in the hills did so on a financial knife edge, eking out their precarious incomes with revenue from the annual crop of wild Whinberries. And there are birds on the edge here too – on the edge of local extinction consequent on the intensification of agriculture over the last few decades. And people have lived here on the edge, the margins, of society, people like Wild Edric, the Saxon warrior and his Lady Godda, in retreat from the Norman conqueror. And you can hear creatures 'on edge' too, whether it is an anxious ewe or a neurotic Stonechat, calling 'tseet ... chack-chack' incessantly from the top of a spiky Gorse bush.

Why sound boxes? Because, having intruded on this wild landscape, we were looking for a low-key interpretive option which offered the widest possible accessibility. Sound boxes also offered the possibility of ease of periodic renewal or seasonal variation. Dog Rose recorded locally-based actor Pete Postlethwaite (Brassed Off, James and the Giant Peach, In the Name of the Father, Jurassic Park etc and now OBE), reading the script, and dovetailed this with sound effects and British Library recordings of Raven, Red Grouse, Buzzard, Lapwing, Curlew and others. The theme of 'the edge' runs through the series of boxes, but each recording is designed to be complete in itself. At the time of writing, the boxes, which are to be mounted on big butts of oak crafted by the Shropshire-based Greenwood Centre, are about to be installed. Pete Postlethwaite's generous involvement is a publicity coup which should generate plenty of interest and we will be on hand to evaluate usage and reaction following the launch.

How does this initiative fit within English Nature's policies on access to the country's National Nature Reserves (NNRs)? English Nature is the government agency which champions the conservation of wildlife and geology throughout England. Its duties include the selection and designation of NNRs, which now number in excess of 200 and occupy some 81,000ha (200,000 acres); most are under English Nature's direct management. A site's designation by English Nature as a NNR is official recognition of its national importance for nature conservation. NNRs encompass some of England's finest and best-loved scenery and most valued areas for wildlife. English Nature aims to provide access to these wondrous places for as many as possible, whilst safeguarding wildlife, preventing habitat damage, working within safety constraints and seeking to retain wild unspoilt countryside. Access has to be assessed on a site-by-site basis and will be intellectual (via, for example, web sites, literature and interpretation) as well as physical.

A few technical details of the trail may be of interest. The design had to take account of existing use, notably occasional vehicle access and of the trail's bridleway status. This steered us in the direction of a 'bound' rather than a 'rolled' surface; it was feared that the latter would soon scuff-up, impeding wheel-chair use. The existing surface was hard and well-compacted but irregular. It was 'regulated' with 100-150mm of 'sub-base' and surfaced with a double layer thickness of 'Fibredec'. This proprietary surfacing is supplied and laid by Colas Ltd; it is less than 20mm thick, whereas a conventional surfacing of 'blacktop' (dense bitumen macadam) would run to 100mm or so. The first coat of 'Fibredec' consisted of bitumen emulsion together with chopped glass fibres and 10mm chippings; the second coat was again of bitumen emulsion but this time with 6mm chippings which provided the final surfacing material. This final surfacing can be specially selected to provide a texture and colour consistent with local conditions. But herein lies a cautionary tale. We agonised over the selection of this final surfacing, putting down many

*The perch works well*

trial bands before making our final choice – a locally derived stone with colours which picked up the tones of adjacent exposed ground and soils. Any self-congratulation was short-lived however, because the material rapidly lost its colour through trafficking and weathering. Nevertheless we ended up with a surfacing which is more sympathetic to the site than a conventional surfacing of 'black top'.

Fibredec is predicted to last 5-15 years, depending on the level of usage and maintenance. The glass fibre reinforcement is said to give the surfacing an improved tensile strength, making it suitable for application directly onto most unbound granular road bases. It is also judged to offer a slight degree of 'give' making it more sympathetic to horse use, which is clearly an important consideration on a bridleway.

Benches or 'perches' (two off-set parallel bars against which one can lean to take a breather) are provided at maximum 50m intervals and the location of each bench is indicated on the ground by a 1.2m wide band of stone setts running across the trial, providing a tactile cue under the feet of walkers with visual impairment. These bench sites double as the location for the 'sound boxes'. A tapping rail runs the length of the trail made up of an 8-10cm wide, half round fencing rail, with a top height of 30cm. The trail incorporates one 'easy access' gate and one wheel-chair accessible kissing gate.

Attention needs to be paid to access to NNRs as well as to access within them. Over recent years access to The Stiperstones has been facilitated by a Shuttle Bus service operating on Spring and Summer weekends, linking the Reserve with public transport, both bus and train. With Dog Rose expertise and Landfill Tax funding (courtesy again of Tarmac), we have developed an audio tour round the surrounding countryside designed to be listened to as the Shuttle Bus plies its circular route round the site.

Since opening the 500m of trail in July 2002 we have extended it by a further 160m, albeit, for financial reasons, to a lower surfacing standard. This takes users further along the edge of a 30ha area of heathland re-created on the site of a former forestry plantation through Back to purple. The re-created heathland is maintained for us by a flock of Hebridean sheep and four Exmoor ponies, and herein lies another cautionary tale. Whether in search of minerals, for fun, for exercise, or whatever, the ponies delight in digging holes in this new, unbound surface, and in re-opening them whenever we rake them over: the best laid plans of mice and men, and, it seems, the best laid surfaces too, 'gang aft a-gley'!

Tom Wall is the Site Manager, English Nature, for The Stiperstones National Nature Reserve.

All photographs are by Paul Glendell, English Nature.

## Live Theatre
## by Eric Sayce

Are you thinking, like I used to, that sadly that's not for the blind and partially sighted? What's the point of going as I wouldn't be able to see the production and even if my friends came with me and described what was going on on stage, I would feel embarrassed by them whispering in my ear, whilst disturbing the people around us. No, it just isn't worth the hassle. That's a sad reflection and a view which I know that many share from my experience of talking to blind and partially sighted people especially the parents of blind and partially sighted children. How to address this problem and open up live theatre to all became a challenge for the Coventry Belgrade Theatre's access group.

A pantomime was the subject chosen to develop as it was felt that this type of show would have maximum appeal to young and old alike. We were fortunate that the pantomime script writer/producer/director at the time shared our enthusiasm for making such productions accessible to all and in this respect was prepared to modify script. He accordingly incorporating any practical suggestions which we felt applicable.

One of these was the now famous 'Scratch and Sniff' cards idea. This came as a result of us trying to find a way of identifying, for the blind or partially sighted audience, the scene that was on stage at any particular time during the performance. After a good deal of deliberation we decided smell was the most effective method, but wafting the smell out into the auditorium through the air conditioning system was not practical. Perfume cards that women's magazines sometimes carry, when a new perfume is being introduced to the market, was an alternative which could be developed. ALL members of the audience would be given a card with a different smell at each corner and on a given signal from the dame on stage during the performance one of these corners could be scratched and the exposed smell sniffed and thus a clue given as to what scene was on stage. An example was the gorgonzola cheese had everyone cringing in their seats and represented the giant's smelly socks drying in his kitchen, whereas sweet rose smells indicated a country garden. Of course this idea, whilst being introduced to assist the blind and partially sighted, was enjoyed by everyone and didn't separate out the visually impaired by making them special.

The design and production of both scenery and costumes needed to be approached from a different perspective. These needed to be tactile and the number of back cloths which had the scenes painted on them to give 3-D effect reduced. These whilst being very effective visually could not be enjoyed by the blind audience. Costume designs needed to incorporate materials of different textures in order to provide tactile clues of both their design and of the character wearing them. For those who are partially sighted, the colours used on both the scenery painting and costume material needed to be bold bright and clean. In this respect the question was raised, 'What colours? And how are they interpreted by blind and partially sighted people?' This latter question led to a good deal of discussion, the result of which was to classify all the good characters in warm colours (nice to touch) e.g. reds, pinks, greens yellows etc,. and the 'baddies' in cold colours such as black, greys, navy blues etc. In deciding to adopt this approach, experience proved that we were also earning an unanticipated bonus. Our pantomime audiences are now commenting on how clean, bright and attractive the settings are, so everyone is benefiting.

How to provide an idea of the scale of things for people who cannot see? For example how large is the giant in Jack and the Beanstalk when compared with the size of Mum or Dad? We solved that one by having separate 'feelies'; we had a spare giant's boot made that the children could examine and feel comparing it to the size of their own shoes. A spare set of giant's cutlery was also made and I well remember one little 4 year old girl's reaction when we placed both the knife and fork. one on each side of her; when she touched them and realised they came up to the top of her shoulders she exclaimed 'What a big mouth he must have'.

So far we had addressed the senses of touch and smell but what about hearing? Audible components incorporated into the costume design would be helpful. Associating a particular bar of music with a specific character would also assist in the recognition of that character when it appeared on stage, for instance when the fairy appears she is accompanied by a tinkling of bells and in contrast, when the dame appears there is a trumpet fanfare and so on, each character having their own signature tune.

Every pantomime has its own special panto' song in which everyone joins, the song sheet usually being suspended high up over the stage where everyone can read the words, with the exception of course of the blind and partially sighted. In order that the blind and partially sighted could join in the singing along with their sighted peers and therefore feel no different, we produced the song sheets in Braille, large print and on audio cassette, issuing them when the seats were booked. The children and the not-so-young children then had the opportunity of learning the simple tune and words before they come to the show.

When a blind or partially sighted person book their seat at the theatre's box office they are shown a tactile seating plan from which they are able to select the seat of their choice. Tactile plans of the foyer, restaurant and service areas have been designed, produced and now installed. The last component to complete our package which is bringing live theatre alive for blind and partially sighted people like me was the installation of an audio description system. This system enables the blind or partially sighted person to understand why people suddenly burst out laughing for no apparent reason, for example when the 'slap-stick' part was taking place.

To assist the actors to feel more comfortable and confident in their new and unusual roles we gave them some basic training in the techniques we were using. We talked about the wide variations in the amount of sight loss, different eye conditions, how to approach a blind or partially sighted person, take their hands and guide them over their costumes as well as simple guiding techniques. A similar training course was implemented for the front of house staff, but with more emphasis on the guiding techniques and general services approach. The overall objective being to provide a warm, caring, friendly and relaxed atmosphere for everyone.

Our script writer/producer ensures that in all our pantomimes the dame's costumes are very outrageous and very, very tactile. An examples of this: Widow Twanky's outfit consisted of an upside-down plastic washing up bowl hat with a sink plunger sticking out of the top, tooth brush ear rings, a necklace made from sink plugs, wide hooped dress in gingham pattern with a plastic apron onto which had been bonded big plastic bubbles like those you find in blister packs, Doctor Martin's boots and football socks completed the very tactile and colourful outfit.

In contrast, the baddies in Dick Whittington were rats from the sewers of London and were named King Rat and his two henchmen Scratch and Sniff, wore very tactile costumes designed to be of a much more sinister nature. King Rat wore a black peaked hat with a visor that came almost flat on his nose with a jewelled name badge on the front and big brown rat ears attached, his jacket and trousers were black leather, the trousers being lace-up on the outside of each leg. A sign of his prowess as king were the rats tails which he wore suspended from the sleeves, waist and back of his jacket indicating his conquests; the jacket had metal studs like a biker's outfit. The trousers were tucked into black leather gaiters and the outfit finished with black leather boots. Of course the rats would not have been complete without false round noses with whiskers projecting from each side, a single large tooth which fitted over the actor's own teeth and a pair of wire half-spectacles and, I nearly forgot, tails which were fitted into the seats of the trousers. King Rat was much larger than Scratch and Sniff and he also wore a sequined vest in a purple colour under his jacket and his tail was longer and thicker than the others; Scratch and Sniff did not have any rat tails to adorn them, neither did they have the peaked cap. Just imagine the fun the children had exploring these costumes!

I will conclude with a typical outline of a pre-show programme:

- Blind and partially sighted people assemble in theatre's main foyer from where they are guided to seats in the auditorium
- Welcome and introduction to the theatre
- Tour of stage, - walk its width and breadth. Feel the specially designed tactile scenery painted with clean bold colours which helps those who are partially sighted
- Experience the size and space of the stage and build your picture of the stage scenery in your mind by using your fingers to feel and touch
- You return to your seats and the principle characters then introduce themselves and describe their individual roles in the panto'. Their entry onto stage is indicated by a bar of music or special sound which relates to them during the panto'
- Meet the principle characters in person, they introduce themselves or rather their tactile costumes to you at your seat. They guide your fingers over their costumes which they are wearing, allowing you to feel the tactile texture of the various materials and very tactile accessories used in their design, thus helping you to build that picture in your mind.
- The popular Belgrade 'Scratch and Sniff' cards help you to identify the scene on stage during the panto'.
- The Belgrade's 'audio description' enables you hear a descriptive commentary through special headsets (no plugs or wires). At the same time you can enjoy the dialogue on the stage, making sure that you don't miss out on the action.

Information in an accessible format completes the package: Braille, large print and audio cassette. Now you can join in and sing those popular panto' songs along with your friends.

Eric Sayce has worked as a consultant with the Dog Rose Trust for many years. The Dorcas Project is named after his first Guide Dog. Before becoming blind Eric was an international marketing executive jetting around the world. He has now put his abilities and energies into helping other blind people and is very involved with the work of Guide Dogs For the Blind and St. Dunstans. He was a prime mover in the project to make theatre more accessible to all at the Belgrade Theatre, Coventry, his home town.

In Access to Leisure, Chapter 2.15, Eric mentions a talking bar code reader and he has been using an i.d.Mate II voice labelling machine for sometime, supplied by Force Ten: http://www.forcetenco.co.uk/home.asp, Telephone: 01372 450887. At present these machines are still rather bulky and expensive for general use, but may well have a useful place in the future.

A leaflet on guiding blind and partially sighted people can be downloaded from the website of Action for Blind people: http://www.afbp.org/Information/Advice/guiding.asp or telephone 020 7635 4800. Guide Dogs for the Blind Association also have leaflet: email guidedogs@guidedogs.org.uk or telephone 0118 983 5555.

## *Theater by the Blind*
## *George Ashiotis*

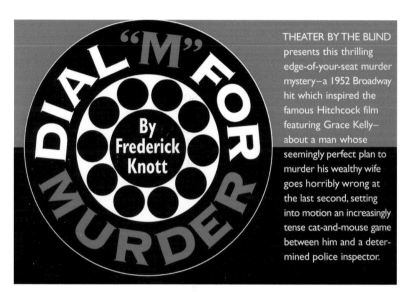

THEATER BY THE BLIND presents this thrilling edge-of-your-seat murder mystery—a 1952 Broadway hit which inspired the famous Hitchcock film featuring Grace Kelly—about a man whose seemingly perfect plan to murder his wealthy wife goes horribly wrong at the last second, setting into motion an increasingly tense cat-and-mouse game between him and a determined police inspector.

In 1983 Theater By the Blind was a troupe of blind and sighted actors touring library theaters like Lincoln Center and other local community-type venues with a 30 to 50 minute show using existing material about blindness. There was, for example, snippets of scenes from Oedipus, King Lear, Butterflies are Free, etc., and included tongue-in-cheek renditions of songs like 'I only have eyes for you' and 'I can see clearly now'.

In 1986 we rented a legitimate theater and mounted our first fully staged production, Crystal Clear. This play had to do with a man losing his sight through diabetes and his struggle to figure out in which world he belonged, as reflected in alternating scenes between his former sighted girlfriend and his current blind one. Since then we have produced all manner of plays from Shakespeare to Agatha Christie.

In 1992 or thereabouts we added a writer's component to our company in order to combat the stereotype image of blindness put forth by Hollywood and started adding original works to our repertoire.

We are a fully integrated company. Our actors use Braille, large print, cassette tapes and regular print to learn their parts. The sight level of our players ranges from total blindness to a considerable amount of sight. Our designers, both lighting and set, are aware of our needs as they talk with us extensively, and do what they can to accommodate us.

For the actors who have some vision, we try to use contrast on the set, like white doilies on a dark wood coffee table, or white molding around a door or window set into a dark colored wall. For our actors who have little or no use of sight, we use tactile markings like area rugs and runners or half-round molding which is painted the same color as the stage floor, so that only the actor who is relying on it knows it's there. The audience never sees it. Other than these adjustments we function like a normal theater company and have gotten great reviews in the <u>New York Times</u> and <u>Post</u>.

In addition to making the performance area accessible, we are equally engaged in making performances themselves accessible to our audience members. To this end we have experimented with various styles of narrating the action on the stage. In Shaw's Misalliance each actor narrated the action of his or her own character. This afforded the visually impaired observer the opportunity to know not only the activity of the character but also the attitude behind the action and, in some instances, the location on stage where the action was taking place.

Wherever possible we try to use props which have a signature sound, like clinking ice cubes in a glass or slamming desk drawers. In other words, if we can do something noisily without impugning the integrity of the piece, we will. Our productions also include a rich sound-track which aids in the establishment of climate and locale.

In our production of Dial 'M' For Murder we tried something different. We employed the use of a single narrator. This was necessary as the central action of this drama, that is to say the murder itself, takes place in the absence of dialog, and both the attacker and the victim are too encumbered with the struggle to describe their own moves. We took advantage of the fact that one of the characters was a TV writer and could easily become a narrator who then related a story to our audiences. It worked really well.

Best of all is when we produce something that has come out of our writers' workshop. As writers, ourselves, we have learned to subtly integrate important information about action in the dialog of the plays we write. For example, why say 'what are you doing here?' when the line can as easily be 'would you put down that knife and tell me what you are doing here?'

Making our performances accessible is an on-going challenge. A technique that works for one show may be inappropriate for another. We have, by no means, solved all the problems. We continue to explore presentational styles. Our goal is to unite performers and audiences of all abilities in a shared aesthetic. We have made great strides toward that end.

George Ashiotis, co-artistic director of Theater by the Blind, has worked in the theatre for thirty years and during that time has played a wide range of parts, including the first blind Hamlet. He had worked with Woody Allen and Richard Harris and his performances have been favorably reviewed by the New York Times among other papers.

For further information look at the website: http://www.tbtb.org/

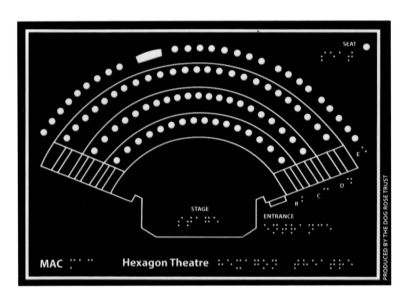

*Theatre and seating plan for the
Hexagon Auditorium at the
Midlands Arts Centre*

## *Coventry - The Shyster View*

This project in Coventry is different again: here the Trust has been working with five members of the Shysters, a well-known ensemble theatre company of actors with learning disabilities.

The aims were:

To produce an audio picture of Coventry, linking Coventry Past with Coventry Present

To have an end product of audio that will promote the work of the Shysters

To enable the Shysters to discover the history of their city and at the same time establish and re-establish their links with and roots in Coventry

**Programme of Work**

Day 1

Discussing the project and gathering ideas for collecting sound and audio interviews around the city

*Listening to the music at the market*

Trying out the mini-disc equipment supplied by the Dog Rose Trust and practising interviewing techniques.

A flexible approach to the work seems to be the right way forward. As much as possible should come from the Shysters themselves.

Day 2

Collecting characteristic sounds around the city, such as clocks, fountains and the market traders, encouraging the Shysters to find out about these for themselves. Discovering the differences in sound in the city between day and night.

Identifying people who could give interviews

Day 3

Interviewing people

Discussing what else needs to be done to create a rounded picture of the city.

We all went out and about in the city recording the Shysters in many different places and getting their comments and reactions to the changes taking place in their city. We recorded in the market, the old Cathedral and the new one, the Transport Museum and by the canal.

We had some very interesting and inspiring moments with the group, such as Lisa singing as she walked across the new Blue Bridge and Catherine carrying out an interview at the Herbert Art Gallery. It has been challenging for all of us to produce a professional recording and the results proved very satisfactory.

We recorded the scripted links and edited the recording together. As part of this project the acoustics of the destroyed cathedral are being reconstructed in conjunction with the University of York in order to take the voices of the actors back into the building as it was 500 years ago.

We all wanted it to be a positive picture of the city, with emphasis on Coventry's place in history, both as a medieval religious centre, major centre for the production of cars and as city of 'firsts'; the Belgrade theatre, shopping centre and the ring road were the first to be rebuilt in the modern style after the war

Taking part in the project were Allan Kelly, Jon Tipton, Katharine Marshall, Lisa Carney and Matthew Granaghan. Kathy Joyce, Assistant Director of the Shysters, was in charge of the training.

*Recording in the studio*

### Out and About

The first stop was Priory Gardens where we talked about the changes that had taken place there and discussed the tactile plan that had been put up to help blind people. We then went down into the gardens and listened to the stories of Coventry lives that has been put into the Cloisters. The wall of water was a fascinating new feature that attracted them all. We also noticed the newly excavated undercroft of the St Mary's Priory. This raised so many questions that we all went back to the Visitor's Centre to ask about a tour of the undercroft and to find out more about it and everyone was a fascinated to learn that they were walking over the medieval city in many places. Christine, an assistant at the centre, explained all about the exhibits and the old buildings to an enthralled audience.

We then went down to Millennium Place and saw the lines of the time clock and walked over the glass bridge; looking down at the Swanswell Gate we talked about the town walls and Lady Herbert's

Garden. We walked back by the new obelisk where there Shyster found their name engraved on a glass plaque.

*Recording at the Transport Museum*

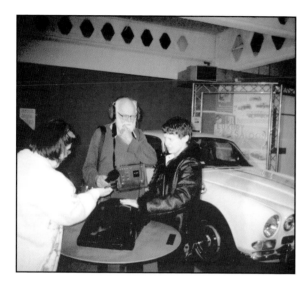

During the walkabout we recorded interviews with the Shysters and gathered as much material as we could. Now that we know them better we need to get more discipline into these interviews and impress on them only to talk one at a time and also to keep quiet when other people are talking.

Over the next two days we visited the canal and the Indoor Market, as well as historic Bond's Hospital and the Cathedrals, old and new, as well as the Transport Museum where Queen Mary's Daimler and the Thrust 2 simulator were the highlights.

The second part of the project involved recording the links for the on-site audio. The Shysters had been rehearsing with their Director, Kathy Joyce and so the session went with a swing, with some excellent work by the group.

**Lessons Learnt and to be learnt**

What did everyone learn from this project? The Trust learnt a great deal, especially that we do not have enough pairs of hands to hold the microphone, operate the audio machine, take photos and keep the person speaking in the right place, addressing at the microphone.

Seriously though, we were unsure, particularly in the early part of the week how much we could get people to pay attention, speak up, keep quiet without precipitating a crisis. As we got to know the Shysters better, we became more confident in telling them these things, but the messages had to be reinforced all the time. There was a need to get everything out in a rush with the rest of the company joining in. This was easier to control in the rehearsal room when there were fewer distractions, but once out in the 'field' this became much more of a problem.

The actors needed to learn how to listen to what is being told to them and not to interrupt when others are speaking and particularly when they are being recorded. Mobile phones must all be off when working: first, they may receive a call which will spoil a take; second, the continuous radio impulses from the phones are picked up by the microphone; third, they are a constant distraction, especially when video is involved.

Everyone, including ourselves, needs more practice with microphone techniques – us to find the best way to get the actors to talk to the microphone and the actors to become more experienced in doing this. Some of the interviews and commentaries have come out very well and we are pleased with them.

Often we found it difficult to get a straight answer. They could describe something, what it looked like and what it did but could not seem to get the idea of giving it a name. We felt we needed to ask that question in a different way.

Listening to the results of the week, in retrospect we think it would have been beneficial to have had a warm-up session each day and a reminder of the techniques they need to use and rules they need to follow to do the job satisfactorily. Their very competent interview techniques, when practised in the rehearsal room, were such that it led us into a slightly false sense of security and we thought that they would retain the information. We know now that we should have done a daily session of recapping.

### Summary
First we must say that the four days working with the Shysters were very interesting and stimulating, if exhausting. Although tinged with exasperation at times, but it has never been dull. It has taught us a great deal and we realise how much we still have to learn. We were all delighted when spontaneous historical or other connections were made between one part of the city and another and they were beginning to think about their city in a different way.

The Shysters are an ensemble company of actors with learning disabilities, whose work is led by Richard Hayhow, artistic director, associate director Kathy Joyce and a team of artists. Through a devising process that encompasses a range of physical theatre methods, the work draws in the actors' experiences and perceptions and transforms them into the stuff of theatre. The Shysters have created their three major touring productions, Scary Antics, Fallen Angels, and Tango Apocalypso through this process.

Since Fallen Angels one of the company's major developments has been our collaboration with other organisations. This began with a production of A Midsummer Night's Dream (October 2001) with the Belgrade Theatre, that paved the way for us to explore an artistic aesthetic that was emerging from our work within a much broader context. Since then we have developed a number of performance projects with, amongst others, Birmingham Rep, Birmingham City Council, regional special schools, Mencap and other dance and theatre companies.

'Shyster' is an obscure word, the original meaning of which is a 'crooked lawyer' or 'conman'. This can translate quite easily to the notion of acting as the deliberate and skilled art of pretence. In some regions of the country the word has quite negative connotations, akin to swearing. For the company it is however a 'positive-negative' word. It implies a degree of craft and cleverness as well as an acknowledgement of the darker side of life, qualities not traditionally acknowledged within the context of learning disability. It's also a name that sticks, once heard it's never forgotten!

Essentially a Shyster looks at the world sideways and through Shyster eyes, it is a place full of marvels, danger, curiosity and the inexplicable. The reality of a Shyster can shake you to the core. Darkness and fear can be just round the corner. A Shyster finds people fascinating. A Shyster is willing to take people as they find them, to be open and non-judgmental. The everyday and the ordinary delight a Shyster, who bends, squishes and shapes it into something surreal to be taken back and shared. This view embraces absurdity, relishes life and turns it into inspired art.'

## CD 1 Examples of Sound

We have written about the Use of Sound in Chapter 2 and in other places. Now you can listen to some of these sounds. All the audio except Track 34, has been recorded and produced by the Dog Rose Trust. Most of the scripting has also been done by the Trust.

1.    The Dog Rose Signature Tune, written by Adrian Williams

### The Use of sound to describe Architecture and Buildings

2.    York Minster, Chapter House and Crypt. This was recorded in the actual building and the acoustics of these two very different spaces are very contrasting. Narrator: Patricia Greene. Chapter 2.12.
3.    York Minster, Lady Chapel. The organ music enhances the space and emphasises the use of the building, as well as being charming in itself. The narrator is Patricia Greene. Chapter 2 12.
4.    The Palace of Westminster, London. A track from the commentary for the interactive model describes Westminster Hall. The narrator is Edward Kelsey. Chapter 3.07
5.    The Palace of Westminster, London. Another track from the commentary, with contrasting acoustics, for the model: St. Stephen's Hall. The narrator is Edward Kelsey. Chapter 3.07
6.    Bolsover Castle, Derbyshire.  The Little Castle Pillar Room with Patricia Greene and Timothy Mowl. Chapter 2.12
7.    Bolsover Castle, Derbyshire. The Little Castle Lantern with Timothy Mowl and Julian Robins playing the lute. Chapter 2.12
8.    Bolsover Castle, Derbyshire. The Little Castle Star Chamber with Patricia Greene and music by John Wilbye sung by Marion Rowlatt and her group of singers from mid-Wales. Chapter 2.12.
9.    Hardwick Hall, Derbyshire. The opening sequence with Gil Sutherland and Patricia Greene with music by Peter Bull. Chapter 2.12.
10.   Hardwick Hall, Derbyshire: An extract from information about the parkland and gardens. Ted Edwards is clearing trees in the park. The narrator is Gil Sutherland. Chapter 2.12
11.   Highbury, Birmingham: Joe Chamberlain's high Victorian house was 'peopled' with characters. Judy Parkin is Lily the maid and narrator Gil Sutherland. Chapter 2.12

# *LIST OF CD TRACKS*

### A Concept of Place

Each space and places has its own acoustics, but often we do not hear them as we are too busy looking or the background noise obscures the ambience. These are some of the examples we have recorded in different places, to capture their sound and produce a soundscape.

12. The Island of Hydra, Greece. With no traffic allowed, the sounds are very distinct: you can hear the goats' bells and the braying donkey. The barking dog defines the shape of the space around it and the day is punctuated by the arrival of the high speed hydro-foils and the slower ferries from Athens. Chapter 2.04.
13. Istanbul, Turkey. Istanbul is a place with a rich medley of sounds. Here the market traders, vying for customers, give way to the Muezzin calling the people to prayer. Chapter 2.04
14. The City of York. An extract from an audio guide to accompany the bronze model of the centre of York. The narration guides the hands around the model as well as giving information about the city. The narrators are Jacqui and Peter Taylor. Chapter 3.07
15. The Accessible Marches, Shropshire. John Kirkpatrick, the narrator, sets the scene in the small Shropshire town of Clun. He points out the different tones of the clocks which act as 'sound icons'. Music by Adrian Williams. Chapter 5.02.
16. Stiperstones Shuttlebus. This recording was made to accompany the Shuttle Bus around the South Shropshire Hills, an area full of legends and the stories of Mary Webb. The narrators are Val Littlehales and Richard Beaumont. Music by Adrian Williams. Chapter 5.04.
17. Coventry - The Shyster View. The actors visit the indoor market in Coventry and remember riding on the roundabout. Taking part are Jon Tipton, Matthew Granaghan, Allan Kelly, Katharine Marshall and Lisa Carney. Chapter 6.03

### Community Involvement

18. Courtroom Scene at Brecknock Museum, Brecon. This is an extract from one of the two short bi-lingual dramatic scenes recorded for a sound and light display in the old Courtroom at Brecon. Local people took part together with museum staff; Edward Kelsey was in charge of direction. Chapter 4.04
19. The Soldiers of Gloucestershire Museum, Gloucester. A dramatic episode from the narration of the audio guide for the museum with a member of the Cheltenham Players. Chapter 4.04
20. Coalport China Museum, Ironbridge, Shropshire. A description of a teacup for the interactive display of tactile tea cups. Local people took part in the recording and the narrators here are Amanda Paterson and Allan Price.* Chapter 4.02
21. Ellesmere, Shropshire. Sound for one of the UTurn wind-up audio units around the Mere. On this track you can hear local residents Gwen Forrester and Graham Beech; the narrator is Ian Ratcliffe. Chapter 4.02
22. Mitchell's Fold Stone Circle, South Shropshire. Paul Saunders tells Eric Sayce the legend of Mitchell's Fold. In the background are the ghostly sound of the bagpipes, played by Paul. Funded by the Shell Better Britain Campaign. Chapter 5.02.
23. Mitchell's Fold Stone Circle, South Shropshire. Stephen Harding relates the story of the boggarts. Funded by the Shell Better Britain Campaign. Chapter 5.02.
24. The Avalon Marshes, Somerset. UTurn wind-up audio units have been placed around this area, using some of the oral history recorded in 2001. This one, with the voices of Ray Sweet and John Coles, describes the ancient trackways that have been  discovered here. The narrator is Paul Rew, prize-winner in the Sunday Times Voice of the Year Competition, 2004. Chapter 3, 2 and Chapter 2.25, Oral History.
25. The Avalon Marshes, Somerset. Another track for a UTurn wind-up audio unit. Describing the train crash are Bob Toogood and Sam Foster. The narrator is Julia Ionides. Chapter 2.25, Oral History.

26. Ham Wall, Somerset. A track for a UTurn wind-up audio unit, describing the birds in the reed-beds for the RSPB. The narrator is Julia Ionides. Chapter 5.03.

## Community Music

27. The Lakelands Schools, Ellesmere, Shropshire. Music of the Mere composed and performed at a workshop at the Lakelands School with Keith Alexander and Lorraine Ross.* Chapter 4.03.
28. The Primary School, Ellesmere, Shropshire. Keith and Lorraine led another workshop to write, compose and perform the Castle of Music.* Chapter 4.03.
29. William Brooks School, Much Wenlock, Shropshire. Here's to Coalport China, written and composed by John Kirkpatrick and performed for the first time at this workshop.* Chapter 4.03.

## Multi-Sensory Descriptions

30. Stiperstones, South Shropshire. Tom Wall of English Nature describes some of the smells and sounds that can be found in the area to Eric Sayce who is totally blind. Chapter 5.04.
31. Cremorne Gardens, Ellesmere, Shropshire. Vernon West, a retired forester, explains how to look at a tree in the arboretum at Ellesmere.* Chapter 4.02.
32. Craven Arms, South Shropshire. On the guide to Craven Arms, Denise Collier asked Bob Milner about the trees that can be found by the River Onny. Funded by the Lottery Awards for All. Chapter 2.12.
33. Who's the Tallest? The audio of the book from Hungry Fingers, written and illustrated by Boguslaw (Bob) Marek of Lublin, Poland. The reader is Paul Rew. Bob describe this in more detail in Chapter 3. 12.
34. And finally: What was Peter recording in the park in Copenhagen where he is holding the microphone towards a black holdall? Listen to this track and you will find out. Chapter 2.07.


*Denotes that this project was funded by the Heritage Lottery Fund


## CD2 . Recording the Voice with Richard Derrington

Track 1 Getting ready
Track 2 Scripting for your audience
Track 3 Writing the script and rehearsing
Track 4 Ready to start
Track 5 Recording hints


Please note that the copyright of these recordings belongs to the Dog Rose Trust and they may not be reproduced without permission. The recordings for Ham Wall also belongs to the RSPB; the Avalon Marshes to Somerset County Council; The Courtroom Scene to Brecknock Museum; the Battle of Corunna to The Soldiers of Gloucestershire Museum; John Kirkpatrick for Here's to Coalport China and to the unknown Danish sound artist for the 'talking holdall'.